THE ECONOMICS OF TOURISM

William S. Reece

*Department of Economics, College of Business
and Economics, West Virginia University*

Prentice Hall
Upper Saddle River, New Jersey

To Wendy

Library of Congress Cataloging-in-Publication Data

Reece, William S.
    The economics of tourism / William S. Reece.—1st ed.
        p. cm.
    Includes bibliographical references and index.
    ISBN-13: 978-0-13-171540-0
    ISBN-10: 0-13-171540-2
    1. Tourism. I. Title.

    G155.A1R44 2010
    338.4'791—dc22   2008027322

Editor in Chief: Vernon Anthony
Acquisitions Editor: William Lawrensen
Editorial Assistant: Lara Dimmick
Marketing Director: David Gesell
Campaign Marketing Manager: Leigh Ann Sims
Curriculum Marketing Manager: Thomas Hayward
Production Manager: Kathy Sleys
Art Director: Jayne Conte
Cover Designer: Bruce Kenselaar
Cover art/image/photo[s]: Getty Images
Full Service/Project Management: Saraswathi Muralidhar/GGS Higher Education Resources, A Division of Premedia Global, Inc.

This book was set in 10pt Minion by GGS Higher Education Resources, A Division of Premedia Global, Inc. and was printed and bound by Bind-Rite, Robbinsville/Command Web. The cover was printed by Bind-Rite, Robbinsville/Command Web.

Pearson Education Ltd., London
Pearson Education Singapore Pte. Ltd.
Pearson Education Canada, Inc.
Pearson Education—Japan

Pearson Education Australia Pty. Limited
Pearson Education North Asia Ltd., Hong Kong
Pearson Educación de Mexico, S.A. de C.V.
Pearson Education Malaysia Pte. Ltd.

Prentice Hall
is an imprint of

www.pearsonhighered.com

10 9 8 7 6 5 4 3 2 1
ISBN-13: 978-0-13-171540-0
ISBN-10:   0-13-171540-2

CONTENTS

Preface   ix

Chapter 1   Introduction   1

Introduction   1

Economic Concepts and Issues in Tourism   2

Creating Value for Consumers and Income for
Workers and Owners   3

Supply   3

Demand   4

Rivalry and Competition   4

Government Regulation   4

Tourism Industry Organizations   5

Summary   6

Bibliography   6

Chapter 2   Creating Value in Tourism   7

What Is an Economy? Why Do We Have
an Economy?   7

Income and Value Added   9

Value Added by Travel Agencies   11

How Much Income Can Travel Agencies Expect
to Earn?   11

Value Added in Tourism in the United States   12

Value Added in Tourism in Canada   12

Summary   14

Bibliography   14

Chapter 3   Tourism Consumers   15

Introduction   15

Profiles of U.S. Travelers   15

The National Household Travel Survey   17

Travel Mode   17

Business Travelers   17

Demand for Tourism   19

The Impact of Price Changes   20

The Impact of Income Changes   20

Factors Affecting Demand   20

Price and Income Elasticities of Demand   22

    Price Elasticity of Demand   22

    Cross Elasticity of Demand   22

    Income Elasticity of Demand   23

    Estimating Elasticities of Demand for Tourism
       Services   23

Customer Loyalty Programs   25

Summary   26

Bibliography   26

**Chapter 4   Supply, Demand, and the Growth
         of Tourism   28**

Introduction   28

Travel and Tourism in the Ancient World   29

Travel in the Middle Ages   31

Travel in the Pre–Modern Era   34

    The Grand Tour   34

Modern Mass Tourism   35

    Supply and Demand   36

Demand   36

Supply   40

    Costs   40

    Strategic Interactions Among Firms   42

Summary   46

Bibliography   47

**Chapter 5   Economic Impact: Output, Income,
         and Sustainability   49**

Introduction   49

Economic Impact Analysis   50

Direct and Indirect Effects   52

Input–Output Analysis   52

    Each Industry Must Have the Outputs of Other
       Industries   54

    What Assumptions Do We Make When Using
       Input–Output Analysis?   56

Sustainable Tourism Development and Ecotourism   57

Intertemporal Economic Analysis   58

Common Property Resources, Externalities, and Property
    Rights   62

Summary   63

Bibliography   71

Chapter 6   Pricing Tourism Services   73

Introduction   73

Demand   74

  Revenue and Marginal Revenue   74

Supply   76

**Yield Management—Price Discrimination with a Capacity
  Constraint   77**

  Planning to Fly with Empty Seats   82

Price Discrimination Through a Two-Part Tariff   82

Summary   84

Bibliography   84

Chapter 7   Airlines   85

Introduction   85

**Growth of U.S. Domestic Scheduled Airline
  Service   86**

  U.S. Federal Regulation of the Airlines   86

  Recent Developments in Commercial Aviation   87

**How Airlines Create Value—The Scheduled Airlines
  Business Model   88**

  Operations   88

  Equipment   88

  Labor   90

  Aircraft Fuel   91

  Maintenance   91

  Airport Landing and Other Fees   91

  Other Operating Expenses   92

  Promoting and Selling Airline Tickets   92

**Overview of the Performance of the U.S. Domestic
  Airline Industry   93**

Industry Structure   95

  Route Structure   95

  Distribution; Reservation Systems   97

  Airline Pricing—Yield or Revenue Management   98

  Overbooking   99

  Understanding Airline Price Differences   101

Consumer Welfare Evaluation of Airline Pricing   102

Airline Pricing with Rising Costs   103

Development of International Airline Markets   104

Open Skies   104

The European Airline Market   106

Rivalry in the Airline Industry   106

The Question of Contestability   107

Rivalry Among Firms   110

Recent Development of the U.S. Scheduled Airline
Industry   115

Summary   119

Bibliography   120

Chapter 8   Tourist Travel by Automobile, Rail, and Bus   123

Introduction   123

Travel by Automobile   124

Travel by Bus and Motorcoach   126

Travel by Train   126

Car Rental   130

Industry Structure   130

Operations   131

Summary   134

Bibliography   134

Chapter 9   Lodging and Restaurants   136

Introduction   136

Lodging   137

Lodging Demand   137

Lodging Supply Combines Three Businesses   138

Real Estate or Property Ownership   139

Real Estate Investment Trusts   139

Integrated Hotel Operating Companies   140

Private Equity and Institutional Investors   140

Buy or Build?   141

Franchising   141

Management of Operations   143

Industry Segments   145

Pricing   146

Competition in the Lodging Industry   148

The Bertrand Model of Oligopoly   148

Complications in the Bertrand Model
of Oligopoly: Differentiated Products
and Capacity Constraints   149

Food and Beverage Service   151

The U.S. Restaurant Industry   152

Costs in the Food and Beverage Industry   153

Using Menus to Capture Restaurant Consumer Surplus   154

Summary   156

Bibliography   157

Chapter 10 Cruise Lines   159

Introduction   159

How Cruise Lines Create Value   161

Structure of the Cruise Line Industry   164

Regulation of the Cruise Industry   166

Freedom of the High Seas   168

Cabotage; Passenger Shipping Act of 1896;
Jones Act of 1920   168

Safety of Life at Sea (SOLAS); the U.S. Coast Guard   170

Cruise Ship Sanitation; Centers for Disease
Control and Prevention   170

Passenger Deposits; Federal Maritime Commission   171

Environmental Regulations   171

Maritime Security   171

Performance, Growth, and Capacity of the Cruise
Line Industry   172

Summary   174

Bibliography   175

Chapter 11 Destinations, Events, and Attractions   177

Introduction   177

Nations, States, Provinces, Cities, Islands   178

Events   180

Attractions   181

Theme Park Economics   181

The Theme Park Industry   182

Operations   184

Optimal Behavior with High Fixed Costs and
Low Marginal Costs   185

Summary   189

Bibliography   189

Chapter 12   **Tourism Intermediaries: Travel Agents, Tour Operators, and Others   191**

Introduction   191

Agency in Tourism   192

Travel Agents Create Value   193

The Travel Agent Industry   193

Travel Management   196

Global Distribution Systems   197

Tour Operators and Tour Wholesalers   198

Tour Operators Create Value for Travelers and Service Providers   199

The Tour Operator Industry   200

Asymmetric Information in the Travel Agent and Tour Operator Industries   201

Some Economics of Asymmetric Information   203

Tourism Intermediaries' Reactions to Asymmetric Information   204

Summary   206

Bibliography   206

Chapter 13   **Casino Gaming   209**

Introduction   209

The U.S. Casino Industry   211

The Global Casino Industry   213

Casino Operations   215

Gaming Revenues   215

Gaming Devices   216

Non-Gaming Revenues   217

Taxation and Regulation of Casinos   218

U.S. State Regulation   218

Casino Taxation   219

Native American Casinos   220

Benefits and Costs of Casinos   220

Summary   222

Bibliography   223

Glossary   225

Index   227

PREFACE

The tourism industry is a global giant which provides services to travelers while also providing opportunities to earn income through useful employment and productive investment. I have written this book to help students use the basic methods of microeconomics to understand what is happening in this important and growing industry. I have been teaching an undergraduate course on the economics of tourism for many years, but I have not found a textbook that could support my undergraduate course on applying mainstream microeconomic analysis to tourism. This book is intended to fill a gap that I see in the array of tourism texts.

For many decades economists have been working on various aspects of tourism. Most notably, economists have studied the airline industry, first examining its regulation and then following the path of the deregulated industry. This large body of work has provided important analysis that students can benefit from. Also, a small industry of researchers applies economic impact analysis to tourism. Other areas of tourism have lacked this depth of attention from economists, but I try to show that much work applied elsewhere has useful applications to tourism. This book shows, for example, that the Nobel-Prize-winning work of George Akerlof, Ronald Coase, and Wassily Leontief is useful for understanding tourism. It also shows how simple concepts and methods that economists have usefully applied to the study of the information industry are equally useful in understanding the behavior of tourism firms. One of the most important areas where students can improve their insights into tourism firm behavior is pricing. Here some simple economic analysis can clearly show how a firm with different kinds of customers and a capacity constraint chooses a price for each kind of customer to maximize profits. This fairly simple economic analysis is important for understanding pricing in tourism, especially for hotels and airlines.

This book is aimed primarily at advanced undergraduates in hospitality and tourism degree programs, but it may also be useful for students in graduate hospitality and tourism programs and undergraduate programs in business and economics. This book is primarily intended as the basis for a course on the economics of tourism, but it could also serve as a resource for other courses in tourism, hospitality management, and other areas of travel and tourism. I am also hopeful that it will stimulate economics of tourism course offerings in many programs that do not offer them now.

The only prerequisite for success in using this book is a course in the principles of microeconomics. Some of the serious work in the economics of tourism requires mathematics beyond elementary algebra, and this book introduces students to some of that work. I have placed the more mathematical parts of the book in appendixes to Chapter 5 to be included in the course or skipped according to the instructor's preferences.

Over the years, students in my economics of tourism course have provided useful feedback on my course materials, and this has helped in my writing of this book. I am grateful for their attention, their work, and their comments. I am also grateful to my reviewers who provided important comments, which helped me improve the text. They are John Bandman, The Art Institute of New York; Russell Brayley, George Mason University; Scott Brunger, Marysville College; Melissa Dallas, Florida Atlantic

University; Peter Dieke, George Mason University; Sotiris Hji-Avgoustis, Indiana University; and Jim Petrick, Texas A&M University. I have also benefited from my collaboration with Russell Sobel on pricing in the presence of a capacity constraint, and I thank him for that. Finally, I thank various people at Prentice Hall, including Vern Anthony, Judy Casillo, Sherry Gerstein, William Lawrensen, and Kathy Sleys who worked to help me bring this book to publication.

CHAPTER 1

Introduction

Learning Goals

- Understand the term *tourism*.
- Know the scope of the world's tourism industry.
- Understand the recurring ideas in the economics of tourism.
- Know the major tourism industry organizations.

INTRODUCTION

Traveling to visit family and friends or going on vacation provides some of our happiest memories. Traveling for business can be an exciting break from the routine of office or factory life. Thus, unlike visiting the doctor or the dentist, we look forward to participating in tourism. It is the industry of roller coasters, fine restaurants, Walt Disney World, cruise ships, Las Vegas, the Eiffel Tower, the Great Barrier Reef, and innumerable other wonderful destinations and attractions. But the tourism industry is not only fun and excitement; it is also serious business.

So what is tourism? The World Tourism Organization (WTO), a branch of the United Nations, defines tourism as the activities of persons traveling outside their usual environment for up to one year for leisure, business, or other purposes except activities for which the traveler is getting paid within the place visited.[1]

Thus, for our purposes, **tourism** is traveling outside one's home area, usually taken to be at least 50 miles or more one way, and returning within one year. The travel may be for business, leisure, visiting family or friends, personal business (weddings, funerals, campus visits, etc.), shopping, or many other purposes. But we exclude changing residence or going to a distant site to work when the traveler expects to be paid at the distant site. Also, short trips in the course of everyday local affairs, such as commuting to work, are not considered tourism.

The tourism industry is a worldwide giant providing services to many millions of people, providing useful employment and investment returns to others, paying

Tourism
Tourism is traveling outside one's home area, usually at least 50 miles or more one way, and returning within one year, except when going to a distant site to work when the traveler expects to be paid at the distant site.

---

[1] World Tourism Organization (2002).

taxes, and upsetting the evolution of local regions. The WTO estimates that in 2005 total global spending on international tourism, including international passenger transport, amounted to more than $800 billion.[2] To this we must add worldwide domestic tourism to see the size of total tourism spending.

The purpose of this book is to help you understand what is happening in the tourism industry. This book is about the economics of the tourism industry; we will see how a few basic ideas and methods of the discipline of economics can promote understanding of tourism. The question is not whether these ideas from economics can help us to understand *everything* about the industry, but rather whether they can help us to understand *anything*. The answer is yes!

We will look at consumers and governments, but our focus will be on business firms participating in the various well defined segments of the industry. We will see that we can make a lot of progress in understanding what we observe about business firm behavior in tourism:

- The firms that we see
- Their structure and operations
- Their interactions with each other
- The services they provide
- The array of prices they charge
- The government regulations they face

I hope you will see that in using these basic ideas from economics we can do a lot with a little. A few concepts and methods, many of which were covered in the prerequisite principles of economics course, will let us make great progress in understanding the tourism industry.

ECONOMIC CONCEPTS AND ISSUES IN TOURISM

Many people and organizations in our society participate in tourism activities. These include consumers, workers, business and property owners, investors, private organizations, governments, and others. We will see that a relatively small number of economic concepts can help us understand the behavior of these participants in the tourism industry. These ideas will appear again and again as we investigate various parts of the industry.

Furthermore, we will see that some of these economic concepts earned their creators Nobel Prizes in Economic Sciences, awarded annually by the Swedish Academy of Sciences. As these ideas arise, we will examine the work of the prize-winning economists and see how this work helps us to understand the tourism industry. For example, Ronald Coase explained that in any industry we expect to observe the firms (big or small, focusing narrowly or integrating many business functions, local or wide ranging, and so on) that do the industry's work at the lowest possible total cost. We will use this idea to help us understand car rental firms and tour operators, among others. To take another example, Wassily Leontief won the Nobel Prize in 1973 for developing "input-output analysis." Tourism analysts often use this type of analysis to measure the economic impact of tourism on regional economies. We will closely examine how this is done.

---

[2] World Tourism Organization (2006a), p. 2.

Creating Value for Consumers and Income for Workers and Owners

An **economy** is the set of institutions that creates the goods and services society wants to consume. The tourism industry's purpose is creating value for tourism consumers by creating tourism goods and services, including restaurant meals, hotels stays, and travel to our destinations, among many other services. By creating this value, the tourism industry creates income for the industry's workers and investors. Labor's wages, salaries, and benefits constitute the majority of the tourism industry's income.

Supply

In most cases supply results from business firm behavior. Costs of producing goods and services are the most important influences affecting business firm behavior. Much of the tourism industry has two special features which will help us to understand what is happening in many segments (including airlines, hotels, amusement parks, and others) of tourism. These ideas are (1) producing the firm's services requires high fixed costs and low marginal costs over a wide range of outputs, and (2) at any point in time the firm has a capacity constraint at the top end of that range.

High **fixed costs** means that producing any level of service at all requires a substantial initial investment in capacity, for example in building a roller coaster. Low **marginal costs** mean that after the firm produces the initial unit of service, additional units of service cost very little. Once again a roller coaster provides a very good example—once the ride is built, it costs very little to serve another rider. Thus, serving the first roller-coaster rider is very costly, while serving the second rider costs almost nothing. Finally, we see the idea of **capacity constraint**. In the case of a roller coaster, the marginal cost of serving another rider is very low until the ride is full. Once the park is jamming as many riders onto the ride per day as can be served, the cost of serving another rider would be extremely high—to serve another rider the park would have to build more capacity in the form of another roller coaster.

As we will see, many tourism firms have developed elaborate behaviors to deal with cost structures that include high fixed costs, low marginal costs, and capacity constraints. These behaviors include very complicated airline fare structures, with air fares changing by the minute and passengers sitting next to each other on a plane discovering that they paid very different prices for the same service. These behaviors also include student and senior citizen discounts, special prices for customers holding coupons, offerings on priceline.com, Orlando theme-park discounts for Florida residents, and many others. Once we understand the basic ideas, the pricing structures of airlines, cruise lines, theme parks, and other tourism firms lose their mystery.

Besides costs, there are other factors affecting business firm behavior. Technical change can have important effects on tourism business firms' costs. But, perhaps more importantly, technical change has from time to time changed the nature of tourism services. More than 200 years ago, technical change in the form of improvements in the steam engine, when later applied to travel, made travel by train and steamship possible. More recently, the invention of the airplane made important changes in tourism possible. But here we emphasize that technical change by itself never changes supply. Before market supply changes, businesses need to adopt technical changes through the creation of new business models or new business strategies. Business models are explanations of

Economy
An economy is the set of institutions that creates the goods and services society wants to consume.

Fixed costs
Costs that do not vary with the level of output produced.

Marginal cost
The additional cost of producing an additional unit of output.

Capacity constraint
Limit on the maximum amount of output that can be produced per period.

how business firms will make profits by serving customers. Business strategies are explanations of how business firms will fit into markets already inhabited by other firms. We will see how business models and business strategies affect supply in tourism markets.

Demand

Demand refers to consumer behavior. In economics, we generally do not find the words "need" or "want" to be very useful. This is not to say that people don't need things like food and medical care. Rather, it means that itemizing what people need does not help us to understand their behavior. For example, one would think that people *need more* water in arid regions, yet certainly we observe that people *use less* water in arid regions. Why? Because water has a higher price in arid regions, and the amount that people use depends on the price. **Demand** is the relationship between the price and the amount of a good or service that people buy. This is an inverse relationship: at higher prices consumers buy less and at lower prices consumers buy more.

Demand
The relationship between the price and the amount of a good or service that people buy.

The most important influence on tourism consumer demand behavior is income. While consumers throughout most of the range of income engage in tourism, higher incomes have a strong effect on increasing tourism demand. We observe this effect through time, as nations with growing average incomes see high rates of tourism growth. We also observe this at any point in time, as consumers with higher incomes have greater demands for tourism services than those with lower incomes.

Rivalry and Competition

A monopoly is an industry dominated by a single firm. We do not find true monopolies in tourism industries, because tourism industries have more than one participating firm. These firms are rivals for the consumers spending. This rivalry affects firms' decisions about the services they provide and the prices they charge. We will examine some ways to understand rivalry among tourism firms and look for the effects of growing numbers of firms on prices and services. One important area is understanding competition between the major airlines that have been flying for many decades and the new low-cost airlines that have entered the industry in recent years.

Government Regulation

Governments have had important impacts on tourism. At times governments have promoted tourism through direct cash subsidies, as with the early airline industry. At other times governments have promoted tourism through subsidized facilities, river and seaport facilities, airports, and roads. Governments have also supported tourism through advertising and other efforts promoting their regions as tourism destinations.

Governments also promote tourism through safety regulation. One important example is the set of important safety requirements that governments around the world imposed on passenger lines following the *Titanic* disaster. Governments also regulate food handling—on cruise ships, in restaurants, and elsewhere. As another example, few things have done more to promote U.S. tourism than the federal and state governments' cooperation in constructing the Interstate Highway System, a far-reaching system of safe, high-speed roadways.

In other ways, governments have discouraged tourism. One of the most direct and frequently seen ways is through taxation, which raises the prices of tourism services. In some cases, governments actively discourage tourism through regulations designed to protect the environment. In other cases, most notably the now defunct U.S. Civil Aeronautics Board, discussed in Chapter 7, government regulation discouraged tourism without a well thought-out rationale.

Finally, governments can vacillate between encouraging and discouraging tourism. The most notable example involves casino gambling. Governments have sometimes chosen to prevent casino operations and in other cases have chosen to promote the growth of casinos. Some governments have chosen both strategies at one time or another. In some cases, governments let voters decide issues of casino gaming through referendums. Casinos are now big business in many parts of the world; as we will see, they are heavily taxed and heavily regulated.

TOURISM INDUSTRY ORGANIZATIONS

Many organizations around the world promote, analyze, measure, and gather information about tourism, or perform some combination of these activities. These organizations are an important source of information about the tourism industry. They provide services to support industry operations, perform analyses, make policy recommendations, compile statistics, and put information into easily accessible forms, often through web sites.

Some of these organizations are government agencies, including branches of local, state, provincial, and national governments. Some are organizations representing the governments of groups of nations. The U.S. Department of Commerce has an Office of Travel and Tourism Industries which promotes tourism to the United States and regularly measures inbound and outbound U.S. tourism by region of the world. Other nations have similar agencies with responsibilities for national tourism promotion and measurement of international travel. For example, Tourism Australia performs these functions for Australia.

The major statistical agencies of the nations of the world often pay special attention to the tourism industry. The U.S. Commerce Department's Bureau of Economic Analysis maintains tourism satellite accounts as part of the national income and product accounts (NIPA) program that produces quarterly measures of gross national product (GNP). Statistics Canada performs the same functions for Canada. New Zealand and many other nations have similar government programs.

The World Tourism Organization, based in Madrid, is an agency of the United Nations. Its goals are to promote tourism around the world through such things as providing technical help to nations seeking to increase the number of tourist arrivals. It also gathers and disseminates statistics on international tourism.

Some of the most important tourism organizations are private associations lacking formal government ties. Many of these are trade associations; that is, associations formed to promote the interests of groups of tourism service providers. In the United States, the Travel Industry Association of America is a large trade association representing the entire industry and promoting travel to the United States. Most tourism industry segments have trade associations representing their interests. One important function of these associations is government relations, including monitoring government policy, informing members about impending government actions, and lobbying on behalf of members. They may also provide technical or operational help with such things as telecommunications and handling payments involving multiple service providers.

The airline industry has some of the largest and most active associations. The International Air Transport Association serves the global air transport industry, including both passenger airlines and air cargo carriers. The Air Transport Association of America performs similar functions for the U.S. air transport industry. Cruise lines, travel agents, tour operators, and many other segments of the tourism industry have active trade associations representing and serving their member firms.

The web sites maintained by these organizations are important sources of information for students and others researching the tourism industry. We will encounter many of these associations in the chapters that follow.

Summary

Tourism, or traveling outside one's home area for business or leisure and returning within one year, provides services, employment, and investment returns to huge numbers of people around the world. The basic ideas and methods of the discipline of economics can help us to understand this industry. These include concepts such as supply and demand, costs, technology, and government regulation.

Many domestic and international organizations promote and analyze tourism. These include the United Nation's World Tourism Organization, national organizations such as the U.S. Department of Commerce and Tourism Australia, and trade associations such as the Travel Industry Association of America. These organizations are important sources of information and analysis about the tourism industry.

In Chapter 2, we will see how the tourism industry creates value for consumers and income for producers.

Bibliography

Air Transport Association of America (2006), "Making Airlines a National Priority," www.airlines.org/home/default.aspx.

American Society of Travel Agents (2006), "Who We Are," www.astanet.com/about/index.asp.

Australian Bureau of Statistics (2006), "Themes," www.abs.gov.au/websitedbs/d3310114.nsf/Home/themes.

Cruise Lines International Association (2006), "Cruise Lines International Association," www.cruising.org/.

National Tour Association (2006), "National Tour Association," www.ntaonline.com/index.php.

Organization of American States (2006), "Tourism Section," www.oas.org/tourism/home/.

Statistics Canada (2006), "National Tourism Indicators Quarterly Estimates," www.statcan.ca/bsolc/english/bsolc?catno=13-009-XIB.

Statistics New Zealand (2006), "Tourism," www.stats.govt.nz/economy/industry/tourism.htm.

Tourism Australia (2006), "Tourism Info," www.tourism.australia.com/AboutUs.asp?sub=0281.

Travel Industry Association of America (2006), "What We Do," www.tia.org/about/what_we_do.html.

U.S. Department of Commerce (2006a), "Office of Travel and Tourism Industries," http://tinet.ita.doc.gov/.

U.S. Department of Commerce (2006b), "Satellite Industry Accounts," www.bea.gov/bea/dn2/home/tourism.htm.

World Tourism Organization (2002), "TSA in Depth: Analysing Tourism as an Economic Activity," http://www.world-tourism.org/statistics/tsa_in_depth/chapters/ch3-1.htm.

World Tourism Organization (2006a), *UNWTO World Tourism Barometer*, June, www.unwto.org/facts/eng/pdf/barometer/WTOBarom06_2_en_ex.pdf.

World Tourism Organization (2006b), "World Tourism Organization," www.unwto.org/.

CHAPTER 2

Creating Value in Tourism

Learning Goals

- Understand what an *economy* is.
- Understand the relationship between *income* and *value added*.
- Understand how travel agents create value.
- See the size of value added in tourism in the United States and Canada.

WHAT IS AN ECONOMY? WHY DO WE HAVE AN ECONOMY?

An economy is the set of institutions that creates the goods and services society wants to consume. If an economy is a set of institutions, we must define *institution*. Some institutions are normal rules of behavior and social interaction. These can be formal, such as laws and regulations, or informal, such as customs and social behaviors. Private property rights and payments for labor services, which are important examples of economic institutions, involve both formal laws and informal social behaviors. Social organizations such as physical markets like a local fish market, or electronic markets like the NASDAQ (National Association of Securities Dealers Automated Quotation System), or more abstract markets, like the labor market, are also institutions. Institutions are often very durable, enduring little-changed for generations or centuries. Or, they can change rapidly. For example, technical change can lead to rapid change in institutions, as with the introduction of the telephone and later the cellular telephone, the Internet, e-mail, and other changes in electronic communications. These changes have caused many changes in the rules of social interaction.

We have an economy and economic institutions because we want to eat, we want to be protected from the weather, we want to be warm in winter and cool in summer, we want to be entertained, we want to be mobile, and so on. We have an economy because we are consumers and nature usually does not give us the things that directly provide consumer satisfaction. At the most basic level, even if we were to subsist on naturally growing fruits and berries we would first have to gather them. The natural foods we gather may also require some kind of preparation. All of this gathering and preparation is economic activity—engaging in production to convert resources into goods and services which are consumed, leading to consumer satisfaction.

Imagine a new reality TV show called *Economy Island*. The show's premise is that the producers drop the contestants off on a small deserted island with nothing but the clothes they are wearing and a TV camera. The island is remote, so the contestants will have no contact with the outside world until the producers return. The producers return six months later to see how the contestants have gotten along and to pick up the camera and its contents. They will discover that the contestants either created an economy or died of starvation, disease, or exposure. Either the contestants engaged in activities to keep themselves alive or they did not. If they survived, they will have done so by doing economic activities like gathering, growing, capturing, preparing, and consuming food. Making shelters and clothing are also economic activities, as are such things as entertaining themselves and treating injuries or illnesses they may contract. In the process of doing these activities, the contestants may have created institutions guiding cooperation or rivalry. They may have divided the resources or assigned responsibilities. Some contestants may have assumed authority for certain actions, or they may have created political institutions, like voting mechanisms, to assign authority and to make decisions. The essence of *Economy Island* is that the contestants create an economy using their own labor and the island's resources or they die.

Economic activity is usually intended to *create value*. In a primitive economy like that on *Economy Island*, the activity of gathering food creates value by converting scattered and distant food items into an accumulation of food items in a place where the contestants can use them. By doing this the economy has created value for consumers. Preparing the food by washing, peeling, or cooking creates additional value by converting the food items into edible and, we hope, enjoyable forms. Usually, economic activity consists of a series of steps that sequentially add value to the gifts of nature, with value determined subjectively by the satisfaction consumers get from consumption of the goods and services.

Value added
A firm's revenue minus what it paid for intermediate goods.

We often measure value created by economic activity as **value added,** a firm's revenue minus what it paid for intermediate goods, to avoid double counting; that is, to avoid counting the same value twice. For example, Ford Motor Company sells cars with CD players, but Ford does not make CD players. Ford buys them from another firm, perhaps Sony. In calculating Ford's value added we subtract the value of its CD player purchases from its car sales. The value added in making cars' CD players belongs to Sony. Subtracting amounts spent on intermediate goods like automobile CD players from total car sales avoids double counting the value of the CD players.

For another example, consider making wooden furniture. The process starts with a forest. A logger creates value by cutting some trees and then selling the logs to a sawmill. The sawmill produces and sells lumber, but its total value added is less than its total sales. To determine the sawmill's value added, we must subtract its purchases of logs from loggers. In general, to calculate a firm's value added, we subtract the value of all intermediate products it buys from other firms. Following the wood to the end product, the "green" lumber next goes to a dry kiln which adds value by reducing the lumber's water content; the dry lumber can then be sold to a furniture maker which adds value by converting the lumber into furniture. At each step a processor adds value to the intermediate products it bought from the prior stage of processing.

INCOME AND VALUE ADDED

Income, the net flow of value created in an economy during a specific time period, is one of the most important concepts in economics. The important thing to note about income and value added is that the value we add or create by our economic activities is the only source of our income. What is the income of the contestants on *Economy Island* while they are on the island? It is whatever value they have created. The same is true everywhere else in the economy—creating value is the only source of income. Note also that income comes in many forms, including wages, salaries, tips, profits, interest, royalties, and rents. For any society, the only source for these varieties of income is the value added during the period.

Students and others often confuse money, wealth, and income, in part because much of income is paid with money and some wealth is held as money. Money, wealth, and income are very different things. Money is the medium of exchange, and it is also a medium for holding some of our wealth. Income, on the other hand, is very different. In the aggregate, income is the flow of value created in the economy during some period. Wealth is the accumulation of value over time out of past income.

Getting a firm grasp of these concepts helps us to understand many important economic issues:

- Can the government increase the nation's income by hiring people into government jobs and paying them with newly created money? Certainly not in times of high employment, because such a policy would increase the supply of money while it would probably not create a lasting increase in the flow of value created in the economy. If the flow of value does not get larger, incomes will not get larger.
- Why do citizens of some nations have very low incomes while citizens of other nations have very high incomes? The typical citizen of a low-income country creates very little value with each hour worked, or works very few hours. The typical citizen of a high-income country creates a lot of value with each hour worked and is able to work many hours per week or per year.
- How much income might someone approaching adulthood expect to earn over his or her working life? It depends on how much value the person will create per period. If he or she becomes a brain surgeon, we would expect a lot of value per hour worked and high income. If he or she works at sweeping the steps of the courthouse, we cannot expect the person to earn much income, because the person is not going to create much value per hour worked.
- How much income should we expect travel agents or engineers or dentists to earn? The answer depends on the value they create.

Value added is centrally important in an economy because value added minus depreciation, no more and no less, is available to be paid out as income. We subtract depreciation from value added in calculating income. For a business firm, **depreciation** is defined as the loss in value of the firm's capital stock during the period, while **capital** is the stock of durable productive inputs such as buildings, tools, machinery, and vehicles the firm uses. A firm such as the sawmill discussed earlier has equipment and other capital stock that will generally decline in value as time passes. For example, the motors on the saws may wear out or become obsolete and as a result become less valuable.

Income
The net flow of value created in the economy during the period.

Depreciation
The loss in value of the firm's capital stock during the period.

Capital
The durable inputs to production, such as buildings, vehicles, machinery, and tools

Thus the firm creates value by using its equipment and loses value as its equipment depreciates. The sawmill's income is then the value of total sales minus purchases of intermediate products and minus depreciation.

The sawmill's value added minus depreciation is all that is available to pay out as wages and salaries to its workers and as interest, rents, and profits to its creditors, landlords, and owners. It may borrow to continue operations with payouts exceeding value added, but in that case it is borrowing value added from the lender. In the aggregate (that is, for the economy as a whole) this must net to zero, so that aggregate income is aggregate value added (minus depreciation). The firm may draw down savings to operate with current payouts exceeding current value added, but here it is shifting value added through time, converting wealth (accumulated value added from the past) to income. There is no avoiding the fact that value added is the only source of income.

We can see the relationship between value added and income in the gross domestic product (GDP) calculations made by the U.S. Department of Commerce. Four times each year the Commerce Department calculates the most recent quarter's GDP and gross domestic income, known together as the national income and product accounts (NIPA). GDP is defined as the total value of goods and services produced, or the sum of the value added of industries and governments, within the nation during the period. Gross Domestic Income measures the same concept by adding income from all sources in the nation.[1]

Suppose the value added of some activity were negative; that is, suppose the value of the goods created by the activity were less than the value of the goods that went into its production process. For example, suppose the value of the lumber produced by a sawmill were less than the value of the logs it bought. Even if it paid no wages to its workers, its profits would be negative. With negative profits, we would expect the firm to go out of business. Eventually it would have to cease operations unless it could get a subsidy from some source to cover the shortfall of revenue from sales relative to costs. Examples of activities with negative value added are rare but not impossible; they existed in non-market economies, such as the former Soviet Union, where profit calculations were rarely made and decisions were often not based on profits. Activities with negative value added can also persist when decision makers do not recognize all costs, for example, when there are substantial negative effects on the environment.

A firm with negative value added is producing output worth less than the value of its intermediate inputs alone. Business firms can, however, engage in economic activities that have positive value added but still lose money. Recall that firms must pay wages to labor and returns to capital (profits and interest) out of value added. Value added may be positive but too small to pay labor and still have something left for a return to capital. The economic profits of a firm show the excess of revenue over total costs, not just the excess over costs of intermediate goods. The normal return to capital is included in total cost, so that a firm earning just the normal rate of return will have economic profits of zero. Negative economic profits, or a rate of return below the normal rate, show that the firm is producing output worth less than the value of the inputs it is using.

---

[1] McCahill and Moyer (2002), p. 23.

VALUE ADDED BY TRAVEL AGENCIES

Travel agencies create value in many ways. Travel agencies are intermediaries between travelers and travel service providers, supplying valuable services to both sides of travel transactions. To the traveler, they provide information on available travel opportunities, on prices, and on many other characteristics of travel. Travel agencies can search through vast amounts of information for flight availabilities, lowest prices, hotel vacancies, and other unknowns. They also provide advice, which is a special kind of information. A highly qualified, experienced travel agent may have visited the destination you are considering, stayed in many of your destination's hotels, sailed on many of the cruise ships, or flown the airlines you are considering. Advice from those with knowledge from personal experience or other sources can be very valuable. Further, the travel agency will often process the transaction. For example, you may go into the travel agency's office with money and leave with an airline ticket, although the ticket is likely to be electronic rather than paper. All of these activities create value for travelers. On the supplier side, the agency is also creating value by processing the transaction. The agency may also be providing services by actively promoting and selling a particular travel supplier's services. In sum, travel agencies create value for both travelers and travel service providers—they provide information, search, advice, promotion, selling, and transactions processing.

How Much Income Can Travel Agencies Expect to Earn?

Now consider the question of how much income travel agencies can expect to earn. The answer will depend on the value they create, and the value created by travel agencies has changed dramatically in recent years. One of the biggest forces changing travel agency value added has been the Internet.

The Internet is a rapidly growing communications network. When combined with personal computers, browser software, and local communications links, the Internet provides consumers, workers, and companies an inexpensive, convenient, ubiquitous means to spread, acquire, and process information. The Internet has had profound effects on information-intensive industries. Publishing, brokerage, telecommunications, and retailing have seen important innovations arise from the powerful and rapidly developing capabilities of the Internet. The travel agency industry is one of the industries most affected. These effects have forced the industry to change.

The nature of the Internet makes it an important source of many kinds of information for travelers. Travelers can use the Internet to get information on available travel opportunities, prices, features, and other characteristics of travel. The Internet and associated software are particularly good at searching. There are many search engines and web portals that organize much of the information available on the World Wide Web and make it easy to search through the astounding volume of this web-published information. Some of this information takes the specialized form of advice. Travel advisors such as Fodor's (www.fodors.com), Frommer's (www.frommers.com), and *Condé Nast Traveler* magazine's Concierge.com (www.concierge.com), among many others, provide a vast array of advice on destinations, travel modes, and the full range of travel service providers. Travel service providers also use the Internet. The World Wide Web and e-mail have created many new ways for providers to promote their services. They have their own web sites, advertise on others' web sites, and distribute e-mail to reach potential customers. Providers not only promote but also sell using the Internet. It is now quite common for travelers and travel service providers to process their transactions, making reservations and buying and selling tickets, through online agencies such as Travelocity, Orbitz, and Expedia.

VALUE ADDED IN TOURISM IN THE UNITED STATES

Earlier we saw a reference to the national income and product accounts, the quarterly accounting of the value created and income earned in the U.S. economy published by the U.S. Department of Commerce. Most nations create similar accounts. See, for example, the Australian Bureau of Statistics (2000).

Over the many years that governments have created accounts of national income and national production, tourism has generally not been separately identified as an industry. Production has been reported for industries such as agriculture, retail trade, manufacturing, transportation, and others. Tourism simply made up a part of transportation, a part of retail trade, and parts of other industries. Recently, the World Tourism Organization, the U.S. government, and other governments around the world have created what are known as *satellite accounts* to break out value added for tourism from the national income and product accounts. That is, tourism satellite accounts are additional accounts that take the parts of industries included in traditional national income and product accounts that are attributable to tourism and combine them into new, separate tourism accounts. In this way we can see the value added and income attributable to tourism.

Periodically the U.S. Department of Commerce estimates travel and tourism satellite accounts for the United States. In 2005, it published estimates for calendar year 2003. Table 2.1 shows some of the Commerce Department's estimates of tourism value added and tourism employee compensation by industry and in total.

Traveler accommodations, food and beverage services, and air transportation combined account for more than half (54 percent) of the value added of the tourism industries. Retail services and travel arrangement and reservation services are also large, with each having about 6 percent of total value added. Note that $172.3 billion of the $285.0 billion in value added of the tourism industries was paid out as compensation to employees. This means that 60 percent of the value added in tourism is paid as wages, salaries, and other compensation to people working in the industry. The remaining 40 percent is available to pay returns to capital through interest, rents, royalties, and profits (including dividends and retained earnings).

VALUE ADDED IN TOURISM IN CANADA

Statistics Canada provides us with similar statistics for 2000 (see Table 2.2). Statistics Canada calculates tourism GDP as the sum of incomes paid by tourism industries rather than the sum of value addeds.[2] In concept, the two methods give the same result.

As with the United States, we see that for Canada accommodations, food and beverage services, and air transportation combined account for more than half (52 percent) of the value added of the tourism industries. About 67 percent of the value added of the Canadian tourism industries was paid out as compensation to employees.

---

[2] Barber-Dueck and Kotsovos (2005), p. 10.

TABLE 2.1 U.S. Tourism Value Added and Employee Compensation by Industry—2003

Industry	Tourism Value Added (Millions of Dollars)	Tourism Compensation (Millions of Dollars)
Traveler accommodations	68,284	36,180
Food and beverage services	36,836	25,393
Air transportation services	50,029	32,901
Rail transportation services	1,174	718
Water transportation services	2,509	1,499
Intercity bus services	880	603
Intercity charter bus services	653	488
Local bus and other transportation services	992	2,355
Taxicab services	2,375	1,491
Scenic and sightseeing transportation services	1,658	786
Automotive equipment rental and leasing	7,516	4,141
Automotive repair services	2,919	1,603
Parking	817	325
Highway tolls	391	152
Travel arrangement and reservation services	17,188	13,962
Motion pictures and performing arts	2,874	2,222
Spectator sports	6,257	3,792
Participant sports	6,029	4,137
Gambling	9,018	4,631
All other recreation and entertainment	7,359	3,691
Petroleum refineries	1,703	588
Industries producing nondurable personal consumption expenditure commodities, excluding petroleum refineries	16,579	8,078
Wholesale trade and transportation services	12,966	7,145
Gasoline service stations	3,550	1,361
Retail trade services, excluding gasoline service stations	18,270	10,493
All other industries	6,201	3,587
Total	285,027	172,324

Data source: Kuhbach and Herauf (2005).

TABLE 2.2 Canadian Tourism GDP and Labor Compensation by Industry—2000

Industry	Tourism GDP (Millions of Dollars)	Labor Income (Millions of Dollars)
Air transportation	3,680	2,949
Railway transportation	683	101
Water transportation	128	96
Bus transportation	419	275
Taxicabs	94	34
Vehicle rental	949	268
Total accommodation	5,247	3,393
Food and beverage services	2,691	2,206
Recreation and entertainment	1,776	1,247
Travel agencies	1,689	1,257
Other industries	5,050	3,304
Total tourism activities	22,407	15,129

Data source: Barber-Dueck and Kotsovos (2005).

Summary

The purpose of the tourism industry is to create value for tourism consumers. In performing this function, the industry creates income for the industry's workers and investors.

Many nations compile tourism satellite accounts to show the size of their tourism industries. These accounts show that labor income, in the form of wages, salaries, and benefits, receives the majority of the tourism industry's income. In the following chapters, we will use these elementary economic concepts of income and value added to help us understand behavior in the various components of the industry, such as lodging and airlines.

Bibliography

Australian Bureau of Statistics, "Australian Tourism Satellite Account," *Australian Economic Indicators*, September, 2000.

Barber-Dueck, Conrad, and Demi Kotsovos (2005), "Canadian Tourism Satellite Account, 2000," Statistics Canada Research Paper, Catalogue no. 13-604-MIE no. 48, www.statcan.ca/english/research/13-604-MIE/13-604-MIE2005048.pdf.

Greif, Avner. "Cultural Beliefs and the Organization of Society: A Historical and Theoretical Reflection on Collectivist and Individualist Societies." *Journal of Political Economy* 102 (1994): 912–950.

———. *Institutions and the Path to Economic Modernity: Lessons from Medieval Trade*. Cambridge: Cambridge University Press, 2006.

Kass, David I., and Sumiye Okubo. "U.S. Travel and Tourism Satellite Accounts for 1996 and 1997." *Survey of Current Business* 80 (2000): 8–24. http://www.bea.gov/bea/ARTICLES/NATIONAL/Inputout/2000/0700tta.pdf.

Kuhbach, Peter, and Bradlee A. Herauf. "U.S. Travel and Tourism Satellite Accounts for 2001–2004." *Survey of Current Business* 85 (2005): 17–29. http://www.bea.gov/scb/pdf/2005/06June/0605_Travel.pdf.

McCahill, Robert J., and Brian C. Moyer. "Gross Domestic Product by Industry for 1999–2001." *Survey of Current Business* 82 (2002): 23–41. http://www.bea.gov/bea/ARTICLES/2002/11November/1102GDPbyIndustry.pdf.

Statistics Canada (2006), "National Tourism Indicators Quarterly Estimates Fourth Quarter 2005," Catalogue no. 13-009-XIB, http://www.statcan.ca/english/freepub/13-009-XIB/13-009-XIB2005004.pdf.

U.S. Bureau of Labor Statistics (2007), "Travel Agents," *Occupational Outlook Handbook 2006–07 ed.*, www.bls.gov/oco/ocos124.htm.

CHAPTER 3

Tourism Consumers

Learning Goals

▪ Be able to describe domestic U.S. travelers.

▪ Know some of the major findings of the National Household Travel Survey.

▪ Understand the factors affecting demand for tourism.

▪ Be able to define price and income elasticities of demand for tourism.

▪ Understand business travel demand.

▪ Understand customer loyalty programs.

INTRODUCTION

During the 2004 U.S. presidential election campaign, many Americans were surprised to learn that candidate John Kerry, a 60-year-old member of the U.S. Senate, owned a snowboard. Few people in Senator Kerry's demographic group own snowboards. Snowboard manufacturers and marketers know their target market well, and it primarily includes boys and men in much younger age groups than we find among members of the U.S. Senate. Tourism firms also need to understand their target markets.

All firms should begin their marketing efforts by identifying their target consumers, or those segments of the population who are most likely to be profitably served. Tourism service providers, including airlines, hotels, destinations, attractions, and many others, know their target markets well. One way tourism firms and marketing organizations such as city convention and visitors bureaus describe their customers is by using visitor profiles. These profiles measure traveler or visitor characteristics along an array of dimensions, including measures describing the demographics, the purpose of the trip, trip length, services consumed, and many others.

PROFILES OF U.S. TRAVELERS

What do we know about travelers? Who are they? Why do they travel? Where do they go? Various travel surveys and research results provide a great deal of information about travelers. The Travel Industry Association of America (TIA) is a trade association and marketing organization that represents the U.S. travel industry. It regularly surveys travelers in the United States and publishes statistics describing these travelers. TIA reports travel behaviors of Americans making trips of 50 miles or more one way; short trips in the course of everyday local affairs, such as grocery shopping, are excluded. TIA reports that in 2004, there were 490 million household trips for leisure and almost 170 million domestic household trips for business purposes in the United States.[1] (A "household trip" is one consisting of one or more persons from the same household. The alternative measure is "person trip," which counts each person separately. Thus, two parents traveling with one child would consist of one household trip and three person trips.) TIA also reports the following additional characteristics of domestic U.S. travel (see Table 3.1).

TABLE 3.1 Characteristics of Domestic U.S. Travelers and Trips—2004

Season of Travel	Percentage of Trips
Winter	20
Spring	23
Summer	33
Fall	24
Purpose of Trip	
Leisure	81
Business or convention	12
Combined business & leisure	7
Mode of Travel	
Automobile, truck, RV	73
Airplane	16
Motorcoach	2
Train, ship, or other	4
Rental car (primary)	3
Duration of Trip	
Same day	23
1 to 2 nights	35
3 to 6 nights	29
7 or more nights	13
Type of Lodging	
Hotel, motel, or B&B	54
Private homes	40
RV or tent	5
Condo or timeshare	4
Other	7

Data source: Travel Industry Association of America (2006).

---

[1] Travel Industry Association of America (2006).

Thus, we see that in 2004 domestic U.S. travel was dominated by short-duration leisure trips, primarily using personal-use vehicles as the travel mode. Summer is the peak travel season and winter is the slowest travel season. Spring and fall have intermediate levels of travel and are often called the "shoulder" seasons, because a graph of tourism activity over the year will show a "head" in the summer with two shoulders on either side during fall and spring. Of course, given that there were nearly 700 million total household trips during the year, the other kinds of trips, including business trips, trips of longer duration, and trips using other travel modes were also very important.

THE NATIONAL HOUSEHOLD TRAVEL SURVEY

In 2001, the U.S. Department of Transportation's Bureau of Transportation Statistics (BTS) conducted the National Household Travel Survey, a very broad survey of American travelers.[2] The survey asked approximately 26,000 randomly selected households for information about all of their travel during the year. The survey included questions about "long-distance" trips, those originating from home and covering a distance of at least 50 miles or more one way. The survey shows that during 2001 Americans took about 2.6 billion trips of 50 miles or more. About 98 percent of long-distance trips were to destinations inside the United States, and 62 percent of those trips were to destinations inside the same state. Fifty-seven percent of long-distance trips were made by men.

Almost 56 percent of long-distance trips during 2001 were for pleasure, which includes vacations, visiting family and friends, rest and relaxation, recreation, and others. About 16 percent of trips were for business. Personal business and commuting to work each accounted for about 13 percent of long-distance trips.

Travel Mode

The BTS survey inquired about modes of long-distance travel. Almost 90 percent of these trips were taken by personal-use vehicle—primarily cars but also including trucks, vans, motorcycles, and other vehicles. Approximately seven percent of trips were by commercial air carrier, although the proportion of trips via air varied greatly with distance traveled. The vast majority of shorter trips were by personal-use vehicle, while almost 75 percent of trips of 2,000 roundtrip miles or more were by air. The survey found that about 2 percent of all household trips were made by intercity bus and less than 1 percent by train.

The proportion of long-distance trips via each mode also varied greatly by the purpose of the trip. Table 3.2 shows the relationship between mode of travel and purpose of travel. Business travelers are least likely to travel by personal-use vehicles and most likely to travel by air.

Business Travelers

The 2001 National Household Travel Survey showed that men made 77 percent of long-distance business trips (see Table 3.3). Thus, business travelers tended to be men, age 30 to 59, in professional, managerial, or technical occupations, and in households with moderate to high incomes.

---

[2] U.S. Department of Transportation, Bureau of Transportation Statistics (2003a).

TABLE 3.2 Distribution of Long-Distance Trips by Purpose and Mode—2001

	Reason for Travel (percentage)				
Mode	Commute	Business	Pleasure	Personal Business	Other
Personal-use vehicle	96.4	79.3	90.4	89.3	96.6
Air	1.5	17.8	6.7	4.7	1.9
Bus	0.5	0.8	2.2	5.6	0.5
Train	1.7	1.6	0.5	0.3	0.0
Other	0.0	0.5	0.2	0.1	1.0

Data source: U.S. Department of Transportation, Bureau of Transportation Statistics, 2003a, p. 26.

TABLE 3.3 Distribution of Business Travelers by Demographic Variables—2001

Occupation	Percentage of Business Travelers
Professional, managerial, technical	53
Sales and service	28
Clerical and administrative	4
Other	15
Age	
18 to 29	16
30 to 39	28
40 to 49	27
50 to 59	18
60 and older	10
Gender	
Male	77
Female	23
Household Income	
$25,000 or less	6
$26,000 to $74,000	49
$75,000 to $99,000	18
$100,000 or more	27

Data source: U.S. Department of Transportation, Bureau of Transportation Statistics, 2003b.

DEMAND FOR TOURISM

Demand for a tourism service is the relationship between the amount of the service that customers will buy and the price of the service. There is an inverse relationship between the quantity of a good demanded and its price, as we will discuss in Chapter 6. We see this in Figure 3.1 in which the demand curve illustrates the relationship between the quantity of a good demanded and its price. The negative slope of the demand curve shows the inverse relationship.

Economists usually assume that tourists buy tourism and all of the other goods and services available to them to maximize the satisfaction they receive from consuming goods and services, given their budget constraints. That is, consumers want to buy food, clothing, housing, transportation, medical care, entertainment, travel, resort vacations, and so on. But they have limited amounts of income and savings of past income, so they cannot have everything they want. The idea of the budget constraint is that the goods and services a consumer wants to buy have prices, and the price of each good and the quantity of each good the consumer wants to buy determine the total amount the consumer will spend to get a particular combination of goods and services. This total amount is the sum of the price of each good multiplied by the quantity of each good, summed over all the goods. If the price of good one is P_1, the price of good two is P_2, and so on, and the quantity of good one that the consumer wants to buy is X_1, and the quantity of good two that the consumer wants to buy is X_2, and so on, then the total amount required to buy these quantities is the following:

$$P_1X_1 + P_2X_2 + P_3X_3 + P_4X_4 + \cdots$$

But the consumer may not have enough income to spend this amount. The consumer can't change the prices, so he or she must adjust the quantities bought to bring this total amount spent to equality with the amount of available income he or she has to spend.

That is, consumers must choose—they must allocate their limited incomes among the alternatives they face. We assume they do so in the way they find most satisfying. Economists refer to this as *maximizing utility subject to a budget constraint.*

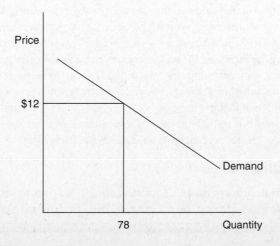

FIGURE 3.1 The Demand Curve.

Adding up the spending on a particular good or service for all consumers in a market gives us the market demand for that good.

The idea that consumers make purchases to get the most satisfaction from their limited incomes has important implications. Let's look at some of these key implications.

The Impact of Price Changes

Suppose that consumers are maximizing utility subject to a budget constraint as just described and that the price of one of the goods increases. At the new higher price of that good, consumers no longer have the income to pay for the combination of goods and services they were buying before the price increase. Consumers will now buy less in total, and more specifically, they will buy less of the good whose price has increased. They will tend to shift their spending away from the good whose price increased in favor of other goods.

This is the law of substitution: when relative prices change, buyers will substitute in favor of what becomes relatively cheaper. Take an example from travel and tourism. Suppose the prices of airline tickets increase for leisure travelers. Then leisure travel consumers will tend to substitute in favor of automobile travel, train travel, and other modes of transportation. They may also substitute in favor of other forms of leisure and entertainment spending, such as audio and video equipment, skipping leisure travel altogether. Goods of this sort are **substitutes;** consumers tend to substitute among them as the goods' relative prices change.

Substitutes
Two goods are substitutes if an increase in the price of one of the goods *increases* the demand for the other.

Complements
Two goods are complements if an increase in the price of one of the goods *decreases* the demand for the other.

Consumers often use goods in combination. In travel and tourism, for example, travelers often use airline services, rental cars, and hotel rooms when making a trip. These goods are not substitutes—they are known as **complements**. If the price of air travel increases, we can expect travelers to make fewer trips, which will require fewer rental cars and fewer hotel rooms. In this case, when the price of airline tickets increases, the demand for rental cars and hotel rooms declines. To take a more familiar example, consider coffee, tea, and sugar. For many people, coffee and tea are substitutes, while coffee and sugar are complements. If the price of coffee were to rise, the demand for tea would increase as consumers, to some extent, substituted tea for coffee. The demand for sugar, however, would decrease as consumers consumed less coffee with sugar.

The Impact of Income Changes

Suppose again that consumers are maximizing utility subject to a budget constraint. What happens when income increases? With higher incomes, consumers can spend more on goods and services. They could buy more of everything. This is not, however, what usually happens when income increases. When incomes increase, consumers tend to add to their purchases unevenly, concentrating their increased income in some areas and, perhaps, even buying less of some things. We refer to goods, such as hotdogs or potatoes, that consumers buy less of when income increases as "inferior" goods. "Normal" goods are those goods that consumers buy more of as income increases. Consumer spending on "luxury" goods increases by a greater percentage than the increase in income.

Factors Affecting Demand

Boeing Corporation studies travel demand each year as part of its annual *Current Market Outlook* for the demand for its aircraft. It has calculated that worldwide the most important factor influencing the growth in *aggregate* demand for air travel is growth in nations' GDP or national income. Other factors, including falling prices for air travel, improved service, and increased international trade account for the remainder of the growth in air travel demand.[3]

The major factors affecting the aggregate demand for leisure travel and tourism goods and services are listed below:

- *Income* Both long-term growth in the incomes of typical citizens and fluctuations in incomes over the business cycle strongly affect demand for leisure travel and tourism goods and services.
- *Season of the year* Leisure tourism is highly seasonal. The strongest demand for leisure tourism is during the summer. The weakest period of demand for leisure tourism in North America is during January through March.
- *Day of the week* Leisure tourism varies strongly during the typical week, with travel peaking on weekends and tailing off midweek. Friday and Sunday are peak travel days.
- *Price of the travel service* There is an inverse relationship between the quantity of a tourism service demanded and its price—a higher price leads to a lower quantity demanded.
- *Prices of substitutes* As with any good or service, the prices of substitutes affect demand for tourism services. When prices change, consumers substitute in favor of the goods and services that become relatively cheaper.
- *Prices of complements* As with substitutes, the prices of complements affect demand for travel and tourism services. When the price of a good or service increases, the demands for that good's complements fall.
- *Quality* Increasing quality increases demand. For example, Boeing's *Current Market Outlook* attributes part of the increase in demand for airline services to increasing frequency of flights and an increasing number of direct flights, which are both quality variables.
- *Security* Changes in security affect the demand for tourism services. For example, improved highway safety through the spread of the U.S. Interstate Highway System and improvements in automobile safety increased the demand for automobile travel in the United States in recent decades.

In addition to these important variables such as prices and income, other variables are important in determining an *individual person's* or *individual household's* tourism demand. These factors include the following:

Demographic variables

- *Age* A traveler's age influences variables such as destination choices, modes of travel, and length of trip.
- *Household type* Families with young children have different demands for tourism services than couples or singles.
- *Education* Household tourism demand, including destination choices and modes of travel, varies with education.

---

[3] The Boeing Company (2005).

- *Occupation* The major occupation classes include managerial, professional, technical, sales, clerical, laborer, production worker, and others. Household tourism demand also varies with occupation.
- *Work status* Whether members of a household are retired, working full time, working part time, unemployed, enrolled as students, or have some other work status influences household tourism choices.

Location variables

- *Distance* Distance has an important influence on destination choices. Typically, travel costs increase with distance. Also, as distance increases, the relative costs of travel to substitute destinations decreases. Thus, for example, relatively few Florida residents travel to Hawaii—the distance is large, and Florida beaches and the Caribbean provide substitutes for many Hawaiian destinations.[4] While California residents may travel to the Caribbean, the relative price of the Caribbean versus Hawaii is higher for California residents than for Florida residents.
- *Other location variables* Urban, suburban, and rural households may also differ in their tourism demands. The climate of the origin region also influences tourism choices.

PRICE AND INCOME ELASTICITIES OF DEMAND

Price Elasticity of Demand

Price elasticity of demand
A measure of the responsiveness of the quantity of a good demanded to a change in the good's price: $\varepsilon_i = \%\Delta Q_i^D \div \%\Delta P_i$.

The **price elasticity of demand** for any good or service is a measure of the responsiveness of the quantity of the good demanded to a change in that good's price. We define the price elasticity for any good as the percentage change in the quantity demanded divided by the percentage change in the price. Thus for good "i", the price elasticity ε_i is defined, using Δ to denote change, as

$$\varepsilon_i = \frac{\%\Delta Q_i^D}{\%\Delta P_i}.$$

Price elasticities of demand are negative, because, as shown above, there is an inverse relationship between the quantity of a good demanded and its price.

A good with a large elasticity of demand, that is greater than 1 in absolute value (ignoring the sign), is said to be "elastic" in demand. This simply means that when the price changes, the quantity demanded changes by a larger percentage. When the price elasticity is less than 1, we say that demand is "inelastic."

Cross Elasticity of Demand

Cross elasticity of demand
A measure of the responsiveness of the quantity of one good demanded to a change in another good's price: $\varepsilon_{ij} = \%\Delta Q_i^D \div \%\Delta P_j$.

As mentioned earlier, changes in the prices of substitutes or complements may change the demand for any good or service. We measure the size of these effects using the **cross elasticity of demand,** which is defined to be the percentage change in the

---

[4] Reece (2003).

quantity demanded of one good divided by the percentage change in the price of another good. Thus for two different goods i and j, the cross elasticity ε_{ij} is defined as

$$\varepsilon_{ij} = \frac{\%\Delta Q_i^D}{\%\Delta P_j}.$$

A positive cross elasticity occurs when the sign of the numerator is the same as the sign of the denominator (both positive or both negative). This happens, for example, when an *increase* in the price of good j causes an *increase* in the demand for good i. We might, for example, expect that an increase in the price of train travel would increase the demand for intercity bus travel. Then these goods are substitutes—when $\varepsilon_{ij} > 0$, the two goods are substitutes.

When $\varepsilon_{ij} < 0$, the goods are complements. This occurs when the numerator and denominator have different signs (one positive and one negative). We would see this, for example, when an *increase* in the price of gasoline *decreases* the demand for car rentals.

Income Elasticity of Demand

The **income elasticity of demand** for any good or service is a measure of the responsiveness of the good's demand to a change in the consumer's income. The income elasticity for any good is defined to be the percentage change in the quantity demanded (holding prices constant) divided by the percentage change in income. Thus, if M is income, the income elasticity η_i for good i is defined as

$$\eta_i = \frac{\%\Delta Q_i^D}{\%\Delta M}.$$

Income elasticity of demand A measure of the responsiveness of the demand for a good to a change in the consumer's income: $\eta_i = \%\Delta Q_i^D \div \%\Delta M$.

While we saw that price elasticities of demand are negative, income elasticities may be positive or negative. The income elasticity for a normal good is positive, and for an inferior good it is negative.

Estimating Elasticities of Demand for Tourism Services

The literature on statistically estimating elasticities of tourism demand is vast, including hundreds of studies published over the last 40 or more years. There have been many excellent reviews of this literature.[5] Most of the technicalities of this literature are beyond the scope of this book. We can, however, briefly examine simplified views of some of the methods that researchers have used and summarize some of the key results.

One of the most popular approaches to estimating price and income elasticities of tourism demand is to create an econometric model (that is, a set of equations based on economic relationships and including some random elements) of tourist spending across regions or through time. These equations explain tourism spending using variables measuring income, prices of tourism services, prices of substitutes, distances, and other variables.

---

[5] See, for example, Crouch (1995), Sinclair and Stabler (1997), pp. 35–57, Lim (1999), Li, Song, and Witt (2005).

While there are a variety of choices for the variables, in many cases the "dependent variables" in the model are "expenditure shares." Expenditure shares are simply the proportions of the aggregate tourism budget spent on tourism in each destination. To take a specific example, suppose residents of the United States may travel to any of three destinations, say Aruba, Bonaire, and Curacao, denoted A, B, and C. Suppose that the total amount spent on this travel in year t is M_t, and the amounts spent in each of the destinations are X_t^A, X_t^B, and X_t^C, respectively. Then we define the expenditure shares, denoted W, as $W_t^A = X_t^A/M_t$, $W_t^B = X_t^B/M_t$, and $W_t^C = X_t^C/M_t$. These could, for example, be ¼, ¼, and ½, indicating that one-fourth of the total spending was for travel to Aruba, one-fourth of the total spending was for travel to Bonaire, and one-half of the total spending was for travel to Curacao.

In this model we will assume that U.S. tourist consumers have already determined that they will spend M_t on travel to these three destinations during year t. Thus, M_t takes on the role of income in determining spending on travel to each location. Deaton and Muellbauer (1980) have shown that, under certain assumptions about consumer behavior, we can express the functions explaining the expenditure shares of the three destinations as functions of parameters to be estimated (α, β, and γ), the prices of tourism services in each of the three destinations (P^A, P^B, and P^C), total expenditure M, and an index of aggregate prices P:

$$W_t^A = \alpha^A + \gamma_A^A \ln(P_t^A) + \gamma_A^B \ln(P_t^B) + \gamma_A^C \ln(P_t^C) + \beta^A \ln(M_t/P_t)$$
$$W_t^B = \alpha^B + \gamma_B^A \ln(P_t^A) + \gamma_B^B \ln(P_t^B) + \gamma_B^C \ln(P_t^C) + \beta^B \ln(M_t/P_t)$$
$$W_t^C = \alpha^C + \gamma_C^A \ln(P_t^A) + \gamma_C^B \ln(P_t^B) + \gamma_C^C \ln(P_t^C) + \beta^C \ln(M_t/P_t)$$

Here, $\ln(x)$ refers to the natural logarithm of the variable x. These equations state that the expenditure share for *each* destination is a function of the logs of *all* of the prices, the log of the real *total* expenditure (the total expenditure deflated by the price index), and a constant.

The dependent variables, W_t^A, W_t^B, and W_t^C, are expenditure *shares*. This means that they will, by construction, add to 1. This implies many restrictions on the possible combinations of values of the parameters, and indeed, it means that we can calculate all of the parameters by estimating the parameters of any two of the equations. Also, there are simple algebraic expressions for the price and income elasticities using the expenditure shares and the estimated parameters.

One could gather data on U.S. tourist spending and prices in each of these destinations over many years. Then one could estimate the parameters using standard econometric methods, which are beyond the scope of this book.

Many researchers have used this model or similar models to estimate the effects of prices and total expenditure on demand for tourism. For example, Papatheodorou (1999) used a model similar to that outlined here to estimate the elasticities of demand of travelers from the United Kingdom, France, and West Germany for tourism in six Mediterranean destination countries for the period 1957 to 1990.[6] Among many other

---

[6] For other examples of research estimating elasticities using the almost ideal demand system, see Fujii, Khaled, and Mak (1985); Syriopoulos and Sinclair (1993); De Mello, Pack, and Sinclair (2002); Han, Durbarry, and Sinclair (2006); Li, Song, and Witt (2006).

			Cross Elasticities		
TABLE 3.4 Selected Elasticity Estimates in Papatheodorou—1999					
Destination	**Price Elasticity**	**Expenditure Elasticity**	**Portugal**	**Spain**	**Italy**
Portugal	−2.85	0.04	–	0.88	0.19
Spain	−1.30	1.15	0.88	–	0.49
Italy	−1.07	1.05	0.19	0.49	–

results, Papatheodorou estimated the elasticities shown in Table 3.4 for travelers from the United Kingdom.

In Table 3.4 we see that expenditure elasticities are near 1.0, except for a value near zero for Portugal. Also, the absolute values of the price elasticities are greater than 1, so that demand is price elastic. Some of the cross elasticities are small, but all of them are positive, indicating that these destinations are substitutes for each other.

CUSTOMER LOYALTY PROGRAMS

One of the key features of tourism consumer behavior is long-term relationships between consumers and many tourism service providers. This involves repeated consumer purchases of similar services over many years, often from a single service provider or a small group of service providers. Airline passengers often use one airline because it is the dominant airline serving the nearest airport. More often, consumers have a choice of airlines and repeatedly choose one of them because of the service provider's prices or services. Hotel guests also may tend to favor one or a small group of hotels for repeated stays.

To encourage repeat purchases and to develop long-term relationships, tourism service providers have created loyalty marketing programs. The first of these were Western Airlines' "Travel Pass" and American Airlines' "AAdvantage" frequent flyer programs.[7] In the ensuing years, these programs have proliferated; so that, today almost every major tourism service provider has a customer loyalty program.

Customer loyalty programs share a variety of features. First, there is a customer registration process through which the customer gives information, including identifying information, demographic information, and information about travel behavior and travel and service preferences to the provider. The customer then receives "points" or "miles" for each subsequent purchase of the company's services. These points accrue over time, and the traveler can at some later time redeem the points for "rewards," such as free travel, free hotel stays, upgrades to a higher class of service, merchandise, or other benefits. The programs often have various levels of membership, sometimes denoted as "Bronze," "Silver," and "Gold," with access to higher levels for more frequent travelers and buyers. The higher levels offer greater rewards for the traveler.

Tourism service providers offering customer loyalty programs anticipate substantial benefits for the company. The first is customer loyalty in the form of more frequent repeat purchases and purchases of the company's complementary products or services.

---

[7] InsideFlyer (2006).

Ideally, the loyalty program will induce the customer to *exclusively* use the services of the loyalty program's sponsor, shifting all of his or her travel business to the sponsor. The second benefit for the service provider is the acquisition of new information about the consumer, which the company can use to customize future offers of services at customized prices. We will return to the use of customer information in personalized pricing in Chapter 11.

Summary

Tourism firms and marketing organizations describe their customers using visitor profiles. These profiles measure many traveler or visitor characteristics, including demographic characteristics, the purpose of the trip, trip length, services consumed, and others. The TIA and the U.S. Department of Transportation's Bureau of Transportation Statistics periodically provide publicly available data on characteristics of travel and tourism in the United States.

The amount of tourism services consumers want to buy depends on the prices of those services, consumers' incomes, prices of substitutes and complements, season of the year, day of the week, and many other factors. It also depends on an individual consumer's location, demographic characteristics, and other individual characteristics. Many researchers have tried to measure consumer responsiveness to price and income changes by estimating elasticities of demand.

Customer loyalty programs are very important in the tourism industry. To encourage repeat purchases and to develop long-term relationships, many tourism service providers have created programs that award benefits such as free services or service upgrades to repeat purchasers.

Bibliography

The Boeing Company (2005), *2005 Current Market Outlook*, www.boeing.com/commercial/cmo/pdf/cmo2005_OutlookReport.pdf.

Crouch, Geoffrey I., "A Meta-Analysis of Tourism Demand." *Annals of Tourism Research* 22 (1995): 103–18.

Deaton, Angus, and John Muellbauer. "An Almost Ideal Demand System." *American Economic Review* 70 (1980): 312–26.

De Mello, Maria, Alan Pack, and M. Thea Sinclair. "A System of Equations Model of UK Tourism Demand in Neighboring Countries." *Applied Economics* 34 (2002): 509–21.

Fujii, Edwin, Mohammed Khaled, and James Mak. "The Exportability of Hotel Occupancy and Other Tourist Taxes." *National Tax Journal* 38 (1985): 169–77.

Han, Zhongwei, Ramesh Durbarry, and M. Thea Sinclair. "Modelling US Tourism Demand for European Destinations." *Tourism Management* 27 (2006): 1–10.

InsideFlyer (2006), "The Big 2–5—Celebrating 25 Years of Frequent Flyer Programs," www.insideflyer.com/articles/o2.php?key=89.

Kotler, Philip, John Bowen, and James Makens. *Marketing for Hospitality and Tourism*. Upper Saddle River, NJ: Prentice Hall, 1996.

Li, Gang, Haiyan Song, and Stephen F. Witt. "Recent Developments in Econometric Modeling and Forecasting." *Journal of Travel Research* 44 (2005): 82–99.

Lim, Christine. "Review of International Tourism Demand Models." *Annals of Tourism Research* 24 (1997): 835–49.

———. "A Meta-Analytic Review of International Tourism Demand." *Journal of Travel Research* 37 (1999): 273–84.

Maritz Loyalty Marketing (2008), "Loyalty Marketing," www.maritz.com/Sales-and-Marketing-Services/Customer-Loyalty.aspx.

Papatheodorou, Andreas. "The Demand for International Tourism in the Mediterranean Region." *Applied Economics* 31 (1999): 619–30.

Reece, William S. "Travelers to Las Vegas and to Atlantic City." *Journal of Travel Research* 39 (2001): 275–84.

———. "Comparing Orlando Leisure Travelers to Travelers to Other Florida Destinations." *Tourism Economics* 8 (2002): 151–64.

———. "Demographics of Hawaii Leisure Travel." *Journal of Hospitality & Tourism Research* 27 (2003): 185–99.

———. "Are Senior Leisure Travelers Different?" *Journal of Travel Research* 43 (2004): 11–18.

Shapiro, Carl, and Hal R. Varian. *Information Rules: A Strategic Guide to the Network Economy.* Boston: Harvard Business School Press, 1999.

Siebel Systems (2006), "SNCF Drives Customer Loyalty with Siebel Systems and Accenture," www.siebel.com/news-events/press_releases/2006/060117_sncf.shtm.

Sinclair, M. Thea. "Tourism and Economic Development: A Survey." *Journal of Development Studies* 34 (1998): 1–51.

Sinclair, M. Thea, and Mike Stabler. *The Economics of Tourism.* London: Routledge, 1997.

Smeral, Egon, and Stephen F. Witt. "Econometric Forecasts of Tourism Demand to 2005." *Annals of Tourism Research* 23 (1996): 891–907.

Song, Haiyan, Stephen F. Witt, and Thomas C. Jensen. "Tourism Forecasting: Accuracy of Alternative Econometric Models." *International Journal of Forecasting* 19 (2003): 123–41.

Syriopoulos, Theodore C., and M. Thea Sinclair. "An Econometric Study of Tourism Demand; the AIDS Model of US and European Tourism in Mediterranean Countries." *Applied Economics* 25 (1993): 1541–552.

Travel Industry Association of America (2006), "Domestic Travel Fast Facts," www.tia.org/pressmedia/domestic_statistics.html; www.tia.org/pressmedia/domestic_statistics.html.

U.S. Department of Transportation, Bureau of Transportation Statistics (2003a), *NHTS 2001 Highlights Report*, BTS03-05, Washington, DC. www.bts.dot.gov/publications/highlights_of_the_2001_national_household_travel_survey/pdf/entire.pdf.

———(2003b), *America on the Go: US Business Travel,* www.bts.gov/publications/america_on_the_go/us_business_travel/.

Witt, Stephen F., and Christine A. Witt. "Forecasting Tourism Demand: A Review of Empirical Research." *International Journal of Forecasting* 11 (1995): 447–75.

CHAPTER 4

Supply, Demand, and the Growth of Tourism

Learning Goals

- Know how tourism has risen and fallen over the centuries.
- Know how tourism has risen as an activity enjoyed by a large proportion of the population.
- Understand how supply and demand can explain the rise and fall of tourism and the development of today's tourism for the masses.
- Understand how tourism demand changes in response to changes in income and other factors.
- Understand the relationship of tourism supply to technology, business models, business strategies, and public policies.

INTRODUCTION

Tourism has existed since ancient times, and in some ways ancient tourism was similar to tourism today. Ancient Greeks, Romans, and others went sightseeing at the pyramids of Egypt, attended distant sporting events and religious festivals, traveled seeking cures for illnesses, or vacationed at seaside resorts. During the early Middle Ages, however, there was little tourism in Western Europe. Now, tourism is perhaps the largest industry among many huge industries. We may wonder why the level of tourism activity has risen and fallen over the centuries. We will see that the simplest kind of economic analysis—analysis of demand and supply—helps us to understand the growth of the tourism industry over the centuries.

TRAVEL AND TOURISM IN THE ANCIENT WORLD

The barbarians who invaded Rome beginning early in the fifth century CE found an advanced civilization with many aspects we would recognize today. They found an active, centralized government with laws, taxes, officials, and plentiful coinage. They found homes and public baths with indoor plumbing. The Roman life they encountered had access to goods from faraway places, books, music, theater, seaside resorts, and many other signs of civilized life. Of course, the Roman civilization of the fifth century also included many practices we find repugnant, including slavery and cruel punishments for criminals and other prisoners.

Much of the travel in the Roman Empire was for military or other government purposes.[1] There was also widespread commerce, especially by ships, both large and small, that served the Mediterranean ports. For overland travel the Romans established a very extensive system of carefully constructed and well-maintained roads. Much of this system was paved, and some stretches included two or three lanes. Some of these roads are still traveled today; one road currently in use travels through a tunnel cut for the original Roman road in the year 77 CE.[2] This system of roads allowed relatively safe travel over great distances. Indeed, these roads covered much of the Western world, from the Holy Land and Egypt to Britain and to Spain. It was true that "all roads lead to Rome," because from Rome the politicians governed the Empire, sending armies and officials to distant regions and supporting commerce of all sorts. Along these routes travelers could find inns of various sorts placed at convenient intervals to accommodate travelers overnight and to provide fresh horses or donkeys. Cities and towns had many inns that travelers could choose from.

Thus, the extensive Roman civil and military administration created an extensive supply of travel and tourism facilities. The prosperous Roman economy created a demand for tourism. As a result, the Romans were also tourists, traveling for rest at resorts and to see the sights. Roman tourists could use the roads and inns that had been put in place primarily for military affairs and official business. They could also board ships carrying cargo around the Mediterranean. They used guidebooks to help spend their time wisely at unfamiliar, distant places; and one of these guidebooks has survived over the millennia. *Description of Greece* by Pausanias, written around 143 to 161 CE, was a Roman guidebook to the cities of Greece.[3] It is still read today.

Scholars and artists of Rome studied the works of the much older civilization of the ancient Greeks, who had accomplished much. The Greeks invented democracy, philosophy, theater, and much of science and mathematics. Over thousands of years Greek architecture and sculpture have remained guides for later artists and standards against which others are compared. Ancient Greece was home to mathematicians Pythagoras and Euclid, philosophers Socrates, Plato, and Aristotle, and the poet Homer, among many other great thinkers and artists with important accomplishments. For example, the mathematician and geographer Eratosthenes knew that the Earth was round, and proceeded to measure its size by measuring changes in the length of shadows at noon as he moved from north to south. His estimate of the size of the

---

[1] See Casson (1994), pp. 115–329, for an extensive description of travel in the Roman world.
[2] Casson (1994), p. 167.
[3] Halsall (1998); Sandbach (1936), p. 689; Casson (1994), pp. 292–299.

Earth was remarkably accurate considering the early date of his efforts, during the third century BCE.[4]

The ancient Greeks were also travelers, and to some extent they were tourists. The ancient Greek world had regularly used travel routes over land and sea, and along these routes there were inns where all travelers could find food and overnight lodging.[5] Casson describes the travel situation in Greece at the beginning of the Classical Era, about 500 BCE:[6]

- merchant ships sailed among eastern Mediterranean ports
- roads linked major cities
- some roads had limited paving, bridges or ferries, road signs, and some facilities for travelers, including inns
- travel modes included wagons, carts, donkeys, horses, and camels
- towns had inns and taverns
- a few people traveled for the sake of travel.

Herodotus, the first historian, traveled widely during the middle of the fifth century BCE from Greece to the Middle East, Egypt, and the fringes of Central Asia, and then wrote about what he saw. In "Herodotus the Tourist," James Redfield writes about ancient Greek tourism, explaining that the ancient Greeks traveled not only for war and commerce but also for sightseeing. He also writes that Herodotus himself traveled to see natural and man-made wonders and to learn about the cultures of the peoples of distant places.[7] Alexander the Great was, of course, also a traveler, having taken his army as far east as India in his conquests. Thus, the ancient Greeks, and the ancient Romans, had extensive first-hand knowledge of much of the world.

Amazingly, after the fall of Rome to the barbarians in the fifth century CE Western Europeans forgot much of this knowledge. Scholarship, the arts, and much learning and high culture nearly disappeared from Western Europe. To illustrate, consider that the ancient Romans built the Pantheon in Rome in the years 118 to 128 CE. It was not until Brunelleschi designed and constructed the great dome of the cathedral of Florence between 1420 and 1436 that anyone would build so large a domed structure in Western Europe.[8] That is, in Europe the ability to build a domed structure like the Pantheon was lost for more than 1,000 years.

The intellectual and cultural losses were vast and astonishing. Following the fall of Rome, the Western Europeans forgot the scientific and mathematical achievements of the ancient world. The ancient idea of perspective in painting was forgotten. It was rediscovered in Italy centuries later as part of the Renaissance. Scholars in the Middle Ages in Western Europe puzzled over fragments of classical texts. In his very charming book *The Making of the Middle Ages,* R. W. Southern relates a story illustrating the depth of loss of ancient learning. He tells of two great eleventh-century scholars, one in a city in present-day Belgium and the other in a city in Germany, who corresponded with each other about a famous text that had survived from the late Roman period.

---

[4] Barber (1928), pp. 262–263.
[5] Constable (2003), pp. 11–22.
[6] Casson (1994), pp. 56–57.
[7] Redfield (1985), p. 98.
[8] King (2000), p. 27.

The text mentioned that the interior angles of any triangle add to 180°. It seems that neither scholar had any idea what the ancient text's interior angles of a triangle were.[9]

In addition to losing most of the writings of the classical Greek and Roman writers, and the mathematical and scientific achievements of Euclid, Eratosthenes, and most of the other classicals, the Western Europeans lost much of the classical knowledge of distant places. For example, Casson notes that in the first century the emperor Nero sent an expedition up the Nile to a point 9° north of the equator—this point on the Nile would not be reached again by Europeans until 1839.[10] Thus, the barbarian invasions ended the Classical Era and, for Western Europe, snuffed out knowledge of the wider world. The fall of the Western Roman Empire also greatly curtailed travel and tourism.

Centralized government largely disappeared from Western Europe for a few centuries until it made a modest comeback with the rise of the Carolingian Empire culminating in Charlemagne (768–814).[11] (The Eastern Roman Empire, based in Constantinople, today's Istanbul, survived for centuries after the decline of the West.) Thus, knowledge that had been gained 15 centuries earlier and carried through the ancient world was a mystery in Western Europe for centuries after the fall of Rome, and it would remain a mystery until rediscovered slowly through contact with ancient learning in the Eastern Empire and the Islamic world. In many ways, the fall of Rome set back the development of Western Europe by at least 1,000 years.

By the end of the seventh century, much of the economy of Western Europe had collapsed, leaving the area with much lower population, production, income, and trade.[12] The decline of the relatively secure Roman road system, with its inns and other facilities, radically decreased the supply of travel and tourism services. The disastrous decline of the Western European economy and plunge in average incomes brought the demand for tourism to near zero.

TRAVEL IN THE MIDDLE AGES

After the fall of the Roman Empire, the West entered what has come to be known as the Middle Ages, a period beginning with centuries of stagnation but then followed by development. During the early Middle Ages, barbarism and local rule by warlords replaced classical life. By a century or two after the barbarian invasions, much of the advanced lifestyle of the ancient world had disappeared in Western Europe. The widespread system of Roman laws and other government activities largely disappeared along with the legions of the Roman army. Road maintenance declined, so that long-distance travel became much more difficult and dangerous.[13] According to Norman Cantor, for 1,400 years no one in Europe knew how to build roads as well as the Romans had, and in the eleventh century the only "real" European roads were a few that had survived from the Roman Empire.[14]

---

[9] Southern (1953), pp. 201–202.
[10] Casson (1994), p. 126.
[11] McNeill (1963), pp. 441–446.
[12] McCormick (2001), pp. 27–119, 782–784.
[13] Feifer (1991), pp. 27–28.
[14] Cantor (1991), p. 21.

The Western European economy began its slow recovery at the end of the eighth century.[15] At that point, population was again growing and agricultural production was increasing. Charlemagne reconnected Italy with northern Europe, and Venice arose as a trading link between Europe and the Mediterranean. Eventually the life of much of Western Europe grew into feudalism, under which the majority of the population was tied to the land through formal obligations to lords.[16] The growth of feudalism created new relationships among people. The Church became a dominant force in most people's lives, and religious pilgrimage became one of the important reasons for long-distance travel in Europe. In the early Middle Ages, incomes, commerce, learning, travel, and many other aspects of life had declined, and in some cases nearly disappeared. The only substantial remnants of the ancient culture in the West could be found in the Church, which preserved some aspects of the old ways, especially Christianity, but also literacy and law.[17] Commerce continued, but on a smaller scale. Much ancient learning and culture lived on in the Eastern Empire and in the Islamic world of the Middle East, North Africa, and Spain, but the Western Europeans had little contact with it.[18] Under feudalism, travel for most people was rare, and few people traveled for leisure.[19]

During the Middle Ages, some Europeans traveled for commerce, warfare, diplomacy, and religious purposes, including pilgrimages and religious study.[20] After the Magyars of Hungary converted to Christianity in the year 1000, the land route from central Europe to Constantinople reopened. This enabled masses of pilgrims to walk to the Holy Land and eventually led to the First Crusade in 1099.[21]

Outside Western Europe, the cultural change in the centuries following the barbarian invasions was different.[22] The Islamic world of Spain, North Africa, and the Middle East thrived during this period. There was much long-distance travel in the region, and lodging places, derived from the ancient Greek model, for travelers and their goods were widely available.[23] In a well known story from the fourteenth century, Ibn Battuta, a lawyer from Tangier on the extreme northwest of Africa, traveled widely in the Middle East, Africa, and Asia.[24] Over the period 1325 to 1355, Ibn Battuta traveled to Arabia, Persia, Central Asia, India, China, and parts of Africa, among other places. On his return, he wrote a book describing his travels.

Invasions from central or northern Asia were also important in India and China. China and India thrived, however, and Chinese and Indian traders visited much of Asia and the east coast of Africa.[25] The most notable of the Chinese travels since ancient times were over land via the network of routes, which later became known as the "Silk Road," through central Asia as far west as the lands just east of the

---

[15] McCormick (2001), pp. 791–798.
[16] North (1981), pp. 126–128.
[17] North (1981), pp. 124–126; Cantor (1991), p. 20.
[18] McNeill (1963), pp. 420–441, 456.
[19] Feifer (1986), pp. 27–61.
[20] McCormick (2001), documents hundreds of early medieval individuals who traveled between Europe and the eastern Mediterranean.
[21] McCormick (2001), p. 796.
[22] McNeill (1963), p. 538.
[23] Constable (2003), pp. 40–67.
[24] Dunn (2005).
[25] Curtin (1984), pp. 109–135.

Mediterranean.[26] Later, the sea voyages of Zheng He in the first few decades of the fifteenth century CE covered much of south Asia, the Persian Gulf, and as far as the east coast of Africa.[27] Of course, there was extensive travel over long distances for many purposes within India and China, and since ancient times there had been trade among Arabia, India, and China.[28]

Europeans had sporadic direct contacts with Asia during the Middle Ages. We can get an idea of the rarity of long-distance travel and the paucity of Western European knowledge of the wider world in the story of Prester John. In 1122, a strange man known as John, and later as Prester John, presented himself in Rome claiming to be the king of a great Asian country. John met with the pope and others, regaling listeners with stories of his Christian kingdom in Asia. Soon he disappeared, and today no one knows who he actually was. Legends of John and his descendents ruling as powerful Christian kings in Asia (or Ethiopia) persisted throughout the Middle Ages, but there was no contact with these fictional fellows.[29]

Venturesome merchants provided some direct contact between Europe and Asia. The most famous of these Western European travelers to the Far East was Marco Polo, a Venetian who traveled to the Chinese court of Kublai Khan in 1271 and returned to Venice in 1295.[30] His book *The Travels of Marco Polo* is still widely read today. But Marco Polo was not the first Western European traveler of the Middle Ages to go to the Far East. An unknown French author of the fourteenth century collected some of the tales of earlier travelers to the East and wild tales from other early collections of travel stories in a falsely autobiographical book known as *Mandeville's Travels*, which was widely read and frequently reprinted.[31]

By the later Middle Ages, travel recovered to some extent, but travelers' knowledge of the world's geography remained skimpy. Postan (1973) notes that medieval travelers used the old Roman roads whenever possible; main roads in fourteenth-century England were largely the same as they had been a 1,000 years before, when England was a Roman colony.[32] Donald Howard (1987) describes the information available to travelers during the lifetime of medieval England's greatest writer, Geoffrey Chaucer (1342–1400), noting that while there were charts for navigating the seas, there were no equivalent maps for overland travel. The few maps that existed were fantasies of no use to travelers.[33]

Chaucer's famous *Canterbury Tales*, written in the 1380s and 1390s, recounts a story of travel in England during the Middle Ages. Chaucer himself, as a royal official, traveled extensively. He traveled at various times from England to France and to Italy, including a trip to Italy through Germany during the winter of 1372–1373. Being an overland trip, the route required Chaucer's party to cross the Alps in winter. Howard (1987) recounts what this entailed, making clear the skimpy supply of tourism services. He relates the difficulty of keeping the passes through the Alps open during the

---

[26] McNeill (1963), pp. 250–252; Foltz (1999), pp. 1–12.
[27] Schell (2003).
[28] Stein (1982), pp. 40–42; Curtin (1984), pp. 122–124.
[29] Southern (1953), pp. 71–73.
[30] Komroff (2001), p. v.
[31] Seymour (1967), pp. xiii–xv.
[32] Postan (1973), pp. 116–117.
[33] Howard (1987), pp. 172–173.

winter, and the constant worries about the weather, caring for horses and mules, poor road conditions, bandits, and the possibility of getting lost.[34]

After centuries of loss, stagnation, some advances, and slow change, Europe began changing more rapidly during Chaucer's lifetime. The Black Death arrived in Europe in 1347 and within a few years killed about one-third of the population. In spite of the loss of life, international trade and trade in local markets continued. Feudalism declined as labor became scarcer and population shifted to cities.[35] Change in Europe was accelerating.

TRAVEL IN THE PRE–MODERN ERA

During the accelerated recovery of intellectual and economic life in Western Europe beginning in the eleventh century, international trade grew.[36] By the Renaissance of the fourteenth and fifteenth centuries which ended the Middle Ages, Western Europeans rediscovered much of the knowledge of the Classical world of the Greeks and Romans. The voyages of discovery by Portuguese, Spanish, Dutch, French, and English explorers during the fifteenth through seventeenth centuries led to a rediscovery of the knowledge of the wider world that had been lost and to a vast expansion of new knowledge of far away places. As cities grew, so did the number of people not tied to the land through feudal relationships. Commerce grew rapidly.[37] Incomes and the demand for travel and tourism grew. Trade between England and the Continent, textile and spice trade, and eventually trade in sugar and tobacco from America all led to increases in travel, and trade also increased the supply of tourism services. Travel within Western Europe and from Europe to distant places grew rapidly. Travel by road in Europe—on old Roman roads where possible—continued to be difficult, but newly constructed canals added to the supply of tourism services in the seventeenth century.[38]

The Grand Tour

One of the most interesting and influential trends in tourism after the Renaissance was the practice throughout the seventeenth and eighteenth centuries of sending wealthy young gentlemen from England to visit the great cities of Europe to finish their educations. This practice became known as the "Grand Tour."[39] At any one time, there might have been as many as 40,000 British tourists on the Continent, and perhaps 100,000 passing through during a single year.[40]

By 1840, wider application of the earlier improvements in the steam engine in the economies of Europe and America, in travel and in other industries, had ended the premodern era of travel. The continuing increase in incomes along with these technology-driven changes in tourism supply opened the opportunity for tourism by the masses.

---

[34] Howard (1987), p. 172.
[35] North (1981), pp. 134–135.
[36] North (1981), pp. 133–135; Cantor (1991), pp. 26–27.
[37] McNeill (1963), pp. 543–547.
[38] Mączak (1995), pp. 4–15, 19–20.
[39] See Feifer (1985), pp. 95–134 for an extensive description of the Grand Tour.
[40] Brendon (1991), pp. 10–11.

MODERN MASS TOURISM

In 1834, King William IV appointed Robert Peel to be Prime Minister of Great Britain. Unfortunately, Peel and his family were vacationing in Italy at the time and had no idea what had happened in London. The Duke of Wellington sent a young official to find Peel and deliver the news. The official arrived at the English Channel after the steamship for the Continent had left; so he hired a boat and was rowed across to France. He proceeded by various horse-drawn and ox-drawn carriages across the Continent until eventually, after a trip lasting 11 days, he located Peel in Rome. Rushing back to London, Peel and his family traveled day and night over a period of 13 days to the coast of France via horse-drawn carriages. There they went by steamship to Dover and then over land to London.[41] Thus, except for the one short steamship ride this adventure proceeded by the same means and probably much of the same route that Julius Caesar had used to travel to Britain in 55 BCE, almost 19 centuries earlier.[42]

Contrast Peel's story to the story, 50 years later, of Britain's reaction to the news of General Charles Gordon's situation in Khartoum in 1884. Late in that year a British force under the command of General Gordon became surrounded by a large, hostile force in Khartoum, Sudan. The British government needed to send a relief expedition from Cairo to Khartoum. What do you think they did to get the job done quickly and efficiently? To get the job done, they called a travel agent! Not just any travel agent, but the Thomas Cook company, which had extensive experience and resources associated with travel in Egypt.[43] Using steamships and railroads, Cook's company accomplished the huge task, but the military mission failed as Khartoum fell and Gordon was killed.[44]

Thus, we see that by 1884 tourism had changed radically from the pre–modern era. Before 1840, tourism was an activity of the aristocracy. Wealthy gentlemen would go on the Grand Tour of the great cities of Europe. Other wealthy people would choose different destinations, but people outside the upper crust of the income distribution rarely engaged in tourism. After 1840, tourism rapidly expanded into an activity of a growing mass of people of many social classes.[45]

The most significant factor promoting change in travel and tourism and leading to the modern era of tourism was the Industrial Revolution in Europe. James Watt's improvements to the steam engine in the 1760s led to huge increases in the productivity of workers, first in textiles but later in many industries, including transportation.[46] Factory owners, merchants, skilled workers, and others earned incomes that matched or exceeded the incomes previously earned only by the landed aristocracy and a few others. With the growth in commerce and the increase in productivity arising from the Industrial Revolution came a substantial growth in incomes and a vast increase in the number of people living outside the grip of subsistence farming and unskilled labor.[47] As a result, many people in Europe had the incomes to pay for luxuries, including travel.

---

[41] Gash (1971).
[42] Brendon (1991), p. 14.
[43] Brendon (1991), pp. 188–190.
[44] Thomas Cook (2007).
[45] Brendon (1991), pp. 182–183.
[46] McNeill (1963), p. 692.
[47] North (1981), pp. 158–162.

In 1840 and 1841, two events rooted in the introduction of steam-powered transportation changed tourism, making it available to large numbers of middle-class consumers. In 1840, Samuel Cunard began scheduled transatlantic steamship service, which eventually replaced the sailing vessels that had previously provided service. This industry grew into today's cruise industry, and Cunard's company also survives as a subsidiary of Carnival Corporation. In 1841, Thomas Cook arranged for a trainload of tourists to travel to a temperance meeting, beginning what would become the tour operator and travel agent industries. Cook's company was the company the British government turned to for help with the 1884 expedition to Khartoum, and the company still operates today. These two events led by Cook and Cunard, and similar applications of steam-powered travel elsewhere, began a transformation of the travel and tourism industry. Today, tourism is readily available to and enjoyed by a wide spectrum of society. By 1995, in the United States alone, travelers took well over one billion trips outside their normal home areas.[48]

Supply and Demand

There are really only two reasons for the growth of the modern tourism industry: changes in supply and changes in demand. The introduction of steam power into transportation at the beginning of the nineteenth century allowed for a radically increased supply of travel and tourism services. There have been many other important changes in the supply of tourism services since 1840. Many of these derive directly from technical change, such as the introduction of powered flight by the Wright brothers. Others are not technical changes, but rather business changes that increase supply, as we will see later in this chapter. On the demand side, the dramatic change accounting for most of the growth of tourism is the growth in income. Together, these changes have transformed travel and tourism and have created a giant industry serving many millions of customers each day.

DEMAND

Boeing, the major aircraft manufacturer, carefully follows the travel market and annually forecasts its future. Its view of demand for air travel, expressed in its 2004 *Current Market Outlook*, is that the major source of growth in air travel is economic growth.[49] Economic growth, or the growth of GDP, determines the incomes of a nation's citizens. For the United States, while there have been ups and downs, economic growth overall has been rapid for long periods. Accumulated over a few centuries, the effect of this income growth has been enormous. This growth has strongly stimulated the demand for travel and tourism.

In 1840, real per capita GDP in the United States was about $1,600 expressed in year-2000 dollars. By 1930, this figure had grown to about $6,000, and by 2004, it was over $36,000.[50] This increase over the period 1840 to 2004 shows a compound annual growth rate of slightly more than 1.9 percent. For the last 75 years the annual growth rate has been more than 2 percent. At that rate of growth, real per capita production in

---

[48] U.S. Department of Transportation (1997), p. 1.
[49] Boeing (2004), p. 5.
[50] Johnston and Williamson (2005).

the economy is growing so fast that it is doubling in about 30 years. At growth rates this fast, an American living into his or her nineties would see real per capita incomes double three times, or *increase by a factor of eight*, over his or her lifetime.

Such rapid and substantial increases in income over extended periods of time have had profound impacts on American consumption of goods and services. The typical household today is many times richer than the typical household a few generations ago. As a result, we now consume a great deal more of most goods and services, including more leisure and more tourism. We see this growth in the increasing size of the average home, the spread of air conditioning to most homes and cars, the increasing number of automobiles per household, the increase in the quality of automobiles, the increased consumption of health care services, and increased consumption of many other goods and services. Young people today might find it hard to imagine their parents growing up with three channels of black-and-white television, one bathroom in the house or apartment, one telephone (wired to the wall), no air conditioning in the house or car, and wisdom teeth being extracted with local anesthetic, a hammer, and a chisel. Their grandparents may have grown up with no television, no car, no air conditioning even in large public buildings, outdoor plumbing, and little medical or dental care. These changes in the everyday lives of Americans result from an annual rate of increase in output in the U.S. economy of 2 percent over many decades.

This rapid growth in incomes over long periods of time has boosted demand for tourism. As we saw earlier, real incomes in America of the 1990s were 18 times larger than they were 150 years earlier. Europe has seen similar changes, as have Canada, Australia, and New Zealand. Recent income growth in much of Asia has been even more extreme. As income is the most important factor influencing the demand for tourism, tourism demand has also dramatically increased. Indeed, the increase in tourism demand is even larger than the increase in income, because, as we will see later, the income elasticity of demand for tourism is greater than one.

The quantity of travel and tourism demanded also depends on prices. Prices of many forms of travel have fallen in recent decades. The price of air travel is one of the most prominent examples. The Air Transport Association, a major aviation trade group, has calculated airline "yield," defined to be pennies per passenger–mile, over the period since 1926. Yield is a useful measure of airline pricing; and, while it has fluctuated up and down at times, it has shown a slow rise over the decades since the introduction of passenger airline service early in the twentieth century. Consumer prices overall, of course, have risen over time; so that, to examine the price of air travel relative to goods in general, we must account for the general rise in prices. Dividing airline yields by the consumer price index gives us the real yield measure of real airline prices. As we see in Table 4.1, domestic U.S. real yield has shown a dramatic decline over long periods. This fall in real airline prices has increased the amount of air travel consumers want to buy.

The real prices of other travel and tourism services have also fallen in recent decades. Perhaps the most important has been the decline in the cost of automobile travel. Real gasoline prices declined over many decades through 2006, and the increase in the quality of cars has reduced maintenance costs and reduced the probability of having to get service on the road. The U.S. Interstate Highway System has radically reduced long-distance automobile travel times. These factors have substantially reduced the price of automobile travel since the introduction of the automobile about one hundred years ago. Whereas a long-distance automobile trip in the 1950s might have

TABLE 4.1 Airline Domestic U.S. Yields—1950–2005

Year	Airline Yield (Cents)	Consumer Price Index 1982–84 = 100	Real Airline Yield
1950	5.56	24.1	15.04
1955	5.36	26.8	13.04
1960	6.09	29.6	13.41
1965	6.06	31.5	12.54
1970	6.00	38.8	10.08
1975	7.69	53.8	9.32
1980	11.49	82.4	9.09
1985	12.21	107.6	7.40
1990	13.43	130.7	6.70
1995	13.52	152.4	5.78
2000	14.57	172.2	5.52
2005	12.29	195.3	4.10

Data source: Air Transport Association (2007).

been an infrequent and hazardous ordeal, today we think nothing of driving hundreds of miles in a single day. Indeed, the 1995 American Travel Survey showed that well over half of household trips between 500 and 1,000 miles round trip were by automobile.[51]

The quality of leisure travel and tourism goods and services affects demand, and quality has shown substantial increases over many years. One important example of this is the dramatic increase in the average quality of roadside motels since Kemmons Wilson created the Holiday Inn motel chain in 1957. Before that, roadside motels varied greatly in quality, so that an overnight stay in an unfamiliar town could become an unwelcome adventure or a disastrous experience. Such experiences led Kemmons Wilson to create a company that would provide the American automobile traveler, especially those traveling with children, with a better experience.[52] We have also seen some improvements in air travel, including increased flight frequencies. The increased speed of jet aircraft over propeller-driven aircraft is another quality improvement that has increased the demand for air travel.

Increases in safety and security of travel have had important effects on tourism demand over the centuries. As mentioned earlier, Cunard's steamships were much safer than the wooden sailing vessels previously used in the transatlantic trade. Rail travel was much safer than travel by horse or horse-drawn carriage. Modern jet aircraft are also much safer than the propeller-driven aircraft they replaced. And this air travel safety record improved regularly over the years as airlines and aircraft manufacturers learned from the few accidents that did occur. In recent years, deaths associated with scheduled airline service have become quite rare. For the 10 years from 1997 to 2006, U.S. scheduled airlines averaged less than 0.017 fatal accidents per 100,000 departures.[53]

---

[51] U.S. Department of Transportation (1997), p. 3.
[52] Lukas (2003).
[53] Author's calculations based on National Transportation Safety Board (2007).

TABLE 4.2 U.S. Highway Fatality Rates—1950–2000

Year	Fatalities	Vehicle Miles Traveled (Millions)	Fatality Rate (per 100 Million Miles)
1950	33,186	458,246	7.24
1955	36,688	605,646	6.06
1960	36,399	718,762	5.06
1965	47,089	887,812	5.30
1970	53,816	1,109,724	4.85
1975	45,500	1,327,664	3.43
1980	51,091	1,527,295	3.35
1985	43,825	1,774,826	2.47
1990	44,599	2,144,362	2.08
1995	41,798	2,422,775	1.725
2000	41,945	2,749,803	1.525

Data source: Weingroff (2003).

Automobile travel has also become much safer over the years. The U.S. Interstate Highway System provided vastly improved safety for long-distance drivers and passengers by eliminating grade-level intersections and traffic lights, by constructing medians to separate vehicles moving in different directions, and by using long acceleration lanes for vehicles entering and leaving the highway. Automobiles themselves have become much safer with the introduction of seat belts and air bags, improved tires, brakes, and steering, safer gas tanks, and many other safety features, both obvious and hidden within the structures and systems of cars. Table 4.2 shows the rapid decline in U.S. fatality rates per 100 million highway vehicle miles traveled in recent decades.

The security situation in travel and tourism changed radically on September 11, 2001, with the terrorist attacks in the United States. The attacks had particularly important implications for travel and tourism, because the terrorists used commercial aircraft as their weapons. Demand for travel and tourism within the United States, and between the United States and other countries fell off dramatically immediately after September 11 and remained depressed for years. While security checks are inconvenient and can cause delays, most travelers feel more secure because of them and welcome the added safety.

Thus, the demand for tourism has varied over time because of changes in incomes, prices, quality, and security. Tourism demand has increased tremendously, particularly over the last two centuries, primarily because of the very rapid rise in incomes since the Industrial Revolution. Rapidly falling prices of travel services and sharp improvements in quality, safety, and security of travel and tourism over long periods have also promoted demand for tourism. The result of these changes has been a much larger demand for tourism services that is no longer confined to narrow segments of unusually wealthy people or small numbers of people with very specialized reasons for travel, such as religious purposes. Today, vast segments of society demand travel and tourism for leisure, business, and many other purposes.

SUPPLY

Supply
The relationship between the price of a good or service and the quantity of the good or service that businesses produce and deliver to the market.

For most goods and services, excluding such things as national defense and public education, the *quantity supplied* refers to the quantity of the good or service that businesses produce and deliver to the market. **Supply** refers to the relationship between that quantity and the price of the good or service. Thus, *supply* generally refers to business firm behavior.

Supply is primarily determined primarily by costs of production and distribution and by the strategic interactions among firms. Public policies also influence supply, even for those goods and services that private firms rather than government provide.

Costs

The two primary factors influencing a business firm's costs are input prices and technology. Thus, changes in input prices and technology strongly affect changes in supply.

SUPPLY 1: INPUT PRICES As we will see later, the wage paid to labor is the most important input price for almost every good and service in the travel and tourism industry. While real wages of labor have risen rapidly over the decades, labor costs in any industry can decline if the productivity of labor increases even faster than wages. Overall, however, we probably cannot say that falling real wages have increased the supply of tourism.

The second notable input price determining costs for much of travel and tourism is the price of fuel. During the first half of the twentieth century, the travel and tourism industry's primary fuel shifted from coal to fuels derived from petroleum, including gasoline and related fuels such as jet fuel. Improvements in transportation fuels and power plants have reduced costs and increased the supply of tourism services over the decades.

SUPPLY 2: TECHNOLOGICAL CHANGE Economic historians have referred to the first half of the nineteenth century as a period of "transportation revolution."[54] This was a period of extraordinarily large investments in transportation infrastructure, including canals, roads, rails, and equipment, including ships and railroad rolling stock. These activities greatly increased the supply of travel and tourism services as prices of transportation fell rapidly and levels of activity increased. Technological change has been the most important factor increasing the supply of travel and tourism since 1840. Samuel Cunard and many others exploited the potential of steam power to change the supply of travel and tourism. Many other technical innovations have had similarly important effects on supply in the industry.

Railroads. Early in the nineteenth century the steam-powered railroads supplied new services to travelers. The rapid development of widespread railroad systems in Europe and America in the 1840s and 1850s vastly increased the supply of tourism services and radically changed travel.[55] Now, great numbers of people could travel at much greater speeds and with much more comfort and safety to places they had never previously considered visiting.[56]

---

[54] Taylor (1951); Tuma (1971), pp. 284–296; Walton and Rockoff (2005), pp. 162–183.
[55] North (1966), pp. 142–143.
[56] Brendon (1991), pp. 12–17.

Steamship. Samuel Cunard increased supply in travel and tourism by applying the then recently developed steam-powered ship to regularly scheduled transatlantic service. Before that time, regular transatlantic service was by wind-powered "packet" ships. These were relatively small sail-driven wooden ships called packet ships because they carried packets of mail between England and the West Indies or New York. They sailed regularly and carried passengers in addition to mail and other cargo. The ships were slow, taking as many as 50 days to cross the Atlantic.[57] They were also uncomfortable. Cunard radically increased the supply of travel services by introducing larger, faster, safer, and more comfortable steam-powered ships into regular transatlantic service linking New York and England.

Transatlantic steamship service quickly grew, and new competitors entered the business. Within a few decades, large and luxurious steel steamships from many nations regularly crossed the Atlantic and the other oceans. The enormously popular 1997 movie *Titanic* realistically showed a portrait of transatlantic passenger travel as it existed in 1912.

Steamships increased the supply of travel and tourism services in many more applications and locations around the world during the early and mid-nineteenth century. The Peninsular Steam Navigation Company provided service between England and the Iberian Peninsula beginning around 1834. Later, as the Peninsular and Oriental Steam Navigation Company, it provided service between England and Egypt, Australia, Hong Kong, and other places.[58] Steamships also provided coastal service, for example, among the cities of the East Coast of the United States, and they provided service on lakes and rivers, including the Mississippi, the Ohio, and the rivers of Europe.[59]

Automobile. The first automobiles date from the late nineteenth century. Henry Ford's introduction of the Model T in 1908 made the automobile accessible to large numbers of Americans who could now pay for a car.[60] For its day, the Model T was remarkably durable and reliable, and millions of Americans found themselves much more mobile after buying one. The auto industry grew rapidly, and with this growth travel and tourism in America changed radically with the reductions in time, increases in comfort, and ease of travel by car now available to a large proportion of American families. Similar increases in auto production and use occurred in Canada, Great Britain, and in continental Europe.

Powered Flight. We recently celebrated the one-hundredth anniversary of the Wright brothers' first powered flight. Within a few years, airplanes were carrying passengers. By the 1920s, airlines offered regularly scheduled service between London and Paris and between cities in the United States.[61] In 1936 Pan American Airways began regular passenger airline service across the Pacific Ocean using the "China Clipper"

---

[57] McCusker (1997), p. 182.
[58] P&O Cruises (undated).
[59] Hughes and Cain (1998), pp. 147–150; Tuma (1971), pp. 288–290.
[60] Weingroff (1996a).
[61] Foldes (1961), p. 165; Air Transport Association (2001).

seaplanes built by the Glenn L. Martin Company.[62] Thus, in a short time, powered flight radically increased the supply of travel and tourism services.

Jet Engine. Pan American Airways began daily transatlantic commercial jet airline service with the Boeing 707 in October 1958.[63] This important event drastically reduced the time required to travel between Europe and the United States and did so with a high level of safety and comfort. The grand era of transatlantic cruising came to an end shortly thereafter, although some crossings continued. Just 66 years after the first powered flight, a Boeing 747 could carry 490 passengers in comfort over a distance of 4,800 miles, cruising at 565 miles per hour.[64] Thus, the jet engine magnified the effects of powered flight on travel and tourism supply.

Air Conditioning and Refrigeration. The development of air conditioning led to a tremendous boost in the supply of tourism services in areas with warm climates. Air conditioning allowed the development of many large hotels and resorts in tropical and semi-tropical areas. In the United States, the Florida tourism industry particularly benefited from this innovation. Refrigeration has allowed for much safer and larger scale food service, especially in warm climates. This supported rapid growth in the supply of food and beverage services, an important component of tourism supply.

Strategic Interactions Among Firms

Costs are not the only important influences on supply. Business firms' behavior in their struggle to make profits and to successfully compete in markets having many rivals also determines the supply of travel and tourism services.

Business model
Explanation of how a business makes a profit by creating value for customers.

SUPPLY 3: NEW BUSINESS MODELS   A **business model** is the story of how a business makes a profit by creating value for its customers.[65] Every successful business firm has a business model, even if its managers cannot verbalize what it is. (Some firms, for example, the Walt Disney Company, may have more than one business model.) Thomas Cook had a business model: he would create value for customers by arranging packaged transportation and lodging, negotiating the prices for these services from the providers. He would then offer the packaged services to travelers at prices they found low enough to be attractive while being high enough for Cook to make a profit. McDonald's developed a business model: it would create value for customer by offering standardized, quickly prepared foods in a clean and inviting environment, in locations that are easily accessible, while charging low prices that, because of low costs, are high enough to allow a profit. As we will see later, new business models have been important in increasing the supply of travel and tourism services.

Airlines. As mentioned earlier, in the 1920s various companies introduced scheduled airline service, which was a new business model. The airlines would buy aircraft, train pilots and cabin crew members, build airport terminal facilities, and sell tickets.

---

[62] Heppenheimer (1995), pp. 70–71.
[63] Heppenheimer (1995), pp. 183–184.
[64] Burns (undated).
[65] Magretta (2002), p. 46.

They would carry paying passengers, along with mail and cargo, on regular schedules between major cities. Juan Trippe of Pan American Airways, among others, seized this new business model to radically increase supply in the travel and tourism industry.

Cruise Lines. Samuel Cunard introduced scheduled steamship service to carry passengers between major ports of call, and his business model was quickly imitated by other steamship lines. In contrast, Ted Arison established Carnival Cruise Lines in 1972 to provide travelers a cruise ship experience, with the ports of call secondary to the on-board "fun ship" experience.[66] His goal was to appeal to the millions of Americans who had never considered a leisurely Atlantic crossing. Cruise lines of this more contemporary type have been enormously successful in developing new markets.

Car Rental. John Hertz operated a taxicab company in Chicago from 1915 through the 1920s—he is the fellow who decided that taxicabs should be painted yellow.[67] In the 1920s he bought a Chicago company that had recently created a new business model. Rather than provide a taxicab, which included a driver, the company would offer daily rentals of a car that renters would drive themselves. Thus, the car rental business model is to buy a fleet of cars and offer them for daily rental at prices high enough to pay the interest, depreciation, and other costs, including a profit. The model was very successful, and Hertz Corporation now operates at 7,000 locations around the world.[68]

Motel Chains. Kemmons Wilson created a new business model when he started the Holiday Inn chain of roadside motels. He had been very disappointed with the shoddy accommodations and service he and his family had received from roadside motels that they had stayed at during a long car trip. His thought was that American families should be able to rely on roadside motels for clean, reasonably priced, high quality accommodations, even in an unfamiliar location. This became the basis for his business model—he would provide clean, reasonably priced accommodations of a uniform high quality, with a standard set of facilities including a swimming pool and a restaurant, and air conditioning and television in each room. Furthermore, he would create a brand name that travelers could recognize throughout the country, so that they could be confident in the quality and price of their accommodation, even in places they had never been before. While the prices would be reasonable, and there would be no extra charge for children, prices would be high enough to earn a profit.[69]

SUPPLY 4: NEW BUSINESS STRATEGIES   Every successful business firm has a business model. To do well a firm should also have a business strategy. A **business strategy** is an explanation of how a business firm is going to make a place for itself in the industry. In her book *What Management Is*, Joan Magretta explains that a firm may create value for customers but not be able to make much profit without a strategy, or a way to operate differently than its rivals.[70] Thus, while a business model is a story of how to make a profit while creating value for customers, a business strategy is a story of how to successfully fit into an industry that may have many strong competitors.

Business strategy
Explanation of how a business firm is going to make a place for itself in an industry with other rival firms.

[66] Dickinson and Vladimir (1997).
[67] Yellow Cab Chicago (2005).
[68] Hertz (2007).
[69] Lukas (2003).
[70] Magretta (2002), p. 78.

Insurance Replacement Car Rental. The car rental business model was well known in 1962 when Jack Taylor added car rental to his car leasing business. Eventually the company grew to become Enterprise Rent-A-Car. There were already a few very large competitors in the industry, including Hertz and Avis, and a large number of smaller firms. But Taylor tried a new strategy or a new way for another firm in the industry—he would serve customers looking for a rental car to replace a car being serviced. The result was the development of a new niche for another large car rental company providing a high level of service at a reasonable price for local car rental customers. The business grew rapidly. While the other car rental companies emphasized rentals at airports, before 1995 Enterprise had no locations at airports.[71] They instead preferred suburban locations which were closer to many customers and had much lower real estate costs than the high fees charged at airports.

Low-Cost Airlines. Southwest Airlines has an explicit business strategy to distinguish itself from most other airlines. Its main distinguishing feature is low fares supported by low costs. It operates a very efficient point-to-point route structure, often using airports that are not the primary airports in the cities they serve. Southwest operates only one type of aircraft—the Boeing 737—which lowers the cost of operation and maintenance. It has low labor costs and low selling costs, as it sells most of its tickets through its own web site.[72]

The final important element determining the supply of tourism services is the behavior of governments.

SUPPLY 5: PUBLIC POLICIES   Governments have often had important roles in promoting the development of travel and tourism industries and have worked to increase supply in the industry. They have done this by direct subsidies, by purchasing services, by building infrastructure, by regulating safety, and in many other ways. (Government policies may also reduce the supply of tourism services, for example, by imposing high taxes on travel or by failing to maintain roads, airports, or other facilities. Overall, however, in the United States, Canada, Europe, Australia, and other parts of the world governments have typically promoted travel and tourism.)

Direct Subsidies. In the early and mid-nineteenth century, the U.S. government and the states heavily subsidized road, canal, and railroad construction.[73] One of the largest industrial subsidies in U.S. history was the grant of land to the railroads in the middle of the nineteenth century.[74] The Pacific Railroad Act of 1862 and other federal laws led to transfers of 131 million acres of land to railroad companies.[75] Over the decades, the railroads used some of the land for their facilities and sold rest of the land for other uses.

For many years the British government subsidized airlines. It began in 1921 by making payments to multiple carriers serving London and Paris. Eventually these carriers combined to form a single subsidized company, Imperial Airways. New unsubsidized

---

[71] Enterprise (2007).
[72] Southwest Airlines (2004), pp. 5–11.
[73] Walton and Rockoff (2005), pp. 170–177.
[74] Engerman (1972); Hughes and Cain (1998), pp. 153, 276.
[75] Walton and Rockoff (2005), pp. 308–314.

airlines entered the market. These, too, eventually combined to form British Airways, which also received subsidy payments from the British Government. In 1939, both British international carriers were nationalized, that is, taken over and operated by the government. Their operations were combined as the British Overseas Airways Corporation (BOAC).[76] In 1974 BOAC and another airline were combined to become British Airways. In 1987 the British government privatized British Airways.[77] The Australian government also operated Qantas Airways as a government-owned corporation after 1947.[78]

The governments of Great Britain and France jointly subsidized the development, beginning in 1962, of the supersonic Concorde aircraft. Its first commercial flights occurred in January 1976. British Airways and Air France operated the only Concorde aircraft in commercial service. The Concorde flew transatlantic routes from 1976 to 2003 and was considerably faster than conventional aircraft, cruising at 1,350 miles per hour, more than twice the speed of conventional jet airliners. The Concorde ended commercial flights in 2003.[79]

Government Purchases. The U.S. government directly promoted the early development of the airlines by buying services from them—specifically by paying them to carry mail. U.S. government airmail payments were $46 million in 1946 and $112 million in 1949, plus another $30 million retroactive payment for pre-1949 airmail. Apparently these airmail payments were about double the cost of carrying the mail.[80] In a similar way, the British government bought postal service from Cunard.[81]

Infrastructure Development. At the beginning of the nineteenth century, Europeans and Americans had looked on canals as the way to lower the price and increase the supply of travel services. In America, the states heavily subsidized canal building and river transportation improvements.[82] The U.S. federal, state, and local governments have also subsidized the building of airports. While air travel taxes and user fees now pay much of the cost of facilities currently used by the airlines, this was not true in the early years of commercial aviation. While the airlines paid some landing fees to municipalities, Berge wrote in 1951 that as of his writing the airlines had paid no user charges for federal airways facilities and other federal air navigation aids.[83]

The U.S. Federal-Aid Highway Act of 1956 was one of the most important pieces of legislation to promote travel and tourism through building infrastructure. It created the U.S. Interstate Highway System, which imposed a federal tax on gasoline purchases and offered the money to the states at a $9 match for every $1 spent by states on highways

---

[76] Foldes (1961), pp. 165–166.
[77] British Airways (2005a).
[78] Qantas (undated).
[79] British Airways (2005b).
[80] Berge (1951), p. 521.
[81] Cunard (2006).
[82] North (1966), p. 143; Hughes and Cain (1998), pp. 143–146.
[83] Berge (1951), pp. 522–523.

meeting certain specifications.[84] The result was an explosion of road building, resulting by 2002 in a network of almost 47,000 miles of limited access highways linking almost every part of the United States.[85]

Travel Safety Regulation. On April 14, 1912, the White Star Line's *Titanic*, at the time the largest passenger ship ever built, sank on its first voyage, having left Portsmouth with an intended destination of New York. Of the 2,223 passengers and crew, only 706 survived, primarily because there were not enough lifeboats on board and those that were available were not fully used.[86] One result of the tragedy was a worldwide effort to improve safety of life at sea. The international regulations and standards put in place after the *Titanic* disaster continue, with periodic adjustments, today; and such safety regulations have promoted development of the cruise industry around the world.

Summary

Tourism as we would recognize it has existed since ancient times, as people visited the great sights such as the pyramids of Egypt or vacationed at seaside resorts. But tourism's history has not seen the volume of tourism activity increase in a straight line, from a low level thousands of years ago to the huge volume today. In the Western world, tourism activity has at times dropped to very low levels, as during the early Middle Ages in Western Europe. At other times tourism has grown rapidly.

The simplest kind of economic analysis, examining demand and supply in the market, goes a long way toward helping us to understand the growth of tourism over the centuries. Demand for tourism is primarily influenced by income. Prices and security are also important in determining tourism demand. Business firm behavior, including new business models and new business strategies, determines the supply of tourism. Cost of production, which arises from the interaction of input prices and technology, is a primary influence on business firm behavior.

The level of tourism activity has been high when demand was high, and demand for tourism is primarily influenced by income. Thus, during the height of the Roman Empire and in England during the eighteenth and nineteenth centuries, there were large numbers of people with high incomes, and their tourism demand was high. The very rapid growth of incomes since the Industrial Revolution of the eighteenth century has spurred rapid growth in tourism demand among very large segments of the population.

The supply of tourism services has risen and fallen over the centuries, but supply leaped forward beginning early in the nineteenth century when steam power replaced horse power in travel. This quantum leap in tourism supply continued later as internal combustion engines powered automobiles, ships, and airplanes. Thus, technology, supported by new business models and new business strategies, became the second major force in the growth of tourism, along with income, after the Industrial Revolution.

[84] Weingroff (1996b).
[85] Federal Highway Administration (2007).
[86] U.S. Senate (1912), p. 5.

Bibliography

Air Transport Association. "Brief History of Aviation." *The Airline Handbook—Online Edition,* 2001. members. airlines.org/about/d.aspx?nid=7946.

——— (2007), "Annual Passenger Yields: U.S. Airlines," www. airlines.org/economics/finance/PaPricesYield.htm.

Barber, E. A. "Alexandrian Literature." In *The Cambridge Ancient History.* Vol. VII, edited by S. A. Cook, F. E. Adcock, and M. P. Charlesworth. New York: The Macmillan Company, 1928.

Bentley, Jerry H. *Old World Encounters: Cross-Cultural Contacts and Exchanges in Pre-Modern Times.* New York: Oxford University Press, 1993.

Berge, Stanley. "Subsidies and Competition as Factors in Air Transport Policy." *American Economic Review* 41 (1951): 519–29.

Boeing (2004), *Current Market Outlook 2004.*

Boyer, Marjorie Nice. "Travel Allowances in Fourteenth-Century France." *Journal of Economic History* 23 (1963): 71–85.

Brendon, Piers. *Thomas Cook: 150 Years of Popular Tourism.* London: Secker and Warburg, 1991.

British Airways (2005a), "British Airways History," www. britishairways.com/travel/bapress/public/en_gb.

———(2005b), "Concorde," www.britishairways.com/travel/ bapress/public/en_gb.

Burns, George E. (undated), "The Jet Age Arrives." *Pan American World Airways History,* www.panam.org.

Cantor, Norman F. *Inventing the Middle Ages.* New York: William Morrow and Company, 1991.

Casson, Lionel. *Travel in the Ancient World.* Baltimore: The Johns Hopkins University Press, 1994.

Constable, Olivia Remie. *Housing the Stranger in the Mediterranean World.* Cambridge: Cambridge University Press, 2003.

Cunard, Samuel (2006), "Cunard Heritage," www.cunard.com/ AboutCunard/default.asp?Active=Heritage&Sub =Samuel.

Curtin, Philip D. *Cross-cultural Trade in World History.* Cambridge: Cambridge University Press, 1984.

David, Paul A. "The Growth of Real Product in the United States Before 1840: New Evidence, Controlled Conjectures." *Journal of Economic History* 27 (1967): 151–97.

Dickinson, Bob, and Andy Vladimir. *Selling the Sea: An Inside Look at the Cruise Industry.* New York: John Wiley & Sons, 1996.

Dunn, Ross E. *The Adventures of Ibn Battuta.* rev. ed. Berkeley: University of California Press, 2005.

Durie, Alastair J. "Leisure Industry." In *The Oxford Encyclopedia of Economic History,* edited by Joel Mokyr, 290–96. Oxford: University Press, 2003.

Engerman, Stanley L. "Some Economic Issues Relating to Railroad Subsidies and the Evaluation of Land Grants." *Journal of Economic History* 32 (1972): 443–63.

Enterprise. "Milestones," 2007. http://aboutus.enterprise. com/who_we_are/milestones.html#.

Federal Highway Administration (2007), "Dwight D. Eisenhower National System of Interstate and Defense Highways," www.fhwa.dot.gov/programadmin/ interstate.cfm.

Feifer, Maxine. *Tourism in History: From Imperial Rome to the Present.* Stein and Day, 1986.

Firebaugh, W. C. *The Inns of Greece & Rome.* Chicago: Pascal Covici, 1928.

Foldes, Lucien. "Domestic Air Transport Policy. Part I." *Economica,* N.S., 28 (1961): 156–75.

Foltz, Richard C. *Religions of the Silk Road.* New York: St. Martins Griffin, 1999.

Gash, Norman. *Sir Robert Peel.* 78–83. London and New York: Longman, 1972; quoted in *A Web of English History.* www.dialspace.dial.pipex.com/town/terrace/ adw03/peel/politics/peelhols.htm.

Goeldner, Charles R., and J. R. Brent Ritchie. *Tourism: Principles, Practices, Philosophies.* 9th ed. Hoboken, NJ: John Wiley & Sons, 2003.

Halsall, Paul (1998), "Ancient History Sourcebook: Pausanias (fl.c.160 CE): Description of Greece, Book I: Attica," www.fordham.edu/Halsall/ancient/pausanias-bk1. html.

Henderson, P. D. "Two British Errors: Their Probable Size and Some Possible Lessons." *Oxford Economic Papers.* N.S., 29 (1977): 159–205.

Heppenheimer, T. A. *Turbulent Skies: The History of Commercial Aviation.* New York: John Wiley and Sons, 1995.

Hertz (2007), "Hertz Corporate Profile," www.hertz.com/ rentacar/abouthertz/index.jsp?targetPage=aboutHertz HistoryView.jsp&leftNavUserSelection=globNav_7_1_5.

Howard, Donald R. *Chaucer: His Life, His Works, His World.* New York: E. P. Dutton, 1987.

Hughes, Jonathan, and Louis P. Cain. *American Economic History,* 5th ed. Reading, MA: Addison-Wesley, 1998.

Johnston, Louis D., and Samuel H. Williamson. "The Annual Real and Nominal GDP for the United States, 1790–Present." *Economic History Services.* October, 2005. www.eh.net/hmit/gdp/.

Kiefer, Nicholas M. "Economics and the Origin of the Restaurant." *The Cornell Hotel and Restaurant Administration Quarterly* August, 43 (2002): 58–64.

King, Ross. *Brunelleschi's Dome: How a Renaissance Genius Reinvented Architecture*. New York: Penguin, 2000.

Komroff, Manuel. *The Travels of Marco Polo*. New York: The Modern Library, 2001.

Lopez, Robert S. *The Commercial Revolution of the Middle Ages 950–1350*. Englewood Cliffs, NJ: Prentice-Hall, 1971.

Lukas, Paul. "Holiday Inns: Be My Guest." *Fortune Small Business*, April 18, 2003.

Mączak, Antoni. *Travel in Early Modern Europe*. Cambridge: Polity Press, 1995.

Maddison, Angus. "A Comparison of Levels of GDP Per Capita in Developed and Developing Countries, 1700–1980." *Journal of Economic History* 43 (1983): 27–41.

Magretta, Joan. *What Management Is*. New York: The Free Press, 2002.

McCormick, Michael. *Origins of the European Economy: Communications and Commerce. A.D. 300–900*. Cambridge: Cambridge University Press, 2001.

McCusker, John J. "New York City and the Bristol Packet." In *Essays in the Economic History of the Atlantic World*. 177–89. London: Routledge, 1997.

McNeill, William. *The Rise of the West*. Chicago: University of Chicago Press, 1963.

National Transportation Safety Board (2007), "Accidents, Fatalities, and Rates, 1987 through 2006, for U.S. Air Carriers Operating Under 14 CFR 121, Scheduled Service (Airlines)," www.ntsb.gov/aviation/Table6.htm.

North, Douglass C. *The Economic Growth of the United States 1790–1860*. New York: W. W. Norton, 1966.

———. *Structure and Change in Economic History*. New York: W. W. Norton, 1981.

Olsen, Michael D. "Macroforces Driving Change Into the New Millennium—Major Challenges for the Hospitality Professional." *Hospitality Management* 18 (1999): 371–85.

P&O Cruises (undated), "History of P&O Cruises," www.pocruises.com.au/html/history.cfm.

Postan, M. M.. *Medieval Trade and Finance*. Cambridge: Cambridge University Press, 1973.

Qantas (undated), "History," www.qantas.com.au/info/about/history/index.

Redfield, James. "Herodotus the Tourist." *Classical Philology* (1985): 97–118.

Sandbach, F. H. "Greek Literature, Philosophy and Science." In *The Cambridge Ancient History*. Vol. XI, edited by S. A. Cook, F. E. Adcock, and M. P. Charlesworth, New York: The Macmillan Company, 1936.

Schell, Orville (2003), "A Ming Emperor Would Have Grounded the Shuttle. Bad Idea." *Washington Post*, March 2, 2003, B02.

Seymour, M. C. *Mandeville's Travels*. Oxford: Clarendon Press, 1967.

Silk Road. http://www.silk-road.com/toc/index.html.

Southern, R. W. *The Making of the Middle Ages*. New Haven: Yale University Press, 1953.

Southwest Airlines. *Southwest Airlines Co. 2003 Annual Report*, 2004.

Stein, Burton. "South India: Some General Considerations of the Region and Its Early History." In *The Cambridge Economic History of India*. Vol. 1, edited by Tapan Raychaudhuri and Irfan Habib. Cambridge: Cambridge University Press, 1982.

Taylor, George R. *The Transportation Revolution 1815–1860*. New York: Holt, Reinhart and Winston, 1951.

Thomas Cook (2007), " A Brief History," www.thomascook.com/content/about-us/thomas-cook-history/brief-history.asp.

Tuma, Elias H. *European Economic History*. New York: Harper & Row, 1971.

"Travel and Tourism: Home and Away." *The Economist*, January 10, 1998.

U.S. Department of Transportation. *1995 American Travel Survey Profile: United States*, Washington, D.C., 1997.

U.S. Senate, Committee on Commerce (1912), *"Titanic" Disaster*. Washington, D.C. www.senate.gov/artandhistory/history/resources/pdf/TitanicReport.pdf.

Vasiliev, A. A. *History of the Byzantine Empire*. Vol. 1, Madison, WI: University of Wisconsin Press, 1952.

Walton, Gary M., and Hugh Rockoff. *History of the American Economy*. 10th ed. Mason, OH: South-Western, 2005.

Weingroff, Richard F. (1996a), "Federal Aid Road Act of 1916: Building the Foundation," www.fhwa.dot.gov/infrastructure/rw96a.htm.

——— (1996b), "Federal-Aid Highway Act of 1956: Creating the Interstate System," www.fhwa.dot.gov/infrastructure/rw96e.htm.

——— (2003), "President Dwight D. Eisenhower and the Federal Role in Highway Safety, Appendix," www.fhwa.dot.gov/infrastructure/safetyap.htm.

Weiss, Thomas. "Tourism in America before World War II." *Journal of Economic History* 64 (2004): 289–327.

Yellow Cab Chicago (2005), "The History of the Yellow Cab," www.yellowcabchicago.com/history.htm.

CHAPTER 5

Economic Impact: Output, Income, and Sustainability

Learning Goals

- Understand why destinations promote tourism.
- Know what is meant by the "economic impact" of tourism.
- Understand how researchers measure the direct, indirect, and induced impacts of tourism on a region's income.
- Learn how input–output models and matrix algebra are used to measure economic impacts.
- Understand some of the environmental impacts of tourism.
- Understand sustainable tourism and be able to use intertemporal economic analysis to see what it implies about regional economic development.
- Understand ecotourism.
- See the relevance of common pool resources, externalities, and property rights for understanding many economic impacts of tourism.

INTRODUCTION

Many tourists have felt that they have found the perfect vacation spot and hope that they can return to it year after year. They hope the place stays unchanged throughout their lifetimes, remaining the same unspoiled, undiscovered paradise for decades into the future. These hopes are rarely realized, as others discover the unspoiled paradise and development proceeds. Indeed, local businesses and property owners actively promote vacation spots.

"I ♥ New York!" "Virginia is for Lovers." We have all seen these famous slogans promoting tourism in New York and Virginia. And we are familiar with the advertising campaigns of many other states. What is surprising is the total volume of such advertising. Each year, the tourism organizations of the 50 state governments spend more than one-half billion dollars on tourism promotion. According to the annual survey of state tourism office budgets conducted by the TIA, the 47 states responding to the survey were planning to spend $602 million in fiscal year 2005.[1]

The one-half billion dollar figure for state spending does not include the spending of cities, counties, or other levels of government. Many government units sponsor "convention and visitors bureaus" (known as CVBs) to promote tourism to their local areas. One of the largest of these is the Las Vegas Convention and Visitors Authority, with total spending of almost $220 million in fiscal year 2006, including more than $115 million in advertising and marketing[2]

Why do the states and cities spend so much money on tourism promotion? Because each of these regions expects the promotional spending to return much more in growth in employment, income, and tax revenue within the region. You may remember seeing images of 500-room hotels in Las Vegas being demolished with explosives to make way for 5,000-room hotels. When developers replace a 500-room hotel with a 5,000-room hotel, they need about 10 times as many hotel employees to staff the new hotel. They will need 10 times as many bed linens, 10 times as many cleaning supplies, and 10 times as many staff and all the things that went into operating the smaller hotel. This spending creates income for the hotel's employees and revenue for the suppliers of the products used in the vastly larger hotel. These employees and suppliers, in turn, spend much of their increased incomes within the region, creating further increases in incomes for others. They will also pay taxes. We refer to these changes in employment, income, tax payments, and other measures of economic activity, along with social and environmental impacts, as the **economic impact of tourism**.

Economic impact of tourism
Changes in regional employment, incomes, tax payments, and other measures of economic activity, along with social and environmental impacts that result from a region's tourism development.

ECONOMIC IMPACT ANALYSIS

The economic impact of tourism is one of the most widely studied areas related to travel and tourism. Tourism is a very large industry; therefore, it has many economic effects. According to the TIA more than 7 million people in the United States work in the travel and tourism industry.[3] Tourism can change the nature of places, as we have seen, for example, in Orlando, Florida, where Walt Disney World, Universal's theme parks, and other attractions have brought tremendous growth. Tourists, tourism industry workers, and tourism firms pay taxes. In some cases, for example in Hawaii, such taxes can be among the most important sources of revenue for state and local governments. The World Travel and Tourism Council estimated that in 1999 tourism accounted for 27% of taxes paid in Hawaii.[4]

Many researchers have tried to measure the impacts of tourism on a variety of measures of economic activity. State agencies have tried to measure the impacts of their programs on their states' economies, including impacts on employment, incomes, and tax revenue. The federal government has tried to measure the impacts of gambling on the U.S. economy. Business firms and academic researchers have tried to

---

[1] Travel Industry Association of America (2006a).
[2] Las Vegas Convention and Visitors Authority (2006).
[3] Travel Industry Association of America (2006b).
[4] World Travel and Tourism Council (1999), p. 17.

measure other impacts. The most important and most often used indicators of economic impacts of tourism are those listed below:

- *Output* researchers often measure the increased levels of output, or production, or gross state product, or similar measures of the total level of economic activity in the region;
- *Income* changes in wages and salaries paid to workers is one of the key measures of economic impact;
- *Employment* researchers are often interested in the changing level of employment brought about by changing tourism activity;
- *Tax revenue* state and local governments are often interested in the additional tax revenue to be earned from increasing tourism spending;
- *Environmental impact* other economic impacts go beyond production, jobs, and wages, including the following:
  - Social and cultural (population, lifestyles, and many others)
  - Physical (construction, pollution, erosion, and others)
  - Biological (destruction of habitat, introduction of exotic species, and others).

Here, we will be concerned primarily with the first of these impacts, the impact of tourism on regional output. While there have been a wide variety of studies of these economic impacts, only a handful of standard methods are used to measure them. We will now look at the most important of these methods and some of their applications.

Tourism in New Zealand—The America's Cup Yacht Race

Tourism is important to New Zealand's economy. The New Zealand government estimates that directly and indirectly tourism contributes about 10 percent of the nation's GDP and about 10 percent of the nation's employment. New Zealand has many natural and other attractions bringing visitors from around the world. In 1995, a New Zealand yacht won the America's Cup yacht race. One result of this victory is that the defending champion gets to defend its title in its home waters. This brought the event, with its participants, spectators, and international media, to Auckland in 1999 and 2000. New Zealand successfully defended, bringing the race back to Auckland in 2003. New Zealand's government contracted with a consulting firm to estimate the economic impact of the build-up to the 2003 America's Cup race on the New Zealand economy.[5] This build-up period primarily attracted participants rather than spectators or media. Nevertheless, the study found a substantial impact including crew accommodations for up to 500 sailing and shore crew members and services for the yachts. In some cases crew members also brought their families with them to Auckland. The study estimated direct, indirect, and induced effects using the standard methods discussed in this chapter. It found that for the period 2000–2002, the build-up to the 2003 race created a direct increase in value-added in the New Zealand economy of $27 million and a total increase of $65 million.[6]

[5] Market Economics (2002).
[6] Market Economics (2002), p. 7.

DIRECT AND INDIRECT EFFECTS

The first step in measuring the economic impact of tourism on regional output is measuring the "direct impact" or "direct effect" of the change in tourist spending within the region. The direct effect, as the name suggests, is the effect of the tourist spending itself. We will see later that there are also "indirect" effects of increased tourist spending, but not all studies examine these. A starting point for almost any study of economic impact of travel and tourism is measuring the change in tourist spending on lodging, meals, attendance at attractions, shopping, and all other types of tourist spending. This can be done by estimating the number of travelers, perhaps by types of travelers, such as vacationers, convention attendees, business travelers, and so on. The researcher then measures spending by type of traveler. This spending may or may not be broken down by type of expenditure, such as lodging, food and beverage, and others. The final step in calculating direct effects is to estimate effects of the spending by category on the variables of interest, such as output, employment, and taxes.

In addition to the direct effects, tourist spending has other effects. For example, we know that tourists spend money on lodging. Hotels and motels, however, spend money within the region for cleaning supplies, linens, and other materials needed for their operations. This second round of spending is an indirect effect of the tourism activity. If, for example, a small city were to construct its first convention center, it would expect an influx of new convention visitors in the coming year. These new visitors would spend money on hotel rooms, restaurant meals, and many other things. This spending leads to the direct effect part of the economic impact of the new convention center as the region's production, employment, and payments of wages and taxes rise. This spending, however, has other effects. The restaurants buy more food and materials needed for their now larger operations. Hotels buy more supplies; their utility bills go up. This additional buying by these firms causes production elsewhere in the local economy to rise. Studies of the economic impact of tourism often refer to this additional production as the "indirect effect" of the increased tourism spending.

Some studies, such as the New Zealand study just mentioned, also refer to an *induced effect* of increased tourism. Tourist spending leads hotels, restaurants, and other tourism service providers to hire workers and to pay wages and salaries. Much of this spending remains within the region as the workers' incomes. These workers spend their incomes on housing, food, and all the other things consumers buy. A larger tourism sector will lead to larger incomes, which will lead to increased spending by consumers within the region. This additional increase in economic activity within the region, the induced effect, adds to the total effect of the increase in tourist spending.

INPUT–OUTPUT ANALYSIS

The most important method for analyzing economic impacts of tourism is input–output analysis. The Royal Swedish Academy of Sciences awarded the 1973 Nobel Prize in Economic Science to Wassily Leontief for his work in developing input–output analysis and for applying it to solve economic problems.[7] Beginning in the 1930s, Leontief developed input–output analysis to describe and understand how production

---

[7] Royal Swedish Academy of Sciences (1973).

in one sector of the economy depends upon production in other sectors. For example, making trucks requires buying steel and truck tires, among many other things. But making truck tires also requires buying steel, rubber, and many other things, including trucks. Steel making requires iron ore, coal, and many other things, again including trucks, and various things made from rubber, such as belts and hoses. We can see that all the sectors—trucks, steel, tires, and rubber—are interconnected in a very complicated way. Leontief created a way to describe and understand these complicated interconnections and to predict what would happen in each of the various sectors of the economy if demand for the output of some sector of the economy were to increase. One of the most notable uses of input–output analysis was in military planning in Washington, D.C. and elsewhere during and after World War II. Then, the problem was to know what would be needed throughout the economy to create huge new levels of war-related materials and then later to predict the effects on the economy when the government stopped buying these war-related materials.

      Input–output analysis uses the interdependence of production among the sectors of the economy to analyze what happens to the economy as a whole when the demand for a good changes. Input–output analysis is a method for measuring these indirect effects by industry sector. We will assume that the demand for the output of the tourism industry in a specified region increases, and we want to use input–output analysis to measure the direct, indirect, and induced effects this increase has throughout the region's local economy.

> **Input–output analysis**
> A method for calculating economic impacts of changes in demand for a region's goods and services on the sectors of the region's economy using information on interindustry sales.

      We can use an input–output model to calculate multipliers. An output multiplier, for example, is the ratio of the total increase in output to the initial change in spending, which tells us how many dollars the value of the region's output rises per dollar of increase in spending. We can use input–output analysis to calculate the direct and other effects of the change in final demand and use this to calculate the multiplier. In a similar way, we can calculate employment and income multipliers. We will see in detail how to make these calculations in Appendix 5.1.

      Travel and tourism provides many opportunities to use these methods to calculate economic impacts, and there are many such studies. One example is Bradley M. Braun's 1992 study of the economic impact of conventions on Orlando, Florida.[8] Braun noted that convention attendance (including meetings and trade shows) in Orlando grew from 36,019 in 1969 to 1.675 million in 1989. Braun's goal was to calculate the effect of the spending of 1.675 million convention delegates on Orlando's employment, income, production, and tax revenues. Braun calculated that the total impact of convention spending was to add 65,000 jobs, $457 million in wages, $2.28 billion in output, and $103 million in state and local tax revenues to the Orlando economy. How did he make such calculation? He used a 494-sector input–output model of the Central Florida regional economy.

      In the next section we will show how input–output analysis of the economic impact of tourism is done. We will see that there is no magic involved and that the process uses simple mathematics accessible to anyone who has studied high school algebra. Appendix 5.1 shows some of the details of input–output analysis using matrix algebra.

---

[8] Braun (1992).

Each Industry Must Have the Outputs of Other Industries

Let's look at how input–output analysis works. First we need to construct an input–output table that describes the sales from each sector to each sector for the region we are considering. Input–output analysis typically uses the term *sector* for what elsewhere might be called an "industry." We can divide the economy very narrowly into industries or sectors such as lodging, travel agents, automobiles, and so on. Or we can divide the economy into broad industries or sectors such as travel and tourism, manufacturing, agriculture, and others. The basic ideas are the same regardless of how narrowly or broadly we define our sectors.

Consider again the steel industry. The steel industry sells its output to the automobile industry, the construction industry, other manufacturing sectors, the mining industry, and many other sectors, including, interestingly, the steel industry. During a specified period, such as one year, the steel industry has certain dollar values of sales to each industry. We can express this mathematically with an equation that shows the total dollar value of output of the sector during the year as the sum of sales to all the other sectors plus sales to buyers outside the industries included among the region's producing sectors, such as household consumers, government, and buyers outside the region. We refer to the sales to household consumers, to government, and to buyers outside the region as **final demand**, because these sales are not used in production within the region.

Final demand
In input–output analysis, sales to buyers outside the industries included among the region's producing sectors. Final demand always includes exports (sales to buyers outside the region), and may include government and households.

Suppose, to keep things simple, that the steel industry sells only to buyers outside the region (final demand) and to three industries inside the region: truck producers, glass producers, and steel producers. Then we can write an equation showing the sales of the steel industry as

Steel sales = sales to trucks + sales to glass + sales to steel + sales to final demand.

$$\text{(1)}$$

Suppose steel sales to the truck industry is some constant proportion, "a," of truck industry sales. Let T denote total revenue from sales of trucks. Then

$$\text{Steel sales to trucks} = aT.$$

Suppose similarly that steel sales to glass and steel are constant proportions, "b" and "c," of the sales revenues of those industries, respectively; then

$$\text{Steel sales to glass} = bG$$

and

$$\text{Steel sales to steel} = cS,$$

where G is the glass industry's sales revenue and S is the steel industry's sales revenue. Then we can rewrite equation (1) as

$$S = aT + bG + cS + F_S, \qquad \text{(2)}$$

where F_S is final demand for steel.

In a similar way, let's express sales of the truck and glass industries:

$$T = jT + kG + mS + F_T$$
$$G = dT + eG + hS + F_G.$$

Then, the following three equations show the relationships among the three industries in the region:

$$T = jT + kG + mS + F_T$$
$$G = dT + eG + hS + F_G$$
$$S = aT + bG + cS + F_S.$$

Perhaps surprisingly, we could use these three simple equations to easily calculate the effects of changes in final demand for any or all of the three products, trucks, glass, or steel, on the total sales of all three of the industries. This is the essence of economic impact analysis: if final demand for any of the region's products changes, what will happen to economic activity in every sector within the region?

Let's take a very simple example involving tourism. Consider a small region that has only two industries—hotels and restaurants. Using the same process described earlier for steel, glass, and trucks, we express sales of the restaurant and hotel industries as sales to restaurants plus sales to hotels plus sales to final demand. In this case we assume that final demand is sales to consumers within the region, sales to government, and sales to consumers from outside the region, or tourists. Call restaurant final demand F_R and hotel final demand F_H. Let H be total sales of the region's hotel industry and R be total sales of the region's restaurant industry. Then we can express the relationships among the region's industries with two equations:

$$R = aR + bH + F_R$$
$$H = cR + dH + F_H.$$

Remember that "a" is the constant proportion of restaurant industry sales that is spent on the restaurant industry, and "b" is the constant proportion of hotel industry sales that is spent on the restaurant industry. Suppose these proportions are 0.1 and 0.2, respectively. Suppose also that c and d are 0.2 and 0.3. Then we can rewrite the two equations as

$$R = 0.1R + 0.2H + F_R$$
$$H = 0.2R + 0.3H + F_H.$$

We can now use simple algebra to solve for R and H, restaurant and hotel sales revenue, in terms of F_R and F_H. Recall that this involves solving the first equation for R in terms of H and F_R and substituting the result in the second equation. This eliminates R from the second equation, allowing us to solve for H in terms of F_R and F_H. We then substitute that result into the first equation to eliminate H, giving us R in terms of F_R and F_H. If we do these operations, we get the following results:

$$H = 0.33898F_R + 1.5254F_H$$

and

$$R = 1.1864F_\mathrm{R} + 0.33898F_\mathrm{H}.$$

These results directly show the economic impact of tourism on the region. They show that if the region's restaurants sell an additional $100 in restaurant meals to tourists, which is part of final demand, then restaurant sales will rise by $118.64 = 1.1864 × $100 and hotel sales will rise by $33.898 = 0.33898 × $100. The total increase in output or sales within the region is the sum of these two changes, or $152.54.

Note that increased sales in restaurants increases hotel sales, because some proportion of restaurant industry sales revenue is spent on hotel rooms. Note also that an increase of $100 in final demand for restaurant meals increases restaurant sales by more than $100. This happens because some proportion of restaurant industry sales is spent in the restaurant industry, in just the same way that the steel industry sells to the steel industry. The fact that the increase in sales exceeds the increase in final demand is known as the **multiplier effect**. The ratio of the total increase in sales within the region to the increase in final demand is called the *output multiplier*. Thus, to summarize, an increase in sales to final demand, including tourists, will have a larger effect within the region than the increase in final demand itself. This occurs because industries within the region sell to themselves in addition to selling to final demand. (As we will see, the multiplier effect also occurs because people receiving increased income from the increased final demand spend part of their increased income within the region.)

Multiplier effect
An increase in sales to final demand will have a larger effect within the region than the increase in final demand itself.

The multiplier effect means that if tourism promoters can get additional tourist spending within the region, then sales of the industries within the region will rise by an even larger amount. The multiplier effect increases the incentive of regional governments to promote tourism sales because it increases the impact on local sales of each dollar spent by tourists to a value larger than one dollar.

We can now see the direct, indirect, and induced effects of an increase in tourism spending in the region. The direct effect is the change in final demand. The indirect effect arises from the fact that changes in final demand spread to other sectors because of interindustry purchases; for example, the tourist may not buy dry-cleaning services in the region, but the waiter in the hotel's restaurant does. The indirect effect is the sum of the changes in the outputs of each sector (calculated with the household sector included in final demand) minus the direct effect. Finally, the induced effect is the sum of the changes in the outputs of each sector (calculated with the household sector as one of the productive sectors) minus the direct effect and minus the indirect effect. Some of the region's households earn income in the region's tourism industry and they spend much of that income within the region. See Appendix 5.1 for a more complete explanation of these effects and an explanation of how the region's household sector is treated in input–output analysis.

What Assumptions Do We Make When Using Input–Output Analysis?

We should review the assumptions we have made to get to this point.

- We have taken a fixed region such as a state or metropolitan area as the area of interest, and the area for which we have defined the interindustry relations, defined by equations like equation (2);

- We have taken a fixed time period, usually one year;
- We have assumed a linear model; that is, the proportions shown by the coefficients such as a, b, and c of equation (2) are constant. Whether the output of some industry, say lodging, is at a very low level or a very high level, the required proportions of each of the intermediate products of the other sectors, say window cleaning or legal services, stay the same per unit of lodging output.
- The effects of changes in final demand are additions to economic activity in the region. These effects are not subtracted from the output, employment, income, and taxes of some other industry that was already operating in the region. That is, for example, we assume that if the lodging industry grows because of higher tourism demand, the additional resources used in the lodging industry will not come from reductions in resource use in some other industry in the region.

SUSTAINABLE TOURISM DEVELOPMENT AND ECOTOURISM

As we saw at the beginning of this chapter, many destinations spend vast amounts of money to promote tourism. We saw that Las Vegas spends well over $100 million annually to promote itself as a tourist destination. Tourism development in Las Vegas has dramatically changed that region from a small, remote town in the desert to one of America's largest cities having one of the nation's busiest airports and many of the world's largest hotels. Tourism has transformed the region to the extent that it is hardly recognizable as the same place from one decade to the next.

Many people are unhappy with tourism's impacts on tourist destinations. In some cases the changes in the nature of destinations are widely viewed as negative, as high-rise buildings, T-shirt shops, and chain restaurants overwhelm localities that were originally appealing in part for their low-key, local flavor. In many places, massive tourist arrivals have made local customs disappear or have converted them to staged reenactments of earlier authentic behaviors. Large-scale tourist arrivals have in many cases diminished or threatened natural features and attractions.

These potentially negative impacts of tourism have led to the emergence of interest in "sustainable tourist development" and "ecotourism." One of the most widely cited studies promoting interest in sustainable development was the 1987 report of the World Commission on Environment and Development, a United Nations commission.[9] The Commission was concerned with continuing the world's economic growth, including especially reducing poverty in developing countries, while sustaining the environment. This report stated that sustainable development satisfies people who are alive today without compromising the ability of people of the future to achieve their own satisfaction.[10] Thus, we can think of **sustainable tourism development** as development that explicitly takes account of the impact of today's tourism activities on the opportunities that will be available to future tourists and local residents. The ideas of sustainable tourism and the concerns about tourism impacts that they arose from involve important economic concepts. Economic analysis can help us to understand the concerns and socially useful ways to deal with them.

Sustainable tourism development
Development that explicitly takes account of the impact of today's tourism activities on the opportunities that will be available to future tourists and local residents.

---

[9] United Nations (1987).
[10] United Nations (1987), Chapter 1, paragraph 49.

Ecotourism
Tourism designed to take advantage of a region's natural attractions while providing income to local residents and leaving the region little changed from its pre-tourism conditions.

Ecotourism is a concept related to, but not the same as, sustainable tourism. **Ecotourism** is tourism designed to take advantage of natural attractions while providing income to local residents and leaving destinations little changed from their pre-tourism conditions. Many analysts also emphasize that ecotourism must have an educational component. Others stress the requirement that ecotourism must provide income to maintain the ecological system that tourists visit. The concerns that prompt regions to promote ecotourism are thus similar to the concerns of those interested in sustainable tourism. The basic idea is that tourism can have important negative impacts on the region.

We can improve our understanding of some of the primary concerns about potential negative economic impacts of tourism using the following concepts from economics:

- intertemporal or intergenerational analysis (explicitly incorporating time into economic analysis)
- common pool resources
- externalities and property rights.

INTERTEMPORAL ECONOMIC ANALYSIS

Intertemporal economic analysis
Economic analysis that explicitly incorporates time.

Intertemporal economic analysis is economic analysis that explicitly incorporates time. In analyzing economic behavior over time, we can look at the behavior of a group of individuals in a series of time periods, such as consumers earning income through time, or the impact of one generation's decisions on the behavior of a later generation. In the case of a group of consumers, these consumers can consume part of this period's income and save the rest, earning interest on the savings which would be available to them in future periods. In the case of multiple generations, earlier generations create income, consume exhaustible natural resources, and leave capital (including machinery, buildings, and knowledge) and remaining natural resources for later generations.

To see how intertemporal economic analysis contributes to understanding of the issues involved in sustainable tourism, consider a local region with undeveloped natural resources having potential value to tourists. This might be a coral reef, beautiful sand beaches, a rainforest, a mountainside with beautiful year-round views and terrain ideal for skiing part of the year, or other natural wonders or attractions. This region has been a largely undisturbed home to local people for many generations. Today a developer appears in the area and inquires about building tourist facilities related to the natural wonder. The concerns of sustainable development are to make good use of the local resources, earning income for local people, without spoiling the area for future generations.

The best use of the region may well include some tourism development. With wise development, the natural resources may provide income to local residents and provide tax revenue for local government. This income and tax revenue could provide increased opportunities for many generations of local residents, including improved education, health care, transportation, and larger quantities of many other goods and services. The potential danger giving rise to concerns about sustainable development is that those making decisions today might grab value for themselves, spoiling the region over time, and leaving neither higher incomes nor natural resources for future inhabitants of the region.

At what rate should the natural resources be developed to well serve today's local residents and those of the future? Economists have studied this type of question for decades in examining the theory of exhaustible resources. Economists have long recognized that exhaustible resources, including minerals, petroleum, and many others, must be used for current production and consumption; but that in doing so we leave less of those resources for the future. Earlier generations do, however, leave inexhaustible (producible) resources including plant and equipment, new knowledge, and many others along with some remaining level of exhaustible natural resources. All of these, not just the exhaustible resource, will have value to future generations.

There is obviously a potential tradeoff between current consumption and future consumption, as current populations could overexploit natural resources for short-term benefits at the expense of the future. We can impose a sustainability restriction, thereby removing this tradeoff from our analysis of tourism development, by requiring that consumption must be the same in all time periods. Thus, in the following we impose the constraint that the current generation and future generations will have the same level of consumption.

This restriction satisfies concerns about present consumers grabbing from the future, but it does not remove the tradeoff between current consumption and the amount of capital that will be left for future generations. Thus, even if $C_1 = C_2$, where C_1 is current consumption and C_2 is future consumption, the current generation's decisions about consumption and investment today can lower or raise both C_1 and C_2. And both today's consumption and investment, and therefore tomorrow's consumption, are in part determined by today's decisions about the use of exhaustible natural resources. Thus, removing the concerns about the people of today shifting consumption from the future to themselves does not remove the issue of the optimal choice of resource development to serve both today and the future.

The four-part Figure 5.1 illustrates both tradeoffs. In Figure 5.1(a), we see the production possibilities frontier which shows the tradeoff between current consumption C_1 and future consumption C_2. To see how we construct this curve, assume that in period 1 there is a fixed level of capital, denoted K_1, and a fixed level of an exhaustible natural resource, denoted R. During period 1, we use K_1 and some portion of R, call it R_1, to produce output. (Assume we cannot produce any output without using some of both inputs, K and R.) Today we can consume a portion of this output and use the remainder as investment in capital for the future. Let I denote this investment part of period 1's output. Note that we can produce new K for the future, but we cannot produce R. The fixed quantity of the exhaustible resource R can only be partly used, with the remainder saved for the future.

Given today's production technology, once we know K_1 and R_1 we also know how much output will be produced. Today we must choose how much of that output to consume and how much to invest in capital to be available in the future. Figure 5.1(b) shows this tradeoff. The straight line shows the constraint that $C_1 + I$ must be equal to a constant, which we set at the level of today's output.

Figure 5.1(c) shows that capital available for production in the next generation will be whatever level of capital survives from period 1 (K_1 minus depreciation) plus investment in period 1, which we have been calling I. In drawing the figure, we assume that K_1 fully depreciates so that none is left for period 2; K_2 then equals I.

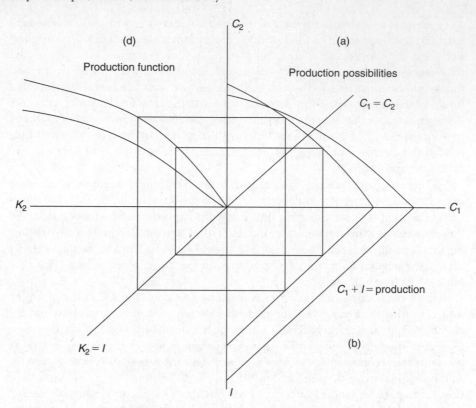

FIGURE 5.1 Production
Possibilities Frontiers for
Various Levels of R_1.

Figure 5.1(d) shows the production function for period 2, or the relationship between output in period 2 and the levels of productive inputs, K_2 and R_2. R_2 is fixed at the level $R - R_1$, so that in the figure production in period 2 depends on K_2 only. Note that because there are only two periods, C_2 equals the amount produced in period 2, as there are no future periods for which we might invest.

To derive the production possibilities frontier, pick a C_1. Then follow this quantity down to Figure 5.1(b) to get I given C_1. Now move left to Figure 5.1(c) to get K_2 given I. Then follow this quantity up to Figure 5.1(d) to get C_2, which equals period 2's output, given K_2. Take this C_2 across to Figure 5.1(a) to give us one point (C_1, C_2) on the production possibilities frontier. To get a second point, begin the process again starting with a different C_1. All possible combinations of (C_1, C_2) taken together form the production possibilities curve, as shown in Figure 5.1(a).

We impose the sustainability constraint by requiring $C_1 = C_2$, and we show this with the diagonal 45° line in Figure 5.1(a). But, as we saw above, this does not remove the issue of the optimal choice of resource development to serve both today and the future. That is, different choices of how much of the natural resource to use today will give us different levels of $C_1 = C_2$.

To see this, recall that we drew the line in Figure 5.1(b) based on the choice of R_1. Given K_1 and our choice of R_1, today's production technology allowed us to produce a specific level of output, and Figure 5.1(b) showed our requirement of dividing that level of output between C_1 and I. With a different choice of R_1 we would get a different level of output, and the line in Figure 5.1(b) would be in a different place. Larger R_1 would move the line in Figure 5.1(b) farther from the origin as shown by the second line in Figure 5.1(b). This would give us a greater I and greater K_2 for any level of C_1. But C_2 would not necessarily be larger, because a larger R_1 means a smaller R_2, so that period 2's production function in part (d) of the figure will move downward, as shown. The resulting change in C_2 given any level of C_1 is ambiguous in general. Figure 5.1(a) also shows a second production possibilities curve associated with the larger value of R_1.

Figure 5.2 shows various production possibilities frontiers for a specific production function. (See Appendix 5.2 for the details of this specific model.) Here we assume in both periods that the production function is $Q = K^{0.7}R^{0.3}$. The figure shows the diagonal line consisting of the points where $C_1 = C_2$. It also shows four production possibilities frontiers for initial capital $K_1 = 90$, exhaustible resource $R = 100$, and four choices of R_1, $R_1 = 70$, $R_1 = 60$, $R_1 = 46$, and $R_1 = 30$. Consider the production possibilities frontier for $R_1 = 70$. This is consistent with $C_1 = C_2 = 56$. But this is using too much of the resource in period 1, because lowering the level of R_1 to $R_1 = 60$ would allow a higher $C_1 = C_2 = 57.5$. Indeed, the highest level of $C_1 = C_2$ is to be found at $R_1 = 46$. Using this level of the resource in the first period allows $C_1 = C_2 = 58.3$.

What is going on here? In this array of production possibilities frontiers, we are observing the second of the tradeoffs discussed previously; that is, we can trade off the natural resource for more reproducible capital. Using more of the natural resource today allows greater production of output today, and some of that output will be used to create new capital for the future. But we must strike a balance, because production in the future will require both capital and the natural resource. By using more of the resource today, we leave less of the natural resource for the future, and we must compensate by creating

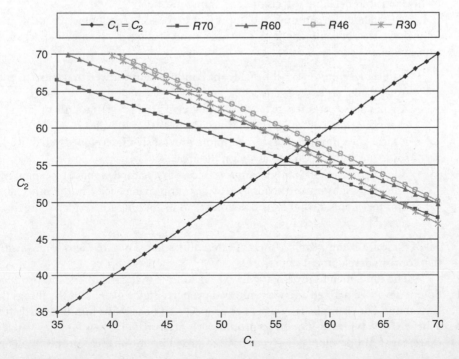

FIGURE 5.2 Production Possibilities Frontiers for Alternative Natural Resource Use R_1.

more capital for the future with a higher level of investment. But in some cases we can get *both more consumption today and the required higher investment* because using more of the resource today yields more output today. This tradeoff between future levels of capital and future levels of the natural resource is the second tradeoff, and this tradeoff exists even if we remove the sustainability issue by requiring $C_1 = C_2$.

Thus, society's concern about the optimal choice of resource development to serve both today and the future goes beyond the potential for earlier generations to behave opportunistically relative to later generations. Optimal resource development requires us to recognize that earlier generations will invest in capital, including new knowledge, that will benefit future generations and that using natural resources in the earlier generations contributes to that investment.

COMMON PROPERTY RESOURCES, EXTERNALITIES, AND PROPERTY RIGHTS

Externality
An effect on the consumption or production of an individual or firm of a transaction to which that individual or firm was not a party.

Have you ever been annoyed by someone else's making a cell phone call in what you regard as an inappropriate time or place? Have you ever been stuck in a traffic jam? We have all been in these situations. Very frequently some consumer or firm in the economy engages in a transaction that affects the consumption or production of other consumers or firms who are not parties to the transaction. When this happens we call this effect an **externality**. As the cell phone and traffic jam examples reveal, examples of externalities are very common. Another common example is when your neighbor spends money on landscaping and regularly mows his lawn, you and the other neighbors benefit. When another neighbor neglects his or her property, the resulting eyesore harms you and the other neighbors. These effects are externalities because you were not involved in your neighbors' decisions and transactions.

Externalities are common and important in tourism development. Consider the following effects of transactions on consumers and producers who are not party to the transactions:

- A developer builds a tall beachfront condominium tower that obstructs the water views of nearby residents.
- A golf course cares for its fairways and greens using vast amounts of lawn care chemicals, some of which run off into nearby bodies of water.
- A local government builds a road into a previously undeveloped valley, leading some species of wildlife to abandon the area.
- A local government wants to improve access to a natural wonder by expanding a previously substandard road, thereby also improving access in the other direction to schools, hospitals, employment, and shopping for residents previously served by the old road.

All of these are examples of the sorts of externalities, some negative and some positive, that tourism development can create.

The fundamental problem with externalities is that consumers and producers do not have well defined and well enforced property rights over all of the things they care about. For example, the owners of property set back a few hundred yards from a beach will typically not have property rights on their view of the water, so that beachfront developers will not have to take account of these property owners' preferences in making building decisions. Of course, beachfront developers could conceivably negotiate with nearby property owners for payments to compensate them for changes in building design to have a smaller impact on the views. Thus, even without a well defined property right, the parties could devise a mutually beneficial transaction. When such negotiations are not feasible because of the large number of parties involved and the accompanying high costs of entering into such a transaction, the harm will occur.

One common example of an externality is congestion. Here, individuals make decisions to use some resource, such as a road or waterway, without regard for the effects of their decisions on the other individuals who might want to use the same resource at the same time. The result can be excessive use of the resource, with all parties feeling the negative effects, such as a traffic jam that brings everyone to a stop.

Another common example of an externality is a common pool resource. In this case, something valuable is widely available but there is no property right that is both well defined and enforced. Once again, use by one party affects others who may not be able to engage in negotiations or transactions to protect their interests. One classic example of a common pool resource is a fishery. Here, fish are available to be taken, and one person's catch reduces the catch of all others fishing the same pool. The result is overfishing, often to the point of devastation of the resource.

New tourism development risks creating or exacerbating such externality problems. Tourism development frequently brings pollution, congestion, overexploitation of common pool resources, along with many other potential problems. Sensible government regulation can improve these situations; but regulations are not always sensible or effective, and they often have important unexpected effects. In some cases, private negotiations can reduce the worst of the negative effects of externalities.

Summary

The economic impact of tourism is one of the most widely studied areas related to travel and tourism. These economic impacts include changes in output, income, employment, tax revenue, and others. Nations, states, provinces, and cities spend vast amounts of money on tourism promotion, because each of these regions expects promotional spending to return much more in growth in employment, income, and tax revenue within the region. But these economic impacts go beyond production and jobs, and include social, cultural, and environmental changes. Regions also contend with adverse impacts as they try to get the benefits of increased tourism activity within their borders.

Researchers measure many of the economic impacts of tourism on regional economies using input–output analysis. This involves using information on inter-industry sales within the region along with information on sales to tourists to measure direct, indirect, and induced changes in the sales of each industry in the region. The direct impact is the tourist spending; the indirect impact is the result of the fact that firms selling services to tourists also buy goods and services from other industries in the region; and the induced impact arises from the employees and owners of tourism firms spending much of their incomes within the region. Matrix algebra using an input–output matrix makes the calculation of these impacts manageable.

Sustainable regional tourism development takes care to preserve the interests of future residents of the region and future tourists. Thus, understanding sustainable tourism requires using intertemporal economic analysis. This analysis reveals two tradeoffs in sustainable tourism development. The first is the tradeoff between the interests of the current generation and the interests of future generations. That is, the current generation can overexploit natural tourism resources to serve their own interests or they can reduce their use of resources today to preserve them for future generations. The second, less obvious, tradeoff is that between future levels of capital and future levels of the natural tourism resource. Earlier generations can use funds generated by using tourism resources today to leave reproducible resources, including physical facilities, new knowledge, and many others, for future generations. All of these resources, not just the natural, exhaustible tourism resource, will have value to future generations. Responsible tourism development will recognize both tradeoffs.

Ecotourism, designed to take advantage of natural attractions while providing income to local residents and leaving destinations little changed from their pre-tourism states, is one approach to socially responsible, sustainable tourism that is growing in popularity.

Tourism development frequently creates externalities—effects of a transaction on the consumption or production of an individual or firm that was not a party to the transaction. Tourism development can bring pollution, congestion, overexploitation of common pool resources, along with many other externalities. The fundamental problem with externalities is that consumers and producers do not have well defined and well enforced property rights over all of the things they care about. Government regulation or private negotiations can mitigate externalities.

APPENDIX 5.1

Solving for Economic Impacts Using Matrix Algebra

Solving for the economic impacts or multipliers by substitution is tedious, and for more than about three sectors it becomes quite impractical. Matrix algebra provides an easy way to solve for economic impacts and this method lends itself readily to solution by computer. Recall that Braun's economic impact study used a 494-sector model, so that only substantial computer resources could ever solve the problem.

A matrix is a rectangular array of numbers. In our uses, the numbers of rows and columns in the matrix will be the same, so that the array of numbers will be square. Recall that our simple two-sector model of the regional economy consisting of only hotels and restaurants was

$$R = aR + bH + F_R$$
$$H = cR + dH + F_H.$$

Now denote the matrix of numbers a, b, c, and d as A:

$$A = \begin{pmatrix} a & b \\ c & d \end{pmatrix} .$$

Denote the vector of output levels R and H as X:

$$X = \begin{pmatrix} R \\ H \end{pmatrix}$$

Finally, denote the vector of final demands as

$$F = \begin{pmatrix} F_R \\ F_H \end{pmatrix}$$

Now we can write our set of equations as a single matrix equation:

$$\begin{pmatrix} R \\ H \end{pmatrix} = \begin{pmatrix} a & b \\ c & d \end{pmatrix} \begin{pmatrix} R \\ H \end{pmatrix} + \begin{pmatrix} F_R \\ F_H \end{pmatrix} \qquad \textbf{(A1)}$$

Or writing the matrix equation more compactly, we can write the equation as

$$X = AX + F \qquad \textbf{(A2)}$$

Recall that to get the element in the first row and first column of X, that is the element R, we multiply the first row of A with the first column of X, which is $aR + bH$, and then add to that result the element in the first row and first column of F, which is F_R. This gives us the original expression for R:

$$R = aR + bH + F_R.$$

Now define the identity matrix, I, as the square matrix consisting of ones on the diagonals and zeroes everywhere else, or for an identity matrix with two rows and two columns

$$I = \begin{pmatrix} 1 & 0 \\ 0 & 1 \end{pmatrix}$$

Using I, we can rewrite the matrix equation (A2) as

$$X - AX = F$$

or

$$(I - A)X = F$$

or

$$X = (I - A)^{-1}F. \qquad \textbf{(A3)}$$

The matrix $(I - A)^{-1}$ is the inverse of the matrix $(I - A)$. The inverse of a matrix M is the matrix which when multiplied by M gives the identity matrix. (This is the matrix equivalent of the number $1/n$ which when multiplied by n yields 1.) This matrix inverse is easy to calculate for a 2 by 2 matrix. In general, the matrix

$$M = \begin{pmatrix} r & s \\ t & u \end{pmatrix}$$

has as its inverse the matrix

$$M^{-1} = \begin{pmatrix} \dfrac{u}{ru - st} & \dfrac{-s}{ru - st} \\ \dfrac{-t}{ru - st} & \dfrac{r}{ru - st} \end{pmatrix} \tag{A4}$$

This inverse exists for any 2 by 2 matrix for which $ru - st \neq 0$.

The key result here is matrix equation (A3), which says that the output of each sector of the regional economy equals final demands for the outputs of all sectors multiplied by factors that take into account all of the interactions between the sectors.

Now let's use equation (A3) to more easily calculate the economic impacts for our simple two-sector example involving hotels and restaurants. In matrix form, our two-sector model is

$$\begin{pmatrix} R \\ H \end{pmatrix} = \begin{pmatrix} 0.1 & 0.2 \\ 0.2 & 0.3 \end{pmatrix} \begin{pmatrix} R \\ H \end{pmatrix} + \begin{pmatrix} F_R \\ F_H \end{pmatrix}$$

Then the matrix $I - A$ is

$$I - A = \begin{pmatrix} 1 & 0 \\ 0 & 1 \end{pmatrix} - \begin{pmatrix} 0.1 & 0.2 \\ 0.2 & 0.3 \end{pmatrix}$$

We subtract matrices term by term, so that $I - A$ is

$$\begin{pmatrix} 1 - 0.1 & 0 - 0.2 \\ 0 - 0.2 & 1 - 0.3 \end{pmatrix} = \begin{pmatrix} 0.9 & -0.2 \\ -0.2 & 0.7 \end{pmatrix}$$

Then, using equation (A4) we see that $(I - A)^{-1}$ is

$$\begin{pmatrix} \dfrac{0.7}{0.63 - 0.04} & \dfrac{0.2}{0.63 - 0.04} \\ \dfrac{0.2}{0.63 - 0.04} & \dfrac{0.9}{0.63 - 0.04} \end{pmatrix} = \begin{pmatrix} 1.1864 & 0.33898 \\ 0.33898 & 1.5254 \end{pmatrix}$$

Then our result $X = (I - A)^{-1}F$ is

$$\begin{pmatrix} R \\ H \end{pmatrix} = \begin{pmatrix} 1.1864 & 0.33898 \\ 0.33898 & 1.5424 \end{pmatrix} \begin{pmatrix} F_R \\ F_H \end{pmatrix} \tag{A5}$$

or, multiplying this gives

$$R = 1.1864 F_R + 0.33898 F_H \tag{A6}$$

and

$$H = 0.33898 F_R + 1.5254 F_H,$$

which is exactly the result we got earlier solving by substitution. The matrix solution, however, is much easier to calculate and lends itself to computer programming which is essential for solving problems involving more than a few sectors.

Recall that when we used substitution to solve for the impact of an increase in the region's restaurants sales to final demand F_R of an additional \$100 we found that restaurant sales would rise by \$118.64 and hotel sales would rise by \$33.898, for a total impact equaling the sum of these two changes, or \$152.54. Then the output multiplier for increased F_R is $152.54/100 = 1.5254$. Note that this is just the sum of the elements in the first column of $(I - A)^{-1}$. The output multiplier for F_H is the sum of the elements in the second column of $(I - A)^{-1}$.

HOW MUST EACH INDUSTRY'S OUTPUT CHANGE TO MEET CHANGING FINAL DEMANDS?

To use the calculations we made above to calculate the effects of changing final demands, especially changing tourism demand, on a local economy, let's begin with final demand at a level we'll call F. Then, as previously shown, the levels of each industry's output required to produce F is

$$X = (I - A)^{-1}F.$$

Now suppose final demand changes; specifically, suppose tourism spending within the region increases. Denote the new level of final demand as F'. Then

$$X' = (I - A)^{-1}F'.$$

To find how output in each sector has changed as a result of this new tourism spending, subtract the previous outputs, X, from these new outputs, X':

$$X' - X = (I - A)^{-1}F' - (I - A)^{-1}F$$
$$X' - X = (I - A)^{-1}(F' - F)$$
$$\Delta X = (I - A)^{-1}\Delta F$$

This last equation says that the change in output of each sector is the change in final demand for the outputs of all sectors multiplied by factors that take into account all of the interactions between the sectors. Given matrix A which shows the interindustry requirements for each industry and the change in final demand ΔF, we can find the change in output of every industry in the region with the straightforward matrix calculation $(I - A)^{-1} \Delta F$.

Returning to the simple numerical example in equations (A5) and (A6), the total increase in output or sales within the region when restaurant final demand rises by $100 is the sum of the changes in restaurant and hotel output, or $152.54. The multiplier for restaurant final demand, 1.5254, is the sum of the elements in the first column of $(I - A)^{-1}$, after rounding to four decimal places. In the same way, the multiplier for the hotel final demand is the sum of the elements in the second column of $(I - A)^{-1}$.

WHAT LABOR INPUTS MUST EACH SECTOR HAVE TO PRODUCE ITS OUTPUT?

The previous discussion showed how we can derive the demand for each industry's output from final demand, taking into account the interindustry demands; that is, taking into account the fact that each industry must have not only the outputs of other industries to maintain its production but it also must have labor. We include labor in the input–output analysis by adding another sector, the household sector. Households within the region sell labor and buy goods and services. We represent these activities by adding a row and a column for the household sector to the input–output matrix.

We have to to account for all of the purchases and sales of the household sector. Let's start with the households' sales of labor services. Let L denote the value of the labor sales of the region's household sector and F_L denote the final demand for the labor services of households. This final demand is the value of the household sector's labor sales to government and to entities outside the region. Assume the value of the household sector's labor sales to the restaurant sector is some proportion e of restaurant sales, and labor sales to the hotel sector is some proportion g of hotel sales. Also, like the other sectors, the household sector sells some proportion of its sales of labor to itself. (Some examples of sales from the household sector to the household sector would be lawn mowing, baby sitting, or domestic help.) Let u represent the proportion of total labor sales from the household sector to itself. Then we add a third equation to represent household sales of labor:

$$L = eR + gH + uL + F_L.$$

Now we turn to household purchases from other sectors. Earlier we lumped these sales together with exports and sales to government as final demand, but now we will break out sales to households within the region. We account for these by adding sales to households to the equations showing sales from restaurants and hotels to other sectors:

$$R = aR + bH + vL + F_R$$
$$H = cR + dH + wL + F_H$$

Here we are assuming that restaurants sell a constant proportion v of labor sales to the household sector and that hotels sell a constant proportion w to households. We now have three equations to describe the regional economy:

$$R = aR + bH + vL + F_R$$
$$H = cR + dH + wL + F_H$$
$$L = eR + gH + uL + F_L$$

Rewriting this in matrix form we get

$$\begin{pmatrix} R \\ H \\ L \end{pmatrix} = \begin{pmatrix} a & b & v \\ c & d & w \\ e & g & u \end{pmatrix} \begin{pmatrix} R \\ H \\ L \end{pmatrix} + \begin{pmatrix} F_R \\ F_H \\ F_L \end{pmatrix}$$

or more compactly

$$X^* = A^*X^* + F^*,$$

where the asterisk distinguishes this equation from equation (A3), which did not have a separate row for sales of the household sector or a separate column for the purchases of the household sector.

As before, we can solve for each sector's output given final demand:

$$X^* = (I - A^*)^{-1}F^*. \tag{A7}$$

The element in the last row of matrix equation (A7) is the value of labor services used to produce final demand F^*, including all of the labor required to produce the intermediate goods needed to produce F^*. That is, the last row, L, is wages and salaries paid within the region.

Again, suppose final demand changes. Suppose tourism spending by consumers from outside the region increases by ΔF^*. Then,

$$\Delta X^* = (I - A^*)^{-1} \Delta F^*$$

and the change in household income is the last element of the column vector ΔX^*.

We can now see the direct, indirect, and induced effects of an increase in tourism spending in the region. The direct effect is the change in final demand, ΔF^*. The indirect effect is the sum of the changes in the outputs of each sector (calculated with the household sector included in final demand), that is the sum of the elements of ΔX, minus the direct effect. Finally, the induced effect is the sum of the changes in the outputs of each sector (calculated with the household sector as one of the sectors in the matrix), that is the sum of the elements of ΔX^*, minus the direct effect and minus the indirect effect.

In more advanced applications, we could also add another row and column to account for investment in capital goods and returns to capital and another row and column to account for government tax revenue and government spending. These new sectors would be treated in the same way as the household sector.

APPENDIX 5.2

Production Possibilities Frontiers Given the Level of Natural Resource Use

We assume there are two periods, the current generation and the future generation. Assume each period's production function is $Q = K^{0.7}R^{0.3}$, so that

$$Q_1 = K_1^{0.7}R_1^{0.3}$$
$$Q_2 = K_2^{0.7}R_2^{0.3}$$

Assume the following level of exhaustible resources: $R = 100$. Use some of the exhaustible resource in period 1 and save the rest for period 2.

$$R_2 = 100 - R_1$$

Begin with capital stock K_1. Capital depreciates; assume that one-half of K_1 will survive to period 2. We can also produce new capital in period 1 (called investment and denoted I which will be available in period 2. Thus, in period 1 we can choose to use the output we produce for consumption in period 1 or for investment in new capital.

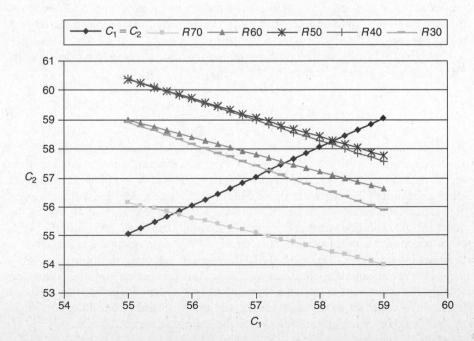

FIGURE A1 Production Possibilities Frontiers for Various Levels of R_1.

$$K_2 = 0.5K_1 + I$$
$$I = Q_1 - C_1$$
$$C_1 = Q_1 - I$$

Generation 2 can consume all of its output:

$$C_2 = Q_2$$

For each level of good 1, the production possibility frontier shows the maximum possible level of good 2. Figure A1 shows a small piece of the production possibilities frontier for various levels of R_1.

Sustainability requires $C_1 = C_2$. What is the optimal level of R_1? That is, how fast should we use up the exhaustible resource? The answer is the level of R_1 that allows the largest $C_1 = C_2$. In this case, the answer is approximately $R_1 = 46$ which allows $C_1 = C_2 = 58.3$.

Bibliography

Archer, B. H. "The Value of Multipliers and Their Policy Implications." *Tourism Management* December (1982): 236–41.

Archer, Brian, Chris Cooper, and Lisa Ruhanen. "The Positive and Negative Impacts of Tourism." In *Global Tourism*, 3rd ed., edited by William F. Theobald, 79–102. Amsterdam: Butterworth-Heinemann/Elsevier, 2005.

Blamey, Russell K. "Ecotourism: The Search for an Operational Definition." *Journal of Sustainable Tourism* 5 (1997): 109–30.

Braun, Bradley M. "The Economic Contribution of Conventions: The Case of Orlando, Florida." *Journal of Travel Research* 30 (1992): 32–37.

Crompton, John L., Seokho Lee, and Thomas J. Shuster. "A Guide for Undertaking Economic Impact Studies: The Springfest Example." *Journal of Travel Research* 40 (2001): 79–87.

Cukier, Judie, Joanne Norris, and Geoffrey Wall. "The Involvement of Women in the Tourism Industry of Bali, Indonesia." *Journal of Development Studies* 33 (1996): 248–70.

Dwyer, Larry, Peter Forsyth, and Ray Spurr. "Evaluating Tourism's Economic Effects: New and Old Approaches." *Tourism Management* 25 (2003): 307–17.

———. "Estimating the Impacts of Special Events on an Economy." *Journal of Travel Research* 43 (2005): 351–59.

Fletcher, John. "Input–Output Models," In *Economic and Management Methods for Tourism and Hospitality Research*, edited by Thomas Baum and Ram Mudambi. Chichester: John Wiley & Sons, Ltd., 1999.

Frechtling, Douglas C. "Assessing the Economic Impacts of Travel and Tourism—Introduction to Travel Economic Impact Estimation." In *Travel, Tourism, and Hospitality Research: A Handbook for Managers and Researchers*, 2nd ed., edited by J.R. Brent Ritchie and Charles R. Goeldner, 359–65. New York: John Wiley & Sons, 1994a.

———. "Assessing the Impacts of Travel and Tourism—Measuring Economic Benefits." In *Travel, Tourism, and Hospitality Research: A Handbook for Managers and Researchers*, 2nd ed., edited by J. R. Brent Ritchie and Charles R. Goeldner, 367–91. New York: John Wiley & Sons, 1994b.

———. "An Assessment of Visitor Expenditure Methods and Models." *Journal of Travel Research* 45 (2006): 26–35.

Frechtling, Douglas C., and Endre Horváth. "Estimating the Multiplier Effects of Tourism Expenditures on a Local Economy through a Regional Input–Output Model." *Journal of Travel Research* 37 (1999): 324–32.

Garrod, Brian, and Alan Fyall. "Beyond the Rhetoric of Sustainable Tourism?" *Tourism Management* 19 (1998): 199–212.

Healy, Robert G. "The Commons Problem and Canada's Niagara Falls." *Annals of Tourism Research* 33 (2006): 535–44.

Hewings, Geoffrey J. D. *Regional Input–Output Analysis*. Beverly Hills: Sage Publications, Inc., 1985.

Howarth, Richard B., and Richard B. Norgaard. "Environmental Valuation under Sustainable Development." *American Economic Review* 82 (1992): 473–77.

Johnston, Robert J., and Timothy J. Tyrrell. "A Dynamic Model of Sustainable Tourism." *Journal of Travel Research* 44 (2005): 124–34.

Krautkraemer, Jeffrey A. "Nonrenewable Resource Scarcity." *Journal of Economic Literature* 36 (1998): 2065–2107.

Las Vegas Convention and Visitors Authority (2006), "Comprehensive Annual Financial Report," http://www.lvcva.com/getfile/2006%20CAFR.pdf?fileID=133.

Liu, Zhenhua. "Sustainable Tourism Development: A Critique." *Journal of Sustainable Tourism* 11 (2003): 459–75.

Market Economics (2002), "The America's Cup Build-up to the 2003 Defence: Economic Impact Assessment," www.tourism.govt.nz/policy/pol-reports/res-ac-2003-eia/res-ac-2003-eia.pdf.

Miller, Ronald E., and Peter D. Blair. *Input–Output Analysis: Foundations and Extensions*. Englewood Cliffs, NJ: Prentice-Hall, Inc., 1985.

Page, Stephen J., and Ross K. Dowling. *Ecotourism*. Harlow: Prentice Hall, 2002.

Pearce, David. "Substitution and Sustainability: Some Reflections on Georgescu-Roegen," *Ecological Economics* 22 (1997): 295–97.

Royal Swedish Academy of Sciences (1973), "Press Release: The Prize in Economic Sciences in Memory of Alfred Nobel to the father of input-output analysis." http://nobelprize.org/nobel_prizes/economics/laureates/1973/press.html.

Sinclair, M. Thea. "Tourism and Economic Development: A Survey." *Journal of Development Studies* 34 (1998): 1–51.

Smeral, Egon. "Tourism Satellite Accounts: A Critical Assessment." *Journal of Travel Research* 45 (2006): 92–98.

Solow, R. M. "Intergenerational Equity and Exhaustible Resources." *Review of Economic Studies* 41 (1974): 29–45.

Stynes, Daniel (1997), "Economic Impacts of Tourism," http://www.msu.edu/course/prr/840/econimpact/pdf/ecimpvol1.pdf.

Travel Industry Association of America (2006a), "What's Hot in State and Territory Tourism Offices Trends & Press," www.tia.org/express/std_hotissues.html.

——— (2006b), "Industry Aims To Educate Millions About Impact Of Travel And Tourism," www.tia.org/pressmedia/pressrec.asp?Item=710.

United Nations (1987), "Report of the World Commission on Environment and Development: Our Common Future," www.un-documents.net/wced-ocf.htm.

U.S. General Accounting Office (2000), "Impact of Gambling: Economic Effects More Measurable Than Social Effects," www.gao.gov/new.items/gg00078.pdf.

Varian, Hal R. *Intermediate Microeconomics: A Modern Approach*, 7th ed., New York: W. W. Norton & Co., 2006.

Victor, David G. "Recovering Sustainable Development." *Foreign Affairs* 85 (2006): 91–103.

Weaver, David. *Ecotourism*. Milton, Queensland: John Wiley & Sons Australia, 2001.

World Travel and Tourism Council (1999), "WTTC Hawaii Tourism Report 1999," http://hawaii.gov/dbedt/info/visitor-stats/econ-impact/WTTC99.pdf.

CHAPTER 6

Pricing Tourism Services

Learning Goals

- Understand the concepts of consumer demand, prices, and revenue, and know how they are related.
- Understand business firm supply—setting prices and quantities of service to maximize profits.
- Understand how a firm sets a single price to maximize profits.
- Understand yield management (or revenue management)—know how firms maximize profits using price discrimination when they have capacity constraints.
- Understand two-part tariffs.

INTRODUCTION

It is well known that passengers sitting side by side in an airplane often pay different prices for their tickets—in many cases the prices may differ by hundreds of dollars. An article in *USA Today* refers to cruise line customers who pay the full price as "chumps."[1] In this chapter, we will see how and why tourism firms separate customers into chumps, who pay high prices, and other groups, who pay discounted prices. We will also see how to set prices for these groups.

We assume here that business firms set their prices and their quantities of services to maximize their profits. In many cases business firms must charge a single price to all consumers and a single price for all units of output they sell. Normally this will occur because consumers may resell the product among themselves, so that anyone who could buy at a low price could buy on behalf of another customer whom the firm is trying to charge a high price. Frequently, however, firms do charge different prices for different sales of the same product or service. This practice is known as **price discrimination**. Student discounts and senior-citizen discounts are two of the most common examples

Price discrimination
Charging different prices for different sales of the same product or service.

---

[1] Stoddart (1999).

of price discrimination. Coupons provide another common example. Business firms that can successfully price discriminate can increase their profits over the level they would get by charging a single price for all units of the product or service they sell.

Price discrimination is very important in tourism pricing. We will first review some of the basics of pricing you learned in your principles of economics course. Then we will look at some of the practices that are common in pricing tourism services.

DEMAND

Demand
The relationship between the price of a firm's product or service and the amount of that product or service that customers will buy.

We use the term **demand** to mean the relationship between the price of a firm's product or service and the amount of that product or service that customers will buy. Suppose you own and operate William's Reptile Petting Zoo. You sell a service—you allow the public to enter your zoo and pet the snakes and lizards. You may also sell products, for example, stuffed snakes and T-shirts with various cool reptile pictures decorating the fronts and backs. Suppose that if you charge $7.00 for admission, then you see that 40 people per hour want to pay for admission. Suppose that as an experiment you lower the admission price to $3.00, and you see that 120 people per hour want to enter and pet the snakes. This relationship between your price and the number of sales is the demand for your service. The graph of your demand, known as the *demand curve* is shown in Figure 6.1.

The graph measures the price along the vertical axis and the quantity customers are willing to pay for on the horizontal axis. We see the two prices and the two quantities that customers demand.

Let's fill in some of the remaining possible prices and quantities demanded. These are shown in Figure 6.2. We see that at a price of $9.00, no one wants to enter your zoo. If you charged a price of only $1.00, however, 160 people per hour would pay for admission.

Revenue and Marginal Revenue

Marginal revenue
The change in total revenue that comes from selling one more unit of output.

Revenue is the money a business firm takes in from sales to its customers. **Marginal revenue** is the change in total revenue that comes from selling one more unit of output. In our example, suppose you were to charge $7.00 and have 40 people per hour visit the zoo. That gives you total revenue, or money received from customers, of

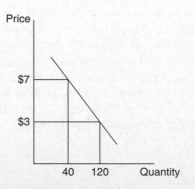

FIGURE 6.1 Consumer Demand.

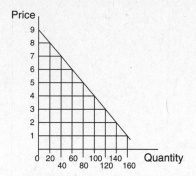

FIGURE 6.2 The Demand Curve.

$7 × 40 or $280. Consider selling one more unit of output, which would be 41 visitors per hour. Given the demand for your service, to get that many customers you would have to lower your price a little. In this case, suppose you would have to lower the price to $6.95 to attract customers at the rate of 41 per hour. Then your total revenue is $6.95 × 41 = $284.95. Then the marginal revenue in going from 40 to 41 units of output is $284.95 − $280 = $4.95.

Note that marginal revenue is made up of two parts. You get more revenue by selling one more unit. But you get less revenue because you had to lower the price on the 40 units you were already going to sell. Figure 6.3 illustrates these two quantities. The darkly shaded box shows the revenue you give up by getting a lower price ($6.95) for the 40 units you were already selling at the old price ($7.00). The lightly shaded box shows the revenue you gain by selling one more unit of service, which is the new price—$6.95. Marginal revenue is the difference between the areas of these boxes, in this case $6.95 − 0.05 × 40 = $4.95. (Of course, you would like to be able to sell additional units at the lower price without having to lower the price for the 40 units you could sell at $7.00. We will consider this possibility later when we examine yield management.) Marginal revenue is always less than the new price because we are subtracting the area of the darkly shaded box from the new price. For cases in which the area of the darkly shaded box is greater than the new price, the marginal revenue will be less than zero. That is, reducing the price in those cases would reduce total revenue.

Figure 6.4 shows demand for the product and also marginal revenue. As we saw earlier, marginal revenue must always be less than the price, so the marginal revenue

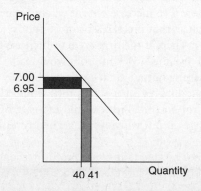

FIGURE 6.3 Marginal Revenue.

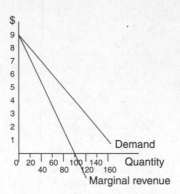

FIGURE 6.4 Demand
and Marginal Revenue.

curve lies below the demand curve. Also marginal revenue can be negative, as in Figure 6.4, when we are selling 120 units of service.

SUPPLY

Having looked briefly at the customer or demand side of the market, now let's look at the business firm or supply side. Supply is the relationship between the price and the amount of the good or service a business firm wants to provide to its customers. In the case of the reptile petting zoo, you could design a zoo with a capacity of 80 people per hour, or 100 people per hour, or many other sizes. The zoo could stay open 60 hours per week, or 70 hours per week, or any other length of time. Thus, you can change the amount of service you provide to the market. The amounts of their products and services business firms provide to the market generally depend on their costs and on their customer demands. It is easy to show how the quantity supplied depends on costs and demand.

To derive the quantity supplied from cost and demand, we need to recall the concepts of marginal cost and marginal revenue from principles of economics. **Marginal cost** is the change in total cost from providing one more unit of output, while marginal revenue, as we saw above, is the change in total revenue from providing one more unit of output. When would a firm want to provide one more unit of output? Suppose marginal revenue is $10 and marginal cost is $9. What happens to profit, which is total revenue minus total cost, when the firm produces and sells one more unit? Total revenue rises by $10, while total cost rises by $9. The difference, in this case $1, is added to profit. The firm wants to make this change, because it increases profit. Thus, one rule firms follow is to increase output whenever marginal revenue is larger than marginal cost, because that increases profit. Suppose marginal revenue is $5, while marginal cost is $7. Then, if the firm were to increase output, total cost would rise more ($7) than total revenue ($5), and profit would fall. Consider decreasing output in this case. By decreasing output, total cost would fall by marginal cost, and total revenue would fall by marginal revenue. Total profit would rise because revenue goes down by less than the drop in cost. Profit would increase by $2. Thus, another rule firms follow is to decrease output whenever marginal revenue is less than marginal cost, because that increases profit.

When will a firm not be able to increase profit by changing output? Only when marginal revenue and marginal cost are equal. If they are not equal, then one of the two

Marginal cost
The change in total cost from producing one more unit of output.

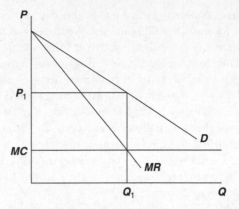

FIGURE 6.5 Profit Maximization when the Firm Charges a Single Price.

rules from the previous paragraph applies. This leads us to the basic rule for finding the output quantity that yields the largest profit: *produce the quantity that equates marginal revenue and marginal cost.*

Figure 6.5 illustrates these ideas. It shows marginal cost set at a constant level denoted MC. It also shows the demand and marginal revenue curves. At very low quantities of output, marginal revenue is higher than marginal cost. At the level of output Q_1, marginal revenue equals marginal cost. At higher levels of output, marginal revenue is less than marginal cost. The firm will earn the highest possible level of profits by producing Q_1 units of output.

YIELD MANAGEMENT—PRICE DISCRIMINATION WITH A CAPACITY CONSTRAINT[2]

The previous discussion reviewed the standard view of setting prices and quantities to maximize profits when a firm can set its own price and sell at that price to all customers. To maximize profits, the firm produces the output that makes marginal revenue equal marginal cost. The firm could, however, make more profits if it could charge different prices to different customers rather than charging a single price to all. (Companies frequently charge different prices to different customers for the same good, as with student or senior citizen discounts.) This price discrimination process is further complicated by the fact that the firm's capacity to serve customers is, in many cases, constant at any one time; it is fixed at a predetermined level. For example, the number of passengers an airline can serve on a particular flight is fixed once the aircraft has been assigned. The number of rooms in a hotel does not usually change from one day to the next, but rather can be changed only after a lengthy construction delay—tonight it is fixed at a predetermined level. We will see that we can simply handle both the possibility of charging different prices to different customers and the capacity constraint at the same time. The process whereby tourism companies having capacity constraints charge different prices to different customers is known as **yield management or revenue management.**

Yield management or revenue management
Price discrimination in the presence of a capacity constraint.

Suppose Southern National Airline has assigned a particular aircraft to Flight 2234, which departs Kansas City, Missouri, on Wednesday at 9:30 A.M. and flies to Tulsa, Oklahoma, where it is scheduled to arrive at 11:30 A.M. The aircraft has exactly 100 coach seats available to passengers. Southern National recognizes from much experience that it serves two broad classes of customers: leisure and business travelers. It serves leisure travelers who make reservations far ahead and are very sensitive to price—if the price is high, they will shop around for a lower fare, perhaps on a flight that has an extra stop, or they might drive or take a bus. Or, if the price is too high they might stay home. The airline also serves business travelers who make their travel plans at the last minute and are not willing to put up with extra stops. These business travelers cannot take the time to travel by road, and they do not have the option to stay home. They are much less sensitive to price.

The airline would like to charge a high price to the business travelers and let the leisure travelers fly at a lower price if there are any seats left. One of Southern National's primary concerns is that it does not want a leisure traveler, paying a low price, to make a reservation that takes a seat away from a business traveler who will call later and be willing to pay a higher price. Allocating seats between classes of customers is known as a *seat assignment problem*. When Southern National begins taking reservations months ahead of the flight time, it must decide how many seats to allocate, or "assign," to business travelers and how many to allocate to leisure travelers. Many leisure travelers will try to reserve their seats early, but Southern National will not let them fill the plane and crowd out business travelers who make last-minute reservations. The airline's solution to the seat assignment problem is known as "yield management." Boeing and American Airlines discovered and began applying yield management during the 1970s.[3] Since then, its use has grown rapidly among the airlines, and it has spread to almost every kind of business in travel and tourism where capacity is an issue; that is, where there is a fixed number of total places for customers. As we will see, capacity is an issue not only in airlines, but also in hotels, theme parks, restaurants, entertainment facilities, and many other tourism businesses. We will examine airlines' yield management in great detail, so that we will be able to apply the principles elsewhere in tourism.

As with Southern National, one of the keys to yield management is that customer groups have different demands for the service. This brings us to the first step: the provider must divide the market into groups of customers having different demands. Often these groups will be business and leisure, but there may be others.

The second key is that the provider must prevent customers from moving between groups. If we charge business travelers higher prices than leisure travelers, we must prevent business travelers from buying tickets at the leisure traveler price. The airline does this by establishing two fare categories, discount and full fare. The discount fare category is available only to travelers meeting specified restrictions. Southern National can, for example, require travelers who want the discount fare to buy their tickets 14 days before the flight time and stay over a Saturday night. Most business travelers will not be willing or able to meet these conditions, so they cannot get the low price. Leisure travelers often can meet the restriction, so they are eligible for the discount fare. Thus, the second step is to create restrictions that keep the groups separate.

---

[3] Kraft, Oum, and Tretheway (1986); Smith, Leimkuhler, and Darrow (1992).

The third step is to set a price for each group of customers. The fourth and last step is to allocate some of the fixed capacity to each of the groups. In the case of Southern National's Flight 2234 from Kansas City to Tulsa, there are 100 coach seats to be allocated between the discount fare category (leisure travelers) and the full fare category (business travelers). We handle the last two steps simultaneously.

To see how this works, let us consider the same two groups of customers—business and leisure travelers. These two groups have different demands as described earlier; that is, business customers are less sensitive to price, or, their demand is *less elastic*. Recall from principles of economics and Chapter 3 that the elasticity of demand is the percentage by which demand decreases when price rises by 1 percent. We assume here that the elasticity of demand for business customers is smaller than the elasticity of demand for leisure fliers, which is generally true in actual practice. We establish two categories of service, which we can call "discount" and "full fare." We establish restrictions for discount service that business travelers will not tolerate, such as a Saturday night stay and advance purchase.

Figure 6.6 shows the demand curves and marginal revenues for the two groups of customers. Suppose the marginal cost of serving an additional passenger on the assigned aircraft is MC. This would be the cost of any meal or other crew service. We can ignore the cost of the aircraft, the flight crew, the fuel, and similar costs, because we assume the flight will occur regardless of the number of passengers on the plane and these costs are constant given that the flight occurs. The profit-maximizing quantities are Q_B business passengers and Q_L leisure passengers. The price that makes the quantity of leisure demand equal to Q_L is P_L, and the price that makes the quantity of business demand equal to Q_B is P_B. Note that the customers with the less elastic demand, in this case the business customers, pay a higher price than the customers (leisure travelers) with the more elastic demand.

Figure 6.6 shows the standard result for this kind of situation. This result, which has different classes of customers paying different prices for the same service, is generally known as *price discrimination*. Pricing behavior of this kind is usually perfectly legal, and it is quite common. Student discounts, senior-citizen discounts, coupon discounts, and other such pricing schemes are some examples of price discrimination. This standard analysis does not work for the airline's seat assignment problem, however. The difficulty with this standard analysis is that it does not impose the requirement that $Q_B + Q_L$ must not be greater than the total number of seats on the aircraft.

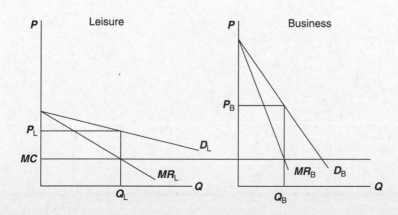

FIGURE 6.6 Price Discrimination with no Capacity Constraint.

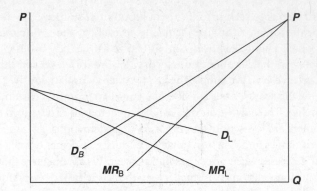

FIGURE 6.7 Imposing a Capacity Constraint with two Categories of Consumers.

We can adjust the standard analysis to make it illustrate the profit-maximizing prices and quantities for the seat assignment problem. We do this by taking the mirror image of the business graph and placing it on the right-hand side of the leisure graph. We do this to make the length of the horizontal Q axis equal to the seating capacity of the aircraft. This forces $Q_B + Q_L$ to be less than or equal to the number of seats on the plane. Figure 6.7 shows how this is done. As before, we have the leisure demand and marginal revenue curves, which we read from left to right. But now we have flipped the business demand and marginal revenue curves, and we read them from right to left.

Now, in Figure 6.8, we add the line showing the cost of having another passenger on the plane, for example, the cost of serving another meal, which is shown as C. What is the marginal cost of having another *leisure* passenger on the plane? Reading from left to right, the marginal cost of letting another leisure passenger on the plane is C up to the point y. For additional leisure passengers beyond the point y, however, the marginal cost is greater than C. The additional cost at this point is not the cost of an additional meal. Because of the limit on the number of passengers, beyond y additional leisure passengers are *taking seats away from business passengers* who would provide revenue higher than C. The marginal cost is then the marginal revenue of business passengers who no longer can be taken on the plane.

Thus, looking from left to right, the marginal cost curve for leisure passengers is the line C up to the point y, and then it follows the business marginal revenue curve beyond y. Figure 6.9 shows the marginal cost curve for leisure passengers without the other curves.

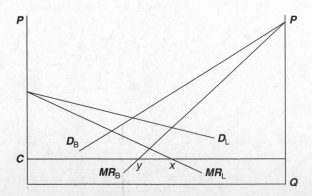

FIGURE 6.8 Marginal Costs and Marginal Revenues with a Capacity Constraint.

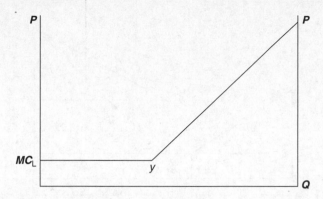

FIGURE 6.9 Marginal Cost for Leisure Travelers with a Capacity Constraint.

In a similar way, we can see the marginal cost curve for business passengers in Figure 6.8. Reading from right to left, it is the line C up to the point x. For business passengers beyond x, the business marginal cost curve is the leisure marginal revenue curve.

Now that we have marginal revenue and marginal cost for both business and leisure passengers, we can read the profit-maximizing prices and quantities from the graph. In Figure 6.10, z is the point where $MR_B = MC_B$ and $MR_L = MC_L$. That point also makes marginal revenue the same for both groups: $MR_B = MR_L$. Reading from left to right, we take Q_L leisure passengers. Reading from right to left, we take Q_B business passengers. Note that because of the way the picture is constructed, $Q_B + Q_L$ must equal the total number of seats on the aircraft. Once we have the quantities, we can move straight up to the demand curves to find the two prices. Note that in this case, as in the standard price discrimination graph, the customers with the less elastic demand pay the higher price.

We have now done the four steps of the yield management process:

1. we have divided the market into groups of customers having different demands for the service;
2. we have created restrictions to keep the groups separate;
3. we have set a price for each group of customers, P_L and P_B;
4. we have allocated the available seats to the groups, Q_L and Q_B.

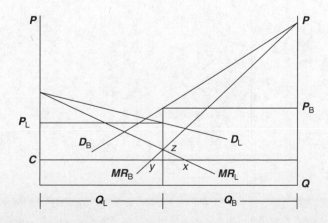

FIGURE 6.10 Price Discrimination with a Capacity Constraint.

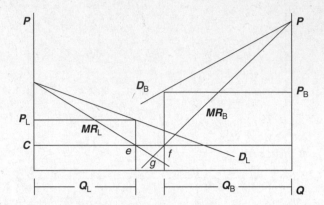

FIGURE 6.11 Price Discrimination with a Non-Binding Capacity Constraint.

Planning to Fly with Empty Seats

Would the airline ever plan to fly a plane with empty seats, even if there were passengers willing to pay something to get on the flight? The answer is yes. Figure 6.11 illustrates such a situation. In this case $MR_L = MC_L$ at a point e where Q_L is not high enough for leisure marginal cost to begin rising along the business marginal revenue curve. The airline will not take any more leisure passengers, because beyond point e marginal revenue is less than marginal cost. Also, Q_B, where $MR_B = MC_B$, is not great enough for business marginal cost to begin rising along the leisure marginal revenue curve. In this case, $Q_B + Q_L$ is less than the total number of seats on the plane. It remains true that at the profit-maximizing Q_B and Q_L marginal revenue is the same for both groups: $MR_B = MR_L$.

PRICE DISCRIMINATION THROUGH A TWO-PART TARIFF

Consumer surplus
The excess of the value to consumers of their consumption of a good over the amount they have to pay to get it.

Price discrimination is possible because consumers almost always receive **consumers' surplus** when they buy goods. Consumer surplus is the excess of the value to consumers of their consumption over the amount they have to pay to get it. Consider the demand curve again, as in Figure 6.12.

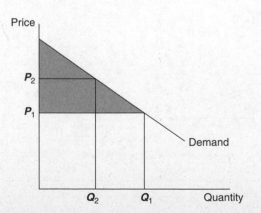

FIGURE 6.12 Consumers' Surplus.

In this case, the consumers in the market are paying a price P_1 and consuming Q_1 of the good. Because the demand curve is downward sloping, some consumers who would have been willing to pay much more than P_1 for some units of the good are paying only P_1. That is, if the price had been higher, for example P_2, consumers would have demanded a positive quantity, Q_2, of the good. Those consumers who would have been willing to buy Q_2 at the higher price are earning consumers' surplus because they are able to buy those units of the good at the lower price. The amount of consumers' surplus when the price is P_1 is the shaded area below the demand curve and above that price. (This amount is a dollar value, because all geometric areas in the $P - Q$ plane are dollar amounts.)

The essence of price discrimination is for the seller to capture as much of the consumers' surplus as possible. In yield management, firms capture consumer surplus by segmenting the market and charging high prices to some segments, often business travelers, and lower prices to others, often leisure travelers. In this way the firms can capture some of the consumer surplus of the business travelers who are willing to pay more than the leisure travelers. A simpler pricing mechanism that does not call for the firm to perform the four steps of yield management is called the *two-part tariff*.[4] The two-part tariff involves two prices paid by all consumers: (1) a flat fee, such as an entrance fee, for the right to buy any number of units of the good and (2) a fee per unit.

The classic example of the two-part tariff is an amusement park that charges both an admissions fee and a fee per ride. Consider the situation shown in Figure 6.13. Here we see a consumer's demand for the amusement park's rides and the marginal cost of providing additional rides. We assume the marginal cost is constant. Also, we assume that all consumers have the same demand for the park's ride.

The amusement park operator will maximize profits by selling the maximum number of rides for which the consumer is at least willing to pay the marginal cost. In Figure 6.13, this is Q_1. Charging the indicated price per ride, equal to marginal cost, makes the quantity demanded equal Q_1. At this price per ride, each consumer would be realizing a level of consumer surplus equal to the large shaded area below the demand curve and above the price. The park operator could then capture this consumer surplus by charging that amount as a fee for admission to the park.

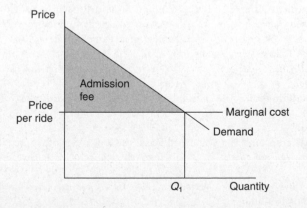

FIGURE 6.13 Optimal Two-Part Tariff: Admission Fee Plus Price Per Unit.

[4] Oi (1971); Varian (2006), pp. 458–459.

Summary

A business firm that must sell all of its output at a single price and wants to maximize profits will produce output at the level that makes marginal revenue equal to marginal cost. The firm will set its price at the level that induces consumers to demand that level of output. If the firm can charge different prices for different units of the same output, it can earn higher profits by dividing the consumers into groups having different demands and setting output to make marginal cost equal to marginal revenue for each group. Charging different prices for different sales of the same product or service is known as price discrimination. This is a common practice as shown by the wide use of student or senior-citizen discounts.

Often in tourism a firm's capacity to serve customers is constant at any one time, as with the seats on a particular airline flight or the rooms in a hotel. In these cases, the firm must take into account this capacity constraint in determining its prices and quantities. Price discrimination in the presence of a capacity constraint is widely practiced in the tourism industry, where it is known as "yield management" or "revenue management." This requires the firm to divide the market into groups of customers having different demands for the service, to create restrictions to keep the groups separate, to set a price for each group of customers, and to allocate the available capacity to the groups. The firm must recognize that marginal revenue for one group is marginal cost for the others. Then the profit maximization rule requiring marginal revenue to equal marginal cost will require the firm to allocate capacity to make marginal revenue the same for all groups.

Tourism firms may also use two-part tariffs to price discriminate. A two-part tariff involves charging all consumers a flat fee for the right to buy any number of units of service and also a fee per unit of service.

Bibliography

Belobaba, Peter P. "Application of a Probabilistic Decision Model to Airline Seat Inventory Control." *Operations Research* 37 (1989): 183–97.

Hanks, Richard D., Robert G. Cross, and R. Paul Noland. "Discounting in the Hotel Industry." *The Cornell Hotel and Restaurant Administration Quarterly* 33 (1992): 15–23.

Kimes, Sheryl E. "The Basics of Yield Management." *The Cornell Hotel and Restaurant Administration Quarterly* 30 (1981): 14–19.

Kraft, Dennis J. H., Tae H. Oum, and Michael W. Tretheway. "Airline Seat Management." *The Logistics and Transportation Review* 22 (1986): 97–130.

Layson, Stephen. "Third-Degree Price Discrimination, Welfare and Profits: A Geometrical Analysis." *American Economic Review* 78 (1988): 1131–32.

Oi, Walter Y. "A Disneyland Dilemma: Two-Part Tariffs for a Mickey Mouse Monopoly." *The Quarterly Journal of Economics* 85 (1971): 77–96.

Orkin, Eric (2001), "Hotel Revenue Management and Market Segmentation." *Hotel Online,* www.hotel-online. com/News/PR2001_1st/Jan01_OrkinRevenueMgmt. html.

Perdue, Richard R. "Perishability, Yield Management, and Cross-Product Elasticity: A Case Study of Deep Discount Season Passes in the Colorado Ski Industry." *Journal of Travel Research* 41 (2002): 15–22.

Reece, William S., and Russell S. Sobel. "Diagrammatic Approach to Capacity-Constrained Price Discrimination." *Southern Economic Journal* 66 (2000): 1001–1008.

Shapiro, Carl, and Hal R. Varian. *Information Rules: A Strategic Guide to the Network Economy.* Boston: Harvard Business School Press, 1999.

Smith, Barry C., John F. Leimkuhler, and Ross M. Darrow. "Yield Management at American Airlines." *Interfaces* 22 (1992): 8–31.

Stoddart, Veronica Gould. "Sea of Options: Savvy Shoppers Faring Well in Search of Extensive Cruise Discounts." *USA Today,* January 22, 1999, 1D–2D.

Varian, Hal R. *Microeconomic Analysis,* 3rd ed. New York: W. W. Norton, 1992.

CHAPTER 7

Airlines

Learning Goals

- Understand the historical development of scheduled airline service.
- Know how the U.S. government has regulated the airlines.
- Know how airlines create value—understand the business model.
- See how the industry has performed in recent years.
- Understand the current structure of the U.S. domestic airline industry.
- Understand the current structure of the European airline market.
- Analyze rivalry in the airline industry.
- Understand the costs of legacy and low-cost airlines.
- Understand recent changes in the airline industry.

INTRODUCTION

We will begin our careful look at the behavior and structure of the travel and tourism industry with the airline industry. There are at least three good reasons to start with the airline industry. First, we know a lot about the airline industry because economists have devoted a lot of attention to it. For 40 years the Civil Aeronautics Board (CAB) heavily regulated the airline industry. Beginning in early 1960s, economists following the lead of George Stigler at the University of Chicago examined the actual effects of economic regulation. The theory of economic regulation was well known, but there had been little or no effort spent on examining what regulation actually did to markets, firms, and consumers. A small group of researchers including George Douglas, Theodore Keeler, Michael Levine, James Miller, and others carefully studied the regulation of the airline industry. This research effort led, over the succeeding years, to a substantial body of work on behavior of the airline industry. This research also led eventually to Congress's abandoning airline price and service regulation and disbanding the CAB. Research on the airline industry has continued even after deregulation.

Our second reason is that the industry is large and is an important, central part of the travel and tourism industry. Finally, the airline industry has been a leader in developing new business methods that were later adopted elsewhere in the travel and tourism industry. Thus, airlines provide a natural starting point.

GROWTH OF U.S. DOMESTIC SCHEDULED AIRLINE SERVICE

Here we ignore military aviation, instead focusing on commercial aviation. General aviation and commercial aviation are the two basic types of civil aviation. General aviation consists of privately owned and operated aircraft, such as those owned by individuals or companies that operate aircraft for their own internal purposes. Commercial aviation carries passengers or cargo for hire. Thus, the scheduled airline industry is part of commercial aviation.

The airline industry is relatively young, with the first scheduled airline service starting in the 1920s. Thus, scheduled airline service has been around for less time than the automobile industry—indeed less than the car rental industry. It is less than half as old as the railroad industry. The short history of this industry, however, has been very eventful, with periods of rapid growth and prosperity, rapid technological change, a long period of heavy-handed federal regulation of prices and routes, entry and exit of a large number of firms, big bankruptcies, giant mergers and acquisitions, safety and security problems, intense rivalry among firms, and heavy financial losses. Indeed, even Hollywood has had a long-standing interest in this intriguing industry, with its oversized personalities and "jet-set" glamour. From 1933's *Flying Down to Rio*, which introduced Fred Astaire and Ginger Rogers as a dance team, to 2004's *The Aviator*, which depicted the rivalry between Howard Hughes's TWA and Juan Trippe's Pan American, the airlines have intrigued screenwriters and audiences. Eventually, both TWA and Pan American failed, with American Airlines acquiring TWA and various airlines acquiring Pan American's assets.

Figure 7.1 shows the rapid growth of the U.S. domestic scheduled airline industry from a tiny novelty to today's giant and centrally important part of America's transportation infrastructure.

U.S. Federal Regulation of the Airlines

From 1938 to 1978, the CAB heavily regulated the U.S. interstate airline industry. In the 1930s, many industry observers feared that the new industry might be harmed by excessive competition. The Civil Aeronautics Act of 1938 created the Civil Aeronautics Authority to regulate all aspects of civil aviation including air traffic control, certification, safety, airline routes, and airline prices. In 1940 the regulatory roles were split into two agencies, including the new CAB which took on the authority to regulate entry and exit in the industry and to regulate the prices the airlines charged. The Federal Aviation Act of 1958 amended the original Act and gave responsibility for aircraft safety regulation to the newly created Federal Aviation Agency, later renamed the Federal Aviation Administration (FAA).

CAB entry and exit regulation involved both entry of new airlines to the industry and existing airlines' entry into or exit from specific routes.[1] For example, the CAB

---

[1] See Bailey (2002).

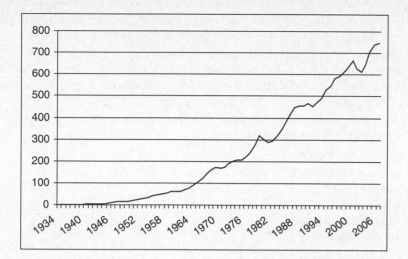

FIGURE 7.1 Annual U.S. Passenger Enplanements by Scheduled Airlines—1934–2006 (Millions of Persons).   *Data source:* Air Transport Association (2007b).

granted United Airlines the right to serve New York to San Francisco via Chicago, and it granted TWA the right to serve New York to San Francisco via St. Louis. These long hauls were known as "trunk" lines. There were four domestic trunk carriers: American, Delta, Eastern, and United. Pan American was the primary U.S.-based international carrier. In addition to the trunk carriers, there were local service carriers, such as Allegheny Airlines (later, part of US Airways), that served large regions of the nation but lacked trunk routes. The CAB created a formal process for considering applications to change airfares. The CAB severely limited competition among airlines by taking as long as four years to render a decision on applications for new routes or major price changes. The agency denied many applications, including all applications to establish new trunk carriers.

After years of study, Congress realized that the CAB was not generally serving the public interest, but rather was stifling competition and maintaining high airfares. One important piece of information was that intrastate carriers, especially Southwest Airlines in Texas and Pacific Southwest Airlines serving California, had much lower fares than the regulated interstate carriers over routes of similar distances. In a very unusual move, with the Airline Deregulation Act of 1978 Congress voted to terminate the CAB and to end its oversight of most aspects of airline behavior. The CAB ceased to exist in 1984. A few types of airline regulation were transferred from the CAB to the FAA in the U.S. Department of Transportation, which had been regulating airline operations and safety since 1958.

Recent Developments in Commercial Aviation

The start of the twenty-first century finds the U.S. airline industry in turmoil. By the end of 2005 we saw about one-half of the U.S. airline industry in bankruptcy. Some of the major names in the history of airlines, including Pan American, Eastern, and TWA, had disappeared through bankruptcy and integration into other carriers. The long-standing "network" carriers, those serving large portions of the nation using hubs, discussed later, face growing competition. One revealing sign of new turmoil in the airline industry is the New York Stock Exchange symbol "LCC" for the airline created by the 2005 merger of US Airways and America West. LCC is the industry's acronym for *low-cost carrier*, which refers to the airlines that have provided the most intense price competition for the long-standing carriers, including these two merger partners. This ticker symbol can be taken to be the symbol of the transition to a new era in the industry.

More recently, rising fuel prices have appeared as the major threat to the industry. During 2007 and 2008 fuel prices rose to record levels, leading to widespread industry losses and a continuing flow of bankruptcies.

The following list shows many of the factors we need to examine in understanding the economics of the airline industry:

- the airlines or carriers
- revenue passenger miles (RPM) and available seat miles (ASM)
- fares or prices
- services, amenities, and classes of service
- hubs and networks
- frequent flyer programs
- low-cost carriers and legacy carriers
- mergers
- domestic and international service
- fuel prices

HOW AIRLINES CREATE VALUE—THE SCHEDULED AIRLINES BUSINESS MODEL

Operations

Firms in the airline industry operate by performing the following major functions or business operations:

1. financing, or getting large sums of money to buy or lease airplanes and other equipment and facilities,
2. hiring pilots, flight attendants, and other staff,
3. promoting their services to customers,
4. selling tickets,
5. buying fuel and other supplies,
6. operating flights,
7. maintaining aircraft, and
8. other activities, perhaps including food service and video rentals.

To get an idea of the size of each of these functions, examine Table 7.1 which shows 2006 operating expenses by major category for AMR Corporation, which includes American Airlines and American Eagle. Note that salaries, wages, and benefits paid to labor makes up the largest expense category, with fuel in second place. By the end of 2008, fuel may overtake labor as the highest category of airline costs.

Equipment

The airline industry operates three basic types of aircraft: turboprop (or propeller-driven) aircraft, single-aisle jets, and twin-aisle jets. The turboprop aircraft, operated by commuter or regional airlines, are small- or medium-sized aircraft accommodating 20 to 40 passengers. Single-aisle jets range from small, regional jets with approximately 50 to 100 seats to much larger aircraft such as the Boeing 757, which has up to 240 seats. Twin-aisle

TABLE 7.1 Operating Expenses—AMR Corporation—2006

Category	Expense (Millions of Dollars)
Wages, salaries, and benefits	6,813
Aircraft fuel	6,402
Maintenance, materials, and repair	971
Commissions, booking fees, and credit card expense	1,076
Aircraft rentals	606
Other rentals and landing fees	1,283
Depreciation and amortization	1,157
Food Service	508
Other operating expenses	2,687
Total	21,503

Source: AMR Corporation (2007), p. 37.

jets, as the name suggests, have two aisles by which passengers get to and from their seats, and these can be intermediate-sized aircraft such as the Airbus A300 or Boeing 767 or large aircraft such as the Boeing 747, which accommodates more than 400 passengers.

The airlines buy many of their aircraft outright, either new aircraft from the manufacturers or used aircraft from other airlines. In other cases, the airlines lease aircraft from financial services companies such as GE Commercial Aviation Service (GECAS).

The Aircraft Manufacturers

The two most important aircraft manufacturers for U.S. airlines, and indeed for most of the world's airlines, are the Boeing Company, based in Chicago, and Airbus, a division of European Aeronautic Defence and Space Company, based in the Netherlands. Boeing and Airbus compete vigorously in the market for large commercial aircraft. These include single-aisle aircraft such as the Boeing 737 (capacity 110 to 177 passengers, short-to-medium range) and 777 (capacity 301 to 368 passengers, range over 9,000 nautical miles), and the Airbus A320 (capacity 150 to 179 passengers, short-to-medium range). The Boeing 737 is the largest selling commercial jet aircraft, with more than 5,500 total sales since the introduction of its first model in 1968. The Airbus A320 has also been popular, selling more than 1,000 aircraft since its introduction in 1988. These competitors also produce larger, twin-aisle aircraft, including the Boeing 747 (capacity 400+ passengers, range 8,000 nautical miles) and Airbus A340 (capacity 313 to 380 passengers, range up to 8,500 nautical miles). In 2007 Airbus delivered its first A380 model, a two-deck aircraft with a typical capacity of 525 passengers and range of 8,000 nautical miles.

Embraer, based in Brazil, and Canada's Bombardier Corporation also are major suppliers of aircraft to the U.S. commercial aviation industry. These companies specialize in the production of regional jets, which are jet aircraft with capacities of 30 to 110 passengers and ranges generally shorter than the large Boeing and Airbus offerings. These aircraft are important in serving smaller markets and in replacing propeller-driven turboprop aircraft. Consumers prefer these regional jets to turboprops because of their greater speed and comfort. The airlines are adopting new regional jet models because of these consumer preferences and because of the regional jets' fuel efficiency and their flexibility in matching demand by route.

TABLE 7.2 American Airlines Operating Flight Equipment—December 31, 2006

Equipment	Average Capacity	Owned	Leased	Total	Average Age
Airbus A300-600R	267	10	24	34	17
Boeing 737-800	148	67	10	77	7
Boeing 757-200	187	87	55	142	12
Boeing 767-200	167	3	12	15	20
Boeing 767-300	220	47	11	58	13
Boeing 777-200	246	46	0	46	6
MD-80	136	138	187	325	17
Entire Fleet		398	299	697	14

Data source: AMR Corporation (2007), p. 18.

Table 7.2 shows American Airlines' aircraft in operation at the end of 2006.

Labor

Labor is the largest single category of costs for the typical airline, making up more than 30 percent of total costs. Many airline employees are covered by union collective bargaining agreements which specify wages, benefits (including health insurance and retirement plans, among others), and aspects of working conditions known as work rules. Some of the major unions operating in the airline industry are the following:

- Air Line Pilots Association International, representing pilots
- Allied Pilots Association, representing pilots
- International Association of Machinists and Aerospace Workers, representing mechanics, customer service agents, ramp employees, flight attendants, and others
- Association of Flight Attendants, representing flight attendants
- Association of Professional Flight Attendants, representing flight attendants
- International Brotherhood of Teamsters, representing mechanics and others
- Transportation Workers Union of America, representing flight attendants and others.

Not all airline employees are covered by collective bargaining agreements with unions, and the proportion of employees represented by unions varies by airline. In 2004, Southwest Airlines and US Airways had heavily unionized airline workforces with each having more than 80 percent of employees covered by collective bargaining agreements. In 2004, about 43 percent of Continental Airlines' employees had union representation, while only 18 percent of Delta Airlines' employees were covered by collective bargaining agreements.[2]

[2] Continental Airlines (2005), p. 11; Delta Air Lines (2005), p. 7; Southwest Airlines (2005), p. 7; U.S. Airways (2005), p. 9.

Of course, these collective bargaining agreements between the unions and the airlines specify wages and benefits, such as pension benefits, health care benefits, and others. But they also in many cases specify certain work rules, or detailed conditions of employment beyond pay rates and benefits. For example, some of these contracts do not allow flight attendants to lift passengers' carry-on luggage into the overhead storage bins.[3]

Aircraft Fuel

Fuel is the second highest category of costs for the airlines. A few years ago, fuel might make up about 15 percent of an airline's costs. In years in which fuel costs are unusually high, such as 2007, fuel can make up over 30 percent of airline operating costs. Swings in fuel prices can have important impacts on the profitability of the airline business. Figure 7.2 shows how the price of aviation fuel has varied in recent years. Notice that average jet fuel prices paid by U.S. domestic airlines reached record levels in 2007. Jet fuel prices continued to rise in 2008.

Maintenance

Airlines either perform their own maintenance on their aircraft or buy maintenance services from other airlines or maintenance companies.

Airport Landing and Other Fees

In 2005 there were 517 U.S. airports with scheduled passenger service and more than 2,500 enplanements.[4] The six largest U.S. airports are shown in Table 7.3.

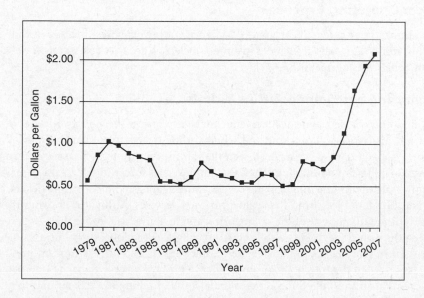

FIGURE 7.2 Average U.S. Domestic Jet Fuel Price per Gallon—1979–2007. *Data source*: U.S. Department of Transportation (2008).

[3] Peterson (2004), p. xv.
[4] U.S. Department of Transportation (2007b).

TABLE 7.3 Largest U.S. Airports—2005

Name	Airport Code	Enplanements
Hartsfield-Atlanta	ATL	41,633,000
Chicago O'Hare	ORD	33,762,000
Dallas/Ft. Worth	DFW	27,713,000
Los Angeles International	LAX	22,966,000
McCarran Intl. (Las Vegas)	LAS	20,705,000
Denver International	DEN	20,206,000

Data source: U.S. Department of Transportation (2007a).

Most major commercial airports are owned by state, municipal, or other government agencies. Airlines pay substantial fees to rent airport facilities for their aircraft and to rent terminal facilities for passenger ticketing, baggage handling, and aircraft boarding. Airlines must also pay airport landing fees, which are based on the weight of the aircraft.

U.S. airlines also pay a Federal Ticket Tax of 7.5 percent of domestic airfares and a Federal Flight Segment Tax of $3.40 per domestic enplanement.[5] These charges are paid into the federal Airport and Airway Trust Fund, which pays for U.S. airport infrastructure. On behalf of the airports, the airlines also collect a Passenger Facility Charge (PFC) of up to $4.50 per domestic enplanement. Each public agency operating a commercial airport is entitled to impose and collect these charges to cover costs of improved airport facilities, including terminal facilities, runways, access roads, and other improvements. In 2006, about 330 U.S. airports collected PFCs, and the total amounted to more than $2.5 billion.[6]

Other Operating Expenses

The airlines' large catch-all category of "other operating expenses" includes a wide variety of important costs. It includes insurance expenses, security costs, crew travel, and many other costs of operating.

Promoting and Selling Airline Tickets

Airlines promote, sell, and collect revenue for their services through a variety of activities and institutions. Promoting and selling airline tickets have changed radically in recent years. Of course, we have all seen that airlines promote their services through television and print advertising. They also employ sales forces to sell air travel services to corporate clients and others. Before 1995, travel agents sold most airline tickets, collecting substantial fees from the airlines for their services. Airline ticket commissions were typically 10 percent of the selling price, and in some cases more than 10 percent. Selling through travel agents also required paying fees to global distribution systems, discussed in Chapter 12, to manage the transactions. In recent years, the airlines have aggressively used the Internet to promote their services. The growth of the Internet and the desire of airlines to reduce the substantial costs of selling led U.S. airlines to phase

[5] Air Transport Association (2007c).
[6] Air Transport Association (2007a).

Airlines Reporting Corporation

The process of using travel agents to sell airline tickets requires extensive coordination among the agents and airlines. This coordination mainly comes from two institutions: global distribution systems and the Airlines Reporting Corporation (ARC).[7] We will examine the global distribution systems later, but the basic idea is that at any point in time the thousands of travel agents needed to know what airline seats were still available at that moment and needed to know the prices. Furthermore, the travel agents needed to make specific reservations for their customers and to sell those seats. The global distribution system allowed each travel agent to search for available seats and to see each seat's price. It also allowed the travel agent to reserve seats and to sell tickets. A travel agent selling a ticket needed to be able to deliver the ticket to the customer, take the customer's payment, and forward the airline's money to the airline. The industry created the ARC to handle the details of travel agent airline ticket sales. First, the ARC accredits travel agents, or certifies that they are qualified to print and deliver tickets to customers. In 2007, there were more than 20,000 travel agencies and corporate travel departments accredited by the ARC. Second, the ARC prints and distributes blank airline ticket stock to accredited travel agents. Finally, the ARC is the central place to which travel agents send the money they collect for airline ticket sales, less any commissions. The ARC then divides the money appropriately and sends it to each airline to compensate them for all airline tickets sold by travel agents.

out travel agent commissions by 2004 and to try to shift sales and transactions processing to their own web sites or call centers. Southwest Airlines, for example, by 2004 was receiving 59 percent of its passenger revenue from its Internet site, southwest.com. Airlines also book a large portion of their ticket sales though their own reservation call centers; and they continue to sell some tickets through travel agents, who now charge ticketing fees to travelers. In 2004, Southwest Airlines received 28 percent of its passenger revenue through its reservation centers and 13 percent from travel agents.[8]

OVERVIEW OF THE PERFORMANCE OF THE U.S. DOMESTIC AIRLINE INDUSTRY

The airline business is cyclical, with demand varying over many years with the business cycle and within each year with the seasons. Each year, summer is the peak season, and midwinter, after New Year's Day, is the low season. Of course, when the business cycle is at its peak and employment and industrial production are relatively high, demand for air travel is high. Conversely, at troughs in the business cycle when employment and production are low, demand for air travel is relatively low. Table 7.4 shows measures of airline financial performance and operating levels for the period 1934 to 2004. Table 7.4 also shows domestic RPM, ASM, domestic load factor, nominal yield, and real yield in 1978 cents (to correct for inflation).

Table 7.4 shows many important facts about the industry's development. First, we see that the amount of U.S. domestic scheduled air travel has grown substantially in recent decades, from 44 million RPM in 1964 to more than 550 million RPM in 2004,

---

[7] Airlines Reporting Corporation (2007); Starr (2000), pp. 62–64.
[8] Southwest Airlines Co. (2005), p. 18.

TABLE 7.4 Operating Data for the U.S. Domestic Airline Industry— 1934–2004

Year	Enplanements (Thousands)	RPM (Millions)	ASM (Millions)	Load Factor (Percent)	Nominal Yield (¢)	Real Yield 1978 (¢)
1934	472	189	368	51.4	5.90	28.71
1944	4,027	2,177	2,435	89.4	5.34	19.78
1954	32,529	16,802	26,922	62.4	5.41	13.11
1964	79,139	44,141	80,524	54.8	6.12	12.87
1974	189,733	129,732	233,880	55.5	7.52	9.95
1984	321,047	243,692	422,507	57.7	12.80	8.03
1994	481,755	378,990	585,438	64.7	13.12	5.77
2004	640,698	551,937	741,677	74.4	12.03	4.15

Data source: Air Transport Association (2007b, d).

a 12.5-fold increase over 40 years. Now there are hundreds of millions of enplanements each year and approaching one trillion ASM flown. Also yields have been generally rising very slowly over the decades. The rise, however, has been so slow that it has not kept up with inflation in general; so that real yields, or yields in 1978 cents, have declined substantially over the decades. Real yields have declined because, corrected for inflation, airline ticket prices have fallen on average in recent decades. Also, real yields have fallen because leisure travel makes up an increasing share of total airline travel, and leisure travelers on average pay less than business travelers.

The load factor is calculated as revenue passenger miles divided by available seat miles multiplied by 100. Thus, if an airplane having 140 seats flies with 70 seats occupied by paying passengers and 70 seats that are empty or occupied by nonpaying passengers, that flight has a load factor of 50 percent. In recent decades, since deregulation, load factors have been rising. Load factors averaged 55 percent for the 1970s, 60 percent for the 1980s, and 65 percent for the 1990s.[9]

Airline operating profits vary widely from year to year. For example, the recession years at the beginning of the 1980s and at the beginning of the 1990s saw declining demand for air travel, declining RPM, and losses for the airline industry. Airline profits also vary inversely with fuel prices, because fuel makes up, when fuel prices are at their highest, as much as 30 percent of an airline's total costs. Figure 7.3 shows the aggregate revenues and net profits of the U.S. domestic scheduled airlines for the years 1970 to 2006.

Through the late 1990s, revenues and net profits rose substantially to record levels. Then the terrorist attacks of September 11, 2001, devastated the U.S. airline industry. From 2000 to 2002, the industry's revenues fell by 18 percent. For the period 2001 through 2005 the industry lost a cumulative total of $35 billion. Note that in 2003 the industry's revenues and profits began to recover, and by 2004 the revenues once again exceeded $130 billion. But profit levels again fell in 2004, as the price of jet fuel increased rapidly. These increased fuel costs prevented the industry from returning to profitability until 2006, in spite of the fact that by 2004 RPM and revenues had exceeded their previous records established in 2000.

---

[9] Author's calculations based on Air Transport Association (2007b).

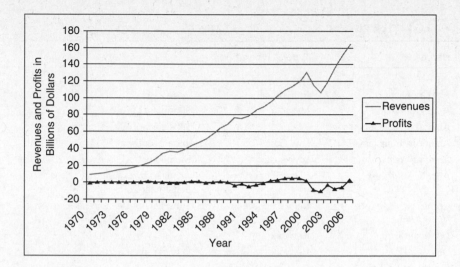

FIGURE 7.3 Revenues and Profits of the U.S. Domestic Airline Industry—1970–2006. *Data source*: Air Transport Association (2007f).

INDUSTRY STRUCTURE

The FAA divides the firms in the airline industry into three categories. The major airlines, also referred to as *Group III*, are those with at least $1 billion in annual revenue. The national airlines (also referred to as *Group II*) are those with annual revenue between $100 million and $1 billion, and the regional airlines (also referred to as *Group I*) are those with less than $100 million in annual revenue. During 2006, the scheduled passenger airlines shown in Table 7.5 were listed in Group III.[10]

During 2006 some of the 32 firms in Group II, or national airlines, included Air Wisconsin, Aloha Airlines, Frontier Airlines, Hawaiian Airlines, Mesa Airlines, Pinnacle, and Spirit Air Lines.

The majors include the "big three" airlines, United, American, and Delta, which hold the top three spots in total operating revenue and RPM. Table 7.6 shows the operating revenue and RPM for the large network and LCCs for 2006.

Route Structure

One of the most important changes in civil aviation that came from deregulation was the changing route structure of scheduled airlines. Before deregulation, airlines had flown primarily "nonstop" and "direct" flights for most city pairs. A city pair is two airports that a passenger might fly between, such as Atlanta and Orlando, or Chicago and Seattle. A nonstop flight from Chicago to Seattle makes no intervening stops. A direct flight from Chicago to Seattle makes one or more stops, but continues on to the destination, so that Chicago to Seattle passengers do not need to change planes. The alternative to nonstop and direct flights is a connecting flight. Connecting flights require the passenger to change aircraft at an intervening stop. For example, our Chicago to Seattle passenger may have a connecting flight with a change of planes in Salt Lake City.

---

[10] U.S. Department of Transportation (2005b, 2006).

TABLE 7.5 U.S. Group III Passenger Airlines—2006

Name	Type of Operation	Notes
Air Tran	Low Cost	
Alaska Airlines	Network	
American Airlines	Network	Subsidiary of AMR Corp.
American Eagle Airlines		Subsidiary of AMR Corp.
American Trans Air (ATA)	Low Cost	In bankruptcy in 2005
America West	Low Cost	Merged with US Airways in 2005
Atlantic Southeast	Delta Connection	Acquired by SkyWest in September 2005
Comair	Delta Connection	Subsidiary of Delta; in bankruptcy in 2005
Continental	Network	
Delta Air Lines	Network	In bankruptcy in 2005
ExpressJet Airlines	Continental Express	
JetBlue	Low Cost	Began operations in February 2000
Northwest Airlines	Network	In bankruptcy in 2005
SkyWest	United Express; Delta Connection	
Southwest Airlines	Low Cost	
United Airlines	Network	In bankruptcy in 2005
US Airways	Network	In bankruptcy in 2005; merged with America West in 2005

Data sources: FAA; company web sites; Air Transport Association (2007e).

TABLE 7.6 U.S. Network and Low-Cost Airline Operating Statistics—2006

Airline	Operating Revenues ($ Millions)	Revenue Passenger Miles
American	22,493	139,392
United	19,334	117,247
Delta	17,339	98,769
Continental	13,010	76,251
Northwest	12,555	72,588
US Airways	11,845	60,895
Southwest	9,086	67,691
Alaska	2,693	17,814
JetBlue	2,363	23,310

Data source: Air Transport Association (2007g), p. 24.

Before deregulation, only about 28 percent of passengers were on connecting flights. About one-half of these passengers changed *airlines* when they changed *planes*. After deregulation, airlines had much more control over their routes, and they changed their route structures to greatly reduce costs of operations. They changed to what is known as a **hub-and-spoke route structure**. This system brought large numbers of passengers from smaller airports and thinner routes to "hub" airports, where the passengers would board larger aircraft that fly heavily traveled routes. The airline could thereby serve thousands of possible city pairs with a relatively small number of routes. This increased the airlines' load factors and provided many choices of departures and routes for passengers, provided they were willing to change planes once or twice. A decade after deregulation, the proportion of passengers flying connecting flights and changing planes had risen to about one-third, but the proportion changing *airlines* to complete their flights fell to near zero.[11]

Only the largest network airlines have route structures that cover most of the United States. Many of the remaining airlines fill in parts of their route structures through a process known as **codesharing.** Codesharing is a process whereby an airline will sell some seats on some of its flights to a second airline. The airline buying the code-share seats will list those seats as flights of their own. Thus passengers for the second airline buy tickets for that airline, but when they show up for their flight they will board an aircraft belonging to the first airline. In this way the second airline can fill out its route structure with seats on another airline rather than an independent flight of its own.

Distribution; Reservation Systems

Information is costly. This fact becomes clear anytime a traveler wants to check the availability of airline seats or hotel rooms or other travel resources. Before the early 1960s, travelers would call the airline or hotel and ask about availability and prices. The operator would check paper records for the information requested. This was slow and cumbersome, particularly because if a traveler wanted to fly to a distant city and stay in a hotel room overnight, the traveler would have to call both the airline and a hotel to ask about availability and prices. The traveler would have to do this serially; that is, calling first one service provider and then another, perhaps repeating the process several times until getting a match between dates of hotel stay and dates of airline flights. In 1960, American Airlines began a process of computerizing its reservation and ticketing processes. By the mid-1960s, a traveler or travel agent calling American Airlines would contact the operator who could search computerized records for availability and prices. The operator could then make the reservation or sale directly into the computer system. American Airlines found this to be a big advantage in reducing costs and increasing efficiency of service.

This computerized system worked so well that by the mid-1970s American Airlines made this service, known as Sabre, available within travel agencies, so that no telephone call to American Airlines' operators was necessary. The travel agents could search for availability and prices, make reservations, and sell tickets themselves using the computerized reservation system directly. Following American Airlines' success, other airlines developed their own computerized reservation systems. Also, American Airlines' parent AMR Corporation allowed other airlines to participate in this computerized reservation system by linking Sabre to their databases of seat availabilities and prices. Finally, AMR Corporation allowed other travel and tourism service providers, such as hotels and car rental companies, to add their services to Sabre. This created a situation in

Hub-and-spoke route structure
An airline route structure that aggregates large numbers of passengers from smaller airports and thinner routes to major or hub airports where the passengers board large aircraft that fly heavily traveled routes.

Codesharing
It is a process whereby one airline sells some seats on some of its flights to another airline, which then lists those seats as if they were on its own flights.

---

[11] Morrison and Winston (1995), pp. 21–23.

which a travel agent with a computer terminal could make all of the most important reservations for the traveler in a single session. This system provided enormous benefits for travelers, travel agents, and service providers by substantially reducing the cost of information gathering and transaction processing.

The development of these computerized reservation systems has led to the situation today in which there are four major computerized reservation systems, known as global distribution systems (GDSs). These are Sabre, Worldspan (which grew out of the Delta Airlines system, and also included Northwest Airlines and TWA), Galileo (which included United Airlines and US Airways), and Amadeus (which included Continental Airlines). (For more on GDSs see Chapter 12.) In 1999, AMR Corporation spun off its Sabre Group as a separate corporation. Sabre is now completely separate from American Airlines and provides a wide variety of services to American Airlines as well as other airlines, hotels, and other service providers in the travel and tourism industry. Industry groups are working to incorporate current information technology into GDSs.[12]

Airline Pricing—Yield or Revenue Management

Airlines provide services to a variety of customer types. Recall the American Travel Survey results in Chapter 3, which state that the major reasons for travel were business, leisure, personal business, and visiting friends or family. We can combine these reasons into two major groups, business and all of the others, which we can call "leisure." These two groups of travelers have very different demands. Business travelers are often willing to pay higher price than leisure travelers, have less elastic demand than leisure travelers, and travel with less advance notice than leisure travelers. Leisure travelers are often more flexible as to time and date of travel and travel mode, that is, whether or not to go by car or air. Thus, for example, a salesperson calling on two or three distant clients will want to travel at specific times to specific places, while a couple planning next summer's vacation can be much more flexible about the time and date of travel, and even about the destination.

Business firms facing different types of customers with different demands will maximize profits by separating those customer groups and offering them customized products or services at customized prices. The airline industry has been one of the most successful industries in segmenting its customers and selling its services at different prices to different segments. In the airline industry this process has been known, as we saw in Chapter 6, as yield management or revenue management. The airline industry uses the term *yield* to mean cents per passenger mile. That is, if a passenger pays $200 for a flight of 1,000 miles, the passenger paid 20 cents per mile. Yield management or revenue management is the process of getting the most revenue possible from the aircraft flown.

To maximize the revenue or yield to be earned from fixed assets, in this case the airline's fleet of aircraft, the airline has to equalize marginal revenue from each category of coach customers. We saw the four steps needed to implement yield management:

1. Divide the market into groups of customers, with different groups having different demands for the service;
2. Create a category of service for each group and restrictions that keep the groups separate;

---

[12] Refer to OpenTravel Alliance (2007) for further information about these efforts.

3. Set a price for each category of service;
4. Assign some portion of total capacity to each of the categories of service.

Thus, within coach class the airline has some categories of service for customers, primarily leisure travelers, who would book their travel weeks or months ahead of departure. It also has categories of coach class service for customers trying to book their trip with little or no advance notice. These last-minute travelers would have a smaller elasticity of demand than those booking months ahead. Therefore the airline would set a much higher price for the category of service aimed at the last-minute traveler than for the leisure traveler. The deeply discounted fare would be available for someone buying a ticket many weeks ahead of the departure, but only a limited number of seats would be allocated to that category. Furthermore, the deeply discounted fare is available only to those meeting restrictions, primarily reservation and purchase weeks ahead of departure and a stay over a Saturday night. Thus last-minute travelers face two obstacles to getting the deeply discounted fare. First, at some point in time all of the seats allocated to the deeply discounted category would be sold, so that the category has no more seats available for later booking. Second, at some point travelers wanting to book at the deeply discounted rate would no longer be able to meet the restriction for advanced reservation and purchase. Also, by limiting the number of seats in the deeply discounted category, the airline is preventing the sale of all of its seats to leisure travelers who are willing to pay only a low price. The airline is in essence saving seats for last-minute travelers willing to pay a much higher price.

Overbooking

The last complication in airline yield management comes from the fact that many travelers cancel or change reservations, and many other passengers simply fail to show up for their flights. To account for changes and no-shows, the airlines overbook their flights; that is, they sell more tickets than there are seats. In the early 1990s American Airlines has estimated that if it did not overbook, then on average its *sold-out* flights would fly with 15 percent of their seats unfilled.[13] **Overbooking** or oversales involves starting selling tickets many months before the flight with many more seats available for sale than the seating capacity of the aircraft. As the flight date approaches, the airline reduces the number of tickets available for sale, but it still may sell more than are available on the flight to allow for changes and no-shows. At flight time for sold-out flights, the airlines expect to have the number of passengers at the gate very close to the number of seats on the flight. The forecasting system is, however, imperfect; so that in some cases there will be more ticketed passengers than seats. In these cases, the airlines may "deny boarding" to ticketed passengers for whom there is no seat and ask for volunteers to wait for the next available flight in exchange for some compensation, such as a free ticket on a future flight. When there are not enough volunteers, the airlines may deny boarding to passengers who have not volunteered. The FAA specifies minimum compensation for those involuntarily denied boarding.

Overbooking
Selling more tickets on a flight than the seating capacity of the aircraft.

---

[13] Smith et al. (1992), p. 11.

The "Bucket" System[14]

In reality, yield management for a major airline is complicated by two additional factors. The first is the fact that many of the airline's most expensive tickets will be for trips of very long distances that involve more than one flight; that is, these trips require the traveler to make connections between flights at hubs. This creates a potential problem—a leisure traveler booking a deeply discounted ticket could conceivably prevent the airline from selling a very expensive ticket to someone who needs the leisure traveler's seat to make a connection. For example, suppose a business traveler from Salem, OR, wants to fly to Jacksonville, FL. There is no direct flight from Salem to Jacksonville so the traveler will have to make connections to complete the flight. Suppose the easiest way for the traveler to make the flight is to fly from Salem to Denver then from Denver to St. Louis on Flight 776 departing at 11:20 A.M. and then from St. Louis to Jacksonville. The flight involves three legs with two changes of planes, one in Denver and one in St. Louis. Suppose the price of this ticket is $1,800. But there is a potential problem; other people have already booked seats on Flight 776 from Denver to St. Louis, and its tickets may be sold out. Some of those passengers may have bought deeply discounted tickets, for example, for $200. The airline does not want a passenger paying $200 to take a seat that could have been sold to a passenger paying $1,800.

Airlines prevent the passenger paying $200 from taking a seat away from the passenger trying to buy a very expensive connecting ticket by using what is known as the "bucket" system. An airline will place all of its coach seats for each flight into buckets, or groups of seats. Suppose there are seven buckets numbered 2 through 8. (Bucket number one is reserved for first-class.) For each flight, the airline places some portion of the available coach seats into each bucket. Seats from bucket number 2 can be sold only to passengers paying at least $1,400 for their tickets. Seats from bucket number 3 can be sold only to passengers paying at least $1,100 for their tickets. This process continues to bucket number 8, from which tickets can be sold to passengers paying the deeply discounted fares or higher. Now the airline begins selling the seats, starting many months before the flight is scheduled to depart. Over the next few months passengers begin buying tickets. When all the seats in bucket number 2 are sold, the airline will reach into a higher-numbered bucket to find another seat for passengers trying to buy a seat from bucket number 2. The airline, however, will never reach into a lower-numbered bucket to take a seat from a high fare category to sell to a passenger paying a lower price. In this way, some seats on each possible connecting flight are saved for future passengers who may want to buy a very expensive ticket requiring a connection. Thus, when the passenger from Salem to Jacksonville tries to buy his or her ticket, there will likely be a ticket available for the Denver to St. Louis leg. Passengers looking for deep discounts on the Denver to St. Louis flight will find that there are no discount seats available even when there are seats remaining for expensive flights requiring a connection.

The number of possible flights that could use a connection on that flight from Denver to St. Louis is very large. The airline is not using the bucket system to save seats on Flight 776 specifically for passengers wanting to travel from Salem to Jacksonville, because such trips are relatively rare. There are, however, thousands of these rare trips, for example, Bisbee, AZ, to Manchester, NH, and Spokane, WA, to Salisbury, MD. While each of these combinations is rare, the airline can forecast the total number of such travelers from all of these rare trips who will want a connection on Flight 776 from Denver to St. Louis. It places the expected number of such seats in bucket number 2. Thus, while there are many thousands of possible trips with passengers who may want coach seats on Flight 776, there are only seven buckets. This boils down an unbearably difficult problem into one that the airline can actually solve for hundreds of flights each day.

---

[14] Smith et al. (1992), pp. 16–20.

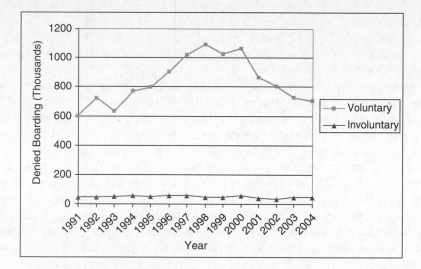

FIGURE 7.4 Passengers Denied Boarding by the Largest U.S. Airlines—1991–2004. *Data source*: U.S. Department of Transportation (2005a), Table 1-58.

To get an idea of the scale and impact of overselling, we can examine the number of ticketed passengers denied boarding. As shown in Figure 7.4, in recent years the largest U.S. domestic carriers alone have denied boarding to hundreds of thousands, and in some years more than 1 million, passengers with confirmed reservations. The vast majority of passengers denied boarding volunteer to accept the offered compensation in exchange for waiting for a later flight.

Understanding Airline Price Differences

Now that we have seen how airlines use yield or revenue management, the bucket system, and overbooking to determine airfares and allocation of seats among classes of customers, we can use this information to understand what we observe in the airline market. News media from time to time report anomalies in airline pricing. For example, they report that two passengers sitting next to each other may have paid wildly different prices for their seats. Or they may report that a round-trip flight from Kansas City to San Francisco costs three or four times as much as a round-trip flight from San Francisco to Kansas City, even though both flights involve the same travel: a flight from Kansas City to San Francisco and a flight from San Francisco to Kansas City. Or they report on the so-called "hidden city" discount. To understand the hidden city discount, suppose a traveler wants to go from Seattle to Detroit. The traveler checks fares and finds that the Seattle to Detroit round-trip costs $800, while a trip from Seattle to Lansing, MI, with a connection in Detroit costs only $500. The traveler gets the hidden city discount by booking a flight from Seattle to Lansing and then getting off in Detroit, not using the Detroit to Lansing leg.

Can we understand what is happening in each of these cases? With an understanding of airline pricing, we can explain these anomalies or seemingly irrational pricing situations. Consider a hypothetical example of a consumer advocacy group that places 400 calls to a variety of airlines and travel agents on a Thursday afternoon to check on airfares for a wide variety of flights. The callers find anomalies. For example, suppose they are quoted fares for a round-trip from Cincinnati to Seattle ranging from $250 to $1,100. They also find that a round-trip from Los Angeles to Boston has a higher price than a round-trip from Boston to Los Angeles.

Can we understand this? Consider what we learned about yield management and the bucket system and add two more facts. First, each airline must set its prices on its own. If airlines were to coordinate their pricing, they could violate antitrust laws that make price-fixing illegal and expose their executives to possible fines and jail sentences. Thus, each airline does its own yield management process based on its own demands and seat availabilities. Since each airline has its own available seats, its own consumer demands, and its own yield management system, we would expect different airlines to come up with different prices even if they are serving the same city pairs at the same time. Second, the airlines' yield management systems determine prices separately for each *origin and destination* combination. For example, Los Angeles to Boston is a different origin–destination combination than Boston to Los Angeles, and the yield management systems will treat them independently. Thus, each will have prices that are set separately depending upon demands and seat availabilities.

Now, at some specific time pick an origin and destination city pair served by more than one airline. At that specific time, is it possible that the various airlines' yield management systems have determined different prices and different seat availabilities for each fare class from the origin to the destination? It is quite likely that these are somewhat different. Will the airlines sell tickets from each fare class at the same rate of sales over time? No, not exactly the same rate—some flights will fill faster than others. Thus, at that specific time, it is quite possible that we are checking fares from different fare classes. For example, looking back at the Cincinnati to Seattle example, it is possible that the $1,100 fare could have been for an airline that had only four full-fare coach seats that it had through codesharing with another airline, while the $250 fare is a promotional discount fare class from an airline that just added that route. For the example involving Boston and Los Angeles, at the time the fares were checked, some discount fare class could be sold out for the Los Angeles origination but still available for the Boston origination. With yield management and the bucket system done by origin and destination, some anomalies such as those described above *must* exist from time to time as airline ticket sales proceed through time, because comparable fare classes on comparable flights will not sell out at exactly the same time. Also, seemingly comparable flights may not have comparable demands and seat availabilities all of the time. With the airline pricing system, some anomalies must pop up all of the time, with a different set of anomalies at different times.

Consumer Welfare Evaluation of Airline Pricing

Yield management has been very good for the airlines, because it has allowed them to get the most revenue from the consumers on each flight. American Airlines estimated that yield management adds $500 million each year to its revenue.[15] Besides making airline passengers pay more in the aggregate for their airline seats, what other effects

---

[15] Smith et al. (1992), p. 8.

does yield management have on consumers? Would consumers benefit from a new law that required airlines to charge a single price for all coach seats? Let's look at some of the effects that we can expect from a system in which the airlines can charge different groups of customers different prices for the same coach service.[16]

1. Some passengers pay less than they would with a single-price system. Consider a situation in which a firm with some monopoly power charges a single price. The firm finds the quantity that makes marginal revenue equal marginal cost and then charges the price that makes the quantity demanded equal to that quantity. A price discriminating firm would want to sell additional units at a lower price as long as it did not have to lower the price on the units it was previously selling and as long as the price for the additional units is greater than marginal cost. Thus, with price discrimination customers buying the additional units are paying less than they would have to pay if the firm were required to charge only one price.

2. If an airline were required to charge a single coach price, some flights would not cover costs and would be canceled. We know that yield management increases the revenue available to the airline from each flight. With a single price, the airline would lose this additional revenue. In some cases, this additional revenue brings the total revenue for the flight above total cost. In those cases, forcing the airline to charge a single price would deprive it of the additional revenue so that the flights would lose money. The airline would cancel those flights.

3. Some passengers can book travel at the last minute. One central feature of yield management is that the airline does not let a consumer willing to pay only a low price prevent sales to consumers willing to pay a high price. Through yield management the airlines typically have high-priced seats available for last-minute travelers, which for those travelers is better than having no seats available at all.

Airline Pricing with Rising Costs

The analysis of airline pricing in this chapter considers maximizing the revenue or yield to be earned from fixed assets. That is, we have considered how to price seats on a flight that the airline has already determined to fly. Note that in the diagram illustrating price determination in yield management, Figure 6.10, there is no role for the cost of operating the flight. (C is the cost of having an additional passenger on the flight.) Then this analysis does not directly show how a rapid rise in fuel prices or other operating costs will affect airline prices. The analysis suggests that modest changes in operating costs will not affect prices, because the airline is already pricing to get the most revenue from each flight.

Changes in operating costs will only affect prices when the airline changes its schedule of flights in response to changing costs. For example, when fuel prices spike upward, the airline may see that for many flights its revenues no longer cover operating costs. It may then cancel some flights. This will increase demand on remaining flights, and with higher demand the yield management system will generate higher prices for those flights. After some reduction in the number of seats flown, the airline may be able to cover its operating costs on its remaining flights.

---

[16] For more on the consumer welfare effects of airline yield management see Botimer (1996).

DEVELOPMENT OF INTERNATIONAL AIRLINE MARKETS

International air travel began early in the history of aviation, with, for example, service between London and Paris beginning as early as the 1920s and "China Clipper" service between the United States and parts of Asia starting in 1936. Such international service raised many problems and policy issues. These included basic issues of national pride and sovereignty, including rights of aircraft from one nation to fly over or into another nation. They also included basic operational issues such as air traffic control and pilot licensing. Finally, they included commercial interests, including protecting the nation's business interests in international transportation and in purely domestic transportation, known as "cabotage." (Restrictions on cabotage have important implications for cruise lines. We will see more on this in Chapter 10.)

Representatives from more than 50 nations met at the International Civil Aviation Conference in Chicago in 1944 to find a workable system of international commercial aviation. The result was a limited agreement, the Chicago Convention, whereby each nation would seek bilateral agreements with other nations to govern commercial air service between them. These agreements would determine what carriers could serve what routes with what capacity and frequency of flights. Pricing was a difficult issue that the negotiating nations left to the new International Air Transport Association (IATA). The United States and Great Britain negotiated the first of these bilateral agreements in Bermuda in 1946. In 1947, the IATA held its first "Traffic Conference" during which the international airlines agreed to airfares for international flights. U.S. airlines were able to participate through antitrust immunity granted for this purpose. The result of the system of bilateral agreements was a system that served narrow, national commercial interests rather than efficiently providing service to potential passengers.[17]

Since the Chicago Conference, international aviation has grown rapidly among all parts of the world, especially within Europe, between Europe and North America, and in the Asia-Pacific region. Table 7.7 shows the world's largest international airlines, ranked by passenger kilometers flown (excluding domestic).

Open Skies

In the 1990s the United States tried to promote improvements in international commercial aviation through its "Open Skies" policies.[18] *Open Skies agreements* are bilateral agreements between the United States and other nations that give both nations' airlines the rights to serve any routes between the two countries and continuing on to points beyond the countries. The Netherlands signed the first Open Skies agreement in 1992. As of the end of 2005, the United States had signed 74 of these agreements. Since 2001, the United States has also participated in one multilateral air commerce liberalization agreement involving the United States, New Zealand, Singapore, Brunei, Chile, Samoa, and Tonga.

The system of bilateral agreements gave each nation power to impose restrictions on air travel between it and all other nations and to protect its own air carriers. Many nations had "national flag carriers" to promote national pride. These and multiple other

---

[17] Yergin et al. (2000), pp. 38–46.
[18] U.S. Department of State (2005).

TABLE 7.7 Largest International Airlines, 2004: International Scheduled Passenger Kilometers Flown

Rank	Airline	Passenger Kilometers (Millions)
1	Deutsche Lufthansa A.G.	103,866
2	British Airways p.l.c.	102,858
3	Air France	96,958
4	Singapore Airlines Ltd.	77,082
5	American Airlines Inc.	70,036
6	United Airlines	67,484
7	Japan Airlines International	64,626
8	KLM Royal Dutch Airlines	63,013
9	Cathay Pacific Airways Ltd.	57,224
10	Northwest Airlines, Inc.	51,704

Data source: International Air Transport Association (2004).

national carriers could operate very inefficiently through protection against international competition and other subsidies. Indeed, during the 1980s Europe had 100 airlines, and such small nations as Belgium, Denmark, and Austria served as home for four airlines each.[19] The European Union (EU) eventually moved to rationalize its airline market, and in 1997 it created a single EU airline market, with any European-based airline free to provide any airline service between cities within the EU.

One of the major developments in international commercial aviation in recent years has been the growth of alliances among carriers of various nations. As we have seen, nations protect their markets, both domestic and international, from service by airlines of other nations. They also protect their airlines by restricting foreign control of the nation's airlines. For example, the U.S. Department of Transportation has regulations restricting citizens of other countries from owning more than 49 percent of the stock and 25 percent of the voting stock of U.S.-based airlines. Also, the presidents and two-thirds of officers of U.S.-based airlines must be U.S. citizens. But travelers of all nations demand international air travel, which may include segments in many nations; and airlines would like to serve these travelers. The IATA supports "interlining," or completing international itineraries having multiple segments through multiple countries on multiple airlines. Its industry clearing services handle the inter-carrier payments to allow passengers to buy one ticket (paid for in one nation's currency) for travel on multiple international carriers.[20]

But interlining is not enough to exploit all of the potential of the industry for efficient service to the public. The airlines would presumably like to form international networks with hubs, spokes, and point-to-point services similar to what we see within the U.S. National restrictions on ownership prevent such fully integrated international operations. The compromise solution has been international alliances, whereby airlines of many nations agree to codesharing, joint scheduling, joint marketing, and cooperating

---

[19] Yergin et al. (2000), p. 49.
[20] International Air Transport Association (2005c).

on other operations. This allows airlines to use cooperating airlines to expand their service networks and increase the density of their routes by accumulating international passengers at partners' hubs. The first of the major international alliances, formed in 1997, was the "Star Alliance," involving United Airlines, Lufthansa, Air Canada, Thai International, SAS, Varig, Air New Zealand, and others. In 1999, American Airlines, British Airways, Qantas, Cathay Pacific, LAN, Finnair, and others formed the "oneworld" alliance.[21] These alliances have been very successful in increasing competition in international airline markets, leading to higher traffic volumes and lower airfares.[22]

The European Airline Market

As mentioned earlier, the EU created a single airline market in 1997, with any European-based airline free to provide any airline service between EU cities. This followed a series of liberalizations of the European airline market over the previous 10 years. These changes included both deregulation of airline markets and privatization of state-owned air carriers, including British Airways, Air France, and Iberia. Deregulation allowed carriers freedom to choose their routes and set airfares and also allowed entry of new airlines. These new entrants are typically LCCs which adopt competitive strategies similar to Southwest Airlines in the United States. That is, they often provide low-fare, point-to-point service between secondary airports. The largest of these new European carriers are Ryanair, easyJet, and Air Berlin.

RIVALRY IN THE AIRLINE INDUSTRY

During the era of CAB regulation of airfares and routes, 1938–1978, the CAB severely limited price competition among U.S. airlines. Carriers could not compete on prices and schedules, although they could compete on services, including food service. The absence of price competition and emphasis on service led to very high costs.

Deregulation led to important shifts in routes and schedules, because airlines were freed to determine the city pairs they would serve and the number of flights, times of flights, and connecting routes the aircraft would travel. This shift of schedules and routes culminated for the largest U.S. airlines in large networks of routes based around hub airports. For example, American Airlines had hub airports in Dallas-Ft. Worth, Chicago, Miami, and San Juan, Puerto Rico.

The carriers emerging from the regulated era retained their very high costs, including high wages and restrictive work rules.[23] Some of the legacy carriers' costs were increased by the hub-and-spoke system, which brought many aircraft to crowded airports at the same time. With multiple classes of service, complicated boarding procedures, and crowded airports and runways, the network carriers' aircraft spent increasing amounts of time on the ground and less time in the air. The legacy airlines also used the traditional means for ticket distribution and, indeed, increased their reliance on travel agents to sell their tickets. The airlines paid travel agents a standard commission of 10 percent for each sale, and this commission could be higher with commission overrides.

---

[21] Oum et al. (2000), p. 22.
[22] U.S. Department of Transportation (2000).
[23] Sprayregen et al. (2002).

Shortly after deregulation came an era of many new entrants and many mergers and bankruptcies.[24] In 1978, the CAB granted permission for Midway Airlines to become the first new airline in 38 years. America West, which merged with US Airways in 2005, entered the industry in 1983. Most of the new airlines that followed deregulation failed. There were more than 50 airline bankruptcies between 1979 and 1986, including such prominent airlines as Continental, which later successfully emerged from bankruptcy, and Braniff, which also emerged only to fail again a few years later.[25] Some airlines that had regional service areas during the regulated era, such as Piedmont and Ozark, later merged into larger carriers. Also, some of the new entrants were acquired by larger airlines, including Morris Air, which Southwest bought in 1993.[26]

The Question of Contestability

After deregulation an airline consumer could typically choose from more than one airline in buying airline tickets for his or her trip; so that, airlines usually competed with each other for consumers. We like competition, because competitive firms keep prices low and they do not earn returns in excess of the normal rate of return that capital can expect. Enough competition in the airline industry would mean that airline consumers would not be paying excessive prices.

The effective amount of competition in an industry does not necessarily depend on the number of firms operating in the industry. One possibility is that the airline industry may be "contestable." A **contestable market** is one that has nothing to prevent entry of new competitors and exit of existing firms, so that any possibilities for high prices and excessive rates of return would attract new entrants. In a contestable market potential entrants exert the same competitive forces on prices and profits as actual entrants.

Contestable market
A market in which potential competition prevents firms from charging high prices and earning above-normal rates of return.

Around the time of deregulation, many analysts expected that the deregulated airline market would be contestable, leading to some new entry into the U.S. domestic airlines industry and much lower airfares, even for travel between city pairs where only a few airlines provided service. That is, many expected that a deregulated market would lead to substantial fare competition, even in markets actually served by few airlines, because potential competition from other large airlines could arise if prices were above competitive levels.

Why might the airline market be contestable? First there are multiple competitors. While each city pair might be served by only three or four airlines, there are more than 10 major airlines and many other airlines that could enter into competition for travelers on any route where prices are too high and rates of return are excessive. Second, there seem to be few barriers to entry or exit in the airline industry and certainly into most city pair markets. In fact, the Department of Transportation reports that between 1992 and 1996 thirteen new firms began scheduled passenger jet service in the United States.[27] Finally, the airlines' capital stock is mobile. The airlines can fly their aircraft into or out of markets without much problem. Thus, there is good reason to believe that airline markets may be contestable; so that potential competition would be just as effective as actual competition in holding prices down.

[24] See Borenstein (1992), pp. 46–52, for a brief survey of industry changes during this period.
[25] Air Transport Association (2007e).
[26] Peterson (2004), pp. 21–22.
[27] U.S. Department of Transportation (1999), p. 7.

What are the implications of the features of the airline market such as yield management, frequent-flier programs, the hub-and-spoke route structure, and airline costs for competition among airlines? Do airlines actually compete with one another? We observe the "big three" airlines, other major airlines, and a variety of smaller airlines. Is this enough airline companies to provide real competition to protect consumers?

Before looking at the evidence on airline prices, potential competition, and actual competition, let us look at how we might measure the amount of market power, or power to hold price above marginal cost, that firms in an industry have. Consider a market with six firms with the shares of total market revenue as shown in Table 7.8.

The four-firm concentration ratio is one of the most commonly used measures of market power. We calculate this as the share of total market sales held by the four largest firms. In this hypothetical market, the four-firm concentration ratio is $0.4 + 0.2 + 0.15 + 0.1 = 0.85$. The Herfindahl Index is another popular measure of market power, and it is one often used by the U.S. Department of Justice in antitrust cases. We calculate the Herfindahl Index as the sum of the squared market shares for all firms in the market. Thus for the market example shown in Table 7.8, the Herfindahl index would be $(0.4)^2 + (0.2)^2 + (0.15)^2 + (0.1)^2 + (0.1)^2 + (0.05)^2 = 0.245$. The inverse of the Herfindahl Index is sometimes called the "number of effective competitors." Consider a market with eight equal-sized firms. The Herfindahl Index would be $8(0.125)^2 = 0.125$. Then the number of effective competitors would be $1/0.125$, which is equal to eight. This is certainly a reasonable estimate for an industry with eight equal-size firms. For our example of six firms shown in Table 7.8, the number of effective competitors would be $1/0.245 = 4.08$. One way to interpret the basic idea here is that the three largest firms provide competition for each other and the other three firms together amount to the competitive pressure of one more large firm.

Finally, the most direct measure of market power we sometimes cite is the so-called Lerner Index, which is calculated as (price − marginal cost) ÷ marginal cost. This directly shows market power, because the effect of market power is pricing above marginal cost. The Lerner Index is zero for a competitive firm and gets larger as firms with monopoly power raise price above marginal cost. The problem with the Lerner Index is that we cannot calculate it directly unless we know marginal cost, and we typically will not know marginal cost. Fortunately, a little algebra shows that the Lerner Index will also be equal to the inverse of the elasticity of demand faced by the firm. We may have estimates of the elasticity of demand, so that we can estimate the Lerner Index for the firm whose market power we are trying to measure.

TABLE 7.8 Market Shares of Six Competitors in a Hypothetical Market

Firm	Proportion of the Market
A	0.40
B	0.20
C	0.15
D	0.10
E	0.10
F	0.05

Let's return now to the question whether airline markets are contestable. Airline markets would be contestable if we observe that the number and size of competitors in the market were irrelevant in determining prices. In a contestable market the Lerner Index would be near zero, and prices and profits would *not* be related to measures of market concentration, including the size of the largest firm, the four-firm concentration ratio, the Herfindahl Index, or the number of effective competitors. Various researchers have examined airline price data to test the relationship between prices and measures of concentration or market power. For example, Peteraf and Reed (1994) examined 345 city pairs that had exactly one airline providing all nonstop, direct, and one-stop service. They looked at the statistical relationship between yield (as a measure of airline prices) and various measures of potential competition. They found that the number of potential competitors, defined as the number of airlines serving at least one of the cities in the pair, and the Herfindahl index of the potential competitors were not significant in determining the yield. This implies that the number and concentration of potential competitors had no significant effect on airline prices. Borenstein (1992) examined average prices in 1990 for airline routes with one, two, and three airlines providing service. He found that prices on routes with two actual competitors were 8 percent lower on average than prices on routes with only a single airline providing service. Further, he found that prices on routes with three actual competitors were again about 8 percent lower on average than prices on routes with two competitors. He concluded that the effect of potential competition on airline prices is only about one-third to one-tenth as strong as the effect of actual competition.

Studies also show that concentration at airports leads to higher prices.[28] The hub-and-spoke route system has led to some cases of substantial concentration for traffic originating or terminating at hubs. Borenstein (1992, pp. 54–56) calculated Herfindahl indexes for travel originating or terminating at hubs and found generally higher fares at more concentrated hubs. In 1999, the U.S. Department of Transportation found high fares for flights between city pairs separated by short distances where one major airline had a large market share and a hub at one of the cities. It concluded that average fares for flights using some of these hub airports were up to 60 percent higher than fares for city pairs involving airports with more competition.[29] Lee and Luengo-Prado (2005) define the "hub premium" as the percentage by which the average fare for traffic originating or terminating at the hub exceeds the average fare for the airline's non-hub traffic for trips of similar distances. Like the Transportation Department, they also calculate some of these hub premiums at more than 50 percent. According to Lee and Luengo-Prado (2005), some of these hub premiums owe to the larger proportion of business travel originating or terminating at hub airports. Nevertheless, after adjusting for this factor they conclude that in 2000 there remained hub premiums even after adjusting for passenger mix.

Thus, examination of the relationships among fares, measures of potential competition, and measures of market concentration revealed that the airline industry was not contestable after deregulation. Actual entry of new carriers, especially LCCs, lowered airfares, but potential entry did not. In spite of potential competition, airlines appeared to be exercising market power in setting fares for travel originating or terminating at hubs.

---

[28] See, e.g., Borenstein (1989, 1992); Evans and Kessides (1993); Morrison and Winston (1995), pp. 43–49; U.S. Department of Transportation (2001); and Lee and Luengo-Prado (2005).

[29] U.S. Department of Transportation (1999), p. 6.

Borenstein (1992, p. 56), for example, attributed this market power to frequent flier programs and travel agent commission policies. Airlines introduced frequent flyer programs to create a preference with each passenger for using a single airline for most flights. At hubs, travelers would prefer the dominant airline. Airlines created travel agent commission overrides, which increased commission rates for travel agents booking a large percentage of their tickets on a particular airline. This created an incentive for travel agents to concentrate their sales on one airline rather than spreading the sales around among many. These and other features of the market could create market power for airlines at their hubs.

The U.S. Department of Transportation concluded in 1999 that the type of competitors is more important to price competition than the number of competitors. It concluded that entry of a low-fare competitor causes average fares to drop regardless of whether this increases the total number of competitors in the market.[30] Low-fare competitors are those like Southwest Airlines that have low costs and compete with substantially lower prices.

Rivalry Among Firms

To further understand what has been happening in the airline market we need to understand how business firms interact with each other in competing for the same customers. Let's look at some simple ways to understand this rivalry.

MONOPOLY   The simplest possibility is a market in which there is a single supplier, so that there is no rival firm. We refer to this as *monopoly*—the pure case of a market consisting of a single seller. Monopolies, lacking rivals, may be in a position to harm consumers by charging excessive prices. We usually understand monopoly behavior as restricting output so as to keep prices high and to earn excessive rates of return on investment. We can see this in Figure 7.5. Here we have shown the price of the good or

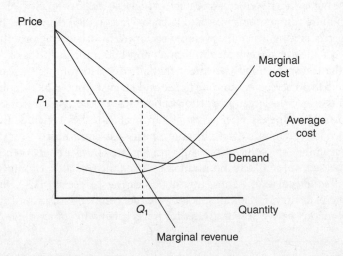

FIGURE 7.5 Monopoly.

---

[30] U.S. Department of Transportation (1999), pp. 3–4.

service on the vertical axis and the quantity produced on the horizontal axis. Of course this quantity is both the quantity produced by the firm and the quantity supplied to the market because there is only a single firm in the market. Profit-maximizing behavior requires the firm to produce the quantity that makes marginal revenue equal to marginal cost. This happens at point Q_1. Then the monopolist will charge price P_1, because that is the price that makes the quantity demanded equal to the quantity the monopolist wishes to supply. Note that the price is far above average cost so that the monopolist earns substantial economic profits.

Examples of pure monopoly are hard to find, unless you define the market very narrowly. For example, if we define the market as the market for a particular book, the publisher has a monopoly over the sale of that book because of copyright laws. In some cases a business firm may have a monopoly because of a franchise granted by a government to provide service within a particular area. For example, a natural gas company may have a franchise to provide natural gas in a particular city or region. Except in such cases of government grants of monopoly through franchises, copyrights, or patents, it is hard to find true monopolies. The reason is that for monopoly to persist there must be "barriers to entry" that prevent other firms from entering the market when the monopolist earns excessive profits.

A **barrier to entry** is a feature of the market that prevents entry by other firms and protects monopoly profits in the long run. Patents, copyrights, and government franchises are often effective barriers to entry. Economies of scale can also be a barrier to entry. If costs for a single firm fall throughout the range of production out to the market demand curve, there will be no room for a second firm to take sales away from the monopolist except by incurring very high costs of production. In those cases, the only way the new entrant could enter is by incurring substantial losses with little hope of ever making profits in the market. Such a situation would discourage entry even if the monopolist were earning an excessive rate of return.

Barrier to entry
A feature of a market that prevents entry by other firms and protects monopoly profits in the long run.

COMPETITION   The other extreme case for market rivalry is the case of pure competition. In the case of **pure competition**, no firm in the industry has any control over price, but rather each takes the market price as given. We refer to purely competitive firms as *price takers*. The classic example pure competition is for agricultural commodities such as wheat. No individual wheat farmer is large enough to have any noticeable influence on the market price. In fact, this is a case in which an individual firm or farmer will actually phone the commodity market or use the Internet to inquire what the market price is at that moment. These firms are literally price takers.

Pure competition
A market in which each firm takes the market price as given and, therefore, unaffected by its own behavior.

Generally, competitive markets are markets in which there are many sellers, none of which is large relative to the size of the market. Each firm can do no more than choose the quantity it wants to produce given the market price. Figure 7.6 illustrates this. Here we see a horizontal line at the market price and we see the firm's marginal cost and average cost curves. In this case price is also marginal revenue, because the firm can sell as much or as little as it wants at the market price. If it sells one more unit it gets the price—thus marginal revenue is the price. To maximize profits, the firm will select that quantity that makes price equal marginal cost as shown in Figure 7.6.

It is important to remember that a price-taking firm chooses its quantity of output to make its marginal cost equal to the market price. This means that the firm's

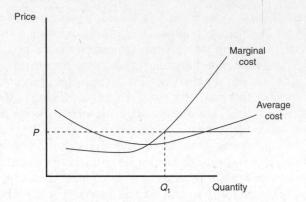

Price

Marginal cost

Average cost

P

Q_1 Quantity

FIGURE 7.6 Pure Competition.

marginal cost curve is the firm's *supply curve*, because it is the curve that shows the quantity of output the firm produces for each level of the price.[31]

There is one extremely significant difference between this situation and the monopoly situation shown in Figure 7.5. In the competitive case, price equals marginal cost. Thus, any consumer who is willing to pay the additional cost of an additional unit of output can do so. This is not true in the monopoly case. In a monopoly case, price is far above marginal cost. Thus, in monopoly, some consumers who are willing to pay the additional cost of additional units of output are denied the opportunity to do so, as the monopolist restricts output so as to charge a higher price and, thereby, to earn higher profits.

OLIGOPOLY   Having dealt with the extreme cases, we can turn to the much more difficult intermediate cases in which there are multiple sellers but there is not enough rivalry to lead to pure competition. The most important of these cases is what we refer to as **oligopoly**, which is an industry consisting primarily of a small number of relatively large firms that are aware of their interactions. In oligopoly markets, a few large sellers dominate.

Oligopolies are often very visible, because their advertising dominates television and other media—beer, soft drinks, breakfast cereals, automobiles, pain relievers, and household cleaning products are all oligopoly industries. Because there are a few large sellers in an oligopoly market, each seller must be aware of the behavior of the other firms in the industry. The firms strategically interact with each other. Each automobile firm knows that if it develops and introduces a successful new product, then the other firms in the industry will respond with similar products of their own. For example, when Chrysler introduced the minivan, consumers eagerly pursued this new product. In response, Ford and General Motors introduced their own versions of the minivan. Surely, this cannot have been a surprise to Chrysler. Thus, the key to understanding oligopoly is trying to understand the interactions of the few rivals.

The airline industry is a good example of an oligopoly. The industry consists of a relatively small number of large firms. Like the automobile manufacturers, airlines

Oligopoly
An industry consisting primarily of a small number of relatively large firms that are aware of their interactions.

[31] Actually, only the portion of the marginal cost curve that lies above average variable cost is the firm's supply curve, because if the firm is not covering its variable costs it will shut down, producing $Q = 0$.

must take into account the potential responses of the other firms in the industry when considering changes in prices or services.

While understanding oligopoly behavior can be extremely difficult, there are a few simple oligopoly market models.[32] The first of these was the model of Cournot. In developing his model, Cournot assumed that there are two firms in the market and that each of these firms selects its profit-maximizing level of output under the assumption that the other firm holds its output at a *constant* level. Cournot wanted to understand what the market outcome would look like under this assumption about business firm behavior. He assumed that the market outcome must be a situation in which each firm makes its assumption about the other firm and *both firms are correct* in their assumptions.

To see Cournot's result, consider Figure 7.7 where we see the market demand curve indicated by D. We also see the demand curve for firm 1, D_1, which we construct by subtracting the quantity firm 1 assumes firm 2 will produce. We subtract Q_2 from the market demand by shifting the demand curve to the left by the amount Q_2. This construction incorporates Cournot's assumption that firm 1 assumes firm 2 produces a constant level of output, which we show as Q_2. After firm 2 takes Q_2, all the market demand remainder shown by curve D_1 is left for firm 1. Firm 1 would then maximize profits subject to this residual demand curve and associated marginal revenue curve in the same manner that any firm facing a downward sloping demand curve would. Firm 1 equates its marginal revenue with its marginal cost to determine Q_1. For example, if firm 1's marginal cost were zero, then Q_1 would be where MR = 0.

Suppose firm 1 assumed that firm 2 would produce a larger quantity of output. Then the remaining demand curve left over for firm 1 would be farther to the left than shown in Figure 7.7. Then its profit maximizing level of output would be smaller than Q_1 shown in Figure 7.7. Alternatively, suppose firm 1 assumed that firm 2 would produce a smaller quantity of output. Then its residual demand curve would be farther to the right than shown in Figure 7.7, and its profit maximizing level of output would be larger than

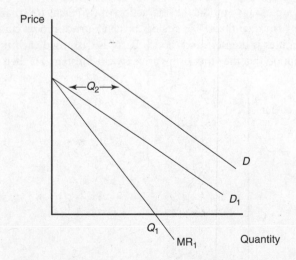

FIGURE 7.7 Cournot's Residual Demand Curve for Firm 1.

---

[32] See Varian (2003), pp. 473–495, for a survey of simple oligopoly models.

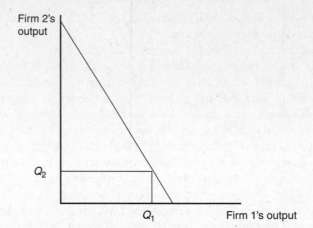

FIGURE 7.8 Firm 1's
Reaction Function.

Q_1. We can trace out this relationship between firm 1's assumption about the production level of firm 2 and firm 1's profit maximizing level of output in Figure 7.8.

Here we see that if firm 2 produces a larger level of output then firm 1 will produce a smaller level of output. At a lower level of output for firm 2, firm 1's profit-maximizing level of output will be larger. This inverse relationship between the assumed level of output for firm 2 and the profit maximizing level of output for firm 1 is known as firm 1's *reaction function*. In the same way, we can construct a reaction function for firm 2. We can then put the two reaction functions on the same figure as shown in Figure 7.9.

The two reaction functions cross at point *E*, which shows the only levels of output for firm 1 and firm 2 at which each firm is maximizing profits given its assumption about the output of the other firm *and* those assumptions are correct. Cournot asserted that this could be the only equilibrium result for such a market. That is, each firm must be maximizing profits given its assumptions about the other firm's behavior and the assumptions about the other firm's behavior must be correct.

Another simple way to model the interaction of two firms in a market is to examine prices rather than quantities. The analog to the Cournot model considering prices rather than quantities is the Bertrand model. Bertrand assumed each firm sets it price under the assumption that the other firm's price is held constant. He then asked what the

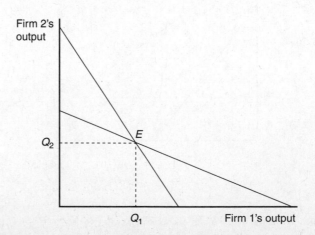

FIGURE 7.9 Cournot
Market Equilibrium.

equilibrium must look like. Suppose firm 2 assumes firm 1 will hold its price at P_1. What would firm 2's profit-maximizing price be? If the two firms are selling the same product and the consumer will buy the lowest price product available, then for firm 2 a price $P_2 = P_1 - 1¢$ will give it the entire market. But this cannot be an equilibrium, because the same option is available to firm 1: set $P_1 = P_2 - 1¢$. The conclusion for the Bertrand model (with the firms producing a homogeneous product) is that the only price that can be an equilibrium is one in which both firms lower their prices to marginal cost—there is no incentive to price below marginal cost, because any additional sales would lower profit, and any price above marginal cost would be undercut by the other firm.

The Cournot and Bertrand models are the simplest ways to model the strategic interactions of two firms in a single market. In spite of their simplicity, these models may help us understand the behavior of airlines. Consider a city pair, say Chicago and Omaha, and suppose exactly two airlines provide nonstop service between them. How will they interact? How many seats will each airline have in service each day? How will they set prices? Brander and Zhang (1990) examined this question using data for 33 city pairs served only by American Airlines and United Airlines and including Chicago as origin or destination. They found that the behavior of the airlines was not consistent with the Bertrand model because prices seemed generally to be above costs. Surprisingly, however, they found the airlines' behavior to be quite consistent with the Cournot model. They found that each airline seemed to act as if changes in the industry's output (number of seats on the route) were equal to changes in its own output, which would be true only if the other firm's output were constant. This is the Cournot assumption.

During the period Brander and Zhang considered, the third quarter of 1985, the main rivals in the U.S. domestic airline industry were the major carriers that had emerged from the CAB-regulated era. In recent years, competition for all of these legacy carriers provided by low-cost carriers, especially Southwest Airlines, has been one of the main features of rivalry in the industry. Cournot's model will probably not explain this rivalry.

RECENT DEVELOPMENT OF THE U.S. SCHEDULED AIRLINE INDUSTRY

After deregulation, Southwest Airlines, which had previously served only intrastate flights within Texas not subject to CAB price and route regulations, expanded into new routes outside of Texas. Southwest had a novel low-fare, low-cost business strategy which included the following elements:

- low fares
- point-to-point rather than hub-and-spoke route structure
- one type of aircraft (the Boeing 737)
- one class of service (coach)
- flights using less crowded, secondary airports in each city served
- no seat assignments
- quick turnaround at the gate, so that the aircraft spent less time on the ground and more time in the air
- increasing sales through the airline's own web site and call centers and declining commissions and fees to travel agents and GDSs

With this strategy, Southwest grew rapidly and provided substantial price competition to the network carriers. The fall in airfares that accompanied Southwest's entry into a new market became known as the "Southwest effect." For example, Southwest entered the Oakland, California, to Los Angeles, California, area market in 1989 by offering flights between the Oakland and Ontario airports. Oakland is near San Francisco; and Ontario International Airport, which is about 35 miles east of downtown Los Angeles, is convenient to many Los Angeles travelers. By 1991 Southwest had added flights between Oakland and Burbank and Oakland and Los Angeles International Airport. Soon, Southwest was carrying more than 40 percent of the traffic between the San Francisco and Los Angeles areas. By 1992 traffic between Oakland and the Los Angeles areas had more than tripled the level preceding Southwest's entry, and airfares had fallen about 50 percent.[33]

The U.S. airline industry saw entry from other new LCCs, including AirTran, American Trans Air, America West, and JetBlue. LCCs grew rapidly during the 1990s, taking customers and revenue from the legacy carriers, or network carriers with their legacy of high costs. The increased price competition from a growing Southwest Airlines and the other LCCs gradually made life increasingly difficult for the legacy carriers. Competition with the LCCs exposed the sources of these high legacy costs:

- hub-and-spoke networks
  - using congested airports with high fees and rentals
  - long turnaround times for aircraft on the ground
- onerous labor contracts
- complicated scheduling and maintenance resulting from diverse fleets of aircraft
- high distribution costs

Differences in labor costs, selling costs, and other operational costs created important differences in costs between legacy, network carriers and LCCs. Table 7.9 shows the operating costs per ASM for Southwest and six legacy carriers during the first quarter of 2004.

TABLE 7.9 Operating Costs per Available Seat Mile, Selected U.S. Airlines—2004

Carrier	Operating Costs per ASM (¢)
Southwest	7.82
American	9.49
Continental	9.76
United	10.18
Northwest	10.23
Delta	10.38
Alaska	10.41
US Airways	11.68

Data source: Boguslaski et al. (2004), p. 321.

---

[33] Bennett and Craun (1993), pp. 6–7.

The network carriers initially tried to meet the competition of the LCCs through new low-cost operations: Shuttle by United, Ted (United), Delta Express, Song (Delta), and MetroJet (US Airways). These new subsidiaries did not, however, succeed in duplicating the low costs of Southwest and other LCCs, and the companies retained some of the legacy problems of their network operations. Eventually, the legacy carriers ceased their separate low-cost operations.

While the legacy carriers were struggling to meet the growing LCC competition, the terrorist attacks of September 11, 2001, substantially reduced demand for air travel. The result was huge losses for the network carriers. Some declared bankruptcy. Bankruptcies allowed network carriers to reduce some of their legacy costs by renegotiating or abrogating old labor contracts and other contracts, including aircraft leases. Carriers in bankruptcy were able to lower their fares, putting more pressure on the few network carriers that had avoided bankruptcy. These carriers, too, sought to renegotiate labor contracts and reduce costs wherever possible. Also, over time, the network carriers generally reduced their reliance on the hub-and-spoke system. For example, US Airways "dehubbed" Pittsburgh, and Delta dehubbed Dallas/Ft. Worth. We now see a large presence of LCCs and slimmed-down network carriers that have substantially reduced their legacy costs.

PRICE LEADERSHIP FROM LCCS   One way to understand the recent events in the U.S. domestic airline industry is through a price leadership model in which the price leader, an LCC, has lower costs than the followers, who are in this case the legacy carriers.[34] Consider a situation in which a legacy carrier has been serving a city pair with high costs and prices that allow it to earn a normal rate of return on its investment. Now an LCC enters the city-pair market, offering much lower fares to consumers. Assume the legacy carrier is going to be a price taker, matching the new lower fare. The supply curve of the price-taking legacy carrier will be the portion of its marginal cost curve extending above average variable costs. We can then find the residual demand curve of the price leading LCC by subtracting the legacy carrier's supply curve from the market demand curve, as in Figure 7.10.

In the diagram, at price a the legacy carrier's quantity supplied is the market quantity demanded, leaving no demand for the LCC. At a price of b or lower, the legacy carrier's quantity supplied is zero, leaving the entire market demand for the LCC. The residual demand curve that the LCC faces is market demand curve for prices below b and is the market demand minus the legacy carrier's supply curve for prices between a and b. It is zero for prices above a.

To maximize profits, the LCC picks the quantity that makes MR = MC, and charges the price, P, on its demand curve above that quantity. This leaves some of the market to be served by the legacy carrier, shown by the legacy carrier's quantity supplied at price P. Depending on the market demand and the firms' costs, it is possible that P will be below the level b, so that the legacy carrier will not serve the market. It is also possible that $P > b$ but below the legacy carrier's average total cost, so that the legacy carrier is covering its variable costs at P but not covering its variable plus fixed costs. In that case, we would expect the legacy carrier to exit eventually.

---

[34] See, e.g., Varian (2003), pp. 480–482.

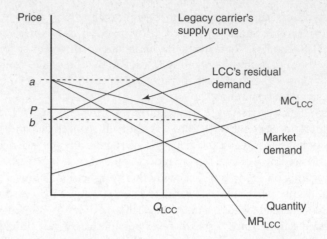

FIGURE 7.10 LCC Price Leadership.

In this model of price leadership by a new entrant with low costs, we see that the legacy carrier becomes a price taker, matching the new lower price of the LCC. It loses much, and possibly all, of the market to the new entrant. Even if it remains in the market, the profit level of the legacy carrier will fall, and perhaps be negative in the short run. The result in the long run is that the legacy carrier must either lower its costs to approach, but not necessarily equal, the costs of the LCC entrant, or it must exit the market. Thus, this model fairly accurately represents the kind of behavior we have seen recently, including entry by LCCs, especially Southwest Airlines, into additional markets and large financial losses, flight schedule reductions, and dramatic efforts to reduce costs by the legacy carriers.

THE FUTURE OF COMPETITION IN THE U.S. DOMESTIC AIRLINE INDUSTRY

Competition from LCCs may determine the future performance of the U.S. domestic airline industry. It appears that the legacy carriers will exit the industry or they will adapt. If they survive, the legacy carriers may continue to shed the burdens they took on during the era of regulation and continue to adopt many of the cost-saving measures of the LCCs. They may continue to lower wage rates and to eliminate some restrictive and burdensome work rules. They may continue to rebalance their mix of hub-and-spoke and point-to-point routes to get lower-cost use of their aircraft and crews. They may continue to reduce the gap between fares charged to business and leisure travelers and to lower their distribution costs.

LCCs, on the other hand, will probably find it harder to grow rapidly at the expense of high-cost legacy carriers. Changes at the legacy carriers will make them harder competitive targets.

During 2007 and 2008, high fuel prices challenged all airlines. If these fuel price increases are permanent, we can expect to see fewer seats flown and higher airfares. If the spike in fuel prices is temporary, future operational changes and aircraft developments may lower costs for all carriers, while increasing demand for air travel may raise revenues. These changes may lead to a new equilibrium in the U.S. domestic airline market in which most carriers can expect to earn normal rates of return on their investments over the business cycle. Travelers meantime could continue to benefit from low fares, service innovations, and many choices of flights and carriers.

Summary

The scheduled airline industry has grown rapidly since its beginnings in the 1920s, only decades after the first powered flight. The U.S. domestic airline industry is a giant; each year there are hundreds of millions of passenger enplanements and approaching 1 trillion ASM flown. In 2006, the U.S. scheduled passenger airline industry consisted of 17 major airlines, each having annual revenues exceeding $1 billion, and many smaller airlines. Airline yields (cents per passenger mile) have been rising slowly over the decades; so slowly that yields have not kept up with inflation. Thus, real yields have declined substantially over the decades.

From 1938 to 1978, the CAB heavily regulated the U.S. interstate airline industry, with authority to regulate entry and exit in the industry and to regulate the prices the airlines charged. In 1978, Congress concluded that the CAB was stifling competition and maintaining high airfares. The Airline Deregulation Act of 1978 ended CAB oversight of most aspects of airline behavior, and in 1984 the CAB was closed. The FAA in the U.S. Department of Transportation regulates airline operations and safety.

One of the most important changes in civil aviation that came from deregulation was the changing route structure of scheduled airlines from mostly point-to-point routes to a hub-and-spoke system. Airlines have been able to substantially increase their load factors since deregulation.

Labor is the highest single category of costs for the typical airline, making up more than 30 percent of total costs. In most recent years, fuel has been the second highest category of costs for the airlines, but in 2007 and 2008 fuel costs competed with labor costs for the highest category. To reduce the costs of selling tickets, U.S. airlines have phased out most travel agent commissions and shifted much of their sales and transactions processing to their own web sites or call centers.

The airline industry has been one of the most successful in segmenting its customers and selling its services at different prices to different segments through a process known as yield management or revenue management. To maximize the revenue or yield to be earned from the airline's current coach capacity, the airline has to equalize marginal revenue from each category of coach customers. Yield management brings greater revenue to the airline, but it also allows some passengers to book air travel at the last minute.

International commercial airline service requires agreements among nations that give the nations' airlines the rights to serve routes between countries and routes that continue on to points beyond the countries. The U.S., the EU, and other countries have been working to increase competition in international airline markets. The EU created a single airline market in 1997, with any European-based airline free to provide any airline service between EU cities.

The immediate post-deregulation U.S. airline industry was not as competitive as some observers had hoped, as fares for service involving hub airports were unusually high. Competition from LCCs was, however, effective in keeping fares low for markets where LCCs provided service. In recent decades, LCCs have grown rapidly.

At the start of the twenty-first century we find the airline industry in turmoil. By the end of 2005 about one-half of the U.S. airline industry was in bankruptcy. LCCs now provide intense competition for the legacy carriers that had emerged from the regulated era. High fuel prices have hurt the airline industry. One way to understand the recent events in the U.S. domestic airline industry is through a price leadership model in which the LCC price leader has lower costs than the legacy carrier followers. In coming years, legacy carriers may continue to shed the burdens they took on during the era of regulation and continue to adopt many of the cost-saving measures of the LCCs.

Bibliography

Air Transport Association (2007a), "Passenger Facilities Charges," www.airlines.org/economics/taxes/PFCs. htm.

——— (2007b), "Annual Traffic and Ops: U.S. Airlines," www.airlines.org/economics/traffic/Annual+US+Traffic.htm.

——— (2007c), "U.S. Aviation Excise Taxes and Fees," www.airlines.org/economics/taxes/excisetaxes.htm.

——— (2007d), "Annual Passenger Yields: U.S. Airlines," www.airlines.org/economics/finance/PaPricesYield. htm.

——— (2007e), "U.S. Airline Bankruptcies," www. airlines.org/economics/specialtopics/USAirlineBankruptcies. htm.

——— (2007f), "Annual Earnings: U.S. Airlines," www.airlines.org/economics/finance/Annual+US+Financial+Results.htm.

——— (2007g), *Balancing the Aviation Equation: 2007 Economic Report*, www.airlines.org/NR/rdonlyres/0E9E7072-ECC6-4CED-8B8E-6857256935E7/0/2007AnnualReport.pdf.

Airbus (2007), "A380: The New-Generation Large Aircraft for the 21st Century," A380 Update press kit, 15 October, www.airbus.com/en/presscentre/presskits/index.jsp

Airliners.net (2005), www.airliners.net.

Airlines Reporting Corporation (2007), "About Us," www.arccorp.com/aboutus/index.html.

American Airlines (2007), "AA Technology Highlights," www.aa.com/content/aboutUs/pressGuide/technical Highlights. jhtml.

AMR Corporation (2005), "Form 10-K, Fiscal Year 2004," http://www.shareholder.com/aa/edgar.cfm?DocType=Annual&SECYear=All.

——— (2007), "Form 10-K, Fiscal Year 2006," www.shareholder.com/aa/edgar.cfm?DocType=Annual&SECYear=All.

Bailey, Elizabeth E. "Aviation Policy: Past and Present." *Southern Economic Journal* 69 (2002): 12–20.

Bailey, Elizabeth E., and John Panzar. "The Contestability of Airline Markets During the Transition to Deregulation." *Law and Contemporary Problems* 44 (1981): 125–45.

Bennett, Randall D., and James M. Craun. "The Airline Deregulation Evolution Continues: The Southwest Effect." U.S. Department of Transportation, May, 1993.

Boeing Company (2007), "About Us," www.boeing.com/companyoffices/aboutus/brief.html.

Boguslaski, Charles, Harumi Ito, and Darin Lee. "Entry Patterns in the Southwest Airlines Route System." *Review of Industrial Organization* 25 (2004): 317–50.

Borenstein, Severin "Hubs and High Fares: Dominance and Market Power in the U.S. Airline Industry." *Rand Journal of Economics* 20 (1989): 344–65.

———. "The Evolution of U.S. Airline Competition." *Journal of Economic Perspectives* 6 (1992): 45–73.

——— (2005), "U.S. Domestic Airline Pricing, 1995-2004," University of California, Berkeley, Competition Policy Center, CPC05-048, http://repositories.cdlib.org/iber/cpc/CPC05-048.

Borenstein, Severin, and Nancy L. Rose. "Competition and Price Dispersion in the U.S. Airline Industry." *Journal of Political Economy* 102 (1994): 653–83.

———. "Bankruptcy and Pricing Behavior in U.S. Airline Markets." *American Economic Review* 85 (1995): 397–402.

Botimer, Theodore C. "Efficiency Considerations in Airline Pricing and Yield Management." *Transportation Research* 30 (1996): 307–17.

Brander, James A., and Anming Zhang. "Market Conduct in the Airline Industry: An Empirical Investigation." *Rand Journal of Economics* 21 (1990): 567–83.

Breyer, Stephen. *Regulation and Its Reform*. Cambridge, MA: Harvard University Press, 1982.

Carey, Susan. "United Airlines Is Flying Past Rival Carriers in Los Angeles." *Wall Street Journal*, January 16, 1998, A1, A9.

Caves, Douglas W., Laurits Christensen, and Michael W. Tretheway. "Economies of Density Versus Economies of Scale: Why Trunk and Local Service Airline Costs Differ." *Rand Journal of Economics* 15 (1984): 471–89.

Continental Airlines, Inc. (2005), "Form 10-K, Fiscal Year 2004," http://ccbn.10kwizard.com/cgi/convert/pdf/CONTINENTALAIRL10K.pdf?pdf=1&repo=tenk&ipage=3334302&num=-2&pdf=1&xml=1&odef=8&dn=2&dn=3.

Delta Air Lines, Inc. (2005), "Form 10-K, Fiscal Year 2004," http://ccbn.10kwizard.com/cgi/convert/pdf/DELTAAIRLINESIN10K.pdf?pdf=1&repo=tenk&ipage=3323686&num=-2&pdf=1&xml=1&odef=8&dn=2&dn=3.

Douglas, George W., and James C. Miller III. *Economic Regulation of Domestic Air Transport: Theory and Policy*. Washington, DC: The Brookings Institution, 1974.

Federal Aviation Administration (undated). "A Brief History of the Federal Aviation Administration," http://www.faa.gov/about/history/brief_history/.

Ito, Harumi, and Darin Lee. "Low Cost Carrier Growth in the U.S. Airline Industry: Past, Present, and Future," 2003. Brown University Working Paper No. 2003-12.

——— (2004), "Incumbent Responses to Lower Cost Entry: Evidence from the U.S. Airline Industry," mimeo.

——— (2005), "Domestic Codesharing, Alliances and Airfares in the U.S. Airline Industry," mimeo.

International Air Transport Association (2004), *World Air Transport Statistics*, www.iata.org/pressroom/wats/ wats_passenger_flown. htm.

——— (2005a), "History," www.iata.org/about/history_2. htm?iata=iata;history_3.htm?iata=iata;history_4.htm? iata=iata.

——— (2005b), "History of Tariff Coordination," www. iata.org/whatwedo/tariffs/history.htm.

——— (2005c), "Industry Clearing Services," www.iata. org/whatwedo/clearing1.htm.

Kahn, Alfred E. *The Economics of Regulation: Principles and Institutions*, Vols. I and II, New York: John Wiley & Sons, 1970, 1971.

Keeler, Theodore E. "Airline Regulation and Market Performance," *The Bell Journal of Economics and Management Science* 3 (1972): 399–424.

Kraft, Dennis J. H., Tae H. Oum, and Michael W. Tretheway. "Airline Seat Management." *The Logistics and Transportation Review* 22 (1986): 115–30.

Lee, Darin. "An Assessment of Some Recent Criticisms of the U.S. Airline Industry." *Review of Network Economics* 2 (2003): 1–9.

Lee, Darin, and María José Luengo-Prado (2005), "The Impact of Passenger Mix on Reported 'Hub Premiums' in the U.S. Airline Industry." *Southern Economic Journal*, 72: 372–94.

Levine, Michael E. "Is Regulation Necessary? California Air Transportation and National Regulatory Policy." *Yale Law Journal* 74 (1965): 1416–47.

———. "Revisionism Revised? Airline Deregulation and the Public Interest." *Law and Contemporary Problems* 44 (1981): 179–95.

Morrison, Steven A., and Clifford Winston. *The Evolution of the Airline Industry*. Washington, DC: The Brookings Institution, 1995.

O'Connor, William E. *An Introduction to Airline Economics*, 5th ed. Westport, CT: Praeger, 1995.

OpenTravel Alliance (2007), www. opentravel. org.

Oum, Tae H., David W. Gillen, and S. E. Noble. "Demands for Fareclasses and Pricing in Airline Markets." *The Logistics and Transportation Review* 22 (1986): 195–222.

Oum, Tae Hoon, Jong-Hun Park, and Anming Zhang. *Globalization and Strategic Alliances: The Case of the Airline Industry*. Pergamon: Amsterdam, 2000.

Peoples, James. "Deregulation and the Labor Market." *Journal of Economic Perspectives* 12 (1998): 111–30.

Peteraf, Margaret, and Randal Reed. "Pricing and Performance in Monopoly Airline Markets." *Journal of Law and Economics* 37 (1994): 193–213.

Petersen, Barbara S. *Bluestreak: Inside JetBlue, the Upstart that Rocked an Industry*. New York: Portfolio, 2004.

———. "Gaming It: How Will the Financial Woes of Major U.S. Airlines Impact Passengers?" *Condé Nast Traveler*, February 2005, 59–68.

Shapiro, Carl, and Hal Varian (1999), *Information Rules: A Strategic Guide to the Network Economy*. Boston: Harvard Business School Press

Simon, Julian L. "The Airline Oversales Auction Plan: The Results," *Journal of Transport Economics and Policy* 28 (1994): 319–23.

Smith, Barry C., John F. Leimkuhler, and Ross M. Darrow. "Yield Management at American Airlines." *Interfaces* 22 (1992): 8–31.

Southwest Airlines Co. (2003), "Form 10-K, Fiscal Year 2002," http://ccbn.10kwizard.com/cgi/convert/pdf/ SOUTHWESTAIRLIN10K.pdf?pdf=1&repo=tenk& ipage=1998572&num=-2&pdf=1&xml=1&cik=92380 &odef=8&secover=0&rid=12&quest=1&dn=2&dn=3

Southwest Airlines Co. (2005), "Form 10-K, Fiscal Year 2004," http://ccbn.10kwizard.com/xml/download. php?repo=tenk&ipage=3238819&format=PDF.

Sprayregen, James H. M., Alexander Dimitrief, and Andrew Kassof. "Informational Brief of United Air Lines, Inc.," filing in U.S. Bankruptcy Court for the Northern District of Illinois, December 9, 2002.

Starr, Nona. *Viewpoint: An Introduction to Travel, Tourism, and Hospitality*. 3rd ed. Upper Saddle River, NJ: Prentice Hall, 2000.

Stigler, George J., and Claire Friedland. "What Can Regulators Regulate? The Case of Electricity." *Journal of Law and Economics* 5 (1962): 1–16, reprinted in Paul W. MacAvoy. *The Crisis of the Regulatory Commissions*. New York: W. W. Norton & Co., 1970.

Tirole, Jean. *The Theory of Industrial Organization*. Cambridge: MIT Press, 1989.

Transportation Research Board (1999), *Entry and Competition in the U.S. Airline Industry: Issues and Opportunities*. Washington: National Academy of Sciences, http://trb.org/publications/sr/sr255/sr255toc. pdf.

US Airways, Inc. (2003), "Form 10-K, Fiscal Year 2002," http://ccbn.10kwizard.com/cgi/convert/pdf/USAIRWA YSGROUPI10K.pdf?pdf=1&repo=tenk&ipage=2075830 &num=-2&pdf=1&xml=1&cik=701345&odef=8&rid= 12&quest=1&dn=2&dn=3

US Airways, Inc. (2005), "Form 10-K, Fiscal Year 2004," http://ccbn.10kwizard.com/xml/download.php?repo=tenk&ipage=3302162&format=PDF.

U.S. Department of Commerce (2005), "Milestones," http://www.commerce.gov/milestones.html.

U.S. Department of State (2005), "Open Skies Agreements," www.state.gov/e/eb/tra/c661.htm.

U.S. Department of Transportation (1999a), "Competition in the U.S. Domestic Airline Industry: The Need for a Policy to Prevent Unfair Practices," http://ostpxweb.dot.gov/aviation/domav/comp_rev.pdf.

——— (1999b), "International Aviation Developments: Global Deregulation Takes Off," http://ostpxweb.dot.gov/aviation/intav/alncrpt3.pdf.

——— (2000), "International Aviation Developments: Transatlantic Deregulation," http://ostpxweb.dot.gov/aviation/Data/transatlantdereg.pdf.

——— (2001), "Dominated Hub Fares," http://ostpxweb.dot.gov/aviation/Data/dominatedhubfares.pdf.

——— (2005a), *National Transportation Statistics 2005,* www.bts.gov/publications/national_transportation_statistics/.

——— (2005b), "Air Carrier Groupings," www.bts.gov/programs/airline_information/accounting_and_reporting_directives/number_279.html.

——— (2006), "Air Carrier Groupings," www.bts.gov/programs/airline_information/accounting_and_reporting_directives/number_281.html.

——— (2007a), "Passengers Boarded at the Top 50 U.S. Airports," www.bts.gov/publications/national_transportation_statistics/html/table_01_41.html.

——— (2007b), "U.S. Airport Runway Pavement Conditions," www.bts.gov/publications/national_transportation_statistics/html/table_01_24.html.

——— (2008), "Airline Fuel Cost and Consumption," http://www.transtats bts.gov/fuel.asp.

Varian, Hal R. *Intermediate Microeconomics,* 6th ed. New York: W. W. Norton, 2003.

Yergin, Daniel, Richard H. K. Vietor, and Peter C. Evans. "Fettered Flight: Globalization and the Airline Industry." Cambridge Energy Research Associates, 2000.

CHAPTER 8

Tourist Travel by Automobile, Rail, and Bus

Learning Goals

- Learn the relative sizes of various modes of long-distance travel.
- Understand the importance of tourist travel by automobile.
- Understand the organization of the bus and motorcoach segment of tourism.
- Know how Amtrak handles U.S. intercity passenger rail service and the importance of subsidies to its operations.
- Understand the organization and operations of the U.S. car rental industry.

INTRODUCTION

Tourists choose from a variety of **travel modes**, or means of moving between the origin and destination. As we have seen in earlier chapters, many tourists travel by commercial airline or by cruise ship. As we will see later in this chapter, airline travelers often rent cars for local travel at the destination. The car rental industry is an interesting one, and we will analyze some of the economics of that industry. Before we get to that, we will examine some of the other major modes of travel between origin and destination. We have already analyzed one of the major travel modes, the airlines, in great detail and will only briefly mention it in this chapter. Our areas of focus will be tourist travel by automobile, train, and bus.

In discussing travelers' choices of travel mode, economists and government analysts typically refer to modes of "intercity passenger transportation," although the tourist's trip may be neither originating nor terminating in a city. Table 8.1 shows recent data on the volume of passenger transportation, both in the number of trips and in the number of passenger miles, by mode for roundtrips to destinations at least 50 miles away.[1]

Travel mode
Way of moving between origin and destination, such as scheduled airline, automobile, bus, or train.

---

[1] TIA (2007) provides similar data on modal choices.

TABLE 8.1 Long-Distance Travel in the United States by Travel Mode—2001

Mode	Person Trips (Millions)	Person Miles (Millions)
Personal-use vehicle	2,336.1	760,325
Airplane	193.3	557,609
Intercity bus	22.9	9,945
Tour or charter bus	32.5	17,136
Train	21.1	10,546
Other and not reported	11.2	5,251
Total	**2,617.1**	**1,360,813**

Data source: U.S. Department of Transportation (2005), Table F-1.

As we can see immediately, travel by personal-use vehicle, primarily automobiles and light trucks (pickups and sport-utility vehicles), dominates travelers' choices with almost 90 percent of person trips. The average length of trip in miles is much shorter for automobile travel, however, so that in person miles travel by personal-use vehicle is less dominant, with 56 percent of the miles. Travelers take most long trips by air; so that, airplane travel, with only 7.4 percent of the trips, approaches the automobile's share of total mileage.

We see that in the United States, intercity bus travel and tour and charter bus travel (often known as motorcoach service) lag far behind in travelers' modal choices, having been chosen for a total among them of only 2 percent of trips. Train travel in the United States lags far behind other modes with less than 1 percent of trips. In part because the marginal cost of an additional automobile passenger is very small, more households choose to travel by automobile as the size of the trip party increases. Demand for travel by air and by automobile both increase with increasing income of the traveler. In contrast, train travel and bus travel are **inferior goods**, which means that in the United States, demand for travel by bus and train declines as income rises (Morrison and Winston, 1985).

Inferior good
Good or service for which consumer demand decreases as consumers' incomes increase.

The travel mode choices of U.S. travelers have been changing. Table 8.2 shows the development of these modes within the United States over recent years. These figures exclude some Amtrak commuter rail passengers, but they include local transit bus, local passenger car, and local light-truck travel.

Here we see that domestic U.S. travel by passenger car, light truck (including sport-utility vehicles), and air has increased substantially in recent years, with air travel bouncing back strongly after 2001. Over this period, passenger miles traveled by air increased by 40 percent, and passenger miles traveled by personal-use vehicle increased by 26 percent, while passenger miles traveled by bus or rail held fairly steady.

TRAVEL BY AUTOMOBILE

Automobile transportation is enormously important in the United States and in other countries. In 2004, U.S. households and businesses owned over 136 million passenger automobiles, and Americans drove a total of almost 2.7 trillion miles

TABLE 8.2 U.S. Passenger Miles by Mode—1994–2004

Year	Mode (All Figures in Millions)				
	Domestic Air	Passenger Car	Light Truck	Bus	Amtrak
2004	556,690	2,693,872	1,758,542	140,716	5,511
2003	505,159	2,641,885	1,706,103	143,801	5,680
2002	482,310	2,620,389	1,674,792	145,124	5,468
2001	486,506	2,556,481	1,678,853	150,042	5,559
2000	516,129	2,544,457	1,467,664	160,919	5,498
1999	488,357	2,494,870	1,432,625	162,445	5,330
1998	463,262	2,463,828	1,380,557	148,558	5,304
1997	450,612	2,389,065	1,352,675	145,060	5,166
1996	434,652	2,337,068	1,298,299	139,136	5,050
1995	403,888	2,286,887	1,256,146	136,104	5,545
1994	388,399	2,249,742	1,269,292	135,871	5,921

Data source: U.S. Department of Transportation (2005), Table B-2.

in passenger cars.[2] Most of this auto travel is not tourism, but only local travel for commuting to work, shopping, and traveling to other places near the home. But as Table 8.1 shows, Americans also use their automobiles for long-distance travel that we consider tourism. For travel up to a few hundred miles one way, automobiles are the primary travel mode. Only for trips of much longer distances do Americans switch to air travel. For most trips of intermediate distances, for example, 100 to 400 miles, there is some intermodal competition among automobiles, buses, and trains.

Automobile travel, over short or long distances, has important advantages over other travel modes. One may be price, especially for parties of three to five people. Once a traveler has made the decision to drive, additional passengers do not have to pay for a ticket. This is typically not true for the other travel modes, for which each additional passenger pays an additional fare. Even for trips involving a single traveler, over some range of distances automobile travel may have the lowest price. Another obvious advantage of driving is that on reaching the destination the traveler does not have to rent a car to maintain his or her mobility. Travel by car also has the advantages of departing on the traveler's own schedule, rather than on the carrier's schedule. Finally, the automobile trip will begin and end at the traveler's origin and destination rather than requiring the traveler to travel to and from air, bus, or train terminals, enduring any associated delays and discomforts.

Interestingly, Morrison and Winston (1985, pp. 224–225) find that vacation travelers do not regard time spent driving to the destination as adding much to the cost of travel—that is, vacation travelers place a very low value on time spent on vacation travel by automobile. The authors attribute this low value on driving time to a recreational value of driving. In contrast, Morrison and Winston find that the perceived cost of time spent traveling to and from the destination using other modes is about the same value as the traveler's hourly wage rate.

---

[2] U.S. Department of Transportation (2006), Tables 1-11, 1-37.

TRAVEL BY BUS AND MOTORCOACH

Motorcoach
A bus designed for carrying passengers (and their luggage) in comfort over long distances.

Here we leave aside local transit buses and school buses, because we do not consider such local travel to be tourism. There are two kinds of bus service relevant for travel and tourism. These are scheduled intercity bus service and **motorcoach** (or tour and charter) bus service.

In the United States, Greyhound Lines, a subsidiary of Laidlaw, Inc., is by far the largest intercity bus or motorcoach service operator and the only nationwide operator. In 1987, Greyhound Lines acquired Trailways Bus System, the other nationwide intercity bus then in operation. In 2006, Greyhound Lines had operating revenues of $1.244 billion (Laidlaw, Inc., 2007a). Greyhound's services compete with automobile travel, and also with regional intercity bus carriers, airlines, and trains.

In early 2007, Laidlaw announced that it was planning to be acquired by the British transportation firm FirstGroup plc. FirstGroup is one of a group of large, integrated companies based in the United Kingdom that provides intercity bus services, along with other transportation services, in the United Kingdom and elsewhere around the world. In addition to FirstGroup, this sector includes Arriva, Go-Ahead Group, National Express Group, and Stagecoach Group. These companies operate many local, charter, and intercity bus services in the United Kingdom, other countries in Europe, Canada, and the United States (along with passenger rail transportation in the United Kingdom).

Motorcoach firms often provide services for hire to organized groups such as groups from schools or similar organizations. In other cases they provide sightseeing tours of tourist destinations, such as Washington, DC, or transportation for individuals or small groups to popular tourist destinations such as Atlantic City, NJ, or Branson, MO. They also provide transportation to and from hotels, airports, resorts, conventions, sporting events, and other events.

The U.S. motorcoach industry consists of a large number, approximately 4,000, of generally small firms operating regionally or locally. A few motorcoach firms are quite large. One of the largest U.S. motorcoach operators is Coach USA, which in 2006 operated about 2,500 motorcoaches in the United States. The company is also affiliated with Coach Canada, which operates another 500 motorcoaches. Coach USA is a subsidiary of the UK's Stagecoach Group plc. Gray Line of Seattle and Gray Line of Alaska, subsidiaries of Holland America Westours, are two other large U.S. motorcoach operators. Many motorcoach service providers are affiliated with Gray Line Worldwide, a worldwide sightseeing and motorcoach tour marketing company. Gray Line's 123 independent operating companies have about $1 billion in annual sales and carry about 25 million passengers per year.[3] The U.S. Department of Transportation regulates the safety of bus and motorcoach operations, including driver qualifications, equipment maintenance, and other aspects of interstate transportation of passengers by bus.[4]

TRAVEL BY TRAIN

While trains have been very important in the history of travel and tourism since shortly after 1840, in recent decades the importance of trains has declined substantially. Intercity passenger rail service remains important in Europe and Japan, but it has

---

[3] Gray Line Worldwide (2007).
[4] U.S. Department of Transportation (2007).

declined in the United States. Nevertheless, American travelers continue to use trains for commuting and, in some situations, for tourism.

In the United States, the most important provider of train service is Amtrak. (The Alaska Railroad provides service in Alaska.) After World War II, passenger travel by rail in the United States resumed its earlier decline, as long-distance travel by automobile and air provided travelers with ever-improving alternatives and rising incomes decreased demand for passenger rail travel. By 1970, U.S. passenger rail service had failed financially, which led to its consolidation, through the Rail Passenger Service Act of 1970, in a new National Railroad Passenger Corporation. This new corporation, which is still operating today, became known as Amtrak. Congress's goal in establishing Amtrak was to consolidate U.S. passenger train service in a single, profit-making, private corporation.

While Congress intended for Amtrak to conduct its operations to make a profit, the company never has. The story of Amtrak is one of continuing losses and substantial annual subsidies, recently over $1 billion per year, from the federal and some state governments. Since its creation in 1971, Amtrak has received about $30 billion in federal funding. Table 8.3 shows the recent annual federal subsidies, including both capital and operating subsidies, for Amtrak.

With the Amtrak Reform and Accountability Act of 1997, Congress removed Amtrak's status as a government corporation and charged it with covering its operating costs with its own revenues by 2002. Amtrak failed to meet that goal and has

TABLE 8.3 Annual U.S. Federal Amtrak Funding (Capital Plus Operating)

Year	Subsidy ($ Millions)
2005	1,203
2004	1,215
2003	1,043
2002	832
2001	520
2000	571
1999	1,701
1998	1,686
1997	843
1996	750
1995	972
1994	909
1993	891
1992	856
1991	815
1990	629
1971–1989	12,731

Data source: Federal Railroad Administration (2007).

TABLE 8.4 Amtrak's Revenue Passengers

Year	Passengers (in Thousands)
2005	25,076
2004	25,215
2003	24,595
2002	23,269
2001	23,444
2000	22,985
1999	21,544
1998	21,248
1997	20,200
1996	19,700
1995	20,349

Data source: U.S. Department of Transportation (2005), Table H-2.

recently been struggling to adjust its operations to try to earn enough revenue to cover its operating costs.

Table 8.4 shows the growth of Amtrak's passenger service in recent years. Amtrak operates passenger rail service in two ways. It provides long-distance service over 14 routes traveling rail lines owned and maintained by freight railroads. It also provides shorter-distance "corridor" services over 27 routes in densely populated regions, or corridors. The most heavily traveled corridor is the Northeast corridor which extends between Washington, DC, and Boston, and also serves Baltimore, Philadelphia, and New York City. Other corridors serve between New York City and Buffalo, NY, Philadelphia and Harrisburg, PA, San Diego and San Luis Obispo, CA (connecting through Los Angeles), and Eugene, OR, and Vancouver, BC (connecting through Seattle and Portland, OR).

Continuing subsidies to Amtrak and the company's continuing operation over thin, unprofitable routes are sources of controversy and political tussling. Amtrak's critics argue that the company's money-losing operations should be shut down rather than continue to be supported by taxpayer subsidies. Supporters argue that Amtrak provides important transportation services that should continue to receive taxpayer support.

There are valid economic arguments that could support some subsidies for scheduled transportation services such as Amtrak. The most important of these is that there are significant **economies of scale** in scheduled passenger rail service. A production process has economies of scale when the long-run average cost of the product or service declines as the level of output increases. Some economies of scale in scheduled passenger rail service come from lowering the railroad's average cost per passenger trip because each additional passenger adds less than the average to equipment and labor operating costs. More importantly, passengers bear much of the cost of scheduled rail service in traveling to and from train stations, in waiting times at the station, and in time spent changing trains. Additional passengers lower these costs by supporting more frequent service and service to more locations.[5]

Economies of scale
A production process in which long-run average cost of producing the good or service declines as the rate of production of output increases.

---

[5] Mohring (1972); Small (2007), pp. 20–21.

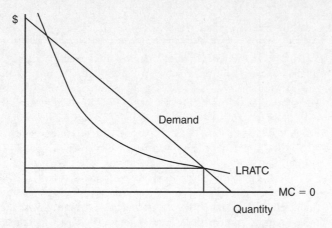

FIGURE 8.1 Economies of Scale in Scheduled Passenger Rail Service.

These factors can make the marginal cost of scheduled passenger train travel lower than the average cost, so that average cost declines with increasing passenger volume. Generally, to achieve a social optimum, price must equal marginal cost. When there are economies of scale, however, marginal cost pricing will not allow the firm to recover its costs. Figure 8.1 shows this case.

Here we take the hypothetical extreme case of a railroad that can serve any number of passengers once it pays the fixed costs of rails, equipment, and labor. In this example, total costs are fixed, marginal costs are zero, and average cost per passenger declines as more passengers are served. Suppose the railroad charged a price that would allow it to just recover its fixed costs, shown at the level where the market demand curve crosses the long run average total cost curve (LRATC). Then some potential passengers who are not willing to pay that price will not travel, even though their travel would cost the railroad nothing. This is not socially optimal, because with price exceeding marginal cost some customers who are willing to pay a price equaling marginal cost or more are not using the service.

Under these circumstances it may be socially useful to subsidize the service by having the taxpayers pay the fixed costs. More generally, it may be economically efficient for taxpayers to subsidize passenger rail service providers to allow them to charge prices below average cost while still breaking even, including a return on their invested capital. This result depends, however, on two important caveats. First, we need to recognize that the taxes themselves will create distortions, which could outweigh the benefits of the subsidized service. Perhaps more importantly, this argument depends on the assumption that the subsidized railroad will use the subsidy wisely in the interests of its passengers. There is a real danger that a firm receiving such a subsidy will dissipate much of the money on excessive costs.[6]

Distortions elsewhere in the transportation system, such as highway congestion (arising from the failure of drivers to pay the cost of their driving) or fuel taxes, could also justify some scheduled passenger rail service subsidies. If prices are not at marginal cost elsewhere, it may be socially optimal to have prices deviate from marginal cost in passenger rail also.

[6] Small (2007), p. 23.

Passenger Rail in Great Britain

In the 1940s Britain had nationalized its rail systems, unifying their management under British Rail and making the public responsible for funding the system. Dissatisfaction with service quality, costs, and high public subsidies led to privatization of the rail system in the 1990s. The ownership of the "infrastructure" of tracks and other facilities was transferred to Railtrack and then later to Network Rail. Network Rail's revenue came from charges levied on the rail service providers and government subsidies, with revenue regulation by the government's Office of Rail Regulation. The government's Strategic Rail Authority franchised the rights to operate trains and provide passenger service to private companies, which bid for the exclusive rights to operate for seven years in their franchise areas. (In 2007, there were 24 train operating companies, including First Great Western, Virgin Trains, and South West Trains.) The winning bidder was the company offering to serve the area with the lowest public subsidy or the highest payment to the government. The train operators leased their engines and rail cars from "rolling stock companies." This complex system, which divided responsibility among a variety of public and private entities, required substantial public subsidies, amounting to nearly $7 billion in 2004.[7]

Between 2004 and 2007, Great Britain again reorganized its extensive system of passenger and freight rail service. The reorganization centralized the regulatory process to give the government more control over rail decisions. It transferred the Strategic Rail Authority's responsibilities to the nation's Department for Transport, and it added responsibility for rail safety to the Office of Rail Regulation.[8]

Where there is sufficient traffic density, some subsidies may make sense. On lightly traveled routes these subsidies would not be justified, because the cost per traveler would be very high. Some of Amtrak's routes are indeed very lightly traveled. In 2000, ten states having Amtrak service averaged 70 or fewer Amtrak passenger boardings per day.[9] The U.S. Government Accountability Office estimates that in 2005 the average operating loss on Amtrak's long-distance routes was $154 per passenger.[10] It may be that in these cases, travelers should choose less costly alternatives such as intercity bus, automobile, or air. Where appropriate, intercity bus could be subsidized at a much lower cost to taxpayers. Using 1977 data, Morrison (1990) found that subsidies to intercity rail travel may be justified on dense routes such as the Northeast corridor, but that they are not justified on low-density or long-haul routes.

CAR RENTAL

Industry Structure

The car rental industry is large and complex, with some features of the industry's operations not found elsewhere in tourism. The industry generates more than one-half of its revenue in the United States, with Europe as the source of most of the remainder.

---

[7] Department for Transport (2004), pp. 12–16, 26; National Rail Enquiries (2007).
[8] Department for Transport (2004), p. 57; Department for Transport (2007), pp. 82–94.
[9] Congressional Budget Office (2003), p. 19.
[10] U.S. Government Accountability Office (2006), p. 24.

TABLE 8.5 Major Car Rental Companies in the United States—2006

Company	Brands	Cars in Service (Average for 2006)	Revenue ($ Billions)
Enterprise Rent-A-Car	Enterprise	630,066	7.0
Avis Budget Group	Avis; Budget	325,000	4.18
Hertz	Hertz	290,000	3.9
Vanguard	Alamo; National	208,400	2.14
Dollar Thrifty Automotive Group	Dollar; Thrifty	85,000	1.53

Data source: Auto Rental News (2007).

In 2006, U.S. car rental revenue was about $20 billion, and Europe's revenue was about $12.5 billion.[11] The largest U.S. car rental companies may also have operations in Canada, Australia, New Zealand, and elsewhere around the globe.

The car rental industry provides a good example of an oligopolistic industry structure, because it is dominated by a handful of very large companies. There are also many smaller regional or local car rental companies. In 2006, there were five very large car rental companies operating in the United States, and they operated eight major brands. (Early in 2007, Enterprise agreed to acquire Vanguard.)

Table 8.5 shows the largest companies, their brand names, and some operational information for the United States for 2006.

Operations

The first step in operating a car rental company is choosing a market segment in which to operate. In this industry there are three primary market segments: business, leisure, and insurance replacement. The largest segment of the car rental industry consists of business travelers picking up rental cars at airports. Many leisure travelers also pick up their rental cars at airports, so that airport rentals account for a very large proportion of car rentals, typically more than 70 percent, for all of the largest car rental companies except for Enterprise. Many leisure travelers also pick up their rental cars at suburban locations to use them to supplement or substitute for their personal vehicles during leisure travel. The insurance replacement market arises from the fact that many people have bought coverage in their personal automobile insurance policies that provides re-placement vehicles in case of accident or theft.

Having chosen the market segment or segments in which to operate, the next thing is to choose locations; there are three general kinds of choices. Car rental locations are generally at airports, at downtown locations, or in suburban areas. Choosing lo-cations is important because of supply considerations and demand considerations, especially the fact that for most companies consumer demand for car rentals is greatest at airports. On the supply side, we see that airport locations are very costly. Airports charge substantial fees to rental car companies for the privilege of locating at the airport. These can be both flat fees and percentages of gross revenues.

[11] Hertz (2007), p. 5.

Downtown locations can also be very costly, while suburban locations can be much less costly.

Many of the large car rental companies have recently been diversifying their revenue sources by expanding their operations outside their traditional areas of focus. A few years ago, Enterprise specialized in serving the insurance replacement market through suburban locations. Most of the remaining large car rental companies concentrated on business and leisure rentals at airports. More recently, Enterprise has been expanding airport rentals, while Hertz and others have been expanding in replacement markets at suburban locations.

With market segments and facilities taken care of, the car rental company then acquires substantial amounts of money to buy its cars. The companies finance these car purchases with cash from operations or by borrowing money in capital markets. Car rental companies typically buy new cars from the manufacturers under one of two types of arrangements. The companies buy the majority of their rental cars under repurchase agreements. Under these agreements the rental companies buy the cars, hold them for many months, and then resell them back to the manufacturers under a predetermined price schedule that depends on the number of months in service and the condition of the cars. The car rental industry refers to these as *program cars*. The alternative is for the car rental company to buy the cars without repurchase agreements. These are known as *non-program* or *at-risk cars*, because the car rental company is taking an unknown risk when it does not know the amount of money it will receive in the future when it sells these cars. Very recently, U.S. auto manufacturers have decided to rely less on "fleet sales" of their cars. For the car rental companies, this means that in the future they will be acquiring a larger percentage of at-risk cars than they have historically.

Car rental companies typically hold their cars for 4 to 12 months and then sell them either through repurchase agreements, in wholesale markets to used car dealers, or through their own retail used car operations. For the largest companies, car buying and selling operates on a mammoth scale. For example, in 2006 Avis Budget Group sold approximately 445,000 cars, and 88 percent of these were program cars.[12]

Car rental companies promote and sell their services through advertising in mass media, through their own sales staffs, who negotiate sales and rates with corporations, through cooperative agreements with hotels and airlines, and through travel agents. They also maintain important customer loyalty programs to attract and serve repeat customers. Internet sales are a large and rapidly growing source of car rental bookings. For 2006, Hertz reports the following distribution of its sources of reservations:[13]

Travel agents	34%
Telephone reservations	30%
Hertz web sites	25%
Third-party web sites	7%
Local booking sources	4%

Car rental companies earn the majority of their revenue from car rentals, but they also earn substantial revenue from selling loss damage waivers, which is similar to insurance and protects renters from some types of liabilities in case rental cars are

---

[12] Avis Budget Group, Inc. (2007), p. 11.
[13] Hertz Corporation (2007), p. 13.

damaged in accidents or stolen. During 2006, Avis Budget Group earned about 4 percent of its revenue from selling loss damage waivers.[14] Car rental companies also earn revenue by selling gasoline and renting equipment such as infant seats, ski racks, and cellular telephones.

Most of the largest car rental companies have both company-owned locations and locations owned and operated by independent entities under franchise or licensing agreements. Generally, but not always, the franchised locations are smaller than the company-owned locations. The franchisees receive the rights to use the company's brand name, the right to access its reservation systems, and other services in exchange for fees based on their revenues or other factors. During 2006, franchisees operated about one-half of the Avis and Budget locations, and the company charged franchisees fees of about 5 to 7.5 percent of rental revenues.[15] As with franchise systems in other industries, car rental franchisees must also meet operating standards established by the company.

Demand for car rental is highly variable over time. Demand varies seasonally, with low points during midwinter and peaks during midsummer. Demand also varies with the business cycle with high levels of demand when employment and business output are high and low levels of demand during low points in the business cycle. The cyclical demand for car rentals closely follows the cyclical demand for air travel, which is not surprising given that such a large proportion of car rentals take place at airports. Demand also varies during the week, with business demand low on weekends and high during the workweek. Car rental companies have at least two basic approaches for dealing with the cyclical changes in demand for their services. Unlike most other firms in travel and tourism, car rental companies have substantial leeway to manage their capacity. Large car rental companies buy and sell hundreds of thousands of cars each year, and they typically keep the cars for no more than one year. This means that, unlike airlines and hotels, car rental companies can vary their capacity at low cost during the year. Car rental companies time their car buying to substantially increase their capacity during the summer and time their selling to decrease their capacity during the winter.

The second approach to dealing with the cyclical changes in demand is to use **peak/off-peak pricing**, lowering prices during off-peak periods and returning them to higher levels during peak periods. Unlike a short-term capacity management described above, peak/off-peak pricing is available not only to car rental companies but also to airlines, hotels, and other service providers in travel and tourism.

We see a simple approach to peak/off-peak pricing in Figure 8.2.

Here we see larger demand and marginal revenue for the peak period, D_p and MR_p, and smaller demand and marginal revenue for the off-peak period, D_o and MR_o. For simplicity, we show constant marginal cost at level MC. In both peak and off-peak periods, the firm maximizes profits by producing output at the point where marginal revenue equals marginal cost. It then charges peak and off-peak prices that make the quantity demanded equal to these quantities. This process determines both peak and off-peak prices as shown in Figure 8.2. The optimal price in the off-peak period is lower than the optimal price in the peak period, and the firm sells less output during the off-peak period. Car rental companies often implement peak/off-peak pricing by offering low weekend rates in areas where peak demand is from business travelers during the workweek.

Peak/off-peak pricing
The process of systematically lowering prices during off-peak periods and returning them to higher levels during peak periods.

---

[14] Avis Budget Group, Inc. (2007), pp. 14–15.
[15] Avis Budget Group, Inc. (2007), p. 7.

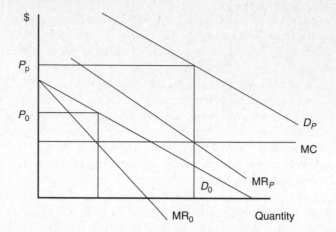

FIGURE 8.2 Peak/Off-Peak Pricing.

Summary

Tourists choose from a variety of travel modes in moving between their origins and destinations. Highway travel by personal-use vehicle (passenger car, motorcycle, or light truck) is the most important mode of tourist travel in the United States. Scheduled airline service is also important, especially for long-distance trips. For intermediate-length trips, tourists can in many cases choose among travel by automobile, train, and bus.

In the United States, Greyhound provides scheduled intercity bus services, and a large number of motorcoach operators provide a variety of tour and charter bus services. These services account for about 2 percent of tourist trips. Train travel provides an important travel mode for many tourists in Europe and to a small extent in the United States, where Amtrak serves intercity passengers. Amtrak provides less than 1 percent of tourist trips. Amtrak's history of financial problems and taxpayer subsidies may eventually require it to focus on serving passengers in densely populated corridors where taxpayer subsidies per passenger are low.

Car rental companies provide important services to tourists and other customers, primarily by renting cars at airport destinations. These companies are unusual in that, unlike airlines or cruise ship operators, they buy and sell a very large proportion of their capital stock each year. That is, they hold their rental cars for typically less than one year, requiring the largest companies to buy and sell hundreds of thousands of cars annually. This flow of car buying and selling allows them to adjust their capital stock to accommodate seasonal cycles of consumer demand. The car rental companies can also use peak/off-peak pricing to maximize profits in the face of cyclical demand.

Bibliography

American Bus Association (2007), "About the American Bus Association," www.buses.org/about_aba/.

Amtrak (2007), "Basic Amtrak Facts," www.amtrak.com/pdf/AmtrakBackgroundInformationFacts-031207.pdf.

Arriva plc (2007), "In Brief," www.arriva.co.uk/arriva/storage/factsheets/corporate.pdf.

Auto Rental News (2007), "2006 US Car Rental Market," www.autorentalnews.com/stats/2006/U.S._Car_Rental_Market.pdf.

Avis Budget Group, Inc. (2007), "Form 10-K, period: December 31, 2006." ccbn.10kwizard.com/cgi/convert/pdf/AVISBUDGETGROUP10K.pdf?pdf=1&repo=

tenk&ipage=4714965&num=-2&pdf=1&xml=1&cik=723612&odef=8&rid=12&quest=1&dn=2&dn=3.

Brown, Chris (2006), "Playing the Market: Rental Car Companies Go Public," *Auto Rental News*, www.autorentalnews.com/t_inside.cfm?action=article_pick&storyID=1050.

Congressional Budget Office (2003), "The Past and Future of U.S. Passenger Rail Service," Washington, DC, www.cbo.gov/ftpdocs/45xx/doc4571/09-26-PassengerRail.pdf.

Department for Transport (2004), *The Future of Rail-White Paper CM 6233*, www.dft.gov.uk/about/strategy/whitepapers/rail/thefutureofrailprintversionc5720.

——— (2007), *Annual Report 2007*, www.dft.gov.uk/about/publications/apr/ar2007/dftannualreport2007.pdf.

Dollar Thrifty Automotive Group (2007), "Form 10-K," http://library.corporate-ir.net/library/71/719/71946/items/240368/2006_AR.pdf.

Enterprise Rent-A-Car (2007), "About Enterprise Rent-A-Car," http://aboutus.enterprise.com/.

Federal Railroad Administration (2007), "Amtrak," www.fra.dot.gov/us/content/274.

Go-Ahead Group plc (2006), "Annual Review for the Year Ended 1 July 2006," www.go-ahead.com/content/doc/cms/Go-Ahead%20Annual%20Review% 202006.pdf.

Gray Line Worldwide (2007), "Fact Sheet," www.grayline.com/grayline/info/au.presscenter.aspx.

Hertz Corporation (2007), Form 10-K, period ending 12/31/2006, http://files.shareholder.com/downloads/HERTZ/148095000x0xS1104659 %2D07%2D24409/47129/filing.pdf.

Hertz Global Holdings, Inc (2007), *2006 Annual Report*, https://images.hertz.com/pdfs/HTZ_2006_annual_report.pdf.

Kahn, Alfred E. *The Economics of Regulation: Principles and Institutions*, vol. I and II, Santa Barbara: John Wiley & Sons, 1971.

Laidlaw, Inc. (2007a), "Laidlaw International Reports Financial Results for Fiscal 2006 and Increases Quarterly Dividend," media.corporate-ir.net/media_files/irol/14/145371/earnings/4Q2006EarningsPRFinal.pdf.

——— (2007b), "Laidlaw International Announces Agreement to Be Acquired by FirstGroup," www.laidlaw.com/phoenix.zhtml?c=145371&p=irol-newsArticle_print&ID=961297&highlight=.

——— (2007c), "Special Meeting of Shareholders," http://library.corporate-ir.net/library/14/145/145371/items/236645/Proxy307.pdf.

Mohring, Herbert. "Optimization and Scale Economies in Urban Bus Transportation." *The American Economic Review* 62 (1972): 591–604.

Morrison, Steven A. "The Value of Amtrak." *Journal of Law and Economics* 33 (1990): 361–82.

Morrison, Steven A., and Clifford Winston, "An Econometric Analysis of the Demand for Intercity Passenger Transportation." *Research in Transportation Economics* 2 (1985): 213–37.

Nathan and Associates (2006), "Motorcoach Census 2005," www.buses.org/files/download/Motorcoach%20Census%202005%2009-21-20061.pdf

National Express Group plc (2007), "Operational Facts," www.nationalexpressgroup.com/nx_as2006/performance/opperf/

National Rail Enquiries (2007), "Train Operating Companies," www.nationalrail.co.uk/tocs_maps/tocs/.

Pindyck, Robert S., and Daniel L. Rubinfeld (2005), *Microeconomics*, 6th ed., Upper Saddle River, NJ: Prentice Hall, 2005.

Schmalensee, Richard. *The Control of Natural Monopolies*. Lexington, MA: Lexington Books, 1979.

Small, Kenneth A. (2007), "Urban Transportation Policy: A Guide and Road Map," www.economics.uci.edu/docs/2006-07/Small-24.pdf.

Stagecoach Group plc (2007), "Annual Report 2007," www.stagecoachgroup.com/scg/ir/finanalysis/reports/.

Travel Industry Association of America (2007), "U.S. Travel Market Overview—Travel Volumes & Trends," http://www.tia.org/researchpubs/us_overview_volumes_trends.html.

U.S. Department of Transportation (2006), Bureau of Transportation Statistics, *National Transportation Statistics 2006*, Washington, DC, www.bts.gov/publications/national_transportation_statistics/2006/.

——— (2007), Federal Motor Carrier Safety Administration "Bus/Passenger Carrier Safety," www.fmcsa.dot.gov/about/outreach/bus/bus.htm.

U.S. Government Accountability Office (2006), "Intercity Passenger Rail: National Policy and Strategies Needed to Maximize Public Benefits from Federal Expenditures," Washington, DC, www.gao.gov/new.items/d0715.pdf.

Winston, Clifford. "Conceptual Developments in the Economics of Transportation: An Interpretive Survey." *Journal of Economic Literature* 23 (1985): 57–94.

———. "Efficient Transportation Infrastructure Policy." *Journal of Economic Perspectives* 5 (1991): 113–27.

CHAPTER 9

Lodging and Restaurants

Learning Goals

- Know what activities make up hospitality.
- Know how lodging firms create value for consumers.
- Know the composition of the lodging industry.
- Understand lodging demand.
- Understand lodging market segments.
- Know how the lodging real estate market operates.
- Understand hotel operations.
- Know how franchising works in the hospitality industry.
- Understand pricing of lodging services.
- Be able to analyze rivalry in the lodging industry.
- Know the basic structure and operations of the restaurant industry.
- Understand how restaurants can use menu bundles to increase profits.

INTRODUCTION

Hospitality industry
The industry that provides business or leisure services to people away from their homes or offices; the industry includes lodging, food service, beverage service, clubs, resorts, casinos, recreation, entertainment, and services for meetings, events, and conventions.

The **hospitality industry** consists of many activities and businesses, which may or may not be operated in combination. These include lodging, food service (including restaurant, catering, and contract food service), beverage service, clubs, resorts, meetings, events, conventions, casinos, recreation, entertainment, and others. One part of tourism that covers all of these activities at the same time is the cruise industry, which we will examine in Chapter 10.

The full range of hospitality is, however, too broad a topic to cover here; so this chapter will look primarily at lodging and, briefly, at restaurant food service. We save casinos for Chapter 13.

LODGING

Lodging firms create value for consumers by providing short-term housing outside the consumers' normal home areas. This can be lodging in hotels, motels, condominiums, bed and breakfasts, campgrounds, resorts, or other accommodations.

The U.S. lodging industry is very large; it is one of the largest components of the tourism industry, similar in size to the U.S. airline industry. Counting properties having 15 or more rooms, in 2005 the industry operated almost 48,000 properties, which contained a total of more than 4.4 million guest rooms. The industry's total revenue was $122.7 billion, and it earned $22.6 billion in pretax profits.[1] On the average weekday in 2003, the U.S. lodging industry sold 2.6 million rooms, and on the average Friday and Saturday the industry sold 2.9 million rooms.[2]

LODGING DEMAND

Lodging demand consists of demand from two main types of travelers—business and leisure. In the United States these types of travelers about evenly split the total demand for room nights, with business travelers occupying about 52 percent and leisure travelers about 48 percent of room nights during 2005.[3] Lodging demand is very cyclical both during the week and during the year. Business demand is relatively strong during the workweek and light on weekends, while leisure demand is the reverse. Overall, including both business and leisure demand, Sunday has the lowest lodging demand while Friday and Saturday have the highest.[4] Both business and leisure demand are weak during the first quarter of the year. Leisure demand for lodging is particularly strong during the summer months.

Lodging demand also varies strongly with the business cycle. Both business and leisure travel demand are high when GDP and incomes are high around the peaks of the business cycle. When GDP rises, we can expect that the demand for lodging will also rise. We define the income elasticity of demand for lodging to be the percentage change in the demand for lodging divided by the percentage change in income. Wheaton and Rossoff (1996) have investigated the effects of income changes on the demand for hotel rooms in the United States. Using GDP to measure the nation's income, they found the income elasticity of demand for hotel rooms to be about 1.8.[5]

Consumers are sensitive to the price of lodging, and we measure this sensitivity with the price elasticity of demand. As with any good or service, we define the price elasticity of demand for lodging to be the percentage change in the quantity of lodging demanded divided by the percentage change in price. Wheaton and Rossoff (1996) estimated this price elasticity for the U.S. lodging industry to be −0.48. Bjorn Hanson (2000) has measured the price elasticity of demand for various segments of the lodging industry using U.S. lodging data from 1987 to 1999. His segments were "upper upscale," "upscale," "midscale with food and beverage," "midscale without food and beverage," and "economy." Hanson found statistically significant price elasticities of demand of

[1] American Hotel & Lodging Association (2006), p. 1.
[2] FelCor Lodging Trust (2004), p. 3.
[3] American Hotel & Lodging Association (2006), p. 4.
[4] Lomanno (2004).
[5] Wheaton and Rossoff (1996), p. 73.

–0.6 for the "upper upscale" segment, –0.9 for the "midscale with food and beverage" segment, and –0.8 for the "midscale without food and beverage." The estimated price elasticities of demand for the other two segments were smaller, but they were not statistically significant. Thus, the demand for lodging in the United States seems to be price inelastic. Using Hanson's results gives a price elasticity of approximately –0.8. This means that a 1 percent increase in the price of lodging would decrease the quantity of lodging demanded by 0.8 percent. Thus, a price increase would increase total room revenue. Lodging firms with monopoly power would increase prices to increase revenue; so that, an inelastic demand implies that there is competitive pressure in the U.S. lodging industry that keeps prices below monopoly levels.

LODGING SUPPLY COMBINES THREE BUSINESSES

Lodging firms perform one or more of three major functions: (1) owning property or real estate, (2) managing lodging operations, and (3) franchising the lodging brand. The lodging industry is in this way substantially different from most other parts of travel and tourism. Most of the large firms in the airline industry, for example, own or lease their own aircraft and operate their aircraft under their own brand names. Car rental firms and cruise lines are similar in that each firm providing the service to consumers owns the capital stock and the brand name, although local car rental operations are frequently franchisees. The lodging industry is different in that, for a typical hotel, ownership of property, management of operations, and franchising are handled by three firms that have no affiliation with each other. Recall from Chapter 1 that Ronald Coase explained that in any industry we expect to observe the firms that do the industry's work at the lowest possible total cost.[6] Apparently, in the lodging industry there are only weak or nonexistent cost advantages to performing property ownership, property management, and franchising the brand name within a single firm.

MeriStar Hospitality Corporation, which private equity firm The Blackstone Group acquired in 2006, provided an excellent example of the split of these three main functions. It owned hotels, but it did not manage any of the hotels it owned. Interstate Hotels and Resorts Corporation, a separate company, managed the MeriStar hotels. Furthermore, neither MeriStar nor Interstate owned any of the brand names on their hotels. The MeriStar hotels carried such names as Courtyard by Marriott, Hilton, Days Inn, and others, which are brand names owned by Marriott, Hilton, and other hotel franchising companies.

Marriott is one of the best-known brands in the lodging industry. In March 1998, the Marriott company split itself into two separate companies, Marriott International and Host Marriott Corp. (Host Marriott Corporation changed its name to Host Hotels & Resorts, Inc., in 2006.) While the old Marriott company was a fully integrated lodging company, owning and operating hotels carrying its brand names, the split separated ownership of property, to be handled by Host Marriott Corporation, from franchising and management, to be handled by the new Marriott International. There are many other examples of the separation among property ownership, hotel operations, and franchising in the lodging industry.

---

[6] Coase (1937).

REAL ESTATE OR PROPERTY OWNERSHIP

Property ownership is the real estate part of the lodging business; that is, someone or some organization owns the hotel property. So, if the company whose name is on the building does not own the building, who does own it? Generally ownership of properties in the lodging industry is very fragmented, with a large number of publicly held companies, private companies, and partnerships owning hotel properties. There are many possibilities. One is that a so-called high-net-worth individual owns the property. For example, in 2004 MSD Capital bought the Four Seasons Maui Wailea resort in Hawaii, and here the MSD stands for Michael S. Dell, founder of Dell Corporation, the computer manufacturer. Many high-net-worth individuals have put some of their investment funds into hotel properties.

Real Estate Investment Trusts

One of the most interesting and important forms of lodging property ownership is through Real Estate Investment Trusts. **Real Estate Investment Trusts** or REITs (pronounced "reets") are specialized businesses with substantial federal income tax benefits and substantial restrictions on their operations. REITs originally were not allowed to earn revenue by operating hotels, although recently the laws have allowed REITs to have subsidiaries that operate hotels. REITs can, however, earn rental income by leasing hotel properties to other companies. To qualify as a REIT, a company must have at least 75 percent of its assets in real estate. REITs must also pay out at least 95 percent of their taxable income to their shareholders as dividends. Furthermore, REITs must have at least 100 owners, and REITs must represent their ownership by transferable shares. Shares of many REITs are traded on stock exchanges including the New York Stock Exchange. There are many other detailed restrictions required for a company to qualify as a REIT, but once a company does qualify as a REIT, it does not pay federal corporate income tax on its income. Rather, the income passes through to the shareholders, where it is taxed along with other income, for example, as personal income when the shareholder is an individual. This is the substantial tax benefit that has encouraged the growth of investment in REITs—this investment does not incur the double taxation of corporate income that most U.S. corporations face. Most corporations pay income tax on their income, and then shareholders pay personal income tax on any dividends the corporations pay. REITs avoid this double taxation because they do not pay corporate income tax.

> **Real estate investment trust**
> A specialized company that owns real estate and receives favorable U.S. federal income tax treatment.

Thus, the idea of a REIT is very simple, it is a company whose purpose is to own real estate and whose shares can be bought and sold. REITs hire management companies to manage their hotels; so that, the REITs themselves do not need the specialized knowledge required to successfully operate hotels. REITs allow individuals and institutional investors, such as pension plans and university endowment funds, to safely diversify into hotel property ownership without knowing anything about hotel management. There is some variation within the lodging REIT industry in how hotel management is handled. In 2001 Congress passed the REIT Modernization Act, which allowed REITs to own taxable subsidiaries that could themselves manage hotels, and some REITs have taken advantage of that opportunity. FelCor Lodging Trust, on the other hand, owns hotels managed by the companies owning the brand names, including Hilton and Starwood.

Hotel REITs grew rapidly in the United States during the 1990s.[7] As of March 2000, Host Marriott Corp., the REIT that emerged from the split of Marriott Corporation, owned 122 hotels containing approximately 58,000 rooms. At the end of 2003, MeriStar Hospitality owned 92 hotels containing almost 25,000 rooms. Hospitality Property Trust is another major lodging REIT.

Integrated Hotel Operating Companies

Some of the major hotel operating companies also own hotels. For example, Hilton Corporation and Starwood Hotels and Resorts are integrated hotel operating companies that own hotels, operate hotels, and franchise their hotel brand names. At the end of 2003, Starwood owned or leased 140 luxury or upscale full-service hotels, managed 286 hotels owned by others, and received franchise fees from an additional 312 hotels. Starwood's brand names include Sheraton, Westin, St. Regis, and others.

Companies owning hotel brand names will not necessarily increase their profits by also owning hotel real estate.[8] Thus, when consumers see value in a lodging company's brand names, such as Marriott or Sheraton, the brand owners can capture some of that value without having their investment funds tied up in the property. Owning hotel properties is a capital-intensive business and the integrated operating companies want to enhance their returns on investment by carefully allocating their capital among alternative uses. Generally, the integrated hotel operating companies want to expand primarily by adding management contracts and franchise contracts rather than by expanding their ownership of properties. For example, Marriott International said in its 2003 annual report that if it buys properties it will quickly sell the properties to recover its investment.[9] Starwood says that it plans to expand as a manager because of the modest capital commitments in that part of the business and to expand its franchise fee income.[10]

Private Equity and Institutional Investors

Private equity funds also own a large number of hotels in the United States and the rest of the world. These firms raise money from wealthy individuals, institutional investors, and others and use the money to buy assets to be held privately; that is, not available for purchase as publicly traded shares on the exchanges. The Blackstone Group is one of the largest and best known of these companies. It is a limited partnership that, among other things, manages private equity and real estate funds. In 2007 Blackstone reorganized itself and issued limited partner shares on the New York Stock Exchange. Since 1992, Blackstone has raised billions of dollars for its real estate funds, and some of this money has been allocated to buying lodging properties. One prominent example was Blackstone's 2004 buyout of all of the shares of Extended Stay America, which had been a publicly traded lodging company. Blackstone paid approximately $3.1 billion in this transaction. In 2007, The Blackstone Group acquired the Hilton Hotels Corporation for approximately $26 billion.

Finally, institutional investors, including insurance companies, pension companies, and other large financial institutions, may themselves directly own lodging properties.

---

[7] McKay (2002), p. 6.
[8] McKay (2002), p. 9
[9] Marriott International (2003), p. 10.
[10] Starwood (2007a), p. 4.

This is in addition to or in place of owning shares of REITs that are available on stock exchanges or investments in private equity funds.

Buy or Build?

There are two ways for a lodging real estate company to get a hotel property—it can buy an existing property or build a new hotel. Usually REITs and other funds look for existing hotels to purchase. They usually look for high-quality properties that will pay a steady return on their investment. Some buyers, on the other hand, look for properties with good prospects for higher earnings after refurbishing, rebranding, or hiring a new management team.

Some of these buying and upgrading opportunities may arise from the current owners' having inadequate capital. Hotel properties need substantial ongoing investments in maintenance and periodic modernization. For example, in a recent year, FelCor Lodging Trust spent more than 7 percent of its room revenue on repair and maintenance of its properties.[11] If owners or operators have failed to keep up with this ongoing requirement, their properties will deteriorate, creating opportunities for improvements, repositioning in the market, and higher room rates.

The other alternative for acquiring new properties is to build new hotels. New construction may be financed with internally generated money, or earnings retained from ongoing operations; but most new hotels' construction relies on some borrowing or debt financing. Normally an individual or company wanting to build a new hotel will put up some of its own money, known as the owner's equity, and will get a mortgage loan from a bank for 60 percent or 70 percent of the value of the property. If there is a gap between the owner's equity and the mortgage loan, the owner will get what is known as *mezzanine financing* to make up the difference. Mezzanine financing is a loan from a financial institution, such as an insurance company; but in the case of a default, or failure of the property owner to pay its required payments on its debt, the mezzanine financing would be paid off only after the first mortgage loan is paid. Thus, mezzanine financing carries a higher risk for the lender and a substantially higher rate of interest to be paid by the borrower.

New construction in the lodging industry is very cyclical. Over the last 50 years or so new construction has gone through periods of boom and bust over long cycles lasting more than 10 years. Designing and building a new hotel property generally takes many years. This long lead time between a decision to build and opening a new hotel for operations creates problems because market supply and demand conditions may change between the time the decision is made and the time the property opens. The hotel business is characterized by long cycles. Part of the cycle is a boom period, during which existing hotels make substantial profits and investors plan new hotels. Then a bust period follows, during which demand is relatively low or supply jumps up as new hotels open and hotels earn lower profits.

FRANCHISING

Well known lodging firms, like restaurants, may offer franchises to others. Franchises are rights to use brand names in selling products or services in a specific place. The franchisee's right to use a nationally known brand name supported by widespread

[11] FelCor (2004), pp. 6, 19.

advertising in mass media and other promotions is an important benefit enhancing the franchisee's prospects for operating successfully. Franchising firms also provide important services to their franchisees, including marketing services, management and staff training, and valuable advice on hotel operations, including designing and building the hotel. Finally, franchisors operate centralized reservation systems which help franchisees communicate with travel agents and guests.

Franchisees pay substantial fees for the rights to use the franchisor's national brand name and for the other services they receive from the franchisors, with the specific terms varying from firm to firm. Generally, a hotel will pay an initial fee and continuing royalty fees, which are a fixed percentage of the hotel's gross room revenue. In the case of Marriott International, this continuing royalty fee is 4 to 6 percent of room revenue along with, in some cases, an additional 2 to 3 percent of food and beverage revenue.[12] Franchisees also pay additional fees to cover costs of promotional programs and for the use of computerized reservation systems. FelCor Lodging Trust reports that its franchise license agreements with the Embassy Suites Hotels brand require a license fee of 4 percent of room revenues, and FelCor pays another 3.5 percent of room revenues as a fee for marketing and reservations system services.[13]

In Europe, hotels have traditionally been owned and operated by families or other closely held companies. One of the most important and famous examples was the Ritz in Paris, owned and operated by César Ritz. European hotels have typically derived the hotel's name from the family or the locale. This has been changing recently as European hotels have moved toward the American model of branding hotels with internationally known brand names. Of course, Ritz has itself become a major brand name, including appearing as part of the Ritz-Carlton name owned by Marriott International. Unlike in Europe, for many decades in the United States most hotel rooms have been in properties operated under a major hotel brand name. Table 9.1 shows some of the major U.S. lodging franchisors and some of their brands.

Marketing representatives and marketing associations are important in creating brand identification in the lodging industry. These marketing companies link independent hotels through joint marketing efforts and centralized reservation systems. They operate around the world and, in many cases, include some of the world's finest lodging establishments. For example, the Rittenhouse Hotel in Philadelphia is a member of the Leading Hotels of the World, while the Lodge at Pebble Beach, the Peabody Hotel in Memphis, and the Dromoland Castle Hotel in Ireland are members of the Preferred Hotels and Resorts Worldwide. Some of the largest and most important of these operations include the following:

- Utell
- Best Western
- Leading Hotels of the World
- Preferred Hotels and Resorts Worldwide
- Relais & Chateaux

---

[12] Marriott International (2007), pp. 4–5.
[13] FelCor (2007), p. 25.

TABLE 9.1 Selected Major U.S. Hotel Brands

Owner: Brand Names

Wyndham Worldwide	Marriott International
Wyndham	Marriott
Days Inn	Courtyard by Marriott
Howard Johnson	Fairfield Inn & Suites
Ramada	Ritz-Carlton
Super 8	Renaissance
InterContinental Hotel Group	Starwood Hotels and Resorts Worldwide
Holiday Inn	Sheraton
Inter Continental	Westin
Crowne Plaza	St. Regis
Choice Hotels International, Inc.	The Luxury Collection
Clarion	Carlson Hotels Worldwide
Comfort Inn	Regent
Sleep Inn	Radisson
Quality Inn	Country Inn & Suites
Hilton Hotels Corporation	Accor North America
Hilton	Motel 6
Doubletree	
Conrad	
Embassy Suites	
Hampton Inn	

Data source: Company web sites and annual financial reports.

MANAGEMENT OF OPERATIONS

The third important piece of the lodging business, and the one we encounter as hotel customers, is management of hotel operations. Management firms, which in the United States often do not own the hotels they operate, work to ensure that basic operations are done well and that guests are satisfied. In some cases, such as Hilton, integrated companies may own the brand name, own the property, and also manage the property. In other cases, a company may franchise the brand name from one company, lease the hotel property from a second company, and then manage the operations of the hotel. Another alternative is that the property owner may franchise the brand name and hire a management firm to operate the hotel.

Hotel management firms take reservations, greet guests, see that rooms are ready to be occupied, provide room service, take customer payments, and so on. As a new hotel approaches its opening, the hotel operator must find people to staff its operations, and the operator must continually train staff and manage labor turnover. Labor is generally the highest single cost category in the hotel industry, and typically a full-service hotel has one person on the staff for each two rooms.

The major operational areas in hotel management are as follows:

- administration (executive management, accounting, human resources)
- sales (business, groups, conventions)
- front desk (guest services, concierge)
- housekeeping
- engineering (heating, ventilation, air conditioning, elevators)
- security
- food and beverage (for full-service hotels only).

Lodging management includes the basic administration of the property, known in the industry as the "back office." These are the important administrative functions that the customer will not normally see, including accounting, human resources management, marketing, and other basic business functions. One important aspect of the back office is the night audit. Each night the accounting department of a hotel will recalculate each customer's bill and, in the case of a customer checking out the next day, will deliver the bill to the customer's room before dawn.

The most obvious of the lodging operations is the front desk, which is responsible for greeting new guests, handling baggage, dealing with customer requests, and other customer service issues. Housekeeping is responsible for cleaning guest rooms, making beds, and similar functions. Engineering is responsible for the most basic physical operations of the hotel, including elevators and heating, ventilation, and air-conditioning, known as HVAC. Hotel managers must also be conscious of hotel security, and the larger properties will have security departments. Finally, hotels will usually have a sales staff whose task is to contact local businesses, travel agents, tour operators, meeting planners, and other groups or institutions to sell the hotel's lodging and other services.

According to Marriott International, there are more than 600 lodging management companies in the United States. Most of these are privately held, but there are, however, some well known publicly traded companies that may also either franchise hotels or own their own hotels.[14] The list below shows some prominent hotel management companies:

- Hilton Hotels Corporation
- Starwood Hotels and Resorts Worldwide
- Marriott International
- Hyatt Corporation
- Interstate Hotels and Resorts
- Crestline Hotels and Resorts
- Kor Hotel Group

The lodging industry promotes its services in ways similar to those used elsewhere and travel and tourism. Lodging companies advertise in mass media, use direct mail, and employ sales staff to promote their services to corporations, groups, and convention organizers. While travel agents book many hotel rooms, they are not as important for the lodging industry as they are for airlines and cruise lines. Lodging companies, like airlines, have loyalty programs for repeat guests. For example, Marriott has "Marriott Rewards" and "Marriott Miles" programs, which provide free stays at Marriott hotels or travel on

---

[14] Marriott International (2007), p. 12.

participating airlines to guests with sufficient stays at Marriott hotels. Hilton and Starwood, among others, also have guest loyalty programs that provide benefits to guests staying at any of the wide range of brand-name hotels owned by these companies.

INDUSTRY SEGMENTS

The hotel industry consists of many segments. One of the most important ways to categorize properties in the industry is by price class, where there are at least four major segments. At the top is the luxury segment, in which rooms are priced at around $250, and in some cases much more, per night. Below this we find the upscale or deluxe segment with prices at around $150 or more per night. The next category is known as the moderate segment with rooms at about $80 or more per night. At the bottom we find the economy or budget segment, with rooms priced typically below $80 per night. Another way to segment the hotel industry is by limited service versus full-service hotels. Full-service hotels include restaurant facilities as part of the hotel and often provide room service, or food service within hotel rooms. They may also have bell personnel to carry travelers' baggage and, perhaps, valet parking. Limited service hotels do not have restaurants as part of the property and provide either limited breakfast service or no food service at all. Limited service hotels do not have bell personnel—travelers carry their bags themselves and park their own cars.

We can also distinguish among hotel segments by location of the hotel properties, and here the major segments are downtown, suburban, airport, highway, and resort. These categories are self-explanatory. Finally, there are a variety of specialty hotels including conference hotels, all-suite hotels, and extended stay hotels. Conference hotels are very large hotels with many guest rooms and extensive conference facilities, including large ballrooms and meeting rooms. All-suite hotels offer only suites consisting of separate sleeping and living areas rather than standard hotel rooms. Extended stay hotels are designed for guests staying more than five consecutive nights; typically they have kitchen facilities and, perhaps, other amenities.

Lodging companies are very conscious of the segments they intend to serve. For example, Starwood Hotels and Resorts Worldwide, Inc., is very clear that it serves the luxury and upscale segments of the lodging market.[15] Companies create brand names to create identity in the minds of particular segments of travelers. For example, the following list shows some of Marriott International's brand names, and it shows brands targeted at many segments:[16]

> *Ritz-Carlton:* luxury hotels and resorts
>
> *JW Marriott:* luxury hotels and resorts
>
> *Marriott:* upper upscale, full-service hotels, resorts, and conference centers
>
> *Renaissance:* upscale, full-service hotels and resorts
>
> *Courtyard by Marriott:* upper-moderate, limited service hotels primarily for business travelers

---

[15] Starwood (2007b).
[16] Marriott International (2007), pp. 8–11.

SpringHill Suites: upper-moderate all-suite hotels

Residence Inn: extended-stay suites with full kitchens

TownePlace Suites: moderate, extended-stay suites with kitchens for business and leisure travelers

Fairfield Inn: lower-moderate hotels for business and leisure travelers

PRICING

Hotels have traditionally had a standard posted room rate, or price for a one-night stay, which is known as the rack rate. This is the rate customer would pay if he or she received no discount or negotiated rate for the room. There are various kinds of negotiated rates. Major corporations negotiate with sales staff from major hotel operators for negotiated corporate rates, which can be substantially below rack rates. Some hotel operators also offer non-negotiated corporate rates, which are discounts off rack rates offered to corporate customers who do not have negotiated rates. Hotel sales staff also negotiate with tour operators, representatives of groups, meeting organizers, and convention organizers for special rates.

In managing their rate structures, hotel managers have typically focused on three measurable quantities. These are the occupancy rate, the average daily rate (ADR), and revenue per available room (RevPAR):

$$\text{Occupancy rate} = \text{number of occupied rooms/total rooms}$$

$$\text{ADR} = \text{room revenue/occupied rooms}$$

$$\text{RevPAR} = \text{room revenue/total rooms}$$

In recent years, average occupancy rates for the U.S. lodging industry have been in the range of 60 percent to 67 percent. From the perspective of a hotel's management, ideally the hotel would have a 100 percent occupancy rate and all rooms would be sold at the rack rate. In this case, both ADR and RevPAR would be the rack rate. The managers, however, can usually only dream of such a situation, as occupancy is normally under 100 percent and the hotel normally sells some rooms at discount rates.

In a few special situations, such as the night before a university's graduation ceremonies, local lodging facilities may be able to sell every room at the rack rate. In reality, facing the law of demand, hotel managers know that usually they can get their occupancy rate very high only by lowering prices. Managers could, for example, send out their sales staffs to fill the hotel with groups paying low negotiated rates. Or they could advertise deep discount packages available to leisure travelers. These marketing activities would raise the occupancy rate, but they would lower ADR and RevPAR, and they would probably not maximize profits available from the property. Alternatively, the managers could give the sales staff opportunities to negotiate low rates with groups for a limited proportion of the available rooms and could promote a few discount packages for leisure travelers. This more moderate approach would raise ADR while lowering the occupancy rate. The effect on RevPAR of such a move is indeterminate. Once again, this would not necessarily maximize profits available from the property. Then we see that the problem for hotel managers is to balance between higher prices with lower occupancy and lower prices with higher occupancy. The general solution to this kind of problem is yield management or revenue management.

Many lodging companies use revenue management or yield management techniques in setting their prices.[17] In this, they are applying knowledge learned from the airline industry. As we saw in Chapters 6 and 7, yield management involves four steps, including dividing customers into groups, using restrictions to keep the groups separate, setting prices, and allocating capacity.

The hotel's revenue manager can identify many groups with different demands, including corporate customers, organized tours, leisure travelers planning far ahead, groups assembling for business meetings or other purposes, and conventioneers. Finally, there are walk-ins, or travelers who appear at the front desk without a reservation, seeking a room for that night. The key to yield management, once again, is to prevent a customer willing to pay only a low price from taking a room away from a customer who is willing to pay a high price. So, for example, the revenue manager does not want to allow the sales staff to sell so many rooms to groups at discount rates that the desk clerk must turn away walk-ins willing to pay the rack rate. Revenue management requires the manager to forecast how many rooms should be held for walk-ins, how many corporate customers will appear at the front desk looking for negotiated rates, and how many rooms remain for the sales staff to sell at discounted rates to groups or to promote at discounted rates to leisure travelers planning ahead.

Marriott was one of the leaders in applying yield management in lodging.[18] Hotel operators have recognized that they were losing revenue under the old system because discounts would be based on the customer's individual negotiating skills and knowledge of industry pricing practices rather than customer demand. The companies were losing revenue when customers haggled with desk clerks for lower rates. To reduce this, the companies have been moving to yield management systems under which discounts are available only to customers meeting restrictions. These restrictions can be things such as advance reservations, nonrefundable advance purchases, length of stay, or day of the week. Discounted rooms are available only when demand is low; when demand is high, management allocates few or no rooms to discount categories. But even when demand is low and discounted categories remain open, with yield management systems in place customers must still satisfy the restrictions to get the discounts. Implementing a formal revenue management process takes away the walk-in traveler's opportunity to negotiate with the desk clerk for an on-the-spot discount.

As with airlines, revenue management increases the revenue to be earned from any fixed number of hotel rooms. It also has certain other advantages for the hotel. The hotel can eliminate on-the-spot discounting, and if necessary the desk clerk can explain the hotel's discounting policies to all customers. The hotel no longer needs to fear that one guest will explain to another guest that he or she got a discount by haggling. Also, guests with nonrefundable advance purchases get discounts for accepting no-show risks that the hotel otherwise accepts with other customers having reservations. Finally, as with the airlines, hotels are saving space for last-minute travelers.

---

[17] Kymes, 1989.
[18] Hanks, Cross, and Noland, 1992.

COMPETITION IN THE LODGING INDUSTRY

Within the United States, as with most other countries, rivalry among lodging firms occurs at two levels—the national level and the local level. There is even rivalry internationally, as when European companies, such as Accor, enter the U.S. market or U.S. firms enter other countries. Within each country there are many vigorous rivals for lodging consumers. In various specific localities, however, there may be only a few rival hotels from which travelers may choose. Lodging firms describe their industry as highly competitive, but they may mean that each of their hotels is in an area that includes other hotels. That is, their individual hotels face rivals in their local markets, which is not the same as being in a highly competitive industry.

As we saw earlier, two of the three basic parts of the lodging industry, property ownership and management of operations, are very competitive at the national level, involving hundreds of firms. Thus, no one firm dominates lodging property ownership or management of lodging operations. Furthermore, there are no barriers to entry into the lodging industry. The third basic part, franchising, is much more concentrated, with a few important firms holding most of the well-known national lodging brands. Over the years, however, new entrants have created new lodging brands.

At the local level, there is a great deal of variety in the competitive conditions lodging firms face. In most cases, we observe rivalry among a few lodging properties that are very much aware of their interactions. That is, each property is aware of the others' service offerings and prices. Each is aware that its decisions affect the others' behavior; for example, a price change by one will affect the prices the others charge. Another important feature of the local rivalry among firms is product differentiation—while some of the lodging properties in a particular place may be very similar, all of them will be somewhat different, at least in brand name. In many cases, the properties may be very different, as when a traveler stopping in a town for the night may be able to choose from among a full-service hotel and a few limited service hotels.

What can we expect in a market of this sort? Do we expect above-normal profits and prices above marginal cost? Recall from your principles of economics course that in a purely competitive market we would see prices at marginal cost and firms earning a normal rate of return. Lodging is not a purely competitive market, as the firms' offerings are differentiated from each other by brand name and other characteristics. Also, in each local market there may be only a few firms, all of which recognize their interdependency. Thus, like airlines and many other markets, this is an oligopoly market.

The Bertrand Model of Oligopoly

One useful model for examining oligopoly markets is the Bertrand model. In the Bertrand model each firm chooses its profit-maximizing price given the prices of the other firms in the industry. As we saw in Chapter 7, the basic Bertrand model is extremely simple. Consider a market consisting of only two firms, firm 1 and firm 2, which are producing a homogenous product—that is, the consumers regard firm 1's hotel rooms as perfect substitutes for firm 2's rooms. For simplicity, assume the two firms have identical costs and let the average cost and marginal cost of offering a hotel room be a constant K. Each firm must choose a price to maximize profits under the assumption that the other firm is also choosing its price to maximize its profits. What will equilibrium look like in this market? Because the rooms are perfect substitutes,

P_1 must equal P_2; otherwise, consumers would only buy the room with the lower price and the firm charging the higher price would sell no rooms at all. Also, in equilibrium P_1 and P_2 must equal K. If either of the prices were above K, the other firm could increase its profits by charging a little less, taking the entire market demand. As the price is going down only a little and the firm is now selling the entire market demand, this would yield higher profits. Also, neither firm would charge less than K because profits would be negative if price were less than average cost. The only outcome that could be a market equilibrium would be $P_1 = P_2 = K$ and both firms earning zero economic profits, or earning a normal rate of return on their investments.

Complications in the Bertrand Model of Oligopoly: Differentiated Products and Capacity Constraints

There are two problems with applying the simple Bertrand model to the lodging industry. First, in the lodging industry the offerings of different firms are not identical, because they vary by brand name at a minimum and perhaps in other ways as well. When products are differentiated, so that consumers no longer regard the products of the two firms as perfect substitutes, price cutting by one firm will not take the entire market away from the other firm. We can use a simple diagram to illustrate the Bertrand model with product differentiation. First we need to derive each firm's reaction function, which in this case will show the firm's profit-maximizing price given the price charged by the other firm. To see one point on firm 1's reaction function, assume firm 2 charges a particular price, which we will call P_2'. Given firm 2's price, firm 1 faces some downward sloping demand curve, because consumers do not regard the output of the two firms as perfect substitutes. Assume marginal cost and average cost are constant at K. Figure 9.1 shows firm 1's situation. Firm 1 maximizes profits by choosing output Q' to make marginal revenue equal to marginal cost, and it charges P_1' to make the quantity demanded equal Q'. (Note that P_1' is greater than marginal cost.) This gives one point (P_1', P_2') on firm 1's reaction function. We graph this point in Figure 9.3.

To get a second point, assume firm 2 charges a higher price, P_2''. If firm 2 charges a higher price than before, then firm 1 will have a greater demand as some consumers substitute firm 1's output for firm 2's. Figure 9.2 shows firm 1's new situation. It will choose output Q' to make marginal revenue equal to marginal cost, and it will charge P_1'' to make the quantity demanded equal Q'. As firm 1's demand is now higher than

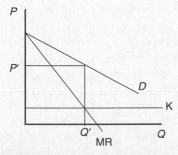

FIGURE 9.1 Firm 1's Output, $P_2 = P_2'$.

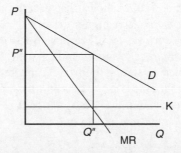

FIGURE 9.2 Firm 1's Output, $P_2 = P_2''$.

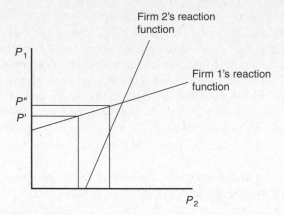

FIGURE 9.3 Bertrand Equilibrium.

before, $P_1'' > P_1'$. We graph this point (P_1'', P_2'') in Figure 9.3. Note that P_1'' is greater than marginal cost.

We now have two points from firm 1's reaction function, which shows firm 1's profit-maximizing prices given firm 2's prices. In the same way, we can graph firm 2's reaction function showing its profit-maximizing prices given firm 1's prices. Figure 9.3 shows both reaction functions. The point at which the two reaction functions intersect shows the combination of P_1 and P_2 at which both firms are maximizing profits given the price being charged by the other firm. This is the Bertrand equilibrium for this market.

Note that in both cases the firm's price exceeds its marginal cost and average cost, K. Thus, unlike the Bertrand equilibrium with no product differentiation, when there is product differentiation firms can charge prices exceeding marginal cost and earn profits. Based on this kind of Bertrand analysis, Jean Tirole develops a "principle of differentiation," whereby firms do not want to compete head on with identical products but rather want to differentiate themselves and establish market niches or clienteles.[19] This allows the firm some market power or protection from being driven by competition to price at marginal cost. We would expect, however, that free entry would tend to drive profits near zero even though the firm retains some pricing power. We certainly see that product differentiation is important in the U.S. lodging industry, as property owners seek to franchise brand names and to use branding and rebranding in their business strategies. Using a more complicated model than we use here and using data from the U.S. highway motel industry, Mazzeo (2002) shows that product differentiation reduces competition and allows motels to charge higher prices.

Firms owning brand names work hard to establish brand names targeted at specific market segments and clienteles. Firms like Starwood, Hilton, and Marriott are explicit in stating their target markets. When they want to enter a new lodging segment, they also create new brand names or acquire brand names with a specific type of customer in mind. Thus, Marriott has created Residence Inn by Marriott, Courtyard

---

[19] Tirole (1988), p. 278.

by Marriott, JW Marriott, and Fairfield Inn as brand names for properties to serve specific market segments. Hilton has acquired the Embassy Suites and Hampton Inn brands. Brand-name owners also have loyalty or frequent guest programs, such as Starwood Preferred Guest, Marriott Rewards, and Hilton Honors, to reward regular customers and encourage travelers to patronize their brands exclusively.

We also see the importance of brand names in the lodging industry in brand-name owners' reactions to the increasing role of the Internet in consumers' search for low prices. Internet hotel room bookings have grown rapidly. Starwood worries that Internet-based intermediaries, such as Priceline or Travelocity, may cause consumers to treat hotel rooms as generic commodities by using general indicators of hotel quality such as "three-star" or "four-star" rather than the company's brand names.[20] Hanson (2004) estimates that the Internet led to a net loss in revenue of U.S. hotels of over $1.2 billion in 2003.

The second problem with applying the simple Bertrand model to the lodging industry is that once the hotels are built, it will generally no longer be true that one firm can serve the entire market demand if it were to lower its price by some small amount. The firm would run into a capacity constraint once all of its rooms were full, leaving the rest of the demand to be served by the other firm, which is charging a higher price. Thus, the equilibrium argument applied above for the simple Bertrand model no longer applies when there is a capacity constraint. Tirole suggests that the Cournot model, in which firms choose quantities rather than prices, is more appropriate than the Bertrand model for industries with rapidly increasing marginal costs, as with firms facing capacity constraints.[21]

FOOD AND BEVERAGE SERVICE

The second major part of the hospitality industry that we will consider here is the restaurant industry. Hospitality firms often provide food and beverage service in combination with lodging services. Full-service hotels have restaurants, bars, and room service, providing food and beverage service to their lodging customers. Airlines, trains, and cruise ships also provide food and beverage service, as do theme parks, stadiums, theaters, and other modes of transportation or attractions. Often, however, food and beverage service is separate from other aspects of travel and tourism, with food and beverage service provided by companies that are independent of the lodging, transportation, or recreation operations.

Commercial food service for tourists and other travelers has been available for millennia. Casson (1994) carefully describes the many varieties of establishments that served food and wine to travelers in the ancient world. A traveler in ancient Rome, for example, could expect to find an inn or *taberna* conveniently spaced along any major travel route. The traveler would find many taverns or other kinds of restaurants in the towns and cities. At Pompeii, the ancient Roman seaside town buried by volcanic ash in the year 79 CE and rediscovered and excavated in modern times, the main street had an eating and drinking establishment of some sort on

---

[20] Starwood (2007a), p. 11.
[21] Tirole (1988), pp. 212–224.

average about every 30 yards along its length.[22] What we would consider restaurants, where diners sit at tables, order from menus, and get served meals that are prepared to order, were present in Hang Zhou, China, by the thirteenth century at the latest.[23] These developed much later in Europe, and developed especially in Paris shortly before and especially after the French Revolution in 1789.[24] Paris was then developing as a commercial and cultural center, and the growth in the numbers of business travelers and the rise in incomes promoted demand for better and more individualized food service. On the supply side, restaurant owners realized they could make higher profits by moving away from the low-quality, communal service that had been common. Also, after the Revolution the aristocracy's kitchen staff had to find other work, and they found their way into a rapidly growing number of restaurants.

Today the food and beverage industry in the United States is huge and diverse.[25] It includes more than 900,000 establishments employing about 13.1 million people, or about 9 percent of the U.S. labor force. Restaurants form the largest category of food and beverage service places. These include what the industry calls "table-service" restaurants, with extensive menus and food cooked to order, and "quickservice," or fast-food restaurants with limited menus and emphasis on speed of the meal's preparation and delivery. As mentioned earlier, lodging operations, transportation facilities, and recreational facilities often provide food and beverage service. Food and beverage retail operations include carryout and vending machines. Educational, health care, and correctional institutions make up important parts of the food service industry. The military, of course, provides food service, as do many businesses and government agencies that provide employee dining.

Food and beverage contract service firms provide substantial services to a wide variety of clients, especially institutional clients. These firms, including Aramark (FY2006 revenues of $11.6 billion)[26] and Sodexo (FY2007 revenues of €13.4 billion, or about $17.7 billion),[27] manage food service operations for corporations, universities, hospitals, correctional institutions, the military, and many other institutions and firms across the United States and elsewhere in the world.

THE U.S. RESTAURANT INDUSTRY

The U.S. restaurant industry consists of two main parts, table service and quickservice. Table-service or full-service restaurants have customers who order from menus with a variety of choices and then wait while the kitchen prepares their selections. There are many kinds of table-service restaurants, from humble seafood shacks to elegant restaurants with extensive wine lists and offerings of haute cuisine. Many table-service restaurants are owned by or franchised from large corporations. These corporations may operate a variety of brand names. For example, Darden Restaurants, Inc., is the parent company operating Red Lobster, Olive Garden, Bahama Breeze,

[22] Casson (1994), p. 211.
[23] Kiefer (2002), pp 63–64.
[24] Kiefer (2002), pp. 59–62.
[25] See National Restaurant Association (2008), and Angelo and Vladimir, 2004, pp. 82–140.
[26] Aramark (2006).
[27] Sodexho Alliance (2007), p. 16.

TABLE 9.2 Large Table-Service Restaurant Chains in the United States—2006

Restaurant Name	Number of Restaurants	Parent Company
Applebee's	1,930	Applebee's International
Red Lobster	680	Darden Restaurants
Olive Garden	614	Darden Restaurants
Chili's Grill and Bar	1,200	Brinker International
Ruby Tuesday	880	Ruby Tuesday, Inc.
International House of Pancakes	1,302	IHOP Corporation
T.G.I. Friday's	833	Carlson Restaurants Worldwide Inc
Denny's	1,545	Denny's Corporation
Bob Evans	580	Bob Evans Farms, Inc.
Cracker Barrel	543	CBRL Group, Inc.

Data sources: Company web sites and annual financial reports.

LongHorn Steakhouse, The Capital Grille, and Seasons 52 restaurants. Other restaurants may independent operations with single locations, and they are often operated by the owners. Table 9.2 shows some of the largest table-service restaurant chains.

Most quickservice restaurants are franchised from or owned by major corporations. The largest of these is McDonald's, with more than 30,000 restaurants located around the world. Table 9.3 shows some of the largest quickservice restaurant chains.

COSTS IN THE FOOD AND BEVERAGE INDUSTRY

Food service providers create value by preparing and serving food and drink for customers. The cost of the average meal in many restaurants is about four times the cost of the ingredients used in preparing it.[28] These ingredients, of course, are not part of value added, because when calculating value added we subtract the value of intermediate

TABLE 9.3 Large Quickservice Restaurant Chains in the United States, 2006

Restaurant Name	Number of Restaurants	Parent Company
McDonald's	31,046	McDonald's Corporation
Burger King	11,129	Burger King Holdings, Inc.
KFC	14,258	Yum! Brands, Inc.
Pizza Hut	12,685	Yum! Brands, Inc.
Taco Bell	5,846	Yum! Brands, Inc.
Wendy's	6,673	Wendy's International, Inc.
Subway	25,000+	Doctor's Associates, Inc.

Data sources: Company web sites and annual financial reports.

---

[28] Daspin (2000).

goods used in production. On average in the United States, value added per employee in the restaurant industry is quite low—in 2006 sales per full-time equivalent restaurant employee were only $61,344.[29] If we attribute 25 percent of total sales to intermediate goods, then this leaves about $46,000 in value added per full-time equivalent employee during the year. This is the amount available to pay all sources of income, including wages, salaries, rents, interest, and profits. As a result of this low value added per employee, average wages and salaries in the restaurant industry, and in food service more generally, are low. Nevertheless, managers in the restaurant industry can be well paid.

Also, profit margins in the restaurant industry are low, and many restaurants fail each year. Restaurant managers face many important challenges in trying to maximize the firm's profits and return at least a normal rate of return to its owners. With low wages, restaurants face high employee turnover. Thus, recruiting, retaining, and training workers are important. Firms must pay special attention to sanitation, food storage, and food handling because of health and safety regulation and the potential for harming customers through contamination. Restaurants face competition from existing restaurants and from new entrants. Either type of competitor may create competitive threats with new menu offerings. Attention to the menu, even in a quickservice restaurant with a limited menu, is important in maximizing profits in the restaurant industry.

USING MENUS TO CAPTURE RESTAURANT CONSUMER SURPLUS

Consumers of any product (or service) may often be able to buy the product for less than the maximum he or she would be willing to pay to get it. We call the maximum price a consumer is willing to pay for a unit of some good or service the reservation price. The best example of this might be a very effective drug that is available in a generic version. Because it is generic, it will probably be available at a low price; because it is very effective in treating the consumer's ailment, it is worth a lot to the consumer and the reservation price will be high. In a case like this, the consumer will be able to buy the drug at a price much lower than the maximum he or she would be willing to pay. Recall from Chapter 6 that we defined consumer surplus as the excess of the value to consumers of their consumption of a good over the amount they have to pay to get it.

For any good or service offered at a particular price, the consumer surplus will normally vary among consumers, because consumers will have different preferences. For example, if diners in a restaurant are all offered an oyster appetizer at $6.00 per serving, some people might regard this as a great treat and a bargain while others would not want oysters at any price. Thus, some of the diners may buy the appetizer and realize a large consumer surplus, some may buy the appetizer and realize a very small surplus, and others may not buy it at all.

While the buyer is very happy to receive consumer surplus, the seller realizes that it could get higher profits by selling its goods at the maximum price each consumer is willing to pay. In the case of generic drugs, competition from other firms prevents each producer from charging a high price. In this case, competition also

---

[29] National Restaurant Association (2008).

prevents the sellers from charging different prices to different consumers. We saw that in the airline industry and the lodging industry firms use yield management to price discriminate, or charge different prices to different customers. How about in the restaurant industry?

Can restaurants increase their profits by capturing consumer surplus? Restaurants normally charge the same prices to all customers—their menus show the prices available to all. Without price discrimination, is there any way to shift the consumer surplus from the consumer to the producer? Yes, there is another way besides price discrimination for sellers to capture consumer surplus, and it is commonly used in the restaurant industry. It is called "bundling." Bundling is the practice of offering to sell a combination of different goods as a package. For example, cable TV companies sell access to stations in packages. The consumer cannot choose among, for example, 150 available channels but, rather, must choose among a few prepackaged combinations of channels. Thus, a consumer who wants a golf channel may only be able to buy it in combination with a few dozen others, including a home-decorating channel which the consumer will rarely watch.

Bundling can shift consumer surplus to sellers, thereby increasing seller profits, when preferences for the available goods are negatively correlated; that is, when consumers who have higher reservation prices for one good have lower reservation prices for another. To see how bundling increases profits, consider a restaurant selling soup and salad. Table 9.4 shows two consumers' reservation prices for the two choices along with the constant marginal and average costs of producing the two choices. If we offer to sell soup at $2 and salad at $2, then both Bob and Ralph would buy both choices, paying a total of $8. If we charged $3 for soup and $3 for salad, Bob would buy salad only and Ralph would buy soup only. Additional revenue from the two sales would be $6. We get additional revenue by charging Bob more for salad and charging Ralph more for soup, but we would lose revenue by charging above the reservation prices on the other two potential sales. Now, suppose we offered only a combination or bundle of "soup and salad," priced at $5. Then we would collect additional revenue of $10, capturing all of Ralph's consumer surplus plus some of Bob's consumer surplus. Thus, we see that when the reservation prices are negatively correlated, the seller can, by bundling, capture some of the consumer surplus without price discrimination.

Restaurants often have separate prices for each item on the menu, known as *a la carte* pricing, and also a bundled price for a combination of menu items. For example, the soup, main course, dessert, and beverage may be offered and priced individually and may also be offered together as a special package. This is an example of mixed bundling, which mixes individual offerings and bundles. This may maximize profits

TABLE 9.4 Reservation Prices with Negative Correlation

	Reservation Price	
Consumer	Soup	Salad
Bob	$2	$4
Ralph	$3	$2

when marginal costs of production exceed some consumers' reservation prices or when reservation prices are not perfectly negatively correlated.[30]

Both bundling and mixed bundling are quite common in tourism and in other industries. In the computer industry, we can buy computers with or without keyboards, monitors, and various types of storage drives. The auto industry offers cars with individual options and option packages. Hotels offer spa packages, golf packages, and many others, in addition to offering rooms and each of these activities separately. In many cases, bundling offers sellers opportunities to increase revenues and profits by capturing consumer surplus for the firm, even in cases when the firm cannot price discriminate.

Summary

The hospitality industry consists of many activities and businesses, and two of the most important are lodging and restaurant food service. The U.S. lodging industry is very large. In 2005 the industry operated almost 48,000 properties and earned over $120 billion in total revenue. Demand for lodging is about evenly split between business and leisure travelers.

Lodging firms perform one or more of three major functions: (1) owning property or real estate, (2) managing lodging operations, and (3) franchising the lodging brand. Ownership of lodging properties is very fragmented, with a large number of publicly held companies, private companies, and partnerships owning hotel properties. Real estate investment trusts, integrated hotel operating companies, and private equity firms are important participants in the lodging property business. In exchange for substantial fees, lodging property owners can franchise well known brand names for their properties. They may also hire one of hundreds of specialized hotel management firms to manage the operations of their lodging properties.

Lodging firms are very conscious of the segment of the market they intend to serve. The hotel industry consists of many segments. These segments are distinguished by price, including luxury, upscale, moderate, and budget segments, by limited service versus full-service hotels, by location, and by special services such as conference hotels, extended stay hotels, and others.

In managing their pricing, lodging establishments offer a standard rack rate and negotiated or other discounted rates. Hotel revenue managers use revenue management techniques learned from the airlines' yield management systems, and they have typically focused on the occupancy rate, the ADR, and RevPAR in judging the performance of their price and revenue management.

Individual hotels face rivals in their local markets and hotel brand owners face substantial competition for consumers' loyalty. The Bertrand oligopoly model is useful for examining hotel market rivalry. Jean Tirole's principle of differentiation says that firms do not want to compete head on with identical products but rather want to differentiate themselves and establish market niches. Hotel brand owners' practice of promoting brand names that are carefully targeted at specific segments and using loyalty programs seems to fit this model well.

Restaurants form the largest category of food and beverage service places. These include table-service restaurants, with extensive menus and food cooked to order, and quickservice restaurants with limited menus and emphasis on speed of the meal's preparation and delivery. Value added per employee in the restaurant industry is often low; so that for most, but not all employees, wages are low. Thus, recruiting, retaining, and training workers are important to success in the industry. Firms must also pay special attention to food storage and handling to meet health and safety regulations and to avoid harming customers through food contamination.

Attention to the menu is important in maximizing profits in the restaurant industry. Restaurants can capture consumer surplus and increase their profits by bundling items offered on their menus.

---

[30] See Pindyck and Rubinfeld, 2005, pp. 408–414, for more on mixed bundling.

Bibliography

American Hotel and Lodging Association (2005a), *History of Lodging*, www.ahla.com/content.aspx?id=4072&ekmensel=935ecbf6_322_332_btnlink.

——— (2007), *2006 Lodging Industry Profile*, www.ahla.com/content.aspx?id=4214

Angelo, Rocco M., and Andrew N. Vladimir. *Hospitality Today: An Introduction*, Lansing, MI: Educational Institute of the American Hotel and Lodging Association, 2004.

Aramark (2006), "ARAMARK Reports Fiscal Year 2006 Results," http://phx.corporate-ir.net/phoenix.zhtml?c=130030&p=irol-newsArticle&ID=931477&highlight=

Baum, Tom, and Ram Mudambi. "An Empirical Analysis of Oligopolistic Hotel Pricing." *Annals of Tourism Research* 22 (1995): 501–16.

Besanko, David, and Ronald R. Braeutigam. *Microeconomics*, 2nd ed. New York: John Wiley & Sons, 2005.

The Blackstone Group (2007), "Form 10-Q," Period Ending June 30, 2007, http://files.shareholder.com/downloads/BX/160754253x0xS1193125%2D07%2D180760/1393818/filing.pdf.

Bob Evans Farms, Inc. (2006), "Form 10-K, Fiscal Year Ending April 28, 2006," http://files.shareholder.com/downloads/BOBE/163220513x0xS950152%2D06%2D5794/33769/filing.pdf.

Burger King Holdings, Inc. (2006), "Form 10-K, Fiscal Year Ending June 30, 2006," http://ccbn.10kwizard.com/cgi/convert/pdf/BurgerKingHoldi10K.pdf?pdf=1&repo=tenk&ipage=4366488&num=-2&pdf=1&xml=1&odef=8&dn=2&dn=3.

Canina, Linda, and Steven Carvell. "Lodging Demand for Urban Hotels in Major Metropolitan Markets." *CHR Reports*, vol. 3, no. 3, Center for Hospitality Research, Cornell University, 2003.

CBRL Group, Inc. (2006), "2006 Annual Report," http://files.shareholder.com/downloads/CBRL/163221611x0x61335/72063B27-6332-44DA-8583-5D5F24302E46/cbrl_2006.pdf.

Cheesecake Factory Incorporated (2006), "Form 10-K," http://ccbn.10kwizard.com/xml/download.php?repo=tenk&ipage=3986645&format=PDF.

Coase, Ronald H. (1937). "The Nature of the Firm." *Economica* n.s. 4 (1937): 386–405.

Crestline Hotels & Resorts (2007), "About: Company Profile," www.crestlinehotels.com/about_company_profile.cfm.

Darden Restaurants, Inc. (2007), "Form 10-K," Fiscal Year 2007, http://investor.dardenrestaurants.com/ir_fi_Edgar.cfm?DocType=Annual&Year=2007.

Daspin, Eileen (2000), "What Do Restaurants Really Pay for Meals?" *The Wall Street Journal*, March 10.

Denny's Corporation (2007), "Form 10-K," Fiscal Year 2006, http://ccbn.10kwizard.com/cgi/convert/pdf/DENNYSCORP10K.pdf?pdf=1&repo=tenk&ipage=4732429&num=-2&pdf=1&xml=1&odef=8&dn=2&dn=3.

Elgonemy, Anwar R. "Debt-financing Alternatives: Refinancing and Restructuring in the Lodging Industry." *Cornell Hotel and Restaurant Administration Quarterly*, June 2002, 7–21.

Frommer, Arthur. *Arthur Frommer's New World of Travel*, 5th ed. New York: Macmillan, 1996.

FelCor Lodging Trust Incorporated (2004), "Form 10-K," Fiscal Year 2003, http://ccbn.10kwizard.com/xml/download.php?repo=tenk&ipage=2670751&format=PDF.

——— (2007), "Form 10-K," Fiscal Year 2006, http://ccbn.10kwizard.com/xml/download.php?repo=tenk&ipage=4714218&format=PDF.

Gee, Chuck Y., James C. Makens, and Dexter J. L. Choy. *The Travel Industry*, 3rd ed. New York: John Wiley & Sons, 1997.

Goeldner, Charles R., and J. R. Brent Ritchie. *Tourism: Principles, Practices, Philosophies*, 9th ed. New York: John Wiley & Sons, 2003.

Gu, Zheng. "Analysis of Las Vegas Strip Casio Hotel Capacity: An Inventory Model for Optimization." *Tourism Management* 24 (2003): 309–14.

Hanson, Bjorn. "Price Elasticity of Lodging Demand." presented to the UCLA Investment Conference, January 20, 2000.

Hanson, Bjorn. "U.S. Lodging Industry Briefing and Forecast." IACVB Outlook Forum, October 5, 2004.

Hanks, Richard D., Robert G. Cross, and R. Paul Noland. "Discounting in the Hotel Industry: A New Approach." *The Cornell Hotel and Restaurant Administration Quarterly* 33 (February 1992): 15–23.

Holloway, J. Christopher. *The Business of Tourism*, 5th ed. Harlow, UK: Addison Wesley Longman, 1998.

Hospitality Properties Trust (2004), Form 10-K, Fiscal Year Ended December 31, 2003.

Interstate Hotels and Resorts (2004), *Annual Report 2003*.

Jones Lang LaSalle Hotels. "Finance Issues in Hotel Real Estate." *Hotel Topics* 1 (September 1999).

———. "Public and Private Hotel Investment." *Hotel Topics*, 10 (March 2002a).

———. "Changing Ownership Structures." *Hotel Topics* 13 (December 2002b).

———. "Global Hotel Investment Debt and Equity Environments." *Hotel Topics* 15 (October 2004a).

——— (2004b), *Hotel Investment Strategy Annual*.

Kiefer, Nicholas M. "Economics and the Origin of the Restaurant." *The Cornell Hotel and Restaurant Administration Quarterly* 43 (August 2002): 58–64.

Kor Hotel Group (2007), "About the Kor Group," http://www.korhotelgroup.com/company/index.html.

Kotler, Philip, John Bowen, and James Makens. *Marketing for Hospitality and Tourism.* Upper Saddle River, NJ: Prentice-Hall, 1996.

Kymes, Sheryl E. "The Basics of Yield Management." *The Cornell Hotel and Restaurant Administration Quarterly,* 30 (November 1989): 14–19.

Lattin, Gerald W. *The Lodging and Food Service Industry,* 5th ed. Lansing, MI: Educational Institute of the American Hotel and Lodging Association, 2002.

The Leading Hotels of the World (2007), "Record Yield Achieves Record Growth," www.lhw.com/download_s/HOTELS%20magazine. pdf.

Lomanno, Mark V. (2004), "US Lodging Industry Overview," Smith Travel Research, ahlaradio.hsyndicate.com/file/152001691.pdf.

Madanoglu, Melih, and Michael D. Olsen. "Toward a Resolution of the Cost of Equity Conundrum in the Lodging Industry: A Conceptual Framework." *Hospitality Management* 24 (2005): 493–515.

Mckay, Melinda (2002), "The Americas," *Hotel Topics,* Jones Lang LaSalle Hotels, 13, December.

Marriott International, Inc. (2004), *Annual Report 2003.*

——— (2007), "Form 10-K," Fiscal Year 2006, http://ir.shareholder.com/mar/downloads/2006_10-K.pdf.

Mazzeo, Michael J. "Competitive Outcomes in Product-Differentiated Oligopoly." *Review of Economics and Statistics* 84 (November 2002): 716–28.

McDonald's Corporation (2009), "Form 10-K," Fiscal Year 2006, www.mcdonalds.com/corp/invest/pub/sec.html.

MeriStar Hotels and Resorts Inc. (2004), "Form 10-K," Fiscal Year Ended December 31, 2003.

Muller, Christopher C. "The Business of Restaurants: 2001 and Beyond." *Hospitality Management* 18 (1999): 401–13.

National Restaurant Association. *State of the Restaurant Industry Workforce: An Overview.* Washington, DC: National Restaurant Association, 2003.

——— (2005a), *Restaurant Spending.* www.restaurant.org/research/consumer/spending.cfm.

——— (2008), "Restaurant Industry—Facts at a Glance," http://www.restaurant.org/research/ind_glance.cfm.

Orkin, Eric (2001), "Hotel Revenue Management and Market Segmentation," *Hotel Online,* www.hotelonline.com/News/PR2001_1st/Jan01_OrkinRevenueMgmt.html.

Pegasus Solutions, Ltd (2008), "Utell Hotels & Resorts," www.utell.com.

Perloff, Jeffrey M. *Microeconomics,* 3rd ed. Boston: Pearson Addison Wesley, 2004.

Perrin, Wendy. *Wendy Perrin's Secrets Every Smart Traveler Should Know.* New York: Fodor's Travel Publications, 1997.

Pindyck, Robert S., and Daniel L. Rubinfeld. *Microeconomics,* 6th ed., Upper Saddle River, NJ: Prentice Hall, 2005.

Relais & Châteaux (2007), "Relais & Châteaux," www.relaischateaux.com/IMG/pdf/PressKit-Corporate.pdf.

Relihan, Walter J., III. "The Yield-Management Approach to Hotel-Room Pricing." *The Cornell Hotel and Restaurant Administration Quarterly* 30 (May 1989): 40–45.

Ruby Tuesday, Inc. (2006), "2006 Annual Report," www.rubytuesday.com/files/2006AR.pdf.

Sims, Kent. *Economics of the San Francisco Restaurant Industry 2003.* San Francisco, CA: Golden Gate Restaurant Association, 2003.

Sodexho Alliance (now Sodexo) (2007), "Reference Document 2006-2007," www.sodexo.com/group_en/Images/sodexo_2007_reference_document_tcm1383943.pdf.

Starr, Nona. *Viewpoint: An Introduction to Travel, Tourism, and Hospitality,* 3rd ed. Upper Saddle River, NJ: Prentice Hall, 2000.

Starwood Hotels & Resorts Worldwide (2004). "Form 10-K," Fiscal Year 2003, http://ccbn.10kwizard.com/xml/download.php?repo=tenk&ipage=2644846&format=PDF.

——— (2007a), "Form 10-K," Fiscal Year 2006, http://library.corporate-ir.net/library/78/786/78669/items/236096/HOT10k.pdf.

——— (2007b), "Company Overview," www.starwoodhotels.com/corporate/company_info.html.

Subway (2006), "Subway® Chain Facts," www.subway.com/subwayroot/AboutSubway/subwayPressKit.aspx.

T.G.I. Fridays (2006), "T.G.I. Friday's® Restaurants Announces New Wine List," http://fridays.mediaroom.com/index.php?s=press_releases&item=87.

Tirole, Jean. *The Theory of Industrial Organization.* Cambridge, MA: MIT Press, 1988.

Vogel, Harold L. *Travel Industry Economics.* Cambridge: Cambridge University Press, 2001.

Wendy's International, Inc. (2007), "Form 10-K," Fiscal Year 2006, www.wendys-invest.com/fin/10k/wen10k07.pdf.

Wheaton, William C., and Lawrence Rossoff. "The Cyclic Behavior of the U.S. Lodging Industry." *Real Estate Economics* 26 (1996): 67–82.

Wilson, Robert H., Linda K. Enghagen, and Prashant Sharma. "Overbooking: The Practice and the Law." *Hospitality Research Journal* 17 (1994): 93–105.

Wyndham Worldwide Corporation (2007), "Form 10-K," Fiscal Year 2006, http://ccbn.10kwizard.com/xml/download.php?repo=tenk&ipage=4728134&format=PDF.

CHAPTER 10

Cruise Lines

Learning Goals

- Understand the historical development of the cruise line industry.
- Understand how cruise lines create value.
- Understand the cruise line business model.
- Know the structure of the cruise line industry.
- Know how international organizations and national governments regulate cruise lines.
- Examine the performance of the industry.
- Analyze growth in capacity and growth in demand in the cruise industry.

INTRODUCTION

When Columbus sailed across the Atlantic in 1492 looking for a shortcut to India, the crossing was not a regularly scheduled event, and he was carrying no passengers. Transatlantic sailings were to remain irregular for centuries more. Regularly scheduled sailings across the Atlantic did not begin until 1818, when the so-called packet ships began scheduled service carrying passengers and cargo between England and New York City. In 1840 Samuel Cunard introduced steam-powered ships to regularly scheduled transatlantic service. Transatlantic steamship service grew rapidly thereafter because the steamships were much faster, safer, and more comfortable than the wind-powered sailing ships they replaced. By the 1950s, thousands of passengers each year sailed across the Atlantic in four days or so on elegant liners such as the *Queen Mary*, the *Queen Elizabeth*, and the *United States*.

The era of the great transatlantic ocean liners came to an end with the growth of transatlantic jet airline service, which began in the late 1950s. By 1959, more people were crossing the Atlantic by air than by sea. During the 1960s, the companies providing transatlantic sailings either shifted their focus to other markets or ceased operations. In the late 1960s and early 1970s, various entrepreneurs created the modern cruise ship industry, which became centered primarily on Caribbean cruising out of Miami.[1] These included Norwegian Caribbean Lines, the predecessor of today's Norwegian Cruise Line, which repositioned its ship *Sunward*, and Royal Caribbean Cruise Lines, which used ships built specifically for cruising rather than point-to-point sea passage.

In 1972, Ted Arison bought one of the grand transatlantic liners, the *Empress of Canada*, and converted it into the *Mardi Gras*, the first of Carnival Cruise Line's "fun ships." The *Mardi Gras* sailed from Miami to the Caribbean with people more interested in enjoying themselves on the cruise ship than in using the ship as a means of transportation to a destination. Thus, the cruise industry has in recent decades converted itself from an elegant mode of transportation into a floating resort experience. In its new form, the industry has grown very rapidly.

The majority of the cruise line industry operates in North America. Most customers of cruise lines are residents of the United States or Canada, and most cruises originate in North America. The Cruise Lines International Association (CLIA), which includes the majority of the world's cruise industry in its membership, reports that in 2005 about 9.7 million of the 11.2 million people who took cruises were in the North American market. Most cruise itineraries involve destinations in the Caribbean, Mexico, or Alaska. There are, however, growing cruise industry segments serving European and Asian consumers. Many of these consumers travel to North America to board Caribbean or Alaskan cruises. European and Asian consumers, along with many North Americans, also cruise the Mediterranean Sea, northern Europe, or the Pacific.

Table 10.1 shows the substantial growth of the North American cruise industry in recent years.

TABLE 10.1 Number of North American Cruise Line Passengers—1994–2005

Year	Passengers (Millions)
1994	4.31
1995	4.22
1996	4.48
1997	4.86
1998	5.24
1999	5.69
2000	6.55
2001	6.64
2002	7.47
2003	7.99
2004	8.87
2005	9.67

Data source: Cruise Lines International Association (2007).

[1] See Dickinson and Vladimir (1997) for the early history and later development of the cruise line industry.

HOW CRUISE LINES CREATE VALUE

Cruise lines create a prepackaged, largely self-contained vacation experience for their customers. Cruise passengers visit pleasant or exotic destinations. But the main activities of cruising are onboard the ship. Passengers eat seemingly unlimited quantities of gourmet food or more casual cuisine, and they take advantage of a wide variety of onboard activities, including casino gaming, dancing, theater shows, shopping, swimming, spa and fitness center activities, reading, and many more. The latest and largest cruise ships offer an amazing range of onboard activities beyond these. One of Royal Caribbean's newest and largest ships, *Liberty of the Seas*, also has a surf park, a water park, full-size boxing ring, a rock climbing wall, an ice-skating rink, and a miniature golf course, in addition to the other many activities and features typically found on large cruise ships.[2]

The first step in operating a cruise line is choosing a **cruise market segment** in which to operate. This determines the broad outlines of the kinds of ships to be designed and built, the kinds of services to provide, and the customers to target. The largest firms in the industry operate in many segments. The cruise line industry has three major segments known as the contemporary, premium, and luxury segments.[3] The nature of the ships, the price, the length of the cruise, level of service and amenities, and destinations distinguish the three segments.

Cruise market segment
A part of the cruise industry distinguished by level of service, price, size of the ship, and destinations; the three main segments are contemporary, premium, and luxury.

One way to look at the price of a cruise is by what the industry calls the per diem, which is the price per day per person. A typical per diem on a contemporary cruise could be well under $200. For a premium cruise, the typical per diem would be $200 to $300. Luxury cruises are often substantially more expensive and can be priced at up to $2,000 per person per day.[4] Prices vary widely depending on the size and location of the guest room, which is referred to as a cabin, stateroom, or, at the high end of the price range, suite or penthouse. Prices for a particular cruise typically also vary over time. Each cruise has a published brochure price, but passengers often pay a discount off the published price. The discounts may vary as the date of the sailing approaches.[5]

Contemporary cruises typically have durations of up to 7 days, while premium cruises typically last 7 to 10 days. Luxury cruises can vary from 7 days up through many months. Most contemporary cruises have destinations in the Caribbean, Mexico, or Alaska. Luxury cruises may also have these destinations, but they often go to more far-flung places. Crystal Cruises, in the luxury segment, describes its 2008 cruise destinations as including South America, Antarctica, the Middle East, the Canary Islands, the Black Sea, Asia, Australia, New Zealand, the South Pacific, the British Isles, the Baltic Sea, the Arctic Circle, New England, and Canada, in addition to the more typical Caribbean, Mexico, Panama Canal, and Mediterranean.[6]

Another factor distinguishing the segment in which the ship operates is the size of the ship. The contemporary segment typically uses larger ships, with today's largest ships accommodating more than 3,000 passengers at a time. Cruise ships in the luxury segment are usually much smaller. Typically, luxury cruises will accommodate only a

[2] Royal Caribbean International (2007).
[3] Carnival Corporation & plc (2005).
[4] Banay (2005).
[5] Coleman et al. (2003), pp. 131–132.
[6] Crystal (2007a).

Gross registered ton
100 cubic feet of enclosed space on a cruise ship.

Berth
A passenger sleeping accommodation on a cruise ship; a double bed counts as two berths.

Space ratio
Gross registered tons per lower berth.

few hundred passengers at a time. The size of a cruise ship is often measured in "gross registered tons." Surprisingly, this is not a measure of weight but rather is a measure of volume. One **gross registered ton** (GRT) equals 100 cubic feet of enclosed space.

Another primary measure of cruise ship capacity in the cruise line industry is the number of lower berths. In the cruise line industry the term **berth** refers to a bed or sleeping accommodation. Most cabins, or cruise ship rooms, have two berths. A passenger traveling alone will ask for a "single," which is a cabin occupied by one passenger even though most cabins have two berths. Some cabins have three or four berths, including two "lower" berths. When reporting their capacities, cruise lines typically report of the number of lower berths only; that is, they report a capacity of two passengers multiplied by the number of cabins.

The size of the ship relative to the number of passengers is another key indicator of cruise market segment. This is measured by the **space ratio**, which is defined as gross registered tons per lower berth. Generally, the space ratio will be in the range of the 30s for contemporary cruises, in the 40 to 50 range for premium cruises, and 50 to low 60s for luxury cruises. For example, luxury operator Crystal Cruises operates the *Crystal Serenity* with 68,000 GRT and 1,080 passengers; so that the ship's space ratio is a remarkably high 63.[7]

Once the firm has determined the segment or segments to be served, it can plan to operate. Firms in the cruise line industry perform the following functions or business operations:

1. financing, or getting large sums of money to buy ships and shore facilities,
2. hiring staff,
3. promoting and selling their services to customers,
4. buying fuel and other supplies, and
5. operating the cruises.

To get an idea of the size of each of these functions, examine Table 10.2, which shows 2004 operating expenses by major category for Royal Caribbean Cruises Ltd., which in 2004 operated two cruise brands, Royal Caribbean International and Celebrity Cruises. In addition to these 2004 operating expenses, the company incurred marketing, selling, and administrative expenses of $588.3 million. Adding these totals gives

TABLE 10.2 FY 2004 Cruise Operating Expenses—Royal Caribbean Cruises Ltd

Category	Expense ($ Millions)
Commissions, transportation, other other	822.2
Onboard and other	300.7
Payroll and related	487.6
Food	269.4
Other ship operating	939.4
Total cruise operating	2,819.4

Data source: Royal Caribbean Cruises Ltd. (2005b), p. F-4.

[7] Crystal Cruises (2007b).

"gross cruise costs" of \$3,407.7 million. This amounts to an average gross cruise cost per available lower berth (two berths per cabin) per day of about \$159.[8]

From Table 10.2, we see that, unlike most of the tourism industry, labor is not the largest cost category in the cruise industry. The figure for "payroll and related," however, includes only labor costs on the ships and excludes the substantial labor costs of shore personnel. These costs, along with advertising and some other expenses, are included in the marketing, selling, and administrative expenses category. The category "commissions, transportation, other" includes travel agent commissions, airline ticket and other transportation costs, and some port costs. Note that this category, which includes commission expenses, is very large, revealing that the cruise industry relies heavily on travel agents to sell their cruises. The category "other ship operating costs" includes fuel, maintenance, insurance, entertainment, and other expenses. The expense category *onboard and other* refers to costs of goods sold on the ship and other related costs.[9]

These operating costs include the costs of *operating* the cruise ships but do not include the costs of *owning* the ships. The accounting cost of owning these ships is the interest on debts incurred to buy the ships plus depreciation, or decline in the value of the ships as time passes. For Royal Caribbean Cruises in 2004, depreciation and amortization amounted to \$394 million and interest expense was \$310 million.[10]

Once the cruise line has selected a segment to serve, the next step is to acquire the vast amounts of money to build the ships. To see the kind of money required, Carnival reports that its *Carnival Freedom*, which entered service in 2007 with a capacity of 2,974 passengers, cost over \$500 million. At the beginning of 2007, Carnival Corp. had commitments for ships under construction or on order for all of its segments costing a total of more than \$10 billion.[11] Royal Caribbean's new "Project Genesis" ships will cost well over \$1 billion each.

The cruise line must then hire the crew and other staff, promote and sell its cruises, and operate its cruises. Let's look at each of these processes.[12]

Cruise ships will typically have approximately one staff person for each two to three passengers. A cruise ship's staff consists of two parts, the "marine crew," which operates the vessel, and the "hotel staff," which serves the passengers. The captain of the ship is responsible for the behavior of both sets of staff, and has help on the hotel side from a hotel manager. These crew members, too, must be fed and housed and provided medical care and other services while the ship is at sea. For example, Royal Caribbean's *Voyager of the Seas* has approximately 1,176 crew members in addition to its 3,114 passengers.[13] Crystal Cruises, in the luxury segment, operates the *Crystal Serenity* with a capacity of 1,080 passengers and 655 crew, for a very low passenger-to-crew ratio of 1.65.[14]

Cruise lines promote their services through mass media, direct mail, and personal selling. Personal selling efforts are aimed primarily at travel agents, as travel agents sell almost all cruises. Travel agents typically receive a commission of 10 percent of the value of each cruise sold, but the commission may go higher for travel agents with unusually

---

[8] Royal Caribbean Cruises Ltd. (2005b), p. 29.
[9] Royal Caribbean Cruises Ltd. (2005c), footnotes.
[10] Royal Caribbean Cruises Ltd. (2005c), p. F-4.
[11] Carnival Corporation & plc (2007), p. F-16.
[12] See Starr (2000), pp. 175–217, for a description of cruise industry operations.
[13] Cruise Lines International Association (2007b).
[14] Crystal Cruises (2007b).

TABLE 10.3 FY 2006 Cruise Revenues—Carnival Corporation (Including Princess)

Revenue Type	Amount ($ Millions)
Passenger tickets	8,903
Onboard and other	2,514
Cruise revenue	11,417

Data source: Carnival Corporation and Carnival plc (2007), exhibit 13.

Onboard sales
Sales of products and services, including alcoholic beverages, spa treatments, casino gaming, photography, and others, to passengers during a cruise.

high sales volumes. Passengers typically book cruises many months in advance. The cruise lines generally require a deposit to be paid shortly after the reservation is made and require a traveler to pay the balance due 45 to 70 days before the sailing date.

On the revenue side of the business model, the main revenue of the cruise line is passenger ticket sales. But a second major source of revenue is what the industry refers to as **onboard sales**. Onboard sales include retail operations, which may vary from gift shops to extensive shopping opportunities on the largest ships. They also include spa treatments, casino gaming, photography, shore excursions, Internet access, and many other sales to passengers. One of the most important categories of onboard sales is alcoholic beverages, which are generally not included in the ticket price outside the luxury cruise category. In 2006, onboard sales made up about 22 percent of cruise revenues for Carnival Corporation (including Princess). See Table 10.3.

STRUCTURE OF THE CRUISE LINE INDUSTRY

Cruise customers come from around the world, but the largest market for cruises is North America. In 2004, Royal Caribbean Cruises received 82 percent of its passenger ticket revenues from the United States.[15] According to Carnival Corporation, the break-down of markets for cruises is as shown in Table 10.4.

The North American cruise industry consists of about 140 ocean-going vessels sailing from Florida ports, San Juan, Puerto Rico, Vancouver, British Columbia, Los Angeles, Honolulu, and other ports. These ships sail primarily to various ports in the Caribbean, Europe and the Mediterranean, Alaska, and the South Pacific. In a few cases, these ships may sail as far as Antarctica, Australia, or even around the world.

TABLE 10.4 Cruise Passengers by Geographic Home Market—2003

Home Market	Passengers (Millions)
North America	8.2
United Kingdom	1.0
Italy, France, and Spain	0.9
Germany	0.5
Australia and New Zealand	0.16

Data source: Carnival Corporation and Carnival plc (2005), pp. 10–13.

[15] Royal Caribbean Cruises Ltd. (2005b), p. F-11.

The industry is made up of a relatively small number of firms, which in some cases are large publicly traded corporations operating in many segments and in other cases are relatively small privately held firms operating in a single segment. The largest participant in the cruise industry is Carnival Corporation, which operates many cruise lines serving every segment. It operates Carnival Cruise Line in the contemporary segment, Holland America Line in the premium segment, and Cunard and Seabourn in the luxury segment. In 2003, Carnival merged with P&O Princess Cruise Lines, which operates many ships, including the *Pacific Princess*. An earlier ship carrying this name was better known as *The Love Boat* from the television show of the same name of the 1970s and 1980s. Carnival Corp. also owns Costa Cruises, which operates primarily in Europe, and AIDA Cruise Line which primarily markets cruises to the German market. Carnival Corporation also operates three cruise line brands, P&O Cruises, Ocean Village, and Swan Hellenic, that primarily market to the United Kingdom.

The second-largest cruise line operator is Royal Caribbean Cruises Ltd., which operates Royal Caribbean International in the contemporary segment and Celebrity Cruises in the premium segment. In 2006 Royal Caribbean Cruises acquired Spanish cruise operator Pullmantur, and Celebrity recently announced the addition of the new Azamara brand cruise line in the luxury segment. Other major operators in the contemporary segment are Norwegian Cruise Line, MSC Cruises, Star Cruises, and Disney Cruise Line. Other major operators in the luxury segment are Crystal Cruises, Regent Seven Seas Cruise Line, and Silversea Cruises.

Capacity of the cruise line industry is growing rapidly as cruise operators continue to add new, and in many cases extremely large, vessels to their fleets. Table 10.5 shows the number of vessels and the number of passenger berths for the major cruise lines.

The cruise line industry is planning a substantial increase in its capacity over the next few years. The operators are ordering new ships, and the ships are in some cases growing ever larger. In October 1999, Royal Caribbean International took delivery of the *Voyager of the Seas*, which at the time was the largest passenger cruise ship ever built, with 3,100 berths and 138,000 GRT, approximately twice the size of the *Queen Elizabeth 2*. Royal Caribbean International's *Freedom of the Seas* entered service in 2006 with 3,630 berths and 160,000 GRT. MSC Cruises has ordered two ships of 133,500 GRT to be delivered in 2008 and 2009. Royal Caribbean's Project Genesis ships will soon sail with 5,400 berths and 220,000 GRT each.

The Shipbuilders

Few companies anywhere in the world can build a cruise ship of more than 50,000 GRT in size. The following three European companies account for almost all of the very large cruise ships in service or on order:

- *Fincantieri Cantieri Navali Italiani:* a company owned by the Italian government
- *Aker Yards:* a Norwegian corporation; it holds various shipyards around the world including two previously owned by Kvaerner Masa-Yards in Finland and two previously owned by Chantiers de l'Atlantique, a subsidiary of France's ALSTOM
- *Meyer Werft:* a family-owned company in Germany

TABLE 10.5 Capacity of Large Cruise Lines—2006

Cruise Lines and Parents	Cruise Ships	Lower Berths
Carnival Corporation	81	143,676
Carnival Cruise Lines	21	47,818
Princess Cruises	15	32,232
Costa Cruises	11	20,218
Holland America Line	13	18,848
P&O Cruises	5	8,840
AIDA Cruises	4	5,378
Cunard Line	2	4,380
P&O Cruises Australia	2	2,474
Ocean Village	1	1,578
Swan Hellenic	1	678
Seabourn Cruise Line	3	624
Windstar Cruises	3	608
Royal Caribbean Cruise Lines	34	67,550
Royal Caribbean International	20	47,900
Celebrity Cruises	9	15,150
Pullmantur Cruises	5	4,500
Star Cruises	21	32,490
Star Cruises	7	7,188
NCL Corporation		
Norwegian Cruise Line	10	20,318
NCL America	3	4,158
Orient Cruises	1	826
MSC Cruises	7	10,758
Disney Cruise Line	2	3,508
Regent Seven Seas Cruise Line	5	2,408
Crystal Cruises	2	2,110
Silversea Cruises	4	1,368

Data sources: Carnival Corporation & plc (2007); Royal Caribbean Cruises Ltd. (2007a); Cruise Line Industry Association (2007); company web sites.

Table 10.6 lists many of the largest new ships under construction or planned for introduction into cruise line fleets as of 2007.

REGULATION OF THE CRUISE INDUSTRY

U.S. government regulation of the cruise line industry provides an interesting opportunity to apply basic economic analysis and to see the power of principles of economics for understanding business behavior. The industry presents a rare opportunity to observe an industry that is both very heavily regulated and in some ways almost completely unregulated. How can this seeming contradiction—being simultaneously heavily

TABLE 10.6 Large Cruise Ships on Order, 2007

Cruise Line	Builder	Year	GRT	Berths	Price ($ Million)
Norwegian	Meyer Werft	2007	93,000	2,384	465
Cunard	Fincantieri	2007	90,000	2,014	513
Carnival	Fincantieri	2008	112,000	3,000	577
Mediterranean	Aker	2008	89,000	2,550	476
Mediterranean	Aker	2008	133,500	3,300	595
AIDA	Meyer Werft	2008	68,500	2,030	375
Holland America	Fincantieri	2008	86,000	2,100	450
Royal Caribbean	Aker	2008	158,000	3,643	750
Princess	Fincantieri	2008	116,000	3,100	616
Celebrity	Meyer Werft	2008	118,000	2,850	641
Mediterranean	Aker	2009	133,500	3,300	595
AIDA	Meyer Werft	2009	68,500	2,030	375
Costa	Fincantieri	2009	92,700	2,260	531
Costa	Fincantieri	2009	112,000	3,000	577
Celebrity	Meyer Werft	2009	118,000	2,850	641
Carnival	Fincantieri	2009	130,000	3,652	666
Royal Caribbean	Aker	2009	220,000	5,400	1,242
Norwegian	Aker	2009	150,000	4,200	935
Silversea	Fincantieri	2009	36,000	540	NA
Seabourn	T. Mariotti	2009	32,000	450	250
Costa.	Fincantieri	2010	92,700	2,260	556
AIDA	Meyer Werft	2010	68,500	2,050	417
P. & O.	Fincantieri	2010	116,000	3,076	700
Celebrity	Meyer Werft	2010	118,000	2,850	698
Norwegian	Aker	2010	150,000	4,200	935
Royal Caribbean	Aker	2010	220,000	5,400	1,242
Oceania	Fincantieri	2010	65,000	1,260	533
Holland America	Fincantieri	2010	86,000	2,100	567
Mediterranean	Aker	2010	89,000	2,550	547
Seabourn	T. Mariotti	2010	32,000	450	250
Carnival	Fincantieri	2011	130,000	3,652	666
Norwegian	Aker	2011	150,000	4,200	890
Celebrity	Meyer Werft	2011	118,000	2,850	798
Oceania	Fincantieri	2011	65,000	1,260	533
Disney	Meyer Werft	2011	122,000	2,500	NA
Oceania	Fincantieri	2012	65,000	1,260	533
Disney	Meyer Werft	2012	122,000	2,500	NA
Silversea	Fincantieri	NA	36,000	540	NA

Data source: www.coltoncompany.com (2007); NA: not available.

regulated and unregulated—occur? The answer is that U.S. regulations are so onerous that there are almost no U.S.-flagged cruise ships. The heavy regulation has driven most of the cruise industry to other countries. Almost all of the cruise ships that call on U.S. ports are foreign-flagged vessels that are not subject to the most onerous U.S. regulations.

Freedom of the High Seas

One of the most well established principles of international relations is that ships of the nations of the world normally have "freedom of the seas"—they have the right to pass unhindered over the open seas from one nation to another. Nations have long claimed rights to control "territorial waters" within some specified distance from their coastlines. Centuries ago this was typically 3 miles, but in recent years many nations have claimed 12 miles or more. These issues are now subject to the 1982 United Nations Convention on the Law of the Sea. This convention codified the 12-mile limit for territorial waters and guaranteed the world's sea travelers the right of "innocent passage" through territorial waters of any nation. It also created the right of "transient passage" through straits, such as the Strait of Gibraltar where the Mediterranean joins the Atlantic and the Strait of Malacca, connecting the Indian and Pacific Oceans between Malaysia and the island of Sumatra.[16]

Cabotage; Passenger Shipping Act of 1896; Jones Act of 1920

Cabotage
Coastal trade within one nation.

This freedom of the seas principle does not apply to **cabotage**, which is coastal, or "coastwise," trade within a nation. For example, carrying cargo or passengers by ship from New York to Baltimore is cabotage, while sailing from Bermuda to Baltimore is not. Each nation is free to restrict its coastal trade in any way it chooses. The United States severely restricts coastal trade through laws such as the Passenger Shipping Act of 1896 and the Jones Act of 1920, which governs the transportation of merchandise. These laws require that ships in U.S. coastal trade must be built in the United States and staffed primarily by U.S. crews and officers. Of course, ships sailing the open seas

Flags of Convenience

All ships sailing the high seas should fly a flag designating their nation of registry. Under the Law of the Sea (Articles 91 to 94),[17] each ship is subject to the jurisdiction of the nation whose flag it is flying, not the jurisdiction of nations whose waters it may be passing through. Each nation may determine the conditions under which it will permit a ship to fly its flag. This process has given rise to the practice of flying "flags of convenience," or flags of nations that have registration fees and laws that are favorable to ship owners. Company web sites show that most cruise ships serving U.S. ports are registered in one of the following nations:

- The Bahamas
- Panama
- Bermuda
- The Netherlands
- Great Britain

[16] United Nations (1998).
[17] United Nations (2008).

from Mexico, for example, to the United States are not subject to the restrictions of the Passenger Shipping Act and the Jones Act because they are not engaged in cabotage.

As it happens, the United States is a very high-cost producer of large ships, and U.S. labor costs for officers and crews are higher than in many other countries. What would the principles of economics suggest would be the result of the imposition of restrictions like U.S. cabotage laws, which would impose very high costs on cruise ship operators? The principle of rational self-interest says that people do the best they can given the constraints they face. It implies that when these constraints change, people's behavior will also change in such a way as to find the new optimal behavior given the new constraints. The result of the attempt to force high-cost labor and high-cost ships on cruise operators is to induce them to shift their operations overseas, which they can generally do very easily by avoiding cabotage. They do this by moving between United States and foreign ports. For example, it is not coastal commerce to pick up passengers in Miami and take them to Nassau in the Bahamas, because the Bahamas is another country. Cabotage laws do not apply in this case. U.S. law allows foreign-flagged cruise ships to serve U.S. ports if they stop in another country on the voyage.

Where do Alaskan cruises originate? Many originate in Vancouver, Canada. The tens of thousands of passengers heading for the many very popular Alaskan cruises

The Strange Case of Hawaiian Cruises

The only place in the United States where the cabotage laws cannot be easily avoided is Hawaii, which is far from any other country. In past years, some cruise lines operating in Hawaii would sail to Fanning Island in the South Pacific, outside the United States, to include a foreign stop in their itineraries. Before September 11, 2001, American Classic Voyages (AMCV) served the Hawaiian cruise market with the only deep-water U.S.-flagged cruise ship, the *Independence*, which was built in the United States in 1951. AMCV declared bankruptcy and ceased Hawaiian operations in October 2001.

In 1999, before bankruptcy, AMCV had contracted for construction of two ships which would have been the first deep-water cruise ships to be built in the United States since 1958, intending to introduce them to service in Hawaii. In 1997, Congress had passed a section of a Department of Defense appropriations bill which encouraged this project, which became known as "Project America." In 1999, the U.S. Maritime Administration provided a $1.1 billion loan guarantee to support the project, and construction on the first of the two ships began in 2000. After AMCV's bankruptcy, construction stopped. In 2002, Norwegian Cruise Line bought the incomplete hull of the first ship and had the hull towed to Germany, where construction on the ship was completed.

Early in 2003, Congress passed a law allowing a subsidiary of Norwegian Cruise Line, NCL America, to flag this ship, which had been completed in Germany, with the U.S. flag. It also allowed the second Project America ship, also to be built in Germany, and another foreign-built ship to be registered under the U.S. flag. These U.S.-flagged ships could then engage in cabotage among the Hawaiian islands. Since mid-2005, NCL America has been sailing the first of the Project America ships in Hawaii as the *Pride of America*. The second Project America ship sailed as the *Pride of Hawaii* but has been been redeployed in Europe as the *Norwegian Jade*. The third foreign-built, U.S.-flagged ship, the *Pride of Aloha*, operated in Hawaii from 2004 to 2008 but has been redeployed in Asia.[18]

[18] Cruise Line Industry Association (2005c); Norwegian Cruise Line (2008a, b).

often fly to Seattle, where buses and ferries take them to Vancouver to board cruise ships. Cruises originating in Seattle stop in Canada at Vancouver, BC, or Prince Rupert, BC, to make the cruise international rather than cabotage. Originating or stopping the cruises at Canadian ports is a rational response by the cruise lines to onerous U.S. cabotage laws.

The result of the potential application of U.S. cabotage laws to the cruise industry is that large, deep-water cruise ships, with the exception of the unusual case of Hawaiian cruisers, are not flagged in the United States. Large cruise ships use predominantly non-U.S. crews and officers. Large cruise ships include foreign ports in their itineraries. Thus, U.S. cabotage laws have done very little to protect U.S. employment in the cruise industry. The main effect of U.S. cabotage laws on the cruise line industry has been to drive most of the industry out of the United States.

Safety of Life at Sea (SOLAS); the U.S. Coast Guard

Have you seen the movie *Titanic*? Not many people have missed it; soon after its release it had the biggest box office gross receipts of any movie ever. Unfortunately, the tragic story of the sinking of the *Titanic* that formed the backdrop for the movie's love story is true. The *Titanic* sank in 1912 after striking an iceberg in the North Atlantic. Over 1,000 people died because there were not enough lifeboats to accommodate all of the passengers and crew, and the available lifeboats were not used effectively. The international community was shocked and outraged by the deadly incompetence revealed by the tragedy, and it took action to prevent a recurrence. In 1914, the maritime nations of the world adopted the Convention on Safety of Life at Sea (SOLAS), which mandated minimum standards for lifeboats, life vests, and other safety equipment on board deep ocean passenger liners. The signatory nations have amended the SOLAS convention from time to time since 1914, most recently in 1974. The International Maritime Organization of the United Nations now administers the international convention, and the U.S. Coast Guard enforces the provisions of SOLAS for cruise ships operating in U.S. ports.

Cruise Ship Sanitation; Centers for Disease Control and Prevention

A cruise ship takes thousands of happy vacationers away from shore and provides all of their needs for food and shelter, usually for a week or more. This involves preparing literally thousands of meals for passengers and crew each day without contact with outside suppliers of food or water. Such a situation creates dangers of food contamination and spoilage, potentially leading to outbreaks of gastrointestinal diseases. During the 1970s as the cruise industry grew rapidly, there were a few cases in which hundreds of cruise passengers at a time suffered from such diseases. The Centers for Disease Control and Prevention (CDC) established its Vessel Sanitation Program in 1975 to regularly monitor sanitary conditions aboard cruise ships serving U.S. ports. Twice a year the CDC performs unannounced inspections of each cruise ship to check on food storage, handling, and preparation along with other sanitary safety issues. Specifically, the inspectors check the following:

- storage and distribution of the ship's water supply;
- food storage, preparation, and service;

- personal hygiene of employees;
- cleanliness and physical condition of the ship;
- the ship's environmental and public health training programs.

After each inspection, the ship gets a score of up to 100 percent, with 86 percent considered acceptable. Each month, the CDC issues its "Green Sheet" showing the results of recent inspections.[19] The Vessel Sanitation Program also monitors reports of illness on cruise ships. The CDC staff investigates if any ship reports more than 3 percent of passengers with diarrheal illness. The Vessel Sanitation Program and the cruise line industry's responses to it seem to have led to substantial reductions in onboard illness.

Passenger Deposits; Federal Maritime Commission

Cruise lines expect customers to pay a deposit soon after reserving their cruises. The remainder of the money due is to be paid well before the cruise starts. This creates risk for the passengers, because they have paid in part or in full before receiving any services. The Federal Maritime Commission regulates cruise lines' handling of customers' money. Specifically, the Commission requires that cruise lines post a bond or other financial surety from which the company may make refunds of deposits when the company fails to deliver the promised cruise.

At any point in time, a large cruise line will be collecting passenger payments on many months of future sailings on many ships. Thus customer deposits amount to a very large sum. To take the most extreme example, on November 30, 2006, Carnival Corporation listed over $2.3 billion in customer deposits on its balance sheet.[20]

Environmental Regulations

Today's modern cruise ships generate enormous amounts of sewage, trash, and other waste products, which potentially could find their way into coastal or deep ocean waters. The United Nations' International Maritime Organization (IMO) sets standards for pollution emanating from cruise ships. The U.S. Coast Guard and the Environmental Protection Agency (EPA) enforce regulations on cruise ship wastewater discharges within U.S. coastal waters.[21] In international waters, the nation in which a cruise ship is registered is responsible for enforcing the ship's compliance with the IMO's International Convention for the Prevention of Pollution from Ships, which was adopted in 1973 and amended in 1978 and is known as MARPOL. The states of the United States may also in some cases specify "no discharge zones" within which cruise ships may not discharge treated or untreated sewage. U.S. federal legislation passed in 2000 and subsequent state action have created special standards for cruise ships operating in Alaskan waters.[22]

Maritime Security

The terrorist attacks of September 11, 2001, and other attacks around the world have profoundly affected the global tourism industry. The United States has recognized the potential for sea-based terrorist attacks. Also, the cruise lines have had an increased

---

[19] Centers for Disease Control and Prevention (2007b).
[20] Carnival Corporation and plc (2007), p. F-2.
[21] Copeland (2005), pp. 7–12.
[22] Copeland (2005), pp. 16–17.

awareness of their vulnerability to terrorist attacks and to piracy.[23] The United States has implemented a wide variety of measures required or authorized under the Marine Transportation Security Act of 2002. While many of these measures deal primarily with cargo transportation, some of these will have an impact on the cruise industry. The United States has also worked with other maritime nations to amend SOLAS to include a new "International Ship and Port Facility Security Code." The code specifies required actions to manage terrorism risks, including implementing ship security alert systems.

PERFORMANCE, GROWTH, AND CAPACITY OF THE CRUISE LINE INDUSTRY

In the last few years, the cruise line industry has seen many mergers, acquisitions, new entrants, and bankruptcies. The Walt Disney Company entered the cruise industry in 1998. More recently, Star Cruises acquired NCL Corporation, parent of Norwegian Cruise Line (NCL); and Carnival and P&O Princess merged. Renaissance Cruises ceased operation on September 25, 2001, while some of its cruises were still in progress.[24]

The more successful cruise lines, however, have been very profitable in recent years, as shown in Table 10.7.

One result of the high profits of successful cruise lines has been the tremendous expansion of the industry through the construction of new ships, as shown earlier in Table 10.6. But how far can the industry expand? Is there danger of over-expansion and excess capacity?

The answer to this important question depends on the relationship between the supply of cruises, which is the total availability of lower berths, and demand for cruises. Recall that demand is the relationship between the price of the good or service and the amount consumers want to buy. For any given growth in availability of lower berths, the industry can reach equilibrium between the quantity supplied and the quantity demanded by either selling all available capacity or sailing with some empty cabins. To sell all cabins with growing capacity, either demand must grow to absorb the capacity, or the price must fall, or both. The main factors influencing demand for cruises are income growth, population growth, and the prices of substitutes and complements. The effectiveness of the cruise lines' marketing efforts in competing with alternative vacations and in inducing vacationers to try cruising for the first time is also important.

Figures 10.1 and 10.2 illustrate the issue facing cruise lines in the future. Figure 10.1 illustrates equilibrium in the cruise market under the assumption that cruise

TABLE 10.7 Net Income of Carnival Corporation and RCCL—2002–2006

Cruise Line Operator	Year and Net Income ($ Millions)				
	2006	2005	2004	2003	2002
Carnival Corporation	2,279	2,253	1,809	1,187	1,011
Royal Caribbean Cruises Ltd	634	716	475	281	351

Data sources: Royal Caribbean Cruises Ltd. (2007b), p. 20; Carnival Corporation and plc (2007), exhibit 12.

---

[23] Klein (2005).
[24] CNN.com (2001).

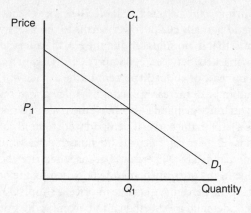

FIGURE 10.1
Equilibrium with Supply
Equal to Fixed Capacity.

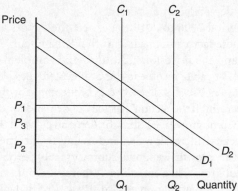

FIGURE 10.2 Market
Equilibrium with
Increased Supply and
Increased Demand.

lines' supply is constant at capacity, which is shown by the vertical line C_1. The price in this market would be P_1 and the quantity Q_1.

In Figure 10.2, we illustrate the increased supply of cruise ship lower berths, retaining the assumption that cruise lines' supply is constant at capacity, by shifting the vertical capacity from C_1 to C_2. If demand were to remain the same, the new equilibrium would be at the intersection of C_2 and D_1. In this case, the cruise lines would have to lower their price from P_1 to P_2 to sell all of their capacity. Suppose alternatively that demand were to increase from D_1 to D_2 while the new ships are under construction, so that the new equilibrium is at the intersection of C_2 and D_2. The cruise lines would only have to lower their price to P_3, which is much higher than P_2.

What can we anticipate about the impact of the new capacity under construction, shown in Table 10.6, on cruise prices? Coleman et al. (2003) note that the cruise line industry capacity increased by a very large amount in 2000 and 2001 with only a small reduction in cruise prices. They estimated the short-run price elasticity of demand to be about −2.0, and speculated that the long-run elasticity of demand might be substantially larger in absolute value (e.g., an elasticity of −3.0 would be larger in absolute value).[25]

Looking at Table 10.5, excluding luxury brands and brands that primarily serve Europe and Asia, the North American market appeared to have almost 200,000 lower

_____
[25] Coleman et al. (2003), pp. 132–133.

berths in the fleet during 2006. Looking at Table 10.6, we see that the brands serving North America will add perhaps 60,000 lower berths to the fleet by 2010. Assume that these are net additions, that is, no ships serving the North American market are retired or diverted to other markets between 2006 and 2010. This increase in lower berths then amounts to an increase of about 30 percent in the capacity of the fleet.

Recall that a fall in price increases the *quantity demanded* but not *demand*. That is, an increase in the quantity demanded is a movement along a demand curve, while a change in demand is a shift in the curve. If demand were to hold constant and the price elasticity of demand is −2.0, we can calculate how much price would have to fall to increase the quantity demanded by 30 percent. Because the price elasticity of demand is the percentage change in the quantity demanded divided by the percentage change in the price, our result for the percentage change in price is simply 30% ÷ 2 = 15%. Thus, if the price elasticity of demand is −2.0, then a 15 percent reduction in the price would increase the quantity demanded by 30 percent.

But over the period 2006 to 2010, we expect the factors affecting demand for cruises to change. These factors that can shift the demand curve are income growth, population growth, and the prices of substitutes and complements. Let us consider income growth alone. Per capita income in the United States has been growing at almost 2 percent per year in recent decades. Then 4 years of income growth at 2 percent per year will be a little over 8 percent. If the income elasticity of demand for cruises is, for example, 1.75, then 8 percent income growth will shift the demand curve to the right by 14 percent (8 × 1.75). Then, because increasing demand owing to income growth will absorb 14 percent of the capacity growth, we should subtract this 14 percent from the 30 percent by which capacity will grow. The remaining 16 percent would need to be accounted for through price reductions. And given a price elasticity of demand of −2.0, this would require a price reduction of 8 percent (16% ÷ 2 = 8%) to absorb the increased capacity not taken up by increasing demand that results from increasing income.

Thus, a rough calculation suggests that North American cruise prices would have to fall by no more than 8 percent to absorb the planned additions to the North American cruise fleet. This downward pressure on price would be mitigated by effects of other factors affecting cruise demand, including population growth. Probably most important among these additional factors is the success of cruise line efforts to promote cruises more widely as alternatives to land-based vacations.

Summary

In the first half of the twentieth century there was a thriving shipping industry carrying passengers between ports, especially New York City and various ports in Europe. Jet aircraft eliminated most demand for this service by the late 1960s. Soon thereafter the modern cruise ship industry arose, primarily with leisure cruises of the Caribbean originating in Miami. Today, most cruises involve destinations in the Caribbean,

Mexico, or Alaska, while European cruises are growing in popularity.

Cruise ships have become giant floating resorts, with today's largest ships accommodating well over 3,000 passengers in a single cruise and costing more than $500 million to build. Carnival Corporation, which operates many cruise lines, including Carnival Cruise Lines and Holland America Lines, serves all segments of the cruise market and has grown to be the largest of the few cruise industry giants.

The main source of revenue of the cruise line is passenger ticket sales. Cruise lines also rely on revenue from onboard sales, which include retail operations, spa treatments, casino gaming, photography, shore excursions, alcoholic beverages, Internet access, and many other sales to passengers.

With the exception of three ships serving Hawaii, all large, ocean-going cruise ships are registered outside the United States. U.S. cabotage and other laws discourage flying the flag of the United States on large cruise ships. Operations on the high seas are governed by international conventions and by the laws of the nation whose flag the ship flies. Cruise lines serving U.S. ports are subject to Coast Guard safety regulation, sanitation regulation, homeland security requirements, and a limited number of other specialized regulations.

Cruise lines are planning large additions to the North American cruise fleet. This increase in supply may cause a small drop in North American cruise prices. Factors increasing demand, including population growth, rising incomes, and cruise line marketing efforts, may reduce this downward pressure on cruise prices.

Bibliography

Aker Yards (2004), "Annual Report 2004," http://hugin.info/134984/R/984901/146779.pdf.

——— (2007), "Annual Report 2006," http://www.akeryards.com/?page=57.

Angelo, Rocco M., and Andrew N. Vladimir. *Hospitality Today: An Introduction.* Lansing, MI: Educational Institute of the American Hotel and Lodging Association, 2004.

Assembly of WEU (2005), "The Future of the European Naval Defence Industry," www.assembly-weu.org/en/documents/sessions_ordinaires/rpt/2005/1916.html.

Banay, Sophia (2005), "World's Most Expensive Cruises 2005," *Forbes.com*, www.forbes.com/travel/2005/10/19/luxury-travel-cruises-cx_sb_1020feat_ls.html.

Bull, Adrian O. "The Economics of Cruising: An Application to the Short Ocean Cruise Market." *Journal of Tourism Studies* 7 (1996): 28–35.

Business Research and Economic Advisors (2005), "The Contribution of the North American Cruise Industry to the U.S. Economy in 2004," August.

Carnival Corporation and plc (2005), "Form 10-K," Fiscal Year 2004, http://ccbn.10kwizard.com/cgi/image?repo=tenk&ipage=3268686&doc=31&fdl=1&cik=1125259&odef=8&rid=12&quest=1&dn=2

——— (2005), *2004 Annual Report*, http://library.corporate-ir.net/library/14/140/140690/items/185374/2004%20Annual%20Report.pdf.

——— (2007), Form 10-K, Fiscal Year 2006, http://ccbn.10kwizard.com/cgi/image?repo=tenk&ipage=4657745&doc=21&fdl=1&odef=8&dn=2.

Carothers, Krista (2005), "When Pigs Float," *Legal Affairs*, July/August, www.legalaffairs.org/issues/July-August-2005/index.msp.

Centers for Disease Control and Prevention (2007a), "Vessel Sanitation Program," www.cdc.gov/nceh/vsp/default.htm.

——— (2007b), "Green Sheet Report: A List of the Most Recent Inspection Scores," wwwn.cdc.gov/vsp/inspectionquerytool/forms/InspectionGreenSheetRpt.aspx.

CNN.com (2001), "Renaissance Cruises Closes," September 26, http://archives.cnn.com/2001/BUSINESS/asia/09/26/aust.cruises.biz/.

Coleman, Mary T., David W. Meyer, and David T. Scheffman. "Economic Analyses of Mergers at the FTC: The Cruise Ships Mergers Investigation." *Review of Industrial Organization* 23 (2003): 121–155.

Copeland, Claudia (2005), "Cruise Ship Pollution: Background, Laws and Regulations, and Key Issues," Congressional Research Service, February 18, www.ncseonline.org/NLE/CRSreports/05feb/RL32450.pdf.

Cruise Line Industry Association (2003), "CLIA Lines Host 8.66 Million Cruise Vacationers in 2002," www.cruising.org/cruisenews/news.cfm?NID=124.

——— (2005b), "CLIA Cruise Lines Ride the Wave of Unprecedented Growth," www.cruising.org/cruisenews/news.cfm?NID=196.

——— (2007a), "Cruise Industry Overview: Marketing Edition—2006," www.cruising.org/press/overview%202006/2.cfm.

——— (2007b), "Cruise Line & Ship Profiles," www.cruising.org/CruiseLines/displayship.cfm~recordID~104.0.cfm.

——— (2007c), www.cruising.org.

——— (2007d), "Technical & Regulatory," www.cruising.org/industry/maritime_industry.cfm.

Crystal Cruises (2007a), "Crystal Cruises Publishes 2008 Worldwide Cruise Atlas," www.crystalcruises.com/mc_release.aspx?PR=403.

——— (2007b), "About the Ship: Crystal Serenity," www.crystalcruises.com/ships.aspx?SH=Serenity&SDL=13.

Cunard Line (2005), "Cunard History at a Glance," www.cunard.com/images/Content/History.pdf.

Dickinson, Bob, and Andy Vladimir. *Selling the Sea: An Inside Look at the Cruise Industry*. New York: John Wiley & Sons, 1997.

Federal Maritime Commission (2005), "Disputes Involving a Cruise Line," www.fmc.gov/bureaus/secretary/DisputesinvolvingaCruiseLine.asp.

Hannafin, Matt (2005), "Norwegian Becomes American, Debuts *Pride of America* with U.S. Hull, U.S. Crew, U.S. Routes and All," *Frommers*, www.frommers.com/articles/2907.html.

International Maritime Organization (2005a), "International Convention for the Safety of Life at Sea (SOLAS), 1974," www.imo.org/Conventions/mainframe.asp?topic_id=250.

——— (2005b), "International Convention for the Prevention of Pollution from Ships, 1973, as Modified by the Protocol of 1978 Relating Thereto (MARPOL 73/78)," www.imo.org/Conventions/mainframe.asp?topic_id=255.

——— (2005c), "Maritime Security," www.imo.org/Safety/mainframe.asp?topic_id=551.

Klein, Debra A. (2005), "After Attack, Cruise Ships Rethink Security," *New York Times*, December 4, http://travel2. nytimes.com/2005/12/04/travel/04prac.html.

McCain, John (2003), "McCain Amendment Strikes Preference for Foreign-Flagged Cruise Line," http://mccain.senate.gov/index.cfm?fuseaction=Newscenter.ViewPressRelease&Content_id=727.

Meyer Werft (2007), "Welcome On Board of the Meyer Werft Website," www.meyerwerft.de/page.asp?main=0&subs=0&websub=m1s0&lang=e.

Norwegian Cruise Line (2007), "About Us," http://www.ncl.com/nclweb/cruiser/cmsPages.html?pageId=AboutUs.

——— (2008a), "Corporate Profile," www.ncl.com/nclweb/cruiser/cmsPages.html?pageId=CorpProfile

——— (2008b), "NCL Corporation Announces Adjustments to Hawai'i Fleet," www.ncl.com/nclweb/pressroom/pressRelease.html?storyCode=PR_021108

Royal Caribbean Cruises Ltd. (2005a), *Annual Report 2004*, http://library.corporate-ir.net/library/10/103/103045/items/146864/2004AR.pdf.

——— (2005b), 2004 Form 10-K, http://ccbn.10kwizard.com/cgi/image?repo=tenk&ipage=3332067&doc=2&fdl=1&cik=884887&odef=8&dn=2.

——— (2005c), "Key Operating and Financial Statistics," http://media.corporate-ir.net/media_files/nys/rcl/Key_Footnotes_102605.pdf.

——— (2007a), 2006 Form 10-K, http://ccbn.10kwizard.com/cgi/image?repo=tenk&ipage=4710110&doc=23&fdl=1&odef=8&dn=2.

——— (2007b), *Annual Report 2006*, http://library.corporate-ir.net/library/10/103/103045/items/248875/06AnnualRep.pdf.

Royal Caribbean International (2007), "Liberty of the Seas," www.royalcaribbean.com/findacruise/ships/class/ship/home.do;jsessionid=0000ggO-HP5ewj3PgOX49dPKo_K:10ktdmpjo?br=R&shipClassCode=FR&shipCode=LB.

Schaal, Dennis (2007), "Ambassadors Closes on Windstar Deal; TPG and Silver Lake Take Sabre Private," *Travel Weekly*, April 9, http://travelweekly.texterity.com/travelweekly/20070409/?pg=18.

Starr, Nona. *Viewpoint: An Introduction to Travel, Tourism, and Hospitality*. Upper Saddle River, NJ: Prentice Hall, 2000.

United Nations (1998), "The United Nations Convention on the Law of the Sea (A Historical Perspective)," www.un.org/Depts/los/convention_agreements/convention_historical_perspective.htm.

——— (2008), "United Nations Convention on the Law of the Sea," http://un.org/Depts/los/convention_agreements/texts/unclos/unclos_e.pdf.

U.S. Department of Homeland Security (2004), "Secure Seas, Open Ports," www.dhs.gov/xlibrary/assets/DHSPortSecurityFactSheet-062104.pdf.

U.S. Maritime Administration (2003), *Compilation of Maritime Laws 2003*, www.marad.dot.gov/publications/complaw03/Table%20of%20Contents.htm.

——— (2005), *Compilation of Maritime Laws 2005*, www.marad.dot.gov/Publications/05%20reports/MaritimeLaws(2005)qxd.pdf.

——— (2006), "North American Cruises 3rd Quarter 2006," http://www.marad.dot.gov/MARAD_statistics/2005%20CRUISE%20UPDATE/cruise%20report%200306.pdf.

www.coltoncompany.com (2007), "Large Cruise Ships on Order," www.coltoncompany.com/

CHAPTER 11

Destinations, Events, and Attractions

Learning Goals

- Understand the importance of destinations in tourism.
- Understand the roles of events and attractions in tourism.
- Know the organization and operations of the U.S. theme park industry.
- Understand the economics of theme park operations.

INTRODUCTION

A **destination** is a well defined place (not a generic place like "the beach") that tourists want to visit. Of course tourists may want to visit a particular destination because it is the home of family and friends or the site of some professional or personal business. In this chapter we will examine features of destinations that appeal to wide segments of the population rather than members of a particular family or employees of a particular business. We will group these features into two categories—attractions and events.

We all know the names of some of the world's most popular and significant destinations, including the nations of Egypt or India, the great cities of the world, including London, Paris, Hong Kong, and New York City, or tropical islands like Hawaii. Tourists want to visit destinations because of the destination's **attractions**, that is, permanent features of the destinations. For example, these could be historical sites, cultural centers, business centers, or extraordinary natural wonders. Tourists also want to visit destinations to attend **events**, which are transitory. Sporting competitions, university graduation ceremonies, and trade shows are a few examples of events that attract tourists. Thus, for example, the Indianapolis Motor Speedway is an interesting and popular attraction every day of the year, and it is also the site of extraordinary events a few days of the year, notably the Indianapolis 500 automobile race on Memorial Day.

Destination
A well defined place that tourists may visit.

Attractions
Permanent features of a destination that draw tourists.

Events
Transitory features of a destination that draw tourists.

The attractions and events that draw visitors to a destination do not have to be as large as Australia's Great Barrier Reef, Niagara Falls, or the Grand Canyon, as significant as the Pyramids of Egypt or the Forbidden City in Beijing, or as exciting as the Las Vegas Strip or the Super Bowl. Consider the example of a small U.S. city, Morgantown, WV. What attractions or events might Morgantown have to bring tourists and other travelers to the area?

There are a surprisingly large number of features that may draw tourists to a small city like Morgantown. The biggest attraction in the area is West Virginia University, with a student population of more than 25,000. Students come to the school, but their parents, other relatives, and their friends also visit Morgantown because the University is there. They come for orientation before classes begin, to bring the students at the beginning of the semester, they come for parents' weekend, and they come for graduation. The university has major sports programs, and visitors travel to the area for football games, basketball games, and other sporting events. It also has theatrical performances, musical performances, and many other events during the year, many of which bring visitors to the area. Morgantown has the county hospital, the University hospital, and other medical facilities, which bring travelers to the area for medical treatment or to visit family members or friends who are receiving medical treatment. Morgantown hosts various fairs and festivals during the year, and from time to time various organizations hold professional meetings in the Morgantown area. Morgantown is the home of a major pharmaceutical manufacturer, and there are banks and other business firms in the area. These businesses also attract visitors, both their own employees normally stationed elsewhere, and salespeople and others who come to Morgantown to interact with the businesses. Thus, while Morgantown is a small city, it attracts a large number of tourists and other visitors, many of whom will require overnight accommodations and, certainly, restaurant meals and other travel and tourism services.

NATIONS, STATES, PROVINCES, CITIES, ISLANDS

In this chapter we will distinguish between destinations (places) and attractions, although in some cases, such as Walt Disney World, the distinction is blurred. Around the world, France and Spain are the destination nations that attract the most tourist arrivals. Each year millions of tourists travel from Northern Europe and the United States to the south of France and Spain's Costa del Sol. Paris, Madrid, Barcelona, and other locations in France and Spain also attract millions of international visitors. Table 11.1 shows the nations with the most international tourist arrivals in 2004.

Some of the most important destinations in U.S. travel and tourism are states and cities. Among U.S. cities, Las Vegas, Orlando, New York City, and San Francisco are some of the most popular destinations. Let us first consider destinations, leaving attractions, such as the Cleveland Museum, Universal Studios Islands of Adventure, and the Statue of Liberty, for later.

Aside from the fact that tourists want to visit these places, an important characteristic of destinations is that they can be marketed. All of the 50 states and the District of Columbia have government-sponsored organizations aimed at marketing the state to tourists and other travelers. In fact, some of the states have more than one such organization. Each state regards tourism as an important part of its economy, and they each spend substantial amounts of money to market itself. The Travel Industry Association

TABLE 11.1 International Tourist Arrivals by Nation—2004

Nation	Arrivals (Millions)
France	75.1
Spain	53.6
United States	46.1
China	41.8
Italy	37.1
United Kingdom	27.8
Hong Kong (China)	21.8
Mexico	20.6
Germany	20.1

Data source: World Tourism Organization (2005).

of America (TIA) annually surveys the states to gather information about their tourism promotion efforts. A recent survey showed that 45 states planned to spend $554 million in total on tourism development and promotion in a single year, fiscal year 2002–2003.[1] Table 11.2 shows the states with the largest tourism office budgets.

The TIA survey showed that the states spent much of this money on domestic and international advertising and related expenditures such as producing, printing, and mailing promotional literature. Many states also have grant programs whereby private companies and organizations can apply for state funds to match some of their own tourism promotion expenditures. States also fund highway welcome centers, Web pages, and many other promotional efforts.

These state-sponsored organizations are some of what are known in the industry as destination marketing organizations or DMOs. In addition to the state organizations,

TABLE 11.2 State Tourism Office Budgets—2002–2003

State	Tourism Budget (Millions of Dollars)
Hawaii	55.98
Illinois	49.69
Pennsylvania	35.13
Texas	31.09
Florida	29.39
Louisiana	17.79
West Virginia	17.03
California	15.70
Missouri	15.19
Virginia	15.00

Data source: Travel Industry Association of America (2006b).

---

[1] Travel Industry Association of America (2006a).

Convention and visitors bureau (CVB)
Local destination marketing organization.

cities, counties, and other subdivisions sponsor DMOs, known generally as **convention and visitors bureaus (CVBs)**. There are many hundreds of CVBs in the United States, ranging from large organizations with substantial programs and expenditures such as the Las Vegas Convention and Visitors Bureau to small organizations representing local areas with fewer tourist attractions, for example, the Greater Morgantown Convention and Visitors Bureau, promoting Morgantown, WV. In the aggregate, CVBs like the state DMOs spend a lot of money making substantial efforts to promote their local areas.

Why do states, cities, counties, and towns spend so much money each year promoting their areas as tourism destinations? The answer is that tourism can bring very large amounts of consumer spending, employment, and income to their areas. Consider one notable example. Bradley Braun (1992) reports that in 1969, Orlando had 36,000 convention visitors who spent about $500,000 while in Orlando. In 1971, Walt Disney World opened near Orlando. By 1989, more than 1.6 million convention visitors visited Orlando, or 47 times as many as 20 years earlier. The spending, income, and employment to support a convention industry that is 47 times larger must be substantially larger. Thus, attracting tourism can have important impacts on the levels of economic activity and the incomes earned in local areas. Researchers have devoted a substantial amount of effort to estimating the actual effects of tourism promotion on tourist spending, local employment, and local income. These efforts are generally known as economic impact studies, which were the subject of Chapter 5.

EVENTS

Throughout history people have traveled to attend events, including religious festivals and sporting events in the ancient world and trade fairs in medieval Europe. Today, the number of events that attract tourists is extremely large, even though many of the events themselves may be small. The total impact of these events on participants, the tourism industry, and on local economies is enormous. Tourism events support tourism industry facilities, including food, beverage, and lodging establishments, in towns and cities around the world; and many tourist destinations, including New York, Orlando, and Las Vegas in the United States, have developed extensive facilities to accommodate events. Universities have in some cases even added event planning as a major field of study in the hospitality curriculum to accommodate the growing demand for qualified people to perform the many tasks needed to conduct a successful event.

The following list gives an idea of the breadth of topics that may be the focus of a tourism event:

- Business (trade show, auto show, boat show, convention)
- Heritage (reenactment, commemoration, celebration)
- Arts and culture (art show, Shakespeare festival, performance)
- Animals (dog or cat show)
- Food (Strawberry festival, wine festival, chili cook-off)
- Sports (championship tournament, golf match, Super Bowl, all-star game, Olympic Games)
- University (graduation, parents' day, move-in day)
- State fair
- Fashion show

- Politics (political convention, demonstration, rally)
- Music (performance, competition, education)

Some giant events, especially cultural or sporting events, draw tourists from around the world. For example, Germany hosted the Fédération Internationale de Football Association (FIFA) World Cup in 2006. This month-long event drew hundreds of thousands of football (soccer) fans from around the world to many host cities in Germany, and it also attracted another 1 billion or more television viewers. Another notable sports event example is cities and nations competing vigorously for the rights to host the summer and winter Olympic Games. The impacts of the Olympic Games on the host cities are huge and long-lasting. Barcelona, Salt Lake City, and Athens, among many other host cities, transformed large parts of their regions by building new facilities to house competitors, competitions, media, and spectators drawn by the Games. One interesting recent example of these large, long-lasting construction projects was the hosting of the 2006 FIFA World Cup final match in the stadium originally built to accommodate the 1936 Berlin Olympic Games.

ATTRACTIONS

As we saw in Chapter 3, there are many reasons why people travel, including business, leisure, visiting family and friends, and personal business. While traveling, people often look for entertainment, cultural heritage sites, shopping, indoor or outdoor recreation, and many other activities. We can think of these travel-related activities as "attractions." In many cases these are natural or historical features. These include ocean beaches, skiing areas, lake or river recreational facilities, historical landmarks, natural wonders, and many others. In other cases, these attractions may be more contemporary constructions, like shopping centers, casinos, theme or amusement parks, museums, sports facilities, and many other kinds of cultural facilities. For example, one of the busiest tourist attractions in the United States is a shopping attraction, the Mall of America near Minneapolis.

Many researchers have studied the economics of recreation facilities, retailing, and, to a smaller extent, museums, and we will not cover those topics here. We will take up the economics of casinos in Chapter 13. Here we will focus on the economic analysis of one major category of attractions—theme and amusement parks.

THEME PARK ECONOMICS

Dorothy Gaiter and John Brecher, wine industry writers for the *Wall Street Journal*, note that Walt Disney World has made a major commitment to developing itself as a wine lovers' destination, with attractions and events for wine lovers, including wines at Epcot's World Showcase and an annual International Food and Wine Festival at Epcot, among others.[2] This illustrates Walt Disney World's role as a destination in itself, a site of theme park attractions, and a site of events such as the food and wine festival. It also gives some hints about key insights of the economics of theme parks, including creating products

---

[2] Gaiter and Brecher (2006).

and services for a variety of categories of customers and cross-selling complementary products and services. Walt Disney World in Orlando is the largest theme park in the world, but the same features of the theme park market dictate the behavior of the entire range of theme parks, from the largest to the smallest.

The Theme Park Industry

Amusement parks began in Europe when developers added entertainment attractions to public gardens. The first mechanical ride that we would recognize as a roller coaster opened in Paris in 1846. In Europe, one of the most significant ancestors of today's theme parks is Tivoli Gardens in Copenhagen, Denmark, which opened in 1843 and still operates today. Chicago's Columbian Exposition of 1893 introduced the first Ferris Wheel. In the United States, Coney Island, New York, was home to some of the major, early amusement parks. In 1927, the famous Cyclone roller coaster was built at Coney Island. Certainly one of the most important events in the development of U.S. theme parks was the opening of Disneyland in Anaheim, California, in 1955. During the 1960s various Six Flags amusement parks opened, and Universal Studios revived their studios tours in California in 1964. Walt Disney World in Orlando opened in 1971.[3]

Today there are approximately 600 theme and amusement parks in the United States, and they are among the country's most important tourist attractions. Europe has another 300 theme parks, and there are a growing number in Asia.[4] These include a wide variety of attractions, including major theme parks, amusement parks, animal parks, aquariums, studio tours, oceanside boardwalks, and many others.

The U.S. theme park industry has grown slowly, both in attendance and in total revenue, in recent years. Table 11.3 shows estimates of U.S. amusement and theme park attendance and revenues since 1996.

TABLE 11.3 U.S. Amusement and Theme Park Industry Growth—1996–2006

Year	Attendance (Million)	Revenue (Billions of Dollars)
1996	290	7.9
1997	300	8.4
1998	300	8.7
1999	309	9.1
2000	317	9.6
2001	319	9.6
2002	324	9.9
2003	322	10.3
2004	328	10.8
2005	335	11.2
2006	335	11.5

Data source: International Association of Amusement Parks and Attractions (2008).

---

[3] National Amusement Park Historical Association (2006); NBC Universal (2006).
[4] International Association of Amusement Parks and Attractions (2006).

TABLE 11.4 Largest North American Theme Parks—2005

Park	State or Province	Attendance (in Millions)
1. Magic Kingdom at Walt Disney World	FL	16.1
2. Disneyland	CA	14.5
3. Epcot at Walt Disney World	FL	9.9
4. Disney-MGM Studios at Walt Disney World	FL	8.6
5. Disney's Animal Kingdom at Walt Disney World	FL	8.2
6. Universal Studios Florida at Universal Orlando	FL	6.1
7. Disney's California Adventure	CA	5.8
8. Universal's Islands of Adventure at Universal Orlando	FL	5.8
9. SeaWorld Orlando	FL	5.6
10. Universal Studios Hollywood	CA	4.7
11. Adventuredome at Circus Circus	NV	4.5
12. Busch Gardens Tampa Bay	FL	4.3
13. SeaWorld San Diego	CA	4.1
14. Paramount Canada's Wonderland	ON	3.6
15. Knott's Berry Farm	CA	3.5
16. Paramount's Kings Island	OH	3.3
17. Morey's Piers	NJ	3.1
18. Cedar Point	OH	3.1
19. Santa Cruz Beach Boardwalk	CA	3.0
20. Six Flags Great Adventure	NJ	2.9
21. Six Flags Great America	IL	2.8
22. Six Flags Magic Mountain	CA	2.8
23. Hersheypark	PA	2.7
24. Busch Gardens Williamsburg	VA	2.6
25. Dollywood	TN	2.3

Data source: Niles, 2005.

The Walt Disney Company owns and operates the largest theme parks in the United States. Table 11.4 shows the approximate number of visitors attending the major North American theme and amusement parks in 2005.

As we have seen, the largest company in the theme park industry is the Walt Disney Company, owner of Walt Disney World in Orlando, Florida, and Disneyland in Anaheim, California. In addition to its U.S. theme parks, it has interests in Disneyland Resort Paris, Tokyo Disney Resort, and Hong Kong Disneyland. The Walt Disney Company is a very large, highly diversified entertainment and media company. It is also a major producer of animated and live action movies and television shows, and it owns ABC television and ESPN cable sports network, among many other activities. Walt Disney is, however, not the only large operator in the theme park industry.

Six Flags, Inc., operates 29 parks in the United States, Mexico, and Canada. The following list shows some of the company's major attractions:

• Six Flags America, MD
• Six Flags Elitch Gardens, Denver

- Six Flags Fiesta Texas
- Six Flags Great Adventure, Six Flags Hurricane Harbor, and Six Flags Wild Safari, NJ
- Six Flags Great America, IL
- Six Flags Hurricane Harbor, Six Flags Magic Mountain, Los Angeles
- Six Flags Marine World, San Francisco
- Six Flags Mexico
- Six Flags Over Georgia, Six Flags White Water Atlanta, Atlanta
- Six Flags Over Texas, Six Flags Hurricane Harbor, Dallas-Ft. Worth

The Anheuser-Busch Company is the third largest U.S. theme park operator, through its wholly owned subsidiary Busch Entertainment Corp. The company owns nine theme parks:

- Adventure Island, Tampa
- Busch Gardens, Tampa
- Busch Gardens, Williamsburg
- Discovery Cove, Orlando
- SeaWorld, Orlando
- SeaWorld, San Antonio
- SeaWorld, San Diego
- Sesame Place, Langhorne, PA, (near Philadelphia)
- Water Country, U.S.A., Williamsburg

NBC Universal, a subsidiary with ownership split between General Electric Corporation (80 percent) and Vivendi Universal (20 percent), is another diversified entertainment company operating music and movie production operations along with its Universal Parks and Resorts. The last includes the Universal Studios Hollywood theme park, the Universal Studios Florida and Islands of Adventure theme parks in Orlando, Universal Studios Japan, and Universal Mediterranea, near Barcelona.

Cedar Fair, L.P., operates 18 amusement parks and water parks in the United States and Canada, having acquired Paramount Parks, which had been previously owned by CBS Corporation. The Cedar Fair parks include Cedar Point and Kings Island in Ohio, Kings Dominion in Virginia, Canada's Wonderland in Ontario, and Knott's Berry Farm in California, among others.

Operations

Theme and amusement parks derive their revenue from admissions charges, food and beverage sales, merchandise sales, charges for some games and rides, charges for some attractions, and other miscellaneous charges. Often games, rides, and attractions are available at no extra charge after the admission fee has been paid. Six Flags reports that in 2005 it received 54 percent of its total revenue from admission charges.[5]

Many U.S. parks operate during the summer season between Memorial Day and Labor Day. Other parks, including those in Orlando and Southern California, operate year round. Although all major theme park operators have some year-round employees,

---

[5] Six Flags (2006), p. 34.

theme park employment is highly seasonal, matching the seasonality of demand and the operating calendar.

Theme and amusement parks have high **fixed costs**, including costs of land, costs of constructing and maintaining facilities, and labor costs required to maintain operations at least at some minimal level. Six Flags estimates that a competitor would need to spend at least $200 million over a two-year period to build a theme park comparable to a Six Flags park.[6]

Most of the costs of operating a theme park fall into the following categories:

Land: In many cases, the theme park operates on land owned by the company, while in other cases the company leases the land from public or private landholders. In the long run, theme park operators can acquire new land, develop previously undeveloped land adjoining existing parks, sell land, or terminate leases.

Rides: Park operators incur substantial capital costs, including interest and depreciation expenses, to install rides. There are also operating costs which include maintenance and repair, insurance, and labor for operations. Ride equipment can be and, from time to time, is moved among parks to create variety from year to year or to respond to changing demands.

Selling: Theme park operators incur costs to sell tickets, including selling to groups along with advertising and other promotions.

Other: Food and beverage operations, merchandise sales, utilities, insurance, licensing fees, security, and others.

Most of these theme park costs are fixed within a wide range of attendance. Revenues, on the other hand, are directly related to park attendance and ticket pricing. Thus, theme and amusement park profits vary widely with attendance and with pricing mechanisms.

Optimal Behavior with High Fixed Costs and Low Marginal Costs

In their book *Information Rules*,[7] Shapiro and Varian discuss optimal business firm behavior in the information industry, where there are high fixed costs and very low marginal costs. They describe much of the information industry, especially online and software firms, as having very high "first copy" costs and very low costs for additional copies, such as when a publisher posts content on the Internet. Here the initial cost of creating the content may be very large, while consumer downloads of the content may cost approximately zero.

Within wide limits up to the capacity of the park, this could also describe the cost structure of the theme park industry. If a theme park is to have mechanical rides such as roller coasters, the cost of the "first ride" is enormous, while the cost of the second ride is near zero. Once the ride is built and staffed, any additional rides up to capacity have little or no additional cost. Thus, like Shapiro and Varian in analyzing the information industry, we can understand much of the behavior of theme park firms as

Fixed costs
Costs that do not vary with the level of output produced.

---

[6] Six Flags (2006), p. 3.
[7] Shapiro and Varian (1999).

optimal reactions to a production process that has high fixed costs and very low marginal costs. Also, the guidance for profit-maximizing behavior that Shapiro and Varian derive from economic analysis of the information industry often applies directly to the theme park industry. Among many other potential actions by the firm, Shapiro and Varian recommend product differentiation, customer lock-in, price discrimination, and cross-selling of complementary products.

PRODUCT DIFFERENTIATION   A firm operating in a highly competitive market may be forced to be a *price taker*; that is, a firm that takes the market price as given. Furthermore, for a purely competitive firm this price will be at the level of marginal cost. When marginal cost is near zero, pricing at this level will be a problem, because earning any revenue will be difficult. One important way to avoid marginal cost pricing is **product differentiation**; that is, selling a product or service that, in the view of consumers, is different in important ways from others available in the market. (A common example of this kind of market is the market for haircuts. Many people, including students, assert that they care a great deal about who cuts their hair, even though the majority of barber shops and beauty salons seem to be quite similar to each other. This is an example of product differentiation in what seems to be a rather uniform service.)

Theme parks differentiate themselves in many ways. One of the most important is location, although in many cases consumers will have more than one choice of theme parks within reach. They also differentiate themselves through rides and amusements, competing, for example, to have the most, or the highest, or the fastest roller coasters.

One important way theme parks differentiate themselves is through themed rides and other attractions based on well known characters designed to appeal to children and their parents. Disney, of course, has a great many characters on which to base themed attractions. These include the many very well known characters that have appeared over many decades in Disney's animated movies, including Mickey Mouse, Donald Duck, Cinderella, Snow White, and many more. Six Flags licenses the rights to popular and well recognized characters featured in popular Warner Brothers cartoons, including Bugs Bunny, Daffy Duck, Yosemite Sam, and in DC Comics comic books, including Superman and Batman. Six Flags uses these exclusive theme park rights to create attractions with themes based on these characters. Universal Studios has exclusive theme park rights to characters from Dr. Seuss's many children's books, including *The Cat in the Hat*, and the cartoon character Popeye. Universal Studios also has exclusive theme park rights to copyrighted material, including characters, logos, and images, from the *Jurassic Park* movies.

CUSTOMER LOCK-IN   In an industry with many competitors selling similar products or services, customers may choose which firm to patronize and also may switch among firms from time to time or product to product. **Customer lock-in** refers to raising their customers' cost of switching to another firm. Firms have tried many methods of customer lock-in. A wide variety of firms in the tourism industry use customer loyalty programs to lock in consumers. In the theme park industry, season passes are one form of loyalty or lock-in program. Once the consumer has bought the season pass for one company's theme parks, he or she may make unlimited visits to those parks at little or no additional cost, while visiting the parks of another firm will require paying another admission charge. In many cases we can expect that consumers will buy the season pass for only one company's theme parks and patronize that company exclusively.

Product differentiation
Making a firm's product or service different in ways important to consumers from other similar products or services available in the market.

Customer lock-in
Raising the customers' cost of switching to another firm.

SELLING COMPLEMENTARY PRODUCTS   In an industry with low marginal costs, there may be pressure to keep some prices low, while there are opportunities to raise prices on other, complementary, products. In the theme and amusement park industry there are many opportunities to do this. Perhaps the most obvious is food and beverage sales. For the larger parks, a typical visit lasts many hours, so customers will be in the parks during meal times. Furthermore, the outdoor, physical activity will make the patrons thirsty and hungry. Theme parks offer their visitors many opportunities to buy food and beverages; and typically prices of food and beverages inside the parks are quite high.

Retail sales of all sorts of goods provide another set of opportunities to sell complementary products. In most cases, theme and amusement parks offer visitors many opportunities for shopping. This includes shopping for batteries, toys and plush replicas of the licensed characters on which the parks base many of their themes. But theme park shopping may also include less obvious opportunities such as jewelry, art work, and even real estate.

Overall, sales of complementary products and services are quite important to the theme park industry. For example, Six Flags reports 2005 total revenue for "theme park food, merchandise, and other" of just over $500 million. This is almost as high as the $588 million in revenue from theme park admissions.[8]

PRICE DISCRIMINATION   As we saw in Chapter 6, price discrimination refers to charging different prices for different sales of the same good or service. There are many ways firms can price discriminate, and these are often grouped into three categories, called first-degree, second-degree, and third-degree price discrimination. Theme parks might use all three forms of price discrimination.

First-Degree Price Discrimination.   First-degree price discrimination entails charging the highest possible price for *each unit* of the good or service sold. While theme parks are not going to be successful in charging the highest possible price for each visit and each ride, they can make some progress in this direction by charging personalized prices, or prices tailored to each individual customer.[9] To do this, the firm must understand consumer demand for its services and have detailed information about the consumer's individual characteristics that are likely to influence demand. Firms can gather and use this information through database marketing. The database of consumer information may be demographic information based on the consumer's address. Or it might be based on personal information gathered through voluntarily disclosed information, for example, during a registration process or, as we saw in Chapter 5, through the consumer's participation in customer loyalty programs. Or the information may be bought from commercial information providers who gather information from publicly available databases, like automobile registrations, or from other sources.

Second-Degree Price Discrimination.   Second-degree price discrimination entails offering various prices for different units of the good or service sold, allowing the consumers to choose prices for themselves. Business firms do this in many ways. Public utilities offer declining block pricing where the price of the first group of kilowatt hours of electricity or thousand cubic feet of gas has one price and the next block of

---

[8] Six Flags (2006), p. 32.
[9] Shapiro and Varian (1999), pp. 40–43.

electricity or gas has a lower price, and so on. In this way, the consumer determines the price along with the quantity bought. Another form of second-degree price discrimination involves offering consumers combinations of goods or services bundled together with prices differing from the sum of the separate prices. As we saw in Chapter 9, restaurants use bundling of products on menus to implement price discrimination. Theme and amusement parks can also use tie-in purchases, which provide discounts to purchasers of another product.

The two-part tariff we saw in Chapter 5 is also a second-degree price discrimination mechanism. In that scheme, the consumer pays a flat fee for the right to buy a variable number of units of the good. Consumers buying different numbers of variable units pay different prices on average. A good example of this is to sell a printer at a low price and sell the ink refills needed to operate the printer at a high price. In this way, the producer charges heavy users more than infrequent users. Theme and amusement parks also use two-part tariffs, charging a flat admissions fee and then charging additional per-use fees for some rides or attractions. Many of these additional fees are set at zero, as many rides and attractions are free once the consumer has entered the park.

One common way to implement second-degree price discrimination is through *versioning*. This entails creating different versions of the product or service, with each version having its own price.[10] This, too, is very common throughout various industries. We see versioning in computer hardware, computer software, automobiles, mail and package delivery, and many others. Versions may differ in performance features, convenience, waiting time, and many other characteristics. Theme and amusement parks can often use versioning. In parks with attached hotels, hotel guests get preferred access to the parks, often getting earlier admission and later closing hours than other visitors. Theme parks use versioning when they offer VIP admissions. VIP customers pay an additional fee, that is, a much higher price, and get a different park experience. For example, the VIP admission may include a host to accompany the consumer while traveling through the park. The VIP may have access to park features not available to other park visitors. The VIP customer will typically access rides and other park attractions through special entrances bypassing the lines of other park visitors.

Third-Degree Price Discrimination. As we discussed extensively in Chapter 6, third-degree price discrimination when there is a capacity constraint is very common in the tourism industry, where it is known as *yield management* or *revenue management*. As elsewhere in the travel and tourism industry, theme and amusement parks can use yield management, because the firms are trying to maximize profits from facilities that are fixed in the short term by serving groups of customers having differing demands.

Once again this involves dividing customers into groups with similar demands, creating rate categories using restrictions, establishing prices for each category, and assigning capacity to categories. One way to implement this is with discount coupons offering lower admissions charges or other discounts during periods of low demand. Coupons entitling the holder to a discount are, of course, very common in a wide variety of industries. Theme parks often use coupons for discounted admission to lower prices for groups of consumers. Other yield management methods are marketing season passes, primarily to nearby residents, and offering group rates during periods with low

---

[10] Shapiro and Varian (1999), pp. 53–81.

demand. Six Flags estimates that during 2005 approximately 31 percent of its theme park attendance resulted from group sales and pre-sold tickets and another 28 percent of attendance resulted from sales of season passes. Six Flags offers discount tickets to members of organizations such as schools or businesses or to customers using coupons.[11]

Theme parks can also use restrictions such as advance purchase requirements as a basis for discounts. One of the key types of restrictions for theme parks' yield management is day of the week, with discounts often not available on weekends or holidays.

Thus, amusement and theme parks offer a very complex set of prices for admissions and amusements, including one-day passes, multiday passes, season passes, special rates for in-state residents, and VIP admissions, among others. Parks also offer coupons and tie-in sales with related businesses. Theme parks have an often surprisingly large number of opportunities for shopping and dining. Theme parks use group sales and impose blackout dates when discounts cannot be used. All of these behaviors can be understood as profit-maximizing behaviors in situations in which the parks find themselves with high fixed costs, low marginal costs, and competing firms offering similar but differentiated products.

Summary

Destinations are well defined places that tourists want to visit. These may be nations (notably France, Spain, the United States, and China), states, cities, or other places. Attractions are permanent features of destinations, such as historical sites, cultural centers, business centers, or natural wonders. Events are transitory features of a destination, such as the FIFA World Cup, the Super Bowl, or a university's graduation ceremony.

National governments, provinces, each of the 50 U.S. states, cities, and other locations have government-sponsored organizations aimed at marketing these areas as tourist destinations.

The Walt Disney Company, Six Flags, Inc., Anheuser-Busch, NBC Universal, and Cedar Fair are some of the largest theme and amusement park operators. Theme and amusement parks have high fixed costs and low marginal costs. Firms competing in a market with this cost situation will try many behaviors in search of profits. Profit-maximizing behavior will require a combination of product differentiation, customer lock-in, price discrimination (first-, second-, and third-degree), and cross-selling of complementary products.

Bibliography

Braun, Bradley M. "The Economic Contribution of Conventions: The Case of Orlando, Florida." *Journal of Travel Research* 30 (1992): 32–37.

Braun, Bradley M., and Mark D. Soskin. "Theme Park Competitive Strategies." *Annals of Tourism Research* 26 (1999): 439–43.

Brunet, Ferran (1995), "An Economic Analysis of the Barcelona'92 Olympic Games: Resources, Financing and Impacts," Barcelona: Centre d'Estudis Olímpics UAB. http://olympicstudies.uab.es/pdf/wp030_eng.pdf.

CBS Corporation (2007), "Form 10-K," Fiscal Year 2006, www.sec.gov/Archives/edgar/data/813828/00010474 6907001525/a2176368z10-k.htm.

Cedar Fair (2008), "Properties," www.cedarfair.com/ir/company/properties/.

---

[11] Six Flags (2006), p. 14.

Gaiter, Dorothy J., and John Brecher (2006), "We're Going to Disney World—For Malbec," July 7, http://online.wsj.com/article/SB115222345421599995.html.

General Electric (2006), "Form 10-K," Fiscal Year 2005, www.ge.com/files/usa/company/investor/secreport/pdfs/ge_10k_2005.pdf.

Goeldner, Charles R., and J. R. Brent Ritchie. *Tourism: Principles, Practices, Philosophies*, 9th ed., Hoboken, NJ: John Wiley & Sons, 2003.

International Association of Amusement Parks and Attractions (2008), "U.S. Amusement Park Attendance & Revenue History," http://www.iaapa.org/pressroom/Amusement_Park_Attendance_Revenue_History.asp.

Kotler, Philip, John Bowen, and James Makens. *Marketing for Hospitality and Tourism*. Upper Saddle River, NJ: Prentice Hall, 1996.

Kotler, Philip, Donald H. Haider, and Irving Rein. *Marketing Places*. New York: The Free Press, 1993.

Milman, Ady. "The Future of the Theme Park and Attraction Industry: A Management Perspective." *Journal of Travel Research* 40 (2001): 139–47.

National Amusement Park Historical Association (2006), "Facts & Figures," http://napha.org/nnn/Library/FactsFigures/GreatMoments/tabid/69/Default.aspx.

NBC Universal (2008), "Company Overview," www.nbcuni.com/About_NBC_Universal/Company_Overview/.

Niles, Robert (2005), "Disney Slams Universal in 2005 Theme Park Attendance," www.themeparkinsider.com/flume/200512/2/.

Oi, Walter Y. "A Disneyland Dilemma: Two-Part Tariffs for a Mickey Mouse Monopoly." *The Quarterly Journal of Economics* 85 (1971): 77–96.

Reece, William S., and Russell S. Sobel. "Diagrammatic Approach to Capacity-Constrained Price Discrimination." *Southern Economic Journal* (April 2000), 1001–1008.

Shapiro, Carl, and Hal R. Varian. *Information Rules: A Strategic Guide to the Network Economy*. Boston: Harvard Business School Press, 1999.

Six Flags (2006), "Form 10-K," Fiscal Year 2005, http://ccbn.10kwizard.com/xml/download.php?repo=tenk&ipage=4035039&format=PDF.

Travel Industry Association of America (2006a), "Executive Summaries—2004–2005 Survey of U.S. State & Territory Tourism Office Budgets," www.tia.org/researchpubs/executive_summaries_budgets.html.

——— (2006b), "Top Ten State Tourism Office Budgets for FY 2002–2003," www.tia.org/researchpubs/executive_summaries_budgets_top10.html.

Vogel, Harold L. *Travel Industry Economics*. Cambridge: Cambridge University Press, 2001.

The Walt Disney Company (2006a), *The Walt Disney Company Fact Book 2005,* http://adisney.go.com/adownload/investorrelations/disney_fb05.pdf.

——— (2006b), "Form 10-K," Fiscal Year 2005, https://clients.moultoncommerce.com/disney/pdfs/2005_10-K.pdf?ebizcatalogsid=8c2d031f43c75d711019f62164892330.

World Tourism Organization (2005), *Tourism Highlights 2005 Edition*, www.unwto.org/facts/wtb.html.

CHAPTER 12

Tourism Intermediaries

Travel Agents, Tour Operators, and Others

Learning Goals

▪ Know what types of firms function as the intermediaries in the tourism industry.

▪ Know how intermediaries create value in tourism.

▪ Understand recent developments in the travel agent and tour operator businesses.

▪ Understand principal-agent problems in tourism.

▪ Understand practical solutions to principal-agent problems in tourism.

INTRODUCTION

Consumers with opportunities or obligations to travel face monumental challenges. The number of potential destinations for a leisure trip is truly mind-boggling. Even a traveler who knows where he or she wants to go often faces a variety of choices about how to travel. Both the mode of travel and the route, including stops along the way, present opportunities for choices. Then, once the traveler arrives at the destination there are often many choices of lodging. Often the consumer will not know the full range of choice available. Even with a good idea of the choices, the consumer will probably not be aware of the costs and benefits of each choice. **Intermediaries** with specialized knowledge about opportunities for travel, including information about destinations, modes of travel, lodging choices and availabilities and prices, can provide valuable help to potentially overwhelmed consumers.

    While consumers have problems making choices, tourism service providers, including airlines, hotels, resorts, and others, face the problem of reaching their potential customers and making the sales. They, like the customers, value the services of

Intermediary
A firm facilitating transactions by offering services to both consumers and service providers.

intermediaries. For tourism service providers, intermediaries can provide the basic functions of the distribution channel, familiar to every marketing student and professional, which include advertising, personal selling, and other services.

AGENCY IN TOURISM

The bewildering array of consumer choices encountered in tourism is particularly large because the choices are often literally worldwide. But the basic problem of consumers facing choices that seem overwhelming is not confined to tourism. Consider a new college graduate accepting a new job in a new town. Such graduates often move to a city and state in which they have never lived and which they visited only for a brief job interview. They will have questions: Where am I going to live? Where do people shop? Where can I get my hair cut? People in such situations seek informal advice from friends, relatives, acquaintances, or employers. They look at publications like real estate and apartment guides, city guides, magazines, and the Internet. They also often seek help from professionals such as real estate and apartment agents and brokers. The role of the agents and brokers is to know their market and to be able to match the consumers to the opportunities available for sale or rent. They provide the professional advice, search, and transaction processing that consumers have trouble doing on their own.

Agents and brokers are intermediaries who stand between the consumers and the providers of goods and services. They are part of what marketers call the distribution channels (see, e.g., Kotler, Bowen, and Makens, 1996). The distribution channels are the broad range of mechanisms that bring goods and services from producers to consumers. The most familiar distribution channel members that we all know about are retailers. Wal-Mart, Kmart, and Target are distribution channel members. So are local auto dealers. Wholesalers and distributors are also important parts of distribution channels. While Wal-Mart may deal directly with Proctor & Gamble to stock its shelves, many smaller retail operations will deal with wholesalers or distributors to get their merchandise. To see a good example of the function of distributors, consider a local auto repair business. From one day to the next, the person operating the business does not know what repair problems will present themselves. Will the repair shop need to repair a radiator on a 1998 Volvo, a 2002 Buick fuel injector, or a broken left-side mirror on a 2003 Honda Accord? It is inconceivable that a local car repairer could keep in stock all of the parts that it might be called upon to use over the next week or month. Keeping a wide variety of parts in stock is the job of the distributors who serve a very large number of auto repair shops over a wide area. On short notice, often the same day, they provide whatever part is needed to whichever repair shop calls for it. The wholesalers and distributors reduce the industry's costs by maintaining centralized inventories and distributing those inventories when and where they are demanded.

Travel agents, travel management companies, tour operators, GDSs, and Internet travel sites are the primary intermediaries serving travelers and the tourism industry. They provide services that link the many millions of travel consumers to the enormous number and variety of hotels, resorts, airlines, restaurants, attractions, and other product and service providers that operate in the tourism industry. They create value by helping consumers make well informed choices and by executing transactions.

TRAVEL AGENTS CREATE VALUE

As we saw in Chapter 2, travel agents create value in many ways. Travel agents, as intermediaries between travelers and travel service providers, supply services to both sides of travel transactions. They provide information on travel opportunities, prices, and many other characteristics of travel to the traveler. Travel agents search through mountains of information. They also provide advice. An experienced travel agent may give the traveler advice based on his or her personal experience, having visited the destination, stayed in the hotel, or sailed on the cruise ship the traveler is considering. Furthermore, the travel agent will often process the transaction, for example, by accepting the traveler's payment and printing the traveler's documents. All of these activities create value for travelers. The agent also creates value for tourism services suppliers by selling their services and processing transactions. Thus, travel agents create value for both travelers and travel service providers—they provide information, searches, advice, promotion, selling, and transaction processing.

THE TRAVEL AGENT INDUSTRY

Travel agents are the most important of the intermediaries in the tourism industry. Today there are two broad classes of travel agencies: the "brick and mortar" agencies with offices consumers can walk into, and the online travel agencies (OTAs) serving travelers only through the Internet. Traditionally, the travel agent's job was to represent sellers of tourism services by presenting information to potential travelers and then executing the transaction. For example, the traveler might be searching for a Caribbean cruise. The agent would explain the types of cruises available, the specific characteristics of each cruise line and ship, the choices of itineraries and departure dates, the prices and payment terms, and all the many details peculiar to the service the customer sought. After making the reservation and the sale and collecting the traveler's payment, the agent would not charge the traveler for his or her services. Rather, as an agent of the cruise line, the agent would receive a commission from the cruise line. Until the mid-1990s, most travel agents earned most of their income selling airline tickets. The travel agent made the reservation, sold the ticket, printed the ticket, and collected payment. The agent collected only the price of the ticket from the traveler and received a commission, usually 10 percent, from the airline. Agents that heavily sold the services of a particular airline or other service provider might also receive a "commission override," which is an extra payment to the agent above the standard commission.

Most travel agencies in 2005 operated from a single location with two to ten employees and $2 million or less in sales.[1] *Sales* here refers to the total value of the agency's bookings, most of which is passed on to the airline, cruise line, or other service providers. The revenue consisting of the agency's commissions and fees earned from bookings goes toward its wages, salaries, other expenses, and profits, if any. Table 12.1 shows the distribution of industry bookings by type of service provider.

Most travel agencies handle both business and leisure travel, with the majority of the bookings for leisure. Some travel agencies are franchisees or licensees operating under well known national brands.

---

[1] *Travel Weekly* (2006).

TABLE 12.1 U.S. Travel Agency Business Mix—2005

Service Provider	Revenue Share (Percentage)
Airline (U.S. and international)	33
Cruise line	25
Tour operator	19
Hotel	13
Car rental	5
Rail	4
Other	1

Data source: *Travel Weekly* (2006).

Eleven states license travel agents.[2] The primary regulation of travel agencies occurs through conference accreditation. Travel agencies must be accredited by conferences of service providers before they can receive commissions. The primary organization for this is the ARC. Since 1984, it has accredited travel agencies to receive commissions from airlines. The ARC also solves a monumentally large practical problem that arises from having tens of thousands of travel agencies collecting money for tickets for travel on dozens of airlines. The problem is to keep track of who owes money to whom and then to make the required payments. The ARC provides the solution by distributing blank ticket stock to travel agencies, collecting airlines' revenue from the agencies that sell the tickets, and distributing the appropriate amounts of revenue to the airlines. The CLIA accredits travel agencies to receive commissions from cruise lines. A subsidiary of the IATA also accredits some travel agencies on behalf of non-U.S. airlines.

The travel agent industry has been changing rapidly in recent years, primarily because of the Internet, which has provided new ways for tourism consumers and service providers to do business. As we saw in Chapter 2, the Internet allows consumers easy access to information, advice, searches, and transactions processing. The Internet also allows service providers to promote and sell their services directly to potential consumers and to process the transaction without, in some cases, the services of an intermediary. These factors have, in some cases, reduced opportunities for travel agents to provide intermediary services. Thus the Internet has reduced the income earning potential of many travel agencies.

Another factor adversely affecting the travel agent industry in recent years has been the reluctance of some service providers to pay commissions. The airline industry, whose commissions provided the majority of income to the travel agent industry before 1995, has steadily reduced its commission payouts to travel agents. In 1995 airlines put a cap on travel agent commissions per ticket sold, and then in 1997 they generally reduced commission rates from 10 percent to 8 percent. By 2002, many airlines had ended traditional commissions paid to travel agents. In 2002, car rental companies reduced commissions to travel agents. According to Transue, agents with 5 to 10 years of experience working for commissions saw their pay fall after 1995.[3]

---

[2] Starr (2000), p. 313.
[3] Transue (1998).

TABLE 12.2 Ten Largest U.S. Travel Agencies—2000

Agency Name	Sales (Billions of Dollars)	Number of Employees
American Express Travel	14.6	15,600
Carlson Wagonlit Travel	12	20,000
Rosenbluth International	4.8	5,805
World Travel BTI	4.6	5,762
Navigant International	3.8	3,936
Travelocity	2.5	1,400
Expedia	1.79	661
TQ3 Maritz Travel Solutions	1.66	2,519
Liberty Travel	1.39	3,000
SatoTravel	1.2	1,818

Data source: *Travel Weekly* (2001).

In the early 1990s, the travel agency industry consisted of about 35,000 firms, most of which were small, local operations. A small number of travel agencies were large, national firms with many branches. In recent years the number of travel agencies operating in the United States has fallen, and the number of very small agencies has declined.[4]

In contrast, a few travel agencies are gigantic. Table 12.2 shows the 10 largest travel agencies operating in the United States in 2000; each had well over $1 billion in annual revenues.

Compare that list with the list of the 10 largest travel agencies operating in the United States in 2006, which is given in Table 12.3.

Note some important facts about these two lists that illustrate the major changes occurring in the industry. First, in 2000 the seventh largest travel agent in the United States was Expedia, an Internet travel agent which began online only in 1996, and achieved its position near the top of the industry with only 661 employees. Travelocity, the

TABLE 12.3 Ten Largest U.S. Travel Agencies—2006

Agency Name	Sales (Billions of Dollars)	Number of Employees
American Express Business Travel	24.2	No data
Carlson Wagonlit Travel	22.1	19,000+
Expedia	17.2	6,600
BCD Travel	12	12,000
Hogg Robinson Group	12	12,000
Travelocity	10.1	5,000+
Orbitz Worldwide	10	1,600
AAA Travel	3.89	5,130
Priceline.com	3.3	No data
Liberty Travel	1.8	2,450

Data source: *Travel Weekly* (2007).

---

[4] *Travel Weekly* (2006).

other Internet travel agent on the list, also began operation in 1996. By 2000 Travelocity had reached sixth place with only 1,400 employees. Thus, these Internet travel agents grew very rapidly between 1996 and 2000. Furthermore, we can see that Expedia and Travelocity had 2000 sales per employee averaging more than $2.2 million. This is three times the sales per employee of the seven traditional travel agencies on the list.

Second, we see that by 2006 half of the names on the 2000 top-ten list had changed. This was because of the presence of new Internet travel agencies. For example, Orbitz, a new Internet travel agency with only 1,600 employees, had grown rapidly enough in the five years after its founding in 2001 to make the top-ten list. Priceline.com, with its trademarked Name Your Own Price pricing system, began operations in 1997 and grew rapidly to enter the top ten within 10 years. The other changes owe to the mergers, acquisitions, and realignments that are consolidating the industry. Since 1995 many travel agencies have consolidated through mergers or through acquisitions of smaller firms by larger firms. Many of the smallest firms have simply shut down. One of the largest of the recent acquisitions occurred when American Express acquired Rosenbluth International, an industry giant, in 2004.

The online travel agencies on the list have become very familiar names after only a few years of operations. These include Priceline.com and Expedia, which was started in 1996 by Microsoft Corporation. Expedia was later spun off as a separate company before being wholly acquired by IAC/InterActive Corp. in 2003 and was spun off again as Expedia, Inc., in 2005. Another OTA on the list, Travelocity, is a subsidiary of Sabre Holdings. In recent years, Cendant Corporation made the top ten list by acquiring CheapTickets.com and other Internet travel firms, including Orbitz in 2004. But Cendant later sold its travel services unit, including CheapTickets and Orbitz, to the Blackstone Group, a private equity firm. Blackstone operates these and other brands under its Travelport company. Travelport sold 40 percent of Orbitz's stock to the public in 2007.

Navigant International was another, more traditional, new entrant into the industry. It formed in 1998 through a spin-off from its parent corporation and grew rapidly through acquisitions, including SatoTravel, which is 10th on the 2000 top-ten list shown in Table 12.2. In 2004, Navigant acquired 50 percent of TQ3, a joint venture with German tourism and shipping giant Touristik Union International (TUI). In 2006, the joint venture terminated as TUI sold its TQ3 operation to the Dutch company BCD Holdings. BCD had operated World Travel BTI, fourth on the 2000 top-ten list, in partnership with Hogg Robinson, but that arrangement ended in 2006. Also in 2006 Carlson Wagonlit Travel, which is jointly owned by Carlson Companies and a private equity affiliate of JP Morgan Chase, acquired Navigant. In recent years there have also been many other mergers and acquisitions involving the largest travel agencies.

TRAVEL MANAGEMENT

Large corporations typically have many employees traveling during the year. They can spend many millions of dollars each year on airline tickets, hotel rooms, and all of the other many expenses associated with travel. Furthermore, their travel needs can be very complicated, with many travelers at any one time going to many different places for varying durations and purposes. The travel and travel expectations of senior executives will often include high levels of service, including first-class air travel, stays at luxury hotels, and similar first-class travel accommodations. Company policies may allow high travel expenses for very senior executives, while requiring more modest accommodations for the typical corporate traveler. This creates the task of enforcing the company's travel policies, and this can be a complicated and thankless job.

For many years, such corporations have hired travel agents to help them with their travel requirements. According to the *Wall Street Journal*, in 1998 the 10 largest travel management companies handled about one-half of business travel of U.S. corporations, totaling more than $40 billion in travel service bookings.[5] In recent decades, some of the largest travel agents have become travel management companies whose job is to manage the travel functions of large corporations. American Express has been one of the largest travel management companies, with operations in the United States and elsewhere around the world. Carlson Wagonlit, BCD Travel, and Hogg Robinson Group are three other very large corporate travel management companies.

Travel management companies provide a long list of services for their clients, including the following:

- search for low prices for air travel and other services
- process transactions
- enforce company travel policies
- negotiate with service providers for low corporate rates
- manage incentive travel
- provide management reports on company travel
- help travelers deal with travel problems

Typically, a travel management company charges its customers fees for its services, rather than relying on commissions from travel service providers. Furthermore, the travel management company may locate its travel agency offices, known as "on-site" agencies, inside the facilities of the customer, where the agency can quickly and conveniently provide very focused service for its largest customers.

One special variety of travel management is incentive travel, which is all-expense-paid travel provided by employers to reward high-performing employees. Maritz Travel is an example of a firm providing incentive travel services. Maritz Travel is part of Maritz, Inc., a privately held company based in St. Louis, MO.[6]

GLOBAL DISTRIBUTION SYSTEMS

During the 1960s and 1970s, travel and tourism grew to the point that people relying on telephone calls and paper records could no longer keep up with the industry's flow of information and transactions at reasonable cost. To do their jobs, travel agents and others had to know in real time what specific travel services were available and what their prices were. They had to be able to make reservations and sell the service. This was a particularly acute problem with airline tickets, as the traveler typically faced many choices, and these choices changed rapidly as seats were sold. Travel agents had to keep up with a complicated and rapidly changing environment.

Computer and communications technology, however, provided solutions to the industry's information and transaction processing problems. The industry developed

[5] Goetz (1998).
[6] Maritz (2008).

computerized reservation systems to handle the large and rapidly growing flow of data. These systems allowed, in an era long before the Internet, online data communications between travel agents and tourism service providers, beginning with the airlines and later adding hotels, car rental companies, cruise lines, and others.

These systems developed into today's GDSs, which are large and complex global data communications networks linking all segments of the tourism industry. There are four major GDSs:

- *Sabre Travel Network:* began in 1964 as American Airlines' computerized reservation system; now owned by Sabre Holdings Corporation, which became a privately held company in 2007 after affiliates of private equity firms Silver Lake and TPG acquired its shares;
- *Galileo International:* began in 1971 as United Airlines' Apollo computerized reservation system; now owned by Travelport, a tourism services company of the private equity firm The Blackstone Group;
- *Amadeus IT Group SA:* began in 1987 as the GDS serving Air France, Lufthansa, Iberia, and SAS; became a publicly traded company before being taken private by WAM Acquisition in 2005;
- *Worldspan:* created in 1990 with the combination of the Delta Airlines, TWA, and Northwest Airlines computerized reservation systems; now owned by Worldspan, L.P.; Travelport has announced plans to acquire the company.[7]

The GDSs, like all participants in the tourism industry, face challenges in adapting to the growth of the Internet. Look for continuing changes in these firms as computing and data communications continue to develop.

TOUR OPERATORS AND TOUR WHOLESALERS

Many of the products or services that travel agents sell have been put together by companies known as tour operators or tour wholesalers. Tourists face many challenges created by the extraordinarily large number of decisions to be made about destinations, routes, travel modes, amenities, and other aspects of travel. Once travelers make decisions, they must execute their plans, which typically requires coordination among many firms in the tourism industry, including lodging, multiple modes of transportation, food, entertainment, shopping, attractions, and possibly many others. Tour operators provide help. Their business is to provide tourists with prepackaged, prepaid travel opportunities. They present an array of thoughtfully designed, appealing, and often favorably priced travel packages from which to choose; once the consumer makes a choice, the tour operator handles almost everything else.

Tour operators have grown rapidly in recent decades and now form a large part of the tourism industry. In 2001 the National Tour Association surveyed U.S. and Canadian consumers' use of packaged travel. The survey found the spending on packaged travel by destination as shown in Table 12.4.

The survey found that packaged travel trips on average lasted more than one night longer than nonpackaged trips and that the average spending on packaged travel

---

[7] Travelport (2006).

TABLE 12.4 Spending on Packaged Travel by U.S. and Canadian Consumers—2001

Destination	Spending (Billions of Dollars)
United States	99
Mexico	13
Canada	9.5
Outside North America	45
Total	**166**

Data source: National Tour Association (2002).

was $2,775 per travel party. Clearly, packaged travel provided by tour operators is an important component of the tourism industry in North America and elsewhere.

TOUR OPERATORS CREATE VALUE FOR TRAVELERS AND SERVICE PROVIDERS

Tour operators create value by prearranging and packaging travel, including transportation, lodging, meals, sightseeing, shopping, and perhaps other activities. Tour operators also handle many details and eliminate inconveniences by arranging transfers between transportation and lodging, arranging for baggage handling, paying tips, taxes, admission fees, and others. They sell these travel packages to consumers, either directly or through other companies, especially travel agents. The package is prepaid, so the traveler knows and pays most of the cost of the trip before departing.

Packaged tours may be for individuals, but they are often for groups. And they may be "hosted" or "escorted." An independent tour is a prepaid package of travel services involving two or more travel services (for example air travel, rental car, and lodging) arranged for one party. A hosted tour is a similar prepaid package of travel services for a group of travelers who are on their own but have the services of a tour representative available if needed. An escorted tour is a package of travel services for a group traveling together along with an escort who leads the group and sees that all arrangements are properly handled.

The growth of tour operators has created opportunities for many travel and hospitality service providers and has created problems for others. As the tourism sector grows, tourism service providers often want to market themselves, for example by hiring sales staff targeting tour operators. Tourism service providers may have separate facilities to handle the peak traffic generated by the arrival or departure of a tour group. The rise of group tours has made market segmentation and price discrimination easier for some providers by effortlessly creating a segment or array of segments that can be built into the yield management process. Thus, a large hotel can at times allocate rooms at discounted rates to group tours of mature travelers or travelers attending a cultural event or some other well defined segment. This is in addition to any other segments in the yield management system. During a peak time, the group sales staff may receive no discount room allocations, so as to reserve rooms for categories paying higher prices.

THE TOUR OPERATOR INDUSTRY

Tour operators of a sort have existed since the Grand Tour, or earlier. Thomas Cook was the pioneer in the industry, creating tour products for a broad spectrum of English consumers in the nineteenth century and expanding since then. The industry, however, grew rapidly during the 1960s and 1970s as incomes grew, the supply of tourism services grew, and opportunities for tourism expanded rapidly. Many tour operators started their operations to provide specialized services to a narrow range of travelers. For example, Collette Vacations, which claims to be the oldest vacation tour operator in the United States, began in 1918 by offering bus tours in the eastern United States.[8] During the 1960s, 1970s, and 1980s, the company expanded its tour offerings in North America, Europe, Australia, Africa, and Asia. American Express also can claim an early entry as a tour operator; by 1922 it had chartered the first round-the-world cruise. It is now a large wholesale and retail tour operator in addition to being a travel management and diversified financial services company. Another of the earliest U.S. tour companies is Tauck World Discovery, which started with New England tours in 1925 and has expanded its offerings in the United States and around the world, especially since the 1960s. ACIS has taken teachers and students on educational tours since 1978. Travcoa, started in 1954, specializes in luxury travel to "exotic" locations, including Libya, Mozambique, and Lapland. As time went on, many narrowly focused tour companies expanded their offerings to serve broader ranges of customers.

Specialty tourism remains a large component of the tour operator's repertoire. The web site of the United States Tour Operators Association (USTOA), www.ustoa.com, allows users to search its members by types of tours, and the results show the following, among many others:

Ecotours	Barging and canals	History tours
Archeology	Photography	Safari
Bicycling	Fall foliage	Whale watching
Bird watching	Rafting	Winery tours
Dog sledding	Hiking	Spa vacation

Some tour operators have operated successfully for decades and have grown into large operations. Some, but not all, of the largest and best known tour operators are members of USTOA. Some of these well established companies are the following:

- Abercrombie and Kent
- Brendan Worldwide Vacations
- Celtic International Tours
- CIE Tours International
- Globus
- GOGO Worldwide Vacations
- Lindblad Expeditions
- Mayflower Tours
- Rail Europe
- SITA World Travel
- Trafalgar Tours

---

[8] Collette Vacations (2008).

The tour industry is a complex network of companies providing a diverse mix of services. Tour operators may market their products directly to travelers though retail operations, including their own web sites. Most are wholesalers who assemble packages by booking large blocks of hotel rooms, airline seats and other tourism services for which they negotiate with the suppliers for low rates. They then resell the services in their packages, which they market through travel agents or other outlets. Travelers ask travel agents about leisure package opportunities, and the agents present an array of opportunities, usually promoted in slick brochures. The agents then try to sell one of the packages to the traveler. With each sale the operators pay commissions to the agents.

Wholesale or retail tour operators may provide the services in the package themselves or, more often, they contract with other companies to provide elements of the package. One of the most integrated of the U.S. tour operators is Holland America Tours. It sells tours to Alaska that involve sailing on Holland America cruise ships, transportation on motorcoaches it owns through Gray Line franchises, transportation in its railroad cars, and lodging in its 10 Westmark hotels and inns. Some tour operators charter their own air transportation. Many tour operators own and operate motorcoaches. But most tour operators contract with other firms for transportation, lodging, and other services. They may even outsource tour operation services for parts of their tours from other tour operators, sometimes known as ground operators. Gray Line sightseeing tours form a large segment of the motorcoach tour operator industry, providing tour services to other tour operators and retail tour services to customers.

One of the largest tour wholesalers in the United States is Mark Travel Corporation, based in Milwaukee. It offers its tours through more than a dozen companies, including United Vacations and Southwest Airlines Vacations. Thus, rather than operate their own tour operations, these airlines contract out for the services of a wholesale tour operator. Here, as elsewhere in the tour operator market, contracting activities out to separate companies shows Coase's theory of the firm, seen earlier in Chapters 1 and 9, in action.

Receptive tour operators are a specialty group of tour wholesalers that market their services to foreign tour operators. They provide the in-country tour services for travelers from other countries, known as inbound tourists. For example, Mark Travel Corporation, mentioned before, operates Mark International as a receptive operator specializing in foreign independent travel. There are many receptive tour operators, and they work with various trade associations, including the Receptive Services Association of America (RSAA) and the TIA. The TIA operates a very large annual trade show, called the International Pow Wow, which brings together companies selling U.S. travel services and foreign tour operators to make business arrangements for the coming year. The 2005 International Pow Wow held in New York City brought more than 5,200 people together, including 1,300 people from 70 countries who buy U.S. tourism services.[9]

ASYMMETRIC INFORMATION IN THE TRAVEL AGENT AND TOUR OPERATOR INDUSTRIES

Tour operators are among the most important intermediaries serving travelers and the tourism industry. The tour operator business also gives us opportunities for interesting economic analysis that helps us understand the industry. The problems that have

---

[9] Travel Industry Association of America (2005).

The British Holiday Market

The tour operator industry in Great Britain is large and diverse, consisting of companies that serve inbound tourists and British tourists going "on holiday," which usually means overseas vacation travel. The Association of British Travel Agents (ABTA) includes more than 1,000 tour operators and 6,000 travel agency offices. British vacationers have often bought packaged travel from tour operators; but while the number of packaged tours sold in the United Kingdom has fallen in recent years, the number of independently booked vacations has risen rapidly and now has a larger share than packaged tours.[10]

The British overseas holiday market is highly concentrated and highly vertically integrated. Until recently four companies have dominated the industry in Great Britain—MyTravel Group (formerly Airtours), TUI (including Thomson Holidays), First Choice, and Thomas Cook. MyTravel operated in Great Britain, elsewhere in Europe, and in North America. In fiscal year 2003, the company earned total revenue of about $7 billion (£4.2 billion), and just over half of that was in the United Kingdom. In 2002, the company had more than 22,000 employees and sold its tourism products and services through more than 100 brand names, including Airtours Holidays. The company is highly vertically integrated. In 2002, it owned or partnered with 120 resorts, and it owned 56 aircraft. The company also owns cruise ships.

In 2007, MyTravel and Thomas Cook merged to form Thomas Cook Group plc. Also, TUI proposed to merge its tour operations with First Choice. The completion of these two mergers would create two integrated giants better able to operate in an environment in which the Internet and low-cost airlines have encouraged more independent travel.[11]

particularly afflicted the tour operator industry come from the fact that consumers rely on the tour operators for detailed arrangements for which the consumers have already paid. The problems arise when the tour operator, for any of a variety of reasons, fails to deliver what the consumer has paid for. The following list shows some of the reasons tour operators may fail to deliver on their promises:

- Bankruptcy of the tour operator or one of the contracted service providers
- Misrepresentation and fraud by the tour operator or one of the contracted service providers
- Unanticipated events

In the United States, the Federal Trade Commission (FTC) regulates business firms to provide some consumer protection against false or misleading claims. During 2006, about 1 percent of the consumer complaints received by the FTC were travel related.[12] Fortunately, according to Starr, there is more honesty in travel advertising now than in the past.[13] Nevertheless, consumers need to exercise some care in making travel arrangements. As we will see, federal regulators, state regulators, and the industry provide some guidance and other help.

Faced with many consumer complaints about travel packages, the FTC has come up with some guidelines to help consumers avoid problems.[14] First, it advises consumers

---

[10] Thomas Cook Group plc (2007), p. 41.
[11] Cogswell (2007).
[12] U.S. Federal Trade Commission (2007), p. 6.
[13] Starr (2000), p. 278.
[14] U.S. Federal Trade Commission (2006).

to buy their travel packages from businesses they trust. It advises consumers to be wary of unsolicited e-mails or faxes offering discounted travel packages. The FTC advises that travelers verify their travel package terms in writing, including the names and addresses of the specific hotels, airlines, and other service providers, and also get the seller's written policies on refunds and cancellations. Also, the consumer should pay with a credit card, because the traveler may be able to dispute any charges for services not received with the credit card company.

Not all tour operator problems involve telemarketing scams. In past years bankruptcies have caused many problems. Indeed the USTOA asserts that one of the major reasons it was founded in 1972 was to protect travelers from tour operator bankruptcies.[15] One of the largest bankruptcies among U.S. tour operators occurred in September 2003 when Far & Wide Travel Corporation failed. Far & Wide had operated many tour companies which it had acquired during the previous four years. The months following the September 11, 2001, terrorist attacks saw rapidly falling demand for tourism services. The war in Iraq and the Severe Acute Respiratory Syndrome (SARS) epidemic also reduced tourism demand after September 11. Soon, with the ensuing substantial drop in sales—the company expected its 2003 revenues would fall by almost half from the level it saw in 2000—Far & Wide could not pay its obligations. At the time of the bankruptcy, the company had 15,000 customers with pending trips or trips in progress. In the months following the bankruptcy, the supervising court sold many of Far & Wide's ongoing tour brands to raise money to pay creditors.

SOME ECONOMICS OF ASYMMETRIC INFORMATION

George Akerlof shared the 2002 Nobel Prize in Economic Sciences for his work on asymmetric information in markets. In his study of the market for lemons, referring to the commonly used term for defective used cars, Akerlof examined the effects of asymmetric information on the development of markets.[16] Here the asymmetric information is the fact that the seller of a used car has a lot of information about the quality of the car, while any potential buyer has very little information about a car with which he or she has no experience. Thus, buyers will be skeptical about claims about the quality of any cars offered to them. They will, probably correctly, assume that sellers on average are trying to unload problem cars—lemons—while owners of unusually good used cars typically keep them for themselves. Thus, given the expectations of buyers, it will be hard for someone selling a high quality used car to get the high price that would be justified by its quality. Akerlof deduced that it might be possible for such behavior to completely force high-quality cars out of the market, because they could never command their true value.

Akerlof generalized his results to credit markets in less developed economies, where asymmetries in information about credit worthiness might prevent credit markets from developing. Economists call the problems Akerlof identified problems of *adverse selection*, because from the perspective of one side of the market, either buyers or sellers, the opportunities presented are selected by the other side to provide adverse results—they are lemons.

---

[15] United States Tour Operators Association (undated c).
[16] Akerlof (1970).

There is another important broad class of problems of asymmetric information in markets. These are problems of information about the actions of other parties to a market transaction, and these are known as problems of *moral hazard*. An example of this is a situation in which a property owner buys property insurance and, because his losses are insured, fails to take care to avoid losses.

Akerlof and others noted that market participants have often developed mechanisms, which Akerlof calls *counteracting institutions* (pp. 499–500), to reduce the effects of adverse selection and moral hazard. Some possible mechanisms or institutions include the following:

- *Guarantees:* The firms in the industry, either individually or in groups, may offer guarantees of performance to reassure consumers that if they get a lemon they can get their money back or receive some other compensation.
- *Brand names and reputation:* Firms can invest in brand names through advertising or other forms of promotion, or they can develop reputations. They can create images in consumers' minds that they are trustworthy and will either not sell lemons or will make good if they do.
- *Chains:* Firms can affiliate with other firms or branch out into new areas, carrying their brand names and reputations with them.
- *Licensing or certification:* Industries can, through their own mechanisms or through government action, create standards of behavior for the industry to counteract information asymmetries.

Also, markets with repeat contracts or repeat sales to each customer are protected from some of the information asymmetry problems because repeat sales give both sides of the transaction information about the other side.

TOURISM INTERMEDIARIES' REACTIONS TO ASYMMETRIC INFORMATION

The tour operator industry has faced the problems arising from asymmetric information. Many tour operators have sold tour packages and failed to deliver on their promises. Many operators have gone bankrupt, leaving travelers without their trips or, worse, stranded in a foreign country. Holloway reports that the 1974 bankruptcy of Britain's largest tour operator left 50,000 travelers stranded in other countries.[17] According to travel writer Wendy Perrin, each year some travel agencies and tour operators fail, leaving travelers without promised services. She notes that California and Florida have important consumer protections against failure of sellers of travel services.[18]

To prosper in spite of the potential problems created by asymmetric information, the tour operator industry has worked hard to develop mechanisms to assure consumers, including all of the counteracting institutions mentioned by Akerlof: guarantees, brand names, reputations, chains, and certification. In a few cases, as Perrin cites earlier, state licensing provides some assurance to travelers, but most states do not license travel agents or tour operators.[19]

---

[17] Holloway (1998), p. 197.
[18] Perrin (1997), pp. 99–100.
[19] Dickerson (2000).

Each major tourism trade association works hard to assure consumers that they can safely deal with the association's members. The associations begin with strict membership requirements. For example, the National Tour Association has North American membership requirements that include meeting any required state licensing or other regulations, employing in a senior management position someone with at least three years of experience in the packaged travel industry, and maintaining comprehensive liability and professional liability insurance coverage with minimum limits of $1,000,000 for each occurrence or a comparable self-insurance program that is independently audited each year. There are additional requirements for membership for firms outside North America.[20]

The trade associations also typically have explicit guarantee programs to protect consumers. The USTOA has a "Travelers Assistance Program" which includes the following:

- Each member will post a $1 million bond with USTOA to protect consumers in case the company becomes insolvent;
- In case a member becomes insolvent, USTOA will inform consumers of their rights and provide a consumer information center for travelers;
- In case a member becomes insolvent, USTOA will ask its members to help the affected travelers by issuing credits, providing free travel, or honoring travelers' deposits.
- USTOA will serve as a clearinghouse of information, informing travelers of options available.[21]

According to Starr, the USTOA has had to use its consumer protection plan several times.[22] Following the 2003 bankruptcy of Far & Wide Travel Corporation, a USTOA member, the USTOA's $1 Million Consumer Protection Plan distributed its $1 million to eligible claimants during 2004.[23]

Tourism intermediaries try to raise standards of behavior and reassure consumers through codes of ethics and through certification of their professionals. The American Society of Travel Agents (ASTA) requires its travel agency and travel professional members to adhere to a comprehensive Code of Ethics which includes the following elements, among others:[24]

- *Accuracy:* Provide accurate information and avoid deceptive practices.
- *Disclosure:* Provide complete details about the terms and conditions of any travel service sold.
- *Responsiveness:* Promptly respond to clients' complaints.
- *Refunds:* Refund any undisputed funds within the specified time limit.
- *Confidentiality:* Treat every client transaction confidentially.
- *Conflict of Interest:* Do not allow relationships with suppliers to interfere with the interests of their clients.

---

[20] National Tour Association (2007).
[21] United States Tour Operators Association (undated a).
[22] Starr (2000), p. 272.
[23] USTOA (2004).
[24] American Society of Travel Agents (2007).

The Code of Ethics includes additional requirements for all ASTA members:

- *Notice:* Members operating tours will promptly advise agents or clients of any change in tour features. If the operator makes substantial changes, the client will be allowed to cancel.
- *Delivery:* Members operating tours will provide the tours stated in their brochures, or provide alternates of equal or greater value, or compensate the consumer.
- *Credentials:* An ASTA member will only provide travel agent credentials to persons who sell or manage the sale of travel services to the public.

These requirements directly address information concerns of consumers as well as concerns of service providers about providing travel agent discounts to people who are not actually travel agents.

Summary

Travel agencies, global distribution systems, travel management companies, incentive travel companies, and tour operators are intermediaries in the tourism industry, providing distribution services to consumers and to tourism service providers. They create value by providing information, searches, transaction processing, promotion, and selling, among many other services. In the United States there are thousands of travel intermediaries, some of which are very large.

The travel agent industry has been changing rapidly in recent years as travel service providers have reduced or eliminated commissions. Travel agents have made wider use of fees for services provided. Many existing firms have combined, while new firms based on the Internet have entered and thrived.

Tour operators create value by packaging tourism services, including travel accommodations and other services, and selling the packages to consumers. Packages are available in many varieties including specialty tours, budget tours to popular locations, and group tours with escorts. Many tour operators are wholesalers, marketing their services through travel agents. Some of the largest tour operators are vertically integrated, providing their own transportation services and, in some cases, their own lodging and other services.

Tourism intermediaries have been plagued for decades by unscrupulous operators misrepresenting their services to consumers. Also, because the industry operates with long lead times, precommitting to travel services and accommodations based on forecasts of sales, unforeseen events can lead to financial difficulties and, in some cases, bankruptcy. This creates uncertainty as to whether or not the company will meet its commitments to its consumers as well as potential problems of adverse selection and moral hazard. In general, industries can mitigate such information problems by offering guarantees, by relying on brand names and reputation, by forming chains of related companies, and by licensing or certification. Tourism intermediaries rely on all of these mechanisms to reassure potential customers. Intermediaries have tried to establish brand names and reputations for reliable service, they affiliate with chains or consortiums, they offer guarantees backed up by programs organized through trade associations, and they have programs to certify their professionals.

Bibliography

ACIS (2007), "About ACIS," http://www.acis.com/about/aboutacis.cfm.

Akerlof, George A. "The Market for 'Lemons': Quality Uncertainty and the Market Mechanism." *Quarterly Journal of Economics* 84 (1970): 488–500.

Amadeus IT Group SA (2005), "Purchase Order," http://www.amadeus.com/amadeus/documents/corporate/Purchase%20order%2006%20Jul%202005.pdf.

—— (2007), "Our History," http://www.amadeus.com/amadeus/x5126.html.

American Express Company (2007a), "Our History," http://home3.americanexpress.com/corp/os/history.asp.

——— (2007b), "*Form 10-K* (Fiscal Year 2006)," http://ir.americanexpress.com/phoenix.zhtml?c=64467&p=IROL-secToc&TOC=aHR0cDovL2NjYm4uMTBrd2l6YXJkLmNvbS94bWwvZ2VudWRHVudHMueG1sP2lwYWdlPTQ3MTQzNDAmcmVwbz10ZW5r.

American Society of Travel Agents (2007), "ASTA Code of Ethics," www.astanet.com/about/codeofethics.asp.

Brannigan, Martha, and Kortney Stringer. "American, Continental Join Delta to End Commissions for Most Travel Agents." *Wall Street Journal*, March 19, 2002.

Buckley, Peter J. "Transactions Cost Analysis of Tourism." In *Economic and Management Methods for Tourism and Hospitality Research*, edited by Thomas Baum and Ram Mudambi, 39–46. Chichester: John Wiley & Sons, 1999.

Business Travel News Online (2006), "BTI Splits, BCD Buys Out TUI's TQ3 Holdings," www.btnmag.com/businesstravelnews/headlines/article_display.jsp?vnu_content_id=1001772713.

Cogswell, David (2003a), "Far & Wide Books Were $100M in the Red," October 6, www.travelweekly.com/Article.aspx?id=102020.

——— (2003b), "Trafalgar Parent Bids for 4 Far & Wide Firms," *Travel Weekly*, October 10, http://www.travelweekly.com/Article.aspx?id=102014.

——— (2003c), "Far & Wide: 5 More Units Auctioned Off," *Travel Weekly*, October 23, http://www.travelweekly.com/Article.aspx?id=101992.

——— (2007), "Europe Mega-Operators TUI and First Choice Propose Merger," *Travel Weekly*, http://travelweekly.texterity.com/travelweekly/20070326/?pg=16.

Collette Vacations (2008), "Collette Vacations Turns 90," www.collettevacations.com/company-history.cfm

Dickerson, Thomas A. (2000), "The Licensing and Regulation of Travel Agents, Tour Operators and Other Travel Sellers in the United States, Canada, Australia, Great Britain, Japan and the members of the European Community," www.courts.state.ny.us/tandv/Aqtaed1.htm.

Dugan, Ianthe Jeanne (2007), "How a Blackstone Deal Shook Up a Work Force," *Wall Street Journal*, July 27.

The Economist. "Travel and Tourism: Home and Away," January 10, 1998, 1–16.

Frommer, Arthur. *Arthur Frommer's New World of Travel*, 5th ed. New York: Macmillan, 1996.

Galileo International (2007), "Our History," www.galileo.com/galileo/en-us/about/History/.

Gee, Chuck Y., James C. Makens, and Dexter J. L. Choy. *The Travel Industry*, 3rd ed. New York: John Wiley & Sons, 1997.

Goeldner, Charles R., and J. R. Brent Ritchie. *Tourism: Principles, Practices, Philosophies*, 9th ed. New York: John Wiley & Sons, 2003.

Goetz, Thomas. "Firms Fire Their Travel Agencies For Slow Service, Missing Low Fares." *Wall Street Journal*, February 6, 1998, B1.

Holloway, J. Christopher. *The Business of Tourism*, 5th ed. Harlow, UK: Addison Wesley Longman, 1998.

Jennings, Lisa, and R. Scott Macintosh (2003), "Far & Wide Bankruptcy Rocks Industry," TravelAgeWest.com, September 29.

Kotler, Philip, John Bowen, and James Makens. *Marketing for Hospitality and Tourism*, Upper Saddle River, NJ: Prentice-Hall, 1996.

Lattin, Gerald W. *The Lodging and Food Service Industry*, 5th ed. Lansing, MI: Educational Institute of the American Hotel and Lodging Association, 2002.

Laws, Eric. "Package Holiday Pricing: Cause of the IT Industry's Success, or Cause for Concern?" In *Economic and Management Methods for Tourism and Hospitality Research*, edited by Thomas Baum and Ram Mudambi, 197–214. Chichester: John Wiley & Sons, 1999.

Lovell, Richard. "The Great GDS Debates." *CWT Vision* 1 (2007): 17–23. http://www.carlsonwagonlit.com/en/global/tmi/cwt_vision_pdf_en/102_gds_en.pdf.

Mak, James, and James E. T. Moncur. "The Demand for Travel Agents." *Journal of Transport Economics and Policy* 14 (1980): 221–30.

Maritz, Inc. (2008), "Company Overview," www.maritz.com/About-Maritz/Company-Overview.aspx.

Mark Travel Corporation (2008) "Fact Sheet," www.marktravel.com/aboutus/factsheet.asp.

MyTravel Group plc (2003) *MyTravel Group plc Annual Report & Accounts 2003*.

National Tour Association (2002), *2001 Packaged Travel in North America, Executive Summary*, www.ntaonline.com/staticfiles/ptna_executive_summary.pdf.

——— (2007), "Tour Operator Requirements and Fees," www.ntaonline.com/index.php?s=&url_channel_id=15&url_subchannel_id=&url_article_id=1586&change_well_id=2.

Perrin, Wendy. *Wendy Perrin's Secrets Every Smart Traveler Should Know*, New York: Fodor's Travel Publications, 1997.

Priceline.com (2007), "Form 10-K, Fiscal Year Ended December 31, 2006," http://ccbn.10kwizard.com/xml/download.php?repo=tenk&ipage=4713489&format=PDF.

Sabre Travel Network (2007), "History," www.sabretravel network.com/about/history.htm.

Schaal, Dennis (2006), "WorldTravel BTI Moves Would Forge Acquisitions into Global $8.5B Brand," *Travel Weekly*, January 9, http://travelweekly.texterity.com/travelweekly/20060109/?pg=14.

——— (2007), "Ambassadors Closes on Windstar Deal; TPG and Silver Lake Take Sabre Private," *Travel Weekly*, April 9, http://travelweekly.texterity.com/travelweekly/20070409/?pg=18.

Sidron, Jorge, and Nadine Godwin (2002), "Giants Dumps Hertz As Car Firms Match Zero," *Travel Weekly*, April 16, http://www.travelweekly.com/Article.aspx?id=90178.

Starr, Nona. *Viewpoint: An Introduction to Travel, Tourism, and Hospitality*, 3rd ed. Upper Saddle River, NJ: Prentice Hall, 2000.

Tauck World Discovery (2007), "Meet the Tauck Family," www.tauck.com/why/meet-the-taucks/.

Thomas Cook Group plc (2007), "Interim Results Presentation," www.thomascookgroup.com/media/tcgpresentationfinal2007.pdf.

Transue, James (1998), "Airline Slashes Wound Commission-only Agents," *Travel Weekly 1998 U.S. Travel Agency Survey*, www.travelweekly.com/harris/blood_transue.htm.

Travel Industry Association of America (2005), "TIA's 2005 International Pow Wow Proves to Be a Big Success," www.tia.org/pressmedia/pressrec.asp?Item=366.

Travel Weekly (2001), "Top Fifty Travel Agencies 2001," www.travelweekly.com/specialreports/top50/index.html.

——— (2006), "2005 U.S. Travel Industry Survey," www.travelweekly.com/multimedia/TWSURVEY2005/index.htm.

——— (2007), "Travel Weekly's 2007 Power List," www.travelweekly.com/Article.aspx?id=56464

Travelport (2006), "Travelport Ltd. and Worldspan, L.P. to Merge to Create Leading Travel Solutions Company," www.travelport.com/en/media/pr/show_release.cfm?id=188.

——— (2007), "About Us," www.travelport.com/en/about/.

TUI AG (2007), "TUI Milestones," http://www.tui-group.com/media/konzern/konzern_ueberblick/meilensteine/Milestones_03_07.

U.S. Bureau of Labor Statistics (2007), "Travel Agents," *Occupational Outlook Handbook 2006-07 ed.* www.bls.gov/oco/ocos124.htm.

U.S. Federal Trade Commission (2006), "Travel tips: How to Gear Up for a Great Tip," www.ftc.gov/bcp/conline/pubs/alerts/trvlalrt.pdf.

——— (2007), "Consumer Fraud and Identity Theft Complaint Data: January–December 2006," www.consumer.gov/sentinel/Sentinel_CY_2006/AppendixB_Sentinel_Complaint_Categories.pdf.

United States Tour Operators Association (2004), "Far & Wide Questions and Answers," February 3, www.ustoa.com/Far&Wide_update.htm.

——— (undated a), "USTOA's Travelers Assistance Program," http://ustoa.com/pressroom/newsreleases/tap_program.html.

——— (undated b), "Tour Operators: A Brief History," http://ustoa.com/pressroom/newsreleases/history.html.

——— (undated c), "USTOA: Over Thirty Years of Integrity in Tourism," http://ustoa.com/pressroom/newsreleases/30years.html.

Varian, Hal R. *Microeconomic Analysis*, 3rd ed. New York: W. W. Norton, 1992.

Worldspan, LP (2007), "Company Profile," http://www.worldspan.com/home.asp?fPageID=5.

CHAPTER 13

Casino Gaming

Learning Goals

▪ Know how commercial and Native American casinos have developed and affected the tourism industry in recent decades.

▪ Know the structure of the U.S. and global casino gaming industries.

▪ Understand how casinos operate.

▪ Know how governments regulate casinos.

▪ Know what taxes casinos pay.

▪ Understand how casinos affect regional economic growth.

▪ Understand some potential social costs of casinos.

INTRODUCTION

While many people object to gambling in general or to casino gaming in particular, it remains true that in recent decades casino gaming has been one of the fastest growing segments of the tourism industry. This growth has two sources. First, long-established casino destinations, especially Las Vegas in the United States and Macao in China, have been growing very rapidly. Second, local authorities, particularly in the United States, have approved many new casino gaming destinations in recent decades.

Gaming consists of a wide variety of activities that involve placing bets on the outcomes of events. These activities include casino gambling, pari-mutuel (horse and greyhound racing and jai alai) gambling, lotteries, and others. In America, betting on horse races must have begun shortly after the arrival of European colonists. The first casino, as we would recognize it today, in the United States opened in New Orleans in 1827.[1] In the ensuing decades many more gambling establishments opened in the large cities of the United States, including New York, Chicago, San Francisco, and Miami. By 1910, however, all of the states had banned almost all forms of gambling.

---

[1] Vogel (2001), p. 122.

The modern gaming industry in the United States had its beginnings when Nevada legalized gambling once again in 1931. This led, over a period of decades, to the development of Las Vegas as a major destination for casino gaming. In 1987 the U.S. Supreme Court affirmed the rights of Native American tribes to operate casinos on their lands. A period of rapid growth of casinos on Indian lands ensued. Also in the decades following Nevada's legalization of gambling, many states allowed pari-mutuel betting. In 1963, New Hampshire established the first state lottery. Once again, over a period of decades, many other states followed New Hampshire's lead with their own lotteries, including participation in multistate lotteries. The result by 2007 was that 12 states had commercial casinos, 11 states had racetrack casinos, 24 states had Class III (including slot machines, table games, and other types of high-stakes gaming) Native American casinos, 41 states and the District of Columbia had lotteries, and 43 states had pari-mutuel betting. In 2008, among the 50 U.S. states only Hawaii and Utah had no form of legal gambling.

For the study of tourism, the expansion of casino gaming is the most important of these developments. In 1976, New Jersey became the second U.S. state in recent history to allow casino gaming when it approved casino gaming operations in Atlantic City. Other states followed with commercial casinos, as shown in Tables 13.1A and B. Commercial casinos can be land-based, as in Las Vegas, or riverboat or dockside casinos, as in Indiana. Eight states have only racetrack-based casinos, sometimes known as *racinos*. Louisiana has all three of these types of casinos. Tables 13.1A and B show 2007 gross commercial and racetrack casino gaming revenue by state.[2]

Table 13.2 shows the development of casino gambling revenue for the United States for the period 1997 to 2007.

TABLE 13.1A U.S. Commercial Casino Gross Gaming Revenue—2007

State	Land-Based and Riverboat Casino Revenue (Millions of Dollars)
Colorado	816
Illinois	1,983
Indiana	2,625
Iowa	908
Louisiana	2,197
Michigan	1,335
Mississippi	2,891
Missouri	1,592
Nevada	12,849
New Jersey	4,921
Pennsylvania	27
South Dakota	98

---

[2] Add the revenues from Tables 13.1A and 13.1B to get total revenues for Iowa, Louisiana, and Pennsylvania.

TABLE 13.1B U.S. Racetrack Casino Gross Gaming Revenue—2007

State	Racetrack Casino Revenue (Millions of Dollars)
Delaware	612
Florida	202
Iowa	455
Louisiana	369
Maine	43
New Mexico	245
New York	828
Oklahoma	79
Pennsylvania	1,063
Rhode Island	448
West Virginia	932

Data source: American Gaming Association (2008e), pp. 12–28.

TABLE 13.2 U.S. Gross Gambling Revenue 1997—2007

Year	Commercial Casino Revenue (Billions of Dollars)
1997	18.2
1998	19.7
1999	22.2
2000	24.3
2001	25.7
2002	26.5
2003	27.0
2004	28.9
2005	30.3
2006	32.4
2007	34.1

Data source: American Gaming Association (2008d).

THE U.S. CASINO INDUSTRY

The casino industry consists of a small number of very large publicly traded or private corporations competing with a variety of smaller firms and Indian tribal casino operations. The industry often distinguishes "commercial" casinos from Indian or tribal casinos. Las Vegas and Atlantic City are home to most of the largest commercial casinos. Las Vegas contains three main casino areas, "The Strip," a section of Las Vegas Boulevard where the giant resort casinos are located, the "Boulder Strip," and "Downtown," home to many casinos and other attractions, especially the Fremont Street Experience. Nevada also has substantial casino operations in Reno, Lake Tahoe,

Laughlin, Mesquite, and along Interstate 15 (in the towns of Primm and Jean, NV). Aside from Nevada and Atlantic City there are also major commercial casino operations at various locations in Mississippi, Indiana, Illinois, Missouri, Michigan, Louisiana, Iowa, and Colorado. The largest tribal casino, and one of the largest of any kind, is Foxwoods in Connecticut. There are also major Indian casinos in California, Minnesota, Michigan, and other states.

Table 13.3 shows the largest U.S. casino markets by annual gross gaming revenue in 2007.

While there are many companies operating U.S. casinos, a small number of large publicly traded corporations owned most of the large U.S. commercial casinos at the beginning of 2007. During the 1990s, some of the major hotel chains divested themselves of their gaming operations. The resulting gaming industry then pursued a frantic pace of consolidation through mergers and acquisitions.

- Harrah's Entertainment, Inc., was the new name of the Promus Companies, Inc., taken after the lodging company spun off its hotel business. Park Place Entertainment Corp. was formed when Hilton Hotels Corp. split its lodging and gaming operations into separate companies at the end of 1998. Park Place later acquired Grand Casinos, Inc., and Caesars World, Inc., and became Caesars Entertainment. Caesars merged with Harrah's Entertainment, Inc., in June 2005. Harrah's had previously merged with Rio Hotel and Casino, Inc. In April 2007, Harrah's agreed to be acquired by private equity firms TPG Capital and Apollo Management. The acquisition was completed in 2008, and the company announced plans to be renamed Caesars Entertainment Corporation.

TABLE 13.3 Largest U.S. Casino Markets—2007

Rank	Casino Market	Revenue (Millions of Dollars)
1	Las Vegas Strip, NV	6,750
2	Atlantic City, NJ	4,921
3	Chicago, IN/IL	2,602
4	Connecticut	1,685
5	Detroit, MI	1,335
6	Tunica/Lula, MS	1,243
7	Biloxi, MS	1,007
8	St. Louis, MO/IL	999
9	Boulder Strip, NV	928
10	Reno/Sparks, NV	928
11	Shreveport, LA	844
12	Lawrenceburg/Rising Sun/Belterra IN	791
13	Kansas City, St. Joseph, MO	758
14	New Orleans, LA	704
15	Lake Charles, LA	641

Data source: American Gaming Association (2008e), p. 8.

- In 1999, MGM Grand acquired Mirage Resorts and the Nevada casino properties of Primadonna Resorts, Inc., including New York-New York. Mandalay Bay
Resorts, Inc., was previously known as Circus Circus, Inc. In 2005, MGM Mirage
acquired Mandalay Bay.

In addition to mergers and acquisitions, there have been important recent entrants into the casino business, including Wynn Resorts, Limited, which opened Wynn
Las Vegas Resort in 2005, and Las Vegas Sands, owner of The Venetian, which opened
in 1999, and The Palazzo Las Vegas, which opened in 2008. Other firms have also
grown through internal growth or acquisitions. The following publicly traded corporations held many of the major U.S. casinos at the end of 2006:

- Harrah's Entertainment
- MGM Mirage
- Las Vegas Sands Corp.
- Wynn Resorts Ltd.
- Station Casinos, Inc.
- Boyd Gaming Corp.
- Penn National Gaming, Inc.
- Aztar Corporation
- Pinnacle Entertainment, Inc.

Table 13.4 shows two of the largest firms operating U.S. casinos as of the end of
2005, along with the names of some of their major U.S. properties, the number of
rooms in attached hotels, and the approximate size of their casinos in square feet. The
totals at the end of the table are approximate values for the companies as of the end of
2005, including casinos not listed in the table.

THE GLOBAL CASINO INDUSTRY

While many of the largest casinos are in the United States, especially Las Vegas, many
other nations around the world have significant casinos. Monaco and its grand Casino
of Monte Carlo have been associated, for many years and around the world, with ele-
gance and sophistication. This reputation grew after the 1958 marriage of Monaco's
ruler Prince Rainier to Hollywood star Grace Kelly. Many of us have seen the Casino of
Monte Carlo in the movies, as the settings of many films have centered around the
casino. Monaco and its Casino of Monte Carlo were the setting for Ian Fleming's James
Bond novel *Casino Royale*.

In recent years, the casino industry of Macao, the former Portuguese colony in
China, has grown dramatically. Since 1999 when Portugal gave up its political rights
over the region, Macao has been a Special Administrative Region of China and the only
place in China with legalized casinos. The government of Macao has granted casino
operating rights or concessions to three companies: Sociedade de Jogos de Macau,
Galaxy Casino Company, and a subsidiary of Wynn Resorts, Ltd, the Las Vegas casino
developer. These companies have granted subconcessions to or entered into partnerships with various others including Las Vegas Sands and MGM Mirage. The results of
these new grants of casino operating rights have been an enormous building boom
and the growth of a very large casino industry—by 2005, Macao's casinos had gross

TABLE 13.4 Selected MGM Mirage and Harrah's Entertainment Casinos—2005

MGM Mirage			Harrah's Entertainment		
Casino	Guest Rooms	Casino Size (Square Feet)	Casino	Guest Rooms	Casino Size (Square Feet)
Bellagio	3,933	155,000	Harrah's Atlantic City	1,630	142,100
MGM Grand Las Vegas	5,044	156,000	Bally's Atlantic City	1,740	225,800
Mandalay Bay	4,756	157,000	Caesars Atlantic City	1,220	130,900
The Mirage	3,044	118,000	Harrah's Las Vegas	2,530	88,400
Luxor	4,403	100,000	Rio	2,520	107,000
Treasure Island	2,885	90,000	Caesars Palace	3,350	129,000
New York-New York	2,024	84,000	Paris Las Vegas	2,920	180,700
Excalibur	3,990	100,000	Flamingo Las Vegas	3,550	76,800
Monte Carlo	3,002	102,000	Reno Hilton	2,000	107,000
Circus Circus Las Vegas	3,764	133,000	Harrah's Lake Tahoe	530	57,600
Primm Valley Resorts	2,642	137,000	Harveys Lake Tahoe	740	63,300
Circus Circus Reno	1,572	69,000	Caesars Indiana	500	87,000
Gold Strike (Jean)	811	37,000	Horseshoe Tunica	510	63,000
Edgewater (Laughlin)	1,356	57,000	Grand Casino Tunica	1,360	136,000
MGM Grand Detroit	N/A	75,000	Grand Casino Biloxi	980	134,000
Beau Rivage (Biloxi)	N/A	N/A	Harrah's St. Louis	500	120,000
Gold Strike (Tunica)	1,133	40,000	Harrah's New Orleans	–	125,100
Borgata—50% owned (Atlantic City)	2,000	125,000	Harrah's Ak-Chin (Arizona)	150	48,000
Approximate MGM Mirage Total	**49,665**	**1,955,000**	**Approximate Harrah's Total**	**42,760**	**3,247,200**

Data source: Harrah's Entertainment, Inc. (2006); MGM Mirage (2006).

revenues of about $5.6 billion.[3] For example, the Sands Macao opened its casino and hotel in 2004, and these facilities have been repeatedly expanded since then. The boom continues and includes development of a new area known as the Cotai Strip, where Las Vegas Sands is building The Venetian Macao. Plans call for Cotai to have more than a dozen giant hotels and casinos similar to those on the Las Vegas Strip.

Singapore will soon be providing new competition for Asian players. In 2006 it granted its first casino license to Las Vegas Sands, Inc.

Canadian provincial governments operate casinos or operate casinos jointly with private partners. For example, British Columbia partners with various private casino operators to operate one racino, fourteen community casinos catering primarily to local players, and four destination casinos aimed at tourists. For their services, the private operators receive 40 percent of the win on table games and 25 percent of the win on slot machines.[4] The Ontario Lottery and Gaming Corporation, a part of the

---

[3] Las Vegas Sands Corp. (2006), p. 2.
[4] British Columbia Lottery Corporation (2006).

provincial government, operates 17 racinos and contracts with private operators to operate four commercial casinos, including the giant Niagara Fallsview Casino Resort. In addition to commercial and racino operations, Canada also allows charity casinos and Native American casinos.[5]

The casino industry in Great Britain is in the process of making substantial changes as the result of its Gambling Act of 2005. South Africa, Australia, and New Zealand also have significant casino industries.

CASINO OPERATIONS

Gaming Revenues

Casinos create value for consumers by providing gaming entertainment along with many associated activities. Today's modern resort casinos combine lodging, food and beverage, meeting and convention facilities, stage entertainment, shopping, outdoor recreation, and other activities. Most of the largest casinos and their related facilities operate 24 hours a day seven days a week. The most popular casino games include blackjack, craps, roulette, poker, and slot machines, along with race and sports betting.

In the United States, slot machines provide by far the largest source of casino gaming revenues. For example, in Nevada casinos, two-thirds of gaming revenue comes from slot machines. Table 13.5 shows the 2007 total casino gaming revenue (win) for Nevada casinos.

Revenue in the gaming industry can be a confusing concept, because not every dollar bet is a dollar of revenue. The industry refers to the total amount wagered as the *handle*. In a casino, the total amount of cash that is converted into chips is known as the drop. But, of course, some bets are winners, so that the person making the bet receives a return greater than the amount of the bet. The gambler often places a succession of bets, some winning and some losing. In the end, on average, the casino holds a portion of the total drop as its winnings, or "win." The casino or lottery's revenue is the total amount the casino or lottery wins.

Casino revenue comes from the "house advantage" associated with each game. In games in which the player bets against the house, such as blackjack or roulette, the expected payout or probability of winning on each play times the amount of the payout for winning is less than the bet. For example, in a typical roulette play, the house

TABLE 13.5 Nevada Casino Gaming Revenue by Source—2007

Source	Revenue (Millions of Dollars)
Win from slot machines	8,451
Win from games and tables	4,230
Win from card games	168
Total win	12,849

Data source: Nevada Gaming Commission and State Gaming Control Board (2008), p. 1.

---

[5] Ontario Lottery and Gaming Corporation (2006).

pays 35 times the bet for selecting the winning number out of 38 possibilities. Over a long run of single-number bets (there are more complicated bets involving a combination of numbers), the casino will pay out $35 for every $38 bet, keeping the remainder as the house advantage. Casinos typically win 10 percent to 25 percent of the drop. In games against other players, the casino takes the house advantage from the pool of bets, or the handle, dividing the rest of the pool among winners according to a fixed formula. These are called pari-mutuel games, and include horse racing, lotteries, and poker. Racetracks typically win 17 percent or more of the handle, while lotteries typically take about 50 percent of the handle.[6]

Some casinos provide free transportation, lodging, and meals to selected groups or individuals, known as "VIPs" or "high rollers," who typically either have high casino credit limits or cash on deposit in the casino and have previously bet substantial amounts of money in the casino. The process of providing complimentary food or lodging is known as "comping." High-end casinos issue "markers" to many table game players. Markers are simply IOUs; that is, the casino is lending the gaming money to the player. This is not important for most slot machine players and most table game players, but it is important for the biggest gaming customers of the most luxurious casinos.

Gaming Devices

The slot machines, or gaming devices, which are so important to the casino industry, are made by a relatively small number of manufacturing companies, including International Gaming Technologies, WMS Industries, Aristocrat Technologies, and Bally Technologies. These casino gaming machines can be traditional slot machines with three, four, or five spinning reels displaying fruits, bars, numbers, or other graphics. Casinos have generally replaced the mechanical slot machines of the past with computerized machines that in many cases simulate the spinning reels on computer displays. More recently, these gaming devices provide much more varied games, including the very popular video poker, which depends to some extent on the skill of the player. Often the most popular casino slot machines are based on games with well known brand names, such as WMS Gaming's Monopoly and Hollywood Squares and International Game Technology's Wheel of Fortune and Star Wars. Other innovations include progressive jackpots with the potential of a very large win with a small bet and cashless machines that print a ticket showing any winnings the player may have rather than the earlier practice of ejecting coins into a tray below the machine.

Gaming machine manufacturers can get their revenue in many ways. They earn revenue from sales of gaming machines to the casino operators. In some cases, the manufacturers can collect daily rental fees on machines. Or, machine manufacturers can charge casino operators either a percentage of the win on each machine or, in some cases, a percentage of the amount wagered on the machine. Also, games manufacturers or third-party owners of intellectual property can charge royalty fees for use of things such as the names, designs, and characters appearing in the games.

Games manufacturers, independent designers, and casinos devote a lot of effort to offering machines that will appeal to players. International Game Technology states

---

[6] Vogel (1998), pp. 250–251.

that in 2005 it had over 1,200 employees working in product development, including game design, graphics, computer technology, and other areas.[7] Casinos and manufacturers carefully monitor play so that they can remove gaming devices with low levels of play and replace them with games generating more revenue. Generally, new gaming devices require regulatory approval before they can be put into operation.

Non-Gaming Revenues

For many decades, Las Vegas casinos have had attached lodging, food, and beverage operations. Many also have had entertainment venues. The newest Las Vegas casinos and casinos around the world are now just parts of gigantic resort destinations with multiple lodging options, convention centers, large entertainment venues, some of the world's finest restaurants, and many other attractions. MGM Mirage recently described its Mandalay Bay resort casino complex as including the following:[8]

- numerous restaurants, including Charlie Palmer's Aureole, Wolfgang Puck's Trattoria Del Lupo, and Hubert Keller's Fleur de Lys
- a 12,000-seat special events arena
- a 1,760-seat showroom featuring a Broadway hit show
- the *House of Blues*
- the Rumjungle restaurant and nightclub
- Shark Reef, home to sharks and other sea predators
- an extensive pool and beach area, including a wave pool and a European-style beach
- a 30,000-square-foot spa
- a Four Seasons Hotel with its own lobby, restaurants and pool and spa
- THEhotel, an all-suite hotel which includes its own spa and fitness center, lounge, and restaurants, including Alain Ducasse's Mix Las Vegas
- convention, exhibit, and meeting facilities including almost 2 million square feet of space
- a retail center that with about 40 boutique stores and restaurants, and the burlesque club Forty Deuce.

Retail operations associated with casinos have also grown substantially, particularly with the Forum Shops at Caesars Palace, the Canal Shoppes at the Venetian, Via Bellagio, the Desert Passage at the Aladdin, the Studio Walk at the MGM Grand, and many more. Las Vegas also has giant shopping malls, including Fashion Show Las Vegas and others, that are separate from the casinos.

In recent years these lodging, entertainment, food and beverage operations have rivaled the casinos in revenue, and in some cases have exceeded casino revenue. MGM Mirage's reported revenue split for 2007 (see Table 13.6) shows that with more than $5 billion in noncasino revenue, its lodging, entertainment, food and beverage, and retailing operations were greater than its revenue from casino operations.

---

[7] International Game Technology (2005), p. 6.
[8] MGM Mirage (2007), p. 2.

TABLE 13.6 MGM Mirage Revenues by Source—2007

Revenue Source	Revenue, Net (Millions of Dollars)
Casino	
Table games	1,228.3
Slots	1,897.6
Other	113.1
Casino total	3,239.1
Noncasino	
Rooms	2,130.5
Food and beverage	1,651.7
Entertainment, retail and other	1,376.4
Noncasino total	5,158.6
Total Revenue	**8,397.7**
Less: promotional allowances	−706.0
Net Revenue	**7,691.6**

Data source: MGM Mirage (2008), p. 20.

TAXATION AND REGULATION OF CASINOS

U.S. State Regulation

Casinos in the United States and around the world are heavily regulated and heavily taxed. In the United States, the states are responsible for regulating casino gambling. Nevada casinos are subject to the Nevada Gaming Control Act and to the regulations of the Nevada Gaming Commission and the Nevada State Gaming Control Board. Nevada regulates the licensing of casino operators, the conduct of card games, the handling of casino money, the design and production of chips and slot machine tokens, the resolution of patron disputes, the operation of casino surveillance systems, and many other details of casino operations.[9]

These regulations are designed to do the following:

- prevent unsuitable persons from being involved with gaming;
- establish responsible accounting practices and procedures;
- maintain controls over the financial practices of licensees, including safeguarding of assets and revenues and maintaining reliable record keeping;
- prevent cheating and fraud; and
- provide a source of state and local revenues through taxes and fees.

Other U.S. states with legalized casino gambling have similar regulatory controls.

---

[9] Nevada Gaming Commission and State Gaming Control Board (2006c).

Casino Taxation

Casinos are a major source of revenue for state, provincial, and national governments. In Canada, for example, the provinces own the commercial casinos and earn income that supports a wide range of government operations. The provinces also share casino revenue with local communities in which the casinos are located. Ontario also operates charity casinos, the net revenues of which go to a provincial charitable foundation. This charity funding amounts to about $100 million each year.[10]

In the United States, the states have revenue-sharing agreements with Indian tribes operating casinos. These agreements provide between 8 and 25 percent of net gaming revenues to state and local governments.[11] In addition, the states levy various taxes and fees on commercial casinos, including percentage fees or taxes on gaming revenue, licensing fees, admissions taxes, and others. For example, Michigan has a 19 to 24 percent tax on gaming revenue, which is roughly evenly split between the state and the city of Detroit.[12] Nevada assesses a "monthly percentage fee" of up to 6.75 percent of the gross gaming revenue. It also levies an annual tax of $250 and a quarterly license fee of $20 per slot machine along with annual and quarterly license fees on table games.[13]

Table 13.7 shows commercial casino tax revenue by state for 2007.

In some cases, states or provinces earmark gaming taxes, including casino taxes, for specific purposes. State and local revenue from casinos typically is split among general funds, education, health care, youth programs, senior-citizen programs, and many other uses.

TABLE 13.7 State Tax Revenue from Commercial Casinos—2007

State	Tax Revenue (Millions of Dollars)
Colorado	115
Illinois	834
Indiana	842
Iowa	315
Louisiana	559
Michigan	366
Mississippi	350
Missouri	417
Nevada	1,034
New Jersey	475
Pennsylvania	473
South Dakota	15
Total	**5,790**

Source: American Gaming Association (2008c).

[10] Ontario Lottery and Gaming Corporation (2006).
[11] Anderson (2005), p. 305.
[12] American Gaming Association (2008a).
[13] Nevada Gaming Commission and State Gaming Control Board (2006b).

Native American Casinos

The U.S. Supreme Court affirmed the rights of Native Americans to own and operate casinos on tribal lands in the case of *California v. Cabazon Band of Mission Indians* (*Cabazon*) in 1987. The following year Congress passed the Indian Gaming Regulatory Act of 1988 which specified terms and conditions for operating tribal gaming establishments. The act also established the National Indian Gaming Commission to regulate Indian gaming at the federal level. The act divided Indian gaming into three classes. Classes I and II involve traditional games such as bingo and other games with smaller stakes. Class III includes casino gaming, such as slot machines, blackjack, roulette, and other table games, and also other types of high-stakes gaming that are not included in Class I or Class II. The Indian Gaming Regulatory Act specifies that tribes may establish Class III casino gaming within any state only after entering into a written agreement, known as a "tribal-state compact," with the state. These tribal-state compacts specify agreements about casino operations on tribal lands. They also include provisions for revenue sharing with the states, in contrast to the states' taxation of commercial casinos. In 2005, there were 28 states with Indian gaming, while 22 of these states had operating Indian casinos.

In 2004, tribal gaming revenues exceeded $19.4 billion in total, and included 55 casino operations that earned $100 million or more during the year.[14]

BENEFITS AND COSTS OF CASINOS

Casinos create both benefits and costs. The primary benefits are the creation of value for consumers by providing gaming entertainment, entertainment of other kinds in venues related to the casinos, food and beverage service, lodging, and other services and products associated with the casinos. The extraordinary example of the attractions on the Las Vegas Strip demonstrates the attractions available for consumers through the introduction of casinos. The level of tourist arrivals and spending on the Las Vegas Strip attest to the value that casinos can create for consumers.

Because casino workers and owners create value for their customers, they also create income for themselves, which shows up as wages, salaries, interest, rents, royalties, corporate profits, and so on. Thus, the growth of casinos in a region can enhance employment, earnings, tax revenue, and other indicators of economic growth. Once again, the phenomenal growth of the City of Las Vegas demonstrates that casinos can bring economic growth to tourist destinations. While Las Vegas is certainly an extreme example, Tunica, MS, provides a second example. Tunica, a county not far from Memphis, TN, was once one of the poorest counties in the United States. Since the first casino's opening in 1992, its nine casinos have brought a great deal of economic development, including employment and income growth.

The extent to which commercial casinos create economic growth is controversial. Some argue that destination casinos attracting primarily tourists from outside the region create economic growth inside the region, but that local's casinos catering primarily to the region's residents do not create growth. Rather, the argument goes, local's casinos simply shift spending and employment away from other businesses, for example local restaurants that operated before the arrival of casinos, to the casinos, with

---

[14] National Indian Gaming Commission (2006b).

little net effect. But is this argument quite correct? Casinos, as with other businesses or industries, create economic growth to the extent that they create new value added. Value added is the only source of income. If as the result of opening new casinos there is more value added within the region, then incomes within the region will rise, regardless of whether the customers are inside or outside the region.

This, of course, does not mean that exports are not important for growth. To the contrary, growing exports can be very important to regional or national growth. We saw this in Chapter 5 where we included total exports as part of final demand. Researchers involved with the contemporary literature on differences in economic growth among nations have carefully examined the sources of economic growth and found openness to external trade to be one of the important sources of growth.

But there are other sources of growth, and all are interrelated. Accumulation of physical and human capital and advancing technology of production have long been associated with regional or national economic growth. That is, regions that use improving technology and have growing physical capital per worker and growing knowledge, skills, and abilities of the workers have growing output per worker, growing output, and growing incomes. Nations or regions that have institutions and policies favoring the accumulation of human and physical capital have these requirements for economic growth. These institutions and policies that favor growth include secure property rights, rule of law, stable monetary policies, stable political institutions, and openness to trade with other nations or regions.

Geographical factors, such as proximity to navigable waters, absence of endemic debilitating diseases, abundance of natural resources, proximity to other high-income areas, and others, also contribute to economic growth and rising incomes. However, as the examples of North Korea and South Korea or, in past years, East Germany and West Germany show, geography itself does not determine economic growth rates. The role in national or regional economic growth of capital accumulation, geography, institutions (including political institutions), technology, and knowledge are subjects of very active research among economists. Helpman (2004) provides an excellent survey of this research.

Clearly, the introduction of commercial casinos in the various states of the United States has brought large investments in physical capital through the construction of facilities and installation of machinery. Casinos have led to education and training that have enhanced workers' knowledge, skills, and abilities. Casinos have introduced advanced technology, not only in gaming machines but also in management, security, and many other areas. All of these developments have increased the productivity of workers and increased value added in regions where modern casinos have been introduced, regardless of whether the customers are locals or tourists.

The impact of the expansion of casino gambling on local regions is quite controversial because of real and potential negative economic and social impacts. Many people have feared a rise in crime rates following the introduction of casino gambling. Another potential problem is rising personal bankruptcy rates as some people lose excessively in casino gambling.

For most casino patrons, gambling is a form of entertainment. Other patrons are problem gamblers who cannot control their behavior and cannot limit their losses to reasonable levels. These problem gamblers may commit crimes to support their gambling, file for personal bankruptcy, disrupt their family life, or contribute to other pathologies. The relationships of casino gambling to all of these issues are the subjects of active research among social scientists and researchers in health-related fields.

In 1996, the U.S. Congress established a National Gambling Impact Study Commission to conduct a comprehensive study of the social and economic impact of gambling in the United States. In April 1999, the National Commission voted to recommend that the expansion of gambling be curtailed. In its June 1999 final report,[15] the Commission recommended the following:

- restrict gaming to those at least 21 years old;
- ban betting on amateur sports;
- prohibit introducing casino-style gambling at pari-mutuel racing facilities primarily to save the pari-mutuel facility;
- ban Internet gaming in the United States;
- allow gaming activities by Indian tribes within each state consistent with the gaming activities allowed to other persons in that state; and
- recognize that casino gaming (but not lotteries, stand-alone slot machines, and Internet gaming) provides economic development, particularly for economically depressed areas.

Casino gaming has been undeniably important for the development of tourism in many regions. We can, however, expect proposals to expand casino gaming to remain controversial.

Summary

In recent decades casino gaming has been one of the fastest growing segments of the tourism industry. Long-established casino destinations, including Las Vegas and Macao, have been growing very rapidly, and local authorities in the United States and elsewhere have approved casinos in new locations. There are many varieties of casinos, including commercial casinos, which may be land-based, riverboat, dockside, or racetrack-based, and Native American casinos. Annual revenue for U.S. commercial casinos now exceeds $30 billion. A few large publicly traded or private corporations own most of the large U.S. commercial casinos. Canada, South Africa, Australia, and New Zealand also have significant casino industries.

Casinos create value for consumers by providing gaming entertainment along with many associated activities. Today's modern resort casinos combine lodging, food and beverage, meeting and convention facilities, stage entertainment, shopping, outdoor recreation, and other activities. Casino revenue comes from the house advantage associated with each game. In the United States, slot machines provide the largest source of casino gaming revenues.

Casinos in the United States and around the world are heavily regulated and heavily taxed. In the United States, the states are responsible for regulating casino gambling. The states have revenue-sharing agreements with Indian tribes operating casinos.

Casinos create value, primarily entertainment, for their customers, and they also create income for their workers, their owners, and others. The expansion of casino gambling is quite controversial, however, because of real and potential negative impacts of casino gambling, including potential increases in bankruptcy and crime rates.

---

[15] National Gambling Impact Study Commission (1999).

Bibliography

American Gaming Association (2008a), "State Information: Statistics," www.americangaming.org/Industry/state/statistics.cfm.

———— (2008b), "States with Gaming," www.americangaming.org/Industry/factsheets/general_info_detail.cfv?id=15

———— (2008c), "Tax Payments," www.americangaming.org/Industry/factsheets/statistics_detail.cfv?id=10.

———— (2008d), "Gaming Revenue: 10-Year Trends," www.americangaming.org/Industry/factsheets/statistics_detail.cfv?id=8.

———— (2008e), "State of the States: The AGA Survey of Casino Entertainment," www.americangaming.org/assets/files/aga_2008_sos.pdf.

Anderson, John E. (2005), "Casino Taxation in the United States." *National Tax Journal* 58: 303–24.

Angelo, Rocco M., and Andrew N. Vladimir. *Hospitality Today: An Introduction*. Lansing, MI: Educational Institute of the American Hotel and Lodging Association, 2004.

Australian Casino Association (2005), "Annual Report 2005," www.auscasinos.com/documents/publications Submissions/ACA_Annual%20Report%202005.pdf.

British Columbia Lottery Corporation (2005), "2004/05 Annual Report," www.bclc.com/documents/annual reports/BCLCAnnualReport0405.pdf.

———— (2006), "Casino Business Unit Snapshot," www.bclc.com/cm/aboutbclc/snapshotCasino.htm.

Collins, David, and Helen Lapsley. "The Social Costs and Benefits of Gambling: An Introduction to the Economic Issues." *Journal of Gambling Studies* 19 (2003): 123–48.

Department for Culture, Media and Sport (United Kingdom) (2006), "Gambling Act of 2005: Introductory note on implementation," www.culture.gov.uk/images/publications/GamblingAct2005Introductorynoteon implementation.pdf.

Eadington, William R. "The Economics of Casino Gambling." *Journal of Economic Perspectives* 13 (1999): 173–92.

————. "Response from William R. Eadington." *Journal of Economic Perspectives* 14 (2000): 225–6.

————. "Measuring Costs from Permitted Gaming: Concepts and Categories in Evaluating Gambling's Consequences." *Journal of Gambling Studies* 19 (2003): 185–213.

Ernst and Young (2006), "United States Gaming Bulletin," www.ey.nl/download/publicatie/Marktinfo_Gaming.pdf.

Garrett, Thomas A. "Casino Gaming and Local Employment Trends." Federal Reserve Bank of St. Louis *Review* 86 (2004): 9–22.

GLS Research (2007), "Las Vegas Visitor Profile, Calendar Year 2007, Annual Report," www.lvcva.com/getfile/VPS-2006%20Las%20Vegas.pdf?fileID=107.

Goeldner, Charles R., and J. R. Brent Ritchie. *Tourism: Principles, Practices, Philosophies*, 9th ed. Hoboken, NJ: John Wiley & Sons, 2003.

Grinols, Earl L., and David Mustard. "Casino Gambling." *Journal of Economic Perspectives* 14 (2000): 223–5.

———— "Casinos, Crime, and Community Costs." *The Review of Economics and Statistics* 88 (2006): 28–45.

Harrah's Entertainment, Inc. (2006), "Form 10-K," Fiscal Year 2005, http://ccbn.10kwizard.com/xml/download.php?repo=tenk&ipage=4028324&format=PDF.

———— (2007), "Harrah's Stockholders Approve Acquisition by Apollo and TPG," http://investor.harrahs.com/phoenix.zhtml?c=84772&p=irolnewsArticle&ID=982363&highlight=.

———— (2008a), "Harrah's Entertainment, Inc. Announces Completion Of Merger," http://phx.corporate-ir.net/phoenix.zhtml?c=84772&p=irol-newsArticle&ID=1100620&highlight=.

———— (2008b), "Harrah's Entertainment To Be Renamed Caesars Entertainment," http://investor.harrahs.com/phoenix.zhtml?c=84772&p=irol-newsArticle&ID=1127757&highlight=.

Helpman, Elhanan. *The Mystery of Economic Growth*. Belknap Press of Harvard University: Cambridge, 2004.

International Game Technology (2005) "Form 10-K." http://ccbn.10kwizard.com/xml/download.php?repo=tenk&ipage=3836008&format=PDF.

Kearney, Melissa Schettini. "The Economic Winners and Losers of Legalized Gambling." *National Tax Journal* 58 (2005): 281–302.

Kwan, Fanny Vong Chuk. "Gambling Attitudes and Gambling Behavior of Residents of Macao: The Monte Carlo of the Orient." *Journal of Travel Research* 42 (2004): 271–78.

Las Vegas Convention and Visitors Authority (2006), "Only Vegas" (The Official Las Vegas Tourism Web Site), www.visitlasvegas.com/vegas/index.jsp.

Las Vegas Sands Corp. (2006), "Form 10-K," Fiscal Year 2005, www.sec.gov/Archives/edgar/data/1300514/000095012306002497/p71940e10vk.htm.

Leone, Richard C., and Bernard Wasow. "Casino Gambling." *Journal of Economic Perspectives* 14 (2000): 223.

Madhusudhan, Ranjana G. "Betting on Casino Revenues." *National Tax Journal* 49 (1996): 401–12.

MGM Mirage (2006), "Form 10-K," Fiscal Year 2005, http://phx.corporate-ir.net/phoenix.zhtml?c=101502&p=irol-seccat&seccat_rs=11&seccat_rc=10.

——— (2007), "Form 10-K," Fiscal Year 2006, http://phx.corporate-ir.net/phoenix.zhtml?c=101502&p=irol-seccat&seccat_rs=11&seccat_rc=10.

——— (2008), "Form 10-K," Fiscal Year 2007, http://phx.corporate-ir.net/phoenix.zhtml?c=101502&p=irol-seccat&seccat_rs=11&seccat_rc=10.

National Gambling Impact Study Commission (1999), http://govinfo.library.unt.edu/ngisc/reports/fullrpt.html.

National Indian Gaming Commission (2006a), www.nigc.gov.

——— (2006b), "Gaming Revenues 2004–2000," www.nigc.gov/TribalData/GamingRevenues20042000/tabid/549/Default.aspx.

——— (2006c), "Annual Report 2004," www.nigc.gov/Portals/0/reading_room/biennial_reports/nigc_2004_annual_report.pdf.

Nevada Gaming Commission and State Gaming Control Board (2006a), "Quarterly Report for the Quarter Ended December 31, 2005," www.gaming.nv.gov/documents/pdf/r5_05dec.pdf.

——— (2006b), "Gaming License Fees and Tax Rate Schedule," http://gaming.nv.gov/taxfees.htm#1a1.

——— (2006c), "Gaming Statutes and Regulations," http://gaming.nv.gov/stats_regs.htm.

Nevada Gaming Commission and State Gaming Control Board (2008), "Gaming Revenue Report," gaming.nv.gov/documents/pdf/1g_07dec.pdf

Ontario Lottery and Gaming Corporation (2006), "OLGC Fact Sheet," http://corporate.olgc.ca/fact/mc_fs_corp_olgc.jsp.

Olson, Mancur. "Distinguished Lecture on Economics in Government: Big Bills Left on the Sidewalk: Why Some Nations are Rich, and Others Poor." *Journal of Economic Perspectives* 10 (1996): 3–24.

Pew Research Center (2006), "Gambling: As the Take Rises, So Does Public Concern," http://pewresearch.org/assets/social/pdf/Gambling.pdf.

Rodrik, Dani, Arvind Subramanian, and Francesco Trebbi. "Institutions Rule: The Primacy of Institutions over Geography and Integration in Economic Development." *Journal of Economic Growth* 9 (2004): 131–65.

Romer, Paul M. "The Origins of Endogenous Growth." *Journal of Economic Perspectives* 8 (1994): 3–22.

Sauer, Raymond D. "The Economics of Wagering Markets." *Journal of Economic Literature* 36 (1998): 2021–2064.

———. "The Political Economy of Gambling Regulation." *Managerial and Decision Economics* 22 (2001): 5–15.

Schuman, Michael (2005), "The Great Game," *Time Asia*, January 31, www.time.com/time/asia/covers/501050207/story.html.

Shoemaker, Stowe, and Dina Marie V. Zemke. "The Locals Market: An Emerging Gaming Segment." *Journal of Gambling Studies* 21 (2005): 379–410.

Suits, Daniel B. "The Elasticity of Demand for Gambling." *The Quarterly Journal of Economics* 93 (1979): 155–62.

Thalheimer, Richard, and Mukhtar M. Ali. "The Demand for Casino Gaming." *Applied Economics* 35 (2003): 907–18.

———. "The Relationship of Pari-Mutuel Wagering and Casino Gaming to Personal Bankruptcy." *Contemporary Economic Policy* 22 (2004): 420–32.

Vogel, Harold L. *Travel Industry Economics*. Cambridge: Cambridge University Press, 2001.

Walker, Douglas M. "Legalized Casino Gambling and the Export Base Theory of Economic Growth." *Gaming Law Review* 3 (1999): 157–63.

Walker, Douglas, and A. H. Barnett. "The Social Costs of Gambling: An Economic Perspective." *Journal of Gambling Studies* 15 (1999): 181–212.

WMS Industries (2005), "Form 10-K." http://ccbn.10kwizard.com/xml/download.php?repo=tenk&ipage=3679028&format=PDF.

GLOSSARY

Attractions. Permanent features of a destination that draw tourists.

Barrier to entry. A feature of a market that prevents entry by other firms and protects monopoly profits in the long run.

Berth. A passenger sleeping accommodation on a cruise ship; a double bed counts as two berths.

Business model. Explanation of how a business makes a profit by creating value for customers.

Business strategy. Explanation of how a business firm is going to make a place for itself in an industry with other rival firms.

Cabotage. Coastal trade within one nation.

Capacity constraint. Limit on the maximum amount of output that can be produced per period.

Capital. The durable inputs to production, such as buildings, vehicles, machinery, and tools.

Codesharing. It is a process whereby one airline sells some seats on some of its flights to another airline, which then lists those seats as if they were on its own flights.

Complements. Two goods are complements if an increase in the price of one of the goods *decreases* the demand for the other.

Consumers' surplus. The excess of the value to consumers of their consumption of a good over the amount they have to pay to get it.

Contestable market. A market in which potential competition prevents firms from charging high prices and earning above-normal rates of return.

Convention and visitors bureau (CVB). Local destination marketing organization.

Cross elasticity of demand. A measure of the responsiveness of the quantity of one good demanded to a change in another good's price: $\varepsilon_{ij} = \%\Delta Q_i^D \div \%\Delta P_j$.

Cruise market segment. A part of the cruise industry distinguished by level of service, price, size of the ship, and destinations; the three main segments are contemporary, premium, and luxury.

Customer lock-in. Raising the customers' cost of switching to another firm.

Demand. The relationship between the price of a firm's product or service and the amount of that product or service that customers will buy.

Depreciation. The loss in value of the firm's capital stock during the period.

Destination. A well defined place that tourists may visit.

Economy. An economy is the set of institutions that creates the goods and services society wants to consume.

Economic impact of tourism. Changes in regional employment, incomes, tax payments, and other measures of economic activity, along with social and environmental impacts that result from a region's tourism development.

Economies of scale. A production process in which long-run average cost of producing the good or service declines as the rate of production of output increases.

Ecotourism. Tourism designed to take advantage of a region's natural attractions while providing income to local residents and leaving the region little changed from its pre-tourism conditions.

Events. Transitory features of a destination that draw tourists.

Externality. An effect on the consumption or production of an individual or firm of a transaction to which that individual or firm was not a party.

Final demand. In input–output analysis, sales to buyers outside the industries included among the region's producing sectors. Final demand always includes exports (sales to buyers outside the region), and may include government and households.

Fixed costs. Costs that do not vary with the level of output produced.

Gross registered ton. 100 cubic feet of enclosed space on a cruise ship.

Hospitality industry. The industry that provides business or leisure services to people away from their homes or offices; the industry includes lodging, food service, beverage service, clubs, resorts, casinos, recreation, entertainment, and services for meetings, events, and conventions.

Hub-and-spoke route structure. An airline route structure that aggregates large numbers of passengers from smaller airports and thinner routes to major or hub airports where the passengers board large aircraft that fly heavily traveled routes.

Income. The net flow of value created in the economy during the period.

Income elasticity of demand. A measure of the responsiveness of the demand for a good to a change in the consumer's income: $\eta_i = \%\Delta Q_i^D \div \%\Delta M$.

Inferior good. Good or service for which consumer demand decreases as consumers' incomes increase.

Input–output analysis. A method for calculating economic impacts of changes in demand for a region's goods and services on the sectors of the region's economy using information on interindustry sales.

Intermediary. A firm facilitating transactions by offering services to both consumers and service providers.

Intertemporal economic analysis. Economic analysis that explicitly incorporates time.

Marginal cost. The change in total cost from producing one more unit of output.

Marginal revenue. The change in total revenue that comes from selling one more unit of output.

Motorcoach. A bus designed for carrying passengers (and their luggage) in comfort over long distances.

Multiplier effect. An increase in sales to final demand will have a larger effect within the region than the increase in final demand itself.

Peak/off-peak pricing. The process of systematically lowering prices during off-peak periods and returning them to higher levels during peak periods.

Price elasticity of demand. A measure of the responsiveness of the quantity of a good demanded to a change in the good's price: $\varepsilon_i = \%\Delta Q_i^D \div \%\Delta P_i$.

Price discrimination. Charging different prices for different sales of the same product or service.

Product differentiation. Making a firm's product or service different in ways important to consumers from other similar products or services available in the market.

Oligopoly. An industry consisting primarily of a small number of relatively large firms that are aware of their interactions.

Onboard sales. Sales of products and services, including alcoholic beverages, spa treatments, casino gaming, photography, and others, to passengers during a cruise.

Overbooking. Selling more tickets on a flight than the seating capacity of the aircraft.

Pure competition. A market in which each firm takes the market price as given and, therefore, unaffected by its own behavior.

Real estate investment trust. A specialized company that owns real estate and receives favorable U.S. federal income tax treatment.

Space ratio. Gross registered tons per lower berth.

Substitutes. Two goods are substitutes if an increase in the price of one of the goods *increases* the demand for the other.

Supply. The relationship between the price of a good or service and the quantity of the good or service that businesses produce and deliver to the market.

Sustainable tourism development. Development that explicitly takes account of the impact of today's tourism activities on the opportunities that will be available to future tourists and local residents.

Travel mode. Way of moving between origin and destination, such as scheduled airline, automobile, bus, or train.

Tourism. Tourism is traveling outside one's home area, usually at least 50 miles or more one way, and returning within one year, except when going to a distant site to work when the traveler expects to be paid at the distant site.

Value added. A firm's revenue minus what it paid for intermediate goods.

Yield management or revenue management. Price discrimination in the presence of a capacity constraint.

INDEX

Adverse selection
  asymmetric information, 203
  counteracting institutions, 204
Agents, 192
Air conditioning, 42
Air flight
  modern mass tourism, 36
  technological change, 41–42
Air Transport Association
  of America, 6
Air travel
  Current Market Outlook factors,
    20–21, 36
  improved safety, 38
  pricing decline, 37, 38t
  value added components, 12, 13t
Airbus, 89
Aircraft, 88–89, 90t
Airline Deregulation Act (1978),
  passage of, 87
Airline industry
  business model, 88–93, 89t, 90t,
    91f, 92t
  contestable markets, 107, 109–115
  deregulation, 106--107
  early history of, 86
  federal regulation of, 85, 86–87
  financial performance, 93–93, 94t,
    95f, 96t
  growth of, 86, 87f, 93–94
  importance of, 85–86
  international market, 104–106, 105
  preferred travel mode, 125t
  recent developments, 87–88,
    115–119, 116t, 118f
  structure of, 95–103, 96t
  trade associations, 6
Airline routes
  CAB regulation, 86
  hub-and-spoke, 96–97, 109–110,
    117, 119
Airlines
  competition, 4
  LCCs, 116t, 116–118, 118f, 119
  low-cost, 44
  major domestic (Group III), 95,
    96t, 117
  major international, 104, 105t
  national (Group II), 95
  new business models, 42–43
  regional (Group I), 95
Airport and Airway Trust Fund, 92
Airports, domestic, 91–92, 92t
Aker Yards, 165, 167t
Akerlof, George, 203
Al la carte pricing, 155
Alaskan cruise lines, 169–170
Alexander the Great, 30
Allegheny Airlines, 87
Amadeus IT Group SA, 98, 198
America's Cup Yacht race, 51
American Airlines
  computerized reservations, 97–98
  domestic carrier, 87
  Group III, 95, 96t

operating expenses, 88, 89t
operating flight equipment, 90t
yield management revenue, 102
American Eagle Airlines
  Group III, 95, 96t
  operating expenses, 88, 89t
American Express Travel agency,
  195t, 196
American Society of Travel Agents
  (ASTA), 205–206
American Travel Survey, 38
AMR Corporation
  computerized reservations, 97
  operating expenses, 88, 89t
Amtrak. *See also* Train
  economies of scale, 128–129, 129f
  federal role, 127t, 127–128
  revenue, 127–128, 128t
  services provided, 128, 130
Amtrak Reform and Accountability
  Act of 1997, 127
Ancient Greece
  culture of, 29–30
  tourism in, 28, 30
Arison, Ted, 43, 160
Association of British Travel Agents
  (ABTA), 202
Asymmetric information
  market study, 203–204
  travel agent/tour operator, 201–203
Atlantic city casino gambling, 210,
  211, 212
Australian Bureau of Statistics, 12
Automobile travel
  improved safety, 39, 39t
  preferred travel mode, 124t,
    124–125, 125t
  price declines, 37–38
  technological change, 41
Aviator, The, 86
Avis Budget Group, 131t

"Back office" functions, 144
Bankruptcies
  airline industry, 87, 107
  tour operator industry, 202, 203,
    204, 205
Barrier to entry, 111
Berths
  cruise line capacity, 165, 166t
  definition of, 162
Bertrand model
  lodging industry, 147–151, 149f,
    150f
  oligopoly, 114–115
Blackstone Group
  and Hilton Hotels Corporation, 140
  and MeriStar Hospitality
    Corporation, 138
  travel agencies, 196, 198
Boeing Corporation
  aircraft manufacturer, 89
  Current Market Outlook, 20–21, 36
Bombardier Corporation, 89
"Boulder Strip," 211

Brands
  counteracting institutions, 204
  in lodging industry, 151
  industry segmentation, 145
  MeriStar Hospitality Corporation,
    138
  Starwood Hotels and Resorts, 140
Braun, Bradley M., 53, 180
British Airways, 44–45
British Overseas Airways
  Corporation (BOAC), 45
Brokers, 192
"Bucket" system, 100
"Bundling," 155, 156
Bureau of Economic Analysis
  statistics, 5
Bureau of Transportation Statistics,
  17, 18t
Bus travel
  preferred mode, 125t, 126
  long-distance trips, 124, 124t
Business strategy, 43
Business traveler
  airline industry, 98
  demographic variables, 17, 18t
  lodging demand, 137

Cabotage
  cruise lines, 168–170
  international aviation, 104
*California v. Cabazon Band of
  Mission Indians*, 220
Canada
  casino industry, 214–215
  casino revenue, 219
  tourism statistics, 5
  value added in tourism, 12, 13t
Canterbury Tales, 33
Cantor, Norman, 31
Capacity constraint, 3
Capital
  definition of, 9
  return on, 12,
Car rental industry
  industry structure, 130–131
  major companies, 131t
  new business models, 43
  operations, 131–133
  replacement insurance, 44
Carnival Cruise lines
  customer deposits, 171
  establishment of, 43, 160
  largest firm, 165
  net income, 172t
  operating expenses, 162t
  revenues, 163–164, 164t
  ships/berths, 166t
  ships on order, 167t
Carnival Freedom, 163
Casino industry
  benefits/costs, 220–222
  domestic, 211–213, 212t
  global, 213–215, 214t
  government regulation, 5, 218
  gross revenues, 210t, 211t

growth of, 208, 210
operations, 215–217, 218t
state revenue, 219, 219t
taxation, 218, 219
Casinos, brief history, 208–209
Centers for Disease Control and
  Prevention (CDC)
  "Green Sheet," 171
  Vessel Sanitation Program, 170, 171
Certification, 204
Chains, 204
Charlemagne, 31, 32
Charter bus, 124, 124t
Chaucer, Geoffrey, 33–34
Chicago Convention. *See*
  International Civil Aviation
  Conference
"China Clipper," 41–42, 104
China. *See also* Macao
  early restaurants, 152
  medieval tourism, 32–33
Civil Aeronautics Act (1938), passage
  of, 86
Civil Aeronautics Authority, 86
Civil Aeronautics Board (CAB)
  airline regulation, 85, 86–87, 119
  price competition, 106
  termination of, 87
Coase, Ronald, 2, 138, 201
Coast Guard, 171
Codesharing, 97
Collette Vacations, 200
Commercial aviation
  definition of, 86
  recent developments, 87–88
Commissions, 193, 194
Common pool resources, 63
Competition
  airlines, 106, 110, 117
  definition, 111, 112f
  industry behavior, 4
  lodging industry, 148
  market power, 111–112
"Comping," 216
Complements
  consumer goods, 20
  tourism factor, 21
Computerized reservation systems,
  98, 198
Congestion, 63
Consumer surplus
  definition, 82, 82f, 154
  restaurant industry, 154–156, 155t
Contestable market, 107
Continental Airlines
  Group III, 95, 96t
  unionized workforce, 90
Convention and visitors bureaus
  (CVBs), 50
Convention for the Prevention of
  Pollution from Ships, 171
Convention on the Law of the
  Sea, 168
Convention on the Safety of Life at
  Sea (SOLAS), 170, 171, 172

"Corridor" services, 128
Cost
　factors of, 40–42
　features of, 3
Counteracting institutions, 204
Cournot model, 113f, 113–114,
　114f, 115
Cross elasticity, 22–23
Cruise lines
　industry structure, 164t, 164–166,
　　166t, 167t
　major ship builders, 165, 166t
　market segments, 161
　modern growth, 159–160, 160t
　new business models, 43
　operations, 162, 162t
　pricing policies, 73
　profitability of, 172t, 172–174,
　　173f,
　regulation of, 166, 168
　value creation, 161–164,
　　162t, 164t
Cruise Lines International Association
　(CLIA)
　cruise statistics, 160, 160t
　travel agency accreditation, 194
Cruise ships
　characteristics of, 161–162
　current capacity, 165–166, 166t
　on order, 166, 167t
Crystal Cruises
　luxury segment, 163
　ships/berths, 166t
Crystal Serenity staff, 163
Cunard, Samuel
　modern mass tourism, 36, 159
　new business models, 43
　ship safety, 38
　technological change, 40
Customer loyalty programs
　lodging industry, 144–145, 151
　value of, 25–26

Delta Air Lines
　domestic carrier, 87
　Group III, 95, 96t
　unionized workforce, 90
Demand
　consumer behavior, 4
　and cross elasticity, 22–23
　definition, 74
　and income elasticity, 23
　and marginal revenue, 74f, 74–76,
　　75f, 76f
　modern mass tourism, 36–39,
　　38t, 39t
　and price elasticity of, 22
　tourist, 19, 20–22
"Deny boarding," 99, 101f
Department of Commerce, 5
Department of Transportation
　airline competition, 110
　airline regulation, 87
　BTS, 17, 18t
Depreciation, 9
Description of Greece, 29
Direct effect/impact
　input-output analysis, 56
　matrix analysis, 69
　economic impact analysis, 52

Disney Cruise line
　recent entrant, 172
　ships/berths, 166t
　ships on order, 167t
Distance variables, 22
Distribution channels, 192
Douglas, George, 85

Eastern Airlines
　bankruptcy of, 87
　domestic carrier, 87
Econometric model, 23–25
Economic impact analysis
　definition, 50
　direct and indirect effects, 52
　indicators, 51
Economies of scale, 128, 129f
Economy
　definition, 3, 7
　purpose of, 7–8
"Ecotourism," 57, 58
Employee compensation, 12, 13t. *See
　also* Labor
Employment
　economic impact indicators, 51
　TIA survey, 50
Enterprise Rent-A-Car, 44, 131t
Entertainment, 217
Environmental impact, 51
Environmental Protection Agency
　(EPA), 171
Environmental regulation, 4–5, 171
Equipment, airline industry,
　88–89, 90t
Eratosthenes, 29–30
Escorted tour, 199
Ethics code, ASTA, 205
European Union (EU), airline
　industry, 105, 106
Exhaustible resources, 59
Expedia, 195t, 195, 196
Externality, 62

Far&Wide Travel Corporation,
　203, 205
Federal Aviation Act (1958), 86
Federal Aviation Administration
　(FAA)
　airline industry categories, 95
　renamed, 86, 87
Federal Flight Segment Tax, 92
Federal Maritime Commission, 171
Federal Ticket Tax, 92
Federal Trade Commission, 202–203
Federal-Aid Highway Act(1956),
　45–46
FelCor Lodging Trust, 139, 141, 142
Final demand
　calculation, 54–56
　definition, 54
　matrix analysis, 67–68
Fincantieri Cantieri Navali Italiani,
　165, 167t
Fixed costs, 3
"Flags of Convenience," 168
Flying Down to Rio, 86
Food and beverage industry
　brief history, 151–152
　casino revenue, 217
　consumer surplus, 154–156

costs, 153–154
　restaurants, 152–153, 153t
　value added components, 12, 13t
Formal institutions, 7
Franchises
　food and beverage industry,
　　152–153
　lodging industry, 138, 141–142,
　　143t
　travel agencies, 193
Freedom of the Seas, 165
"Freedom of the seas," 168
Fuel
　airline industry, 88, 91, 91f, 103,
　　118–119
　input prices, 40

Galileo International, 98, 198
Gaming Act (2005) (UK), 215
Gaming devices, 216–217
GE Commercial Aviation Service
　(GECAS), 89
General aviation, 86
Glenn L. Martin Company, 41–42
Global distribution systems (GDSs),
　192, 197–198
Gordon, General Charles, 35
Grand Tour, 34, 35
Great Britain. *See also* United
　Kingdom
　gaming laws, 215
　holiday market, 202
　passenger rail service, 130
"Green Sheet," 171
Greyhound Lines, 126
Gross domestic product, 36–37
Gross Domestic Income, 10
Gross Domestic Product (GDP), 5, 10
Gross registered tons (GRT), 162

Hanson, Bjorn, 137–138
Harrah's Entertainment, 212,
　213, 214t
Hawaiian cruise lines, 169, 170
Herfindahl Index, 108, 109
Hertz, John, 43
Hertz Car Rental company, 131t
"Hidden city" discount, 101
Hilton Corporation, 140, 143
Holiday Inn chain, 38, 43
Hospitality industry, 136
Host Marriott Corporation
　property ownership, 138
　REITs, 140
Hotel management
　major companies, 144
　operational areas, 144
　services, 143
"Hotel staff," cruise lines, 163
"House advantage," 215
"Household trip," TIA
　definition, 16
Howard, Donald, 33
"Hub premium," 109
Hub-and-spoke route system
　creation of, 96–97, 119
　"dehubbed," 117
　price premium, 109–110
Hughes, Howard, 86

Ibn Battuta, 32
Imperial Airways, 44–45
Income
　and change impact, 20
　and consumer demand, 4
　definition, 9
　economic impact indicators, 51
　GDP, 9
　modern growth, 36–37
　tourism factor, 21
　workers/investors, 3
Income elasticity
　demand factor, 23
　lodging demand, 137
India, 32, 33
Indian Gaming Regulatory Act
　(1988), 220
Indirect effect
　economic impact analysis, 52
　input-output analysis, 56
　matrix analysis, 69
Induced effect
　economic impact analysis, 52
　input-output analysis, 56
　matrix analysis, 69
Industrial Revolution, 35–36
Inexhaustible resources, 59
Inferior goods, 20, 124
Informal institutions, 7
Infrastructure development, 45
"Innocent passage," 168
Input prices, 40
Input–output analysis
　assumptions of, 56–57
　calculation of, 53–56, 64–69
　definition, 53
　development of, 52–53
Institutions, 7
"Intercity passenger transportation,"
　123
"Interlining," 105
Intermediary, 191
International Air Transport
　Association (IATA)
　"interlining," 105
　trade association, 6
　travel agency accreditation, 194
International Civil Aviation
　Conference, 104
International Maritime Organization
　(IMO)
　pollution standards, 171
　SOLAS, 170
International Pow Wow, 201
"International Ship and Port Facility
　Security Code," 172
Internet
　airline ticket sales, 92–93
　and lodging industry, 151
　and travel agency industry, 11–12,
　　193, 194–196
　travel sites, 192
Interstate Highway System, 4, 37
Intertemporal economic analysis
　definition, 58
　tradeoffs, 59–62, 60f,
Italy, 25t

Jet Engine, 42
"Jet set" glamour, 86

JetBlue Airlines, 95, 96t
Jones Act of 1920, 168–169

Keeler, Theodore, 85

Labor
  and the airline industry, 90–91, 119
  and cruise lines, 162t, 163
  and the hotel industry, 143
  matrix analysis, 68–69
Laidlaw, Inc., 126
Las Vegas
  casino gambling, 211
  legalized gambling, 210
  tourist promotion, 57
Las Vegas Convention and Visitors
    Authority, 50
Las Vegas Sands Corp., casino
    industry, 213
Leading Hotels of the World, 142
Leisure traveler
  airline industry, 98
  lodging demand, 137
Leontief, Wassily, 2, 52–53
Lerner Index, 108
Levine, Michael, 85
Licensing, 204
Lodging,
  casino revenue, 217
  demand side, 137–138
Lodging firms
  franchises, 138, 141–142, 143t
  management operations, 138,
    143–145
  real estate/property ownership,
    138, 139–141
  traveler characteristics, 16t
  value creation, 137
Lodging industry
  competition, 148
  pricing, 146–147
  segments of, 145
Low cost carriers (LCC)
  airline industry, 87–88
  entry of, 116, 116t
  major firm competition, 117
  price leadership, 117–118,
    118f, 119

Macao casino industry, 209,
    213–214
Magretta, Joan, 43
Making of the Middle Ages, The, 30
Mandeville's Travels, 33
Mardi Gras, CCL, 160
Marginal costs
  calculation, 76–77, 77f
  capacity constraint, 80f
  definition, 76
  supply, 3
Marginal revenue
  components of, 75
  constraint capacity, 80f, 81
  definition, 74
"Marine crew," 163
Marine Transportation Security Act
    (2002), 172
Mark Travel Corporation, 201
Market power measurements,
    108, 108t

Marriott International
  brand segmentation, 145–146
  franchising/management, 138, 142
  yield management, 147
"Marriott Rewards," 144–145
Matrix, 64
Matrix algebra, 53, 63, 64–69
MeriStar Hospitality Corporation,
    138
Meyer Werft, 165, 167t
Mezzanine financing, 141
MGM Mirage, 213, 214t, 218t
Middle Ages, tourism in, 28, 31–34
Miller, James, 85
Mixed bundling, 156
Monopoly
  definition of, 4
  market structure, 110f, 110–111
Monte Carlo, 213, 214t
Moral hazard, 204
Motel chains, 38, 43
Motorcoach travel, 126
Multiplier effect, 56

National Association of Securities
    Dealers Automated Quotation
    System(NASDAQ), 7
"National flag carriers," 104
National Gaming Impact Study
    Commission recommendations,
    222
National Household Travel Survey
  business travelers, 17, 18t
  travel mode, 17, 18t
National income and products
    accounts (NIPA)
  calculation of, 10
  tourism statistics, 5
National Indian Gaming
    Commission, 220
National Railroad Passenger
    Corporation, 127
National Tour Association
  membership requirements, 203
  packaged tours, 198–199, 199t
Native Americans, casinos, 210, 211,
    212, 220
Natural resources
  matrix analysis, 70f, 70–71
  sustainable development, 59, 61
Navigant International, 195t, 196
Nevada
  casino gambling, 211–212
  casino regulation, 218
  gaming revenue, 215t, 215–216
Nevada Gaming Commission, 218
Nevada Gaming Control Act, 218
Nevada State Gaming Control
    Board, 218
New Zealand, 51
Night audit, 144
"No discharge zones," 171
"Normal" goods, 20
Northwest Airlines, 95, 96t
Norwegian Caribbean Lines (NCL)
  acquired by Star Cruises, 172
  and Hawaiian cruise ships, 169
  major firm, 165
  modern cruise industry, 160
  ships/berths, 166t

Oligopoly
  lodging industry, 147–148
  market power, 112–115, 113f, 114f
Onboard sales, 164, 164t
Online travel agencies, 193, 194–196
Ontario Lottery and Gaming
    Corporation, 214–215
Open skies agreements, 104–106
Orbitz Worldwide, 195t, 196
Orlando (FL) input-output analysis, 53
Output multiplier, 53, 56
Overbooking, 99, 101

Pacific Railroad Act (1862), 44
Pacific Southwest Airlines, 87
Pan American Airways, 41–42, 86–87
Papatheodorou, Andreas, 24–25, 25t
Passenger car. *See* Automobile
Passenger Facility Charge (PFC), 92
Passenger Shipping Act (1896),
    168–169
Pausanias, 29
Peak/off-peak pricing, 133, 134f
Peel, Robert, 35
Peninsular and Oriental Steam
    Navigation Company, 41
Peninsular Steam Navigation
    Company, 41
Person trip, 16
Portugal, 25, 25t
Preferred Hotels and Resorts World
    Wide, 142
Price
  airline industry, 101–102
  definition, 20
  decline in, 37–38
  tourism factor, 21
Price discrimination
  constraint capacity, 77, 80, 81f
  definition, 73
  no constraint capacity, 79f
  two-part tariff, 82–83
Price elasticity
  demand factor, 22
  lodging demand, 137–138
Price takers, 111
Priceline.com, 195t, 196
Pride of America, 169
Production possibilities frontiers
  derivation of, 60f, 60–62, 61f
  matrix analysis, 70f, 70–71
Profits
  airline industry, 94
  cruise lines, 172t, 172–174, 173f
Program cars, 132
"Project America," 169
"Project Genesis," 163
Property rights, 62–63
Pure competition, 111, 112f

Qantas Airways, 45
Quality
  improvement in motels, 38
  tourism factor, 21
Quantity supplied, 40
Quick service restaurants, 152,
    153, 153t

Race tracks, 211t
Rack rate, 146

Rail Passenger Service Act (1970), 127
Railroads, 40. *See also* Trains
Real Estate Investment Trust (REIT),
    139–140
Receptive Services Association of
    America (RSAA), 201
Redfield, James, 30
Refrigeration, 42
Refunds, ASTA code, 205
Reservation price, 154
Reservation services, 12, 13t
Reservations
  airline computerization, 97–98,
    197–198
  car rentals, 132
Restaurants
  casino revenue, 217
  types of, 152–153, 153t
Retail operations, 217
Retail services, 12, 13t
Revenue management. *See also* Yield
    management
  airline industry, 98–99, 102
  calculation of, 77–78
  lodging industry, 147
RITZ, César, 142
Rivalry, 4. *See also* Competition
Rome (Ancient) 28, 29, 151
Royal Caribbean Cruises, Ltd.,
  consumer base, 164, 164t
  net income, 172
  operating expenses, 162t, 162–163
  second largest firm, 165
  ships/berths, 166t
  ships on order, 167t

Sabre Travel Network, 97–98, 198
Safety
  cruise lines, 170–171
  government regulation, 4
  improved, 38–39
  public policy, 46
Sanitation, 170–171
Satellite accounts, 12, 14
Season, 16t, 21
Seat assignment problem, 78
Security
  cruise lines, 171–172
  improved, 38–39
  tourism factor, 21
Senior-citizen discounts, 73–74
September 11, 2001
  airline industry impact, 94, 117
  tourism impact, 39, 171, 203
Severe Acute Respiratory Syndrome
    (SARs), 203
"Shoulder" seasons, 17
"Silk Road," 32–33
Slot machine manufactures, 216–217
Sobel, Russell, 83
Southern, R. W., 30
Southwest Airlines
  business strategy, 115–116
  Group III, 95, 96t
  intrastate carrier, 87
  LCC, 44
  ticket sales, 93
  unionized workforce, 90
"Southwest effect," 116
Space ratio, 162

Spain, 25t
Star Alliance, 106
Star Cruises
  acquisition of NCL, 172
  major firm, 165
  ships/berths, 166t
Starwood Hotels and Resorts, 140
State government
  casino tax revenue, 219, 219t
  tourism promotion, 49–50
Statistics Canada, 5, 12, 13t
Steam power, 36
Steamships
  safety of, 38, 41
  technological change, 36, 40, 41
Stigler, George, 85
"Strip, The," 211
Student discounts, 73–74
Subsidies, 4, 44–45
Substitutes, 20, 21
Supply
  definition, 40
  marginal cost, 75–77
  modern mass tourism, 36
  new business models, 42–43
  new business strategies, 43–44
  public policies, 44–46
  technological change, 40–42
Sustainability restriction, 59
Sustainable tourist development, 57, 58–59

Taberna, 151
Table service restaurants, 152–153, 153t
Tauck World Discovery, 200
Taxation
  airline industry, 92
  casino revenue, 219
  economic impact indicators, 51
  government regulation, 4–5
  tourism, 50
Taylor, Jack, 44
Technical change
  cost factors, 40
  institutional impact, 7
  modern mass tourism, 36
  and supply, 3–4
"Territorial waters," 168
Thomas Cook, 35, 36
Thomas Cook Group plc., 202
Ticket sales
  airline industry, 92–93
  cruise lines, 164, 164t

Titanic
  government regulations, 4
  safety regulation, 46, 170
  and transatlantic travel, 41
Tour bus, 124, 124t
Tour operators
  information asymmetry, 201–203
  low cost providers, 2
  packaged tours, 198–199, 199t
  tourism intermediary, 192
  value creation, 199
Tour operators industry
  retail/wholesale tours, 201
Tourism Australia, 6
Tourism
  definition of, 1
  demographic variables, 21–21
  economic impact analysis, 50–51
  estimating elasticities of, 23–25
  factors affecting, 21
  global spending, 1–2
  location variables, 22
  negative effects, 57
  organizations, 5–6
  participants, 2
  purpose of, 3, 14
  value added components, 12
Tourist industry
  Ancient Greece, 28, 30
  Ancient Rome, 28, 29
  Grand Tour, 34, 35
  Middle Ages, 30–34
  modern mass, 35–36
  Renaissance, 34
Tourist intermediaries
  asymmetrical information, 204–206
  GDSs, 197–198
  role of, 191–192
  tour operators, 198–201, 199t
  travel agents, 193–196, 194t
  travel management companies, 196–197
Trade Associations, 5–6
"Traffic conference," 104
Train
  economies of scale, 128–129, 129f
  long-distance trips, 124, 124t
  preferred travel mode, 125t, 126–130, 127t, 128t, 129f
"Transient passage," 168
Transportation
  preference of modes, 17, 18t
  price declines, 37–38, 38t
  traveler characteristics, 16t

"Transportation revolution," 40
Travel agencies, 11–12
Travel agent industry
  leading firms, 195t, 195–196
  recent changes, 194–196
  regulation, 194
  services, 193–194, 194t
Travel agents
  airline ticket commission, 92–93
  computerized reservations, 97–98
  cost of, 163–164
  information asymmetry, 201–203
  tourism intermediary, 192
  value creation, 193
Travel arrangement component, 12, 13t
Travel Industry Association of America (TIA)
  industry employment, 50
  state tourism spending, 50
  trade association, 5, 6
  travel profiles, 15–17, 16t
Travel management companies, 192, 196–197
Travel mode
  definition, 123
  long distance transportation, 124, 124t
  National Household Travel Survey, 17, 18t
"Travelers Assistance Program" 205
Travelocity, 195t, 195–196
Travels of Marco Polo, The, 33
"Tribal-state-compact," 220
Trippe, Juan, 86
"Trunk lines," 87
TWA, 86–87
Two-part tariff, 83, 83f

Unions, 90–91
United Airlines
  domestic carrier, 88
  Group III, 95, 96t
United Airlines, 86–87
United Kingdom, 24. *See also* Great Britain
United Nations
  International Maritime Organization, 170, 171
  Law of the Sea Convention, 168
  sustainable tourism, 57
  WTO, 1, 5
United States
  casino industry, 211–213, 212t

food and beverages industry, 152
GDP growth, 36–37
lodging industry, 137
Office of Travel and Tourism Industries, 5
restaurant industry, 152–153, 153t
value added in tourism, 12, 13t
visitor profiles, 15–17, 16t
United States Tour Operators Association (USTOA)
  bankruptcy protection, 203
  specialty tours, 200
  "Travelers Assistance Program" 205
US Airways, 90
Utility, 19

Value added, 8, 9–10
Vessel Sanitation Program, 170, 171
Vessels, cruise lines, 165, 166t
Visitor profiles, TIA data, 15–17, 16t
Voyager of the Seas, 163, 165

Wages, input prices, 40
Western Europe
  medieval period, 30–31
  medieval tourism, 28, 31–34
  Renaissance tourism, 34
Wilson, Kemmons, 38, 43
Work rules, 90, 91
World Commission on Environment and Development, 57
World Tourism Organization (WTO)
  organizations, 5
  satellite accounts, 12
  tourism definition, 1
World Travel and Tourism Council, 50
Worldspan, 98, 198
Wright brothers, 36, 41
Wynn Resorts Ltd., 213

"Yield," 37, 38t
Yield management
  airline industry, 98–99, 102, 119
  calculation of, 77–78
  consumer impact, 103
  lodging industry, 147
  process steps, 78–81
Yields, 94t, 94

Zheng He, 33